THIS IS NO LONGER THE PROPERTY
OF THE SEATTLE PUBLIC LIBRARY

THE PAUL A. BARAN – PAUL M. SWEEZY MEMORIAL AWARD

John Smith's book, *Imperialism in the Twenty-First Century*, is the inaugural winner of the Paul A. Baran–Paul M. Sweezy Memorial Award. This award, established in 2014, honors the contributions of the founders of the *Monthly Review* tradition: Paul M. Sweezy, Paul A. Baran, and Harry Magdoff. It supports the publication in English of distinguished monographs focused on the political economy of imperialism. The aim is to make available in English important work written in the tradition of Paul M. Sweezy, Paul A. Baran, and Harry Magdoff, broadly conceived. It will also apply to writings previously unpublished in English, and will include translations of new work first published in languages other than English.

Paul M. Sweezy co-founded *Monthly Review* in 1949, and, with Paul A. Baran, developed the fundamental analysis of accumulation under monopoly capitalism. Baran's *The Political Economy of Growth*, published in 1957, set the template for understanding imperialism in the latter part of the twentieth century—an argument that was to be further developed in Baran and Sweezy's *Monopoly Capital* (1966). Harry Magdoff, who would become the co-editor of *Monthly Review*, carried this project forward in *The Age of Imperialism* (1969) by investigating the historical trajectory of imperialism and tracing the contours of monopoly capitalism as a world system of exploitation. Their collective effort helped form a current of independent socialist thought of increasing importance on a global scale.

Today, the struggle continues against a global capitalist system that has created conditions of increased exploitation in the countries of the global South, alongside a vast transfer of wealth to imperialist centers of the global North. While untold profits accrue to imperialism's ruling elite—the 1 percent of society at home and abroad—the 99 percent of the world's population experience greater hardship and misery. The imperial system of the twenty-first century is one marked by growing uncertainty, instability, and ecological disaster. The promise of national emancipation through independence has not been fulfilled in general. Capitalist globalization is in fact imperialism without colonies.

Please visit our website for complete details of the award.

THIS IS NO LONGER THE PROPERTY
OF THE SEATTLE PUBLIC LIBRARY

IMPERIALISM

in the Twenty-First Century

Globalization, Super-Exploitation, and Capitalism's Final Crisis

John Smith

MONTHLY REVIEW PRESS

New York

Copyright © 2016 by John Smith
All Rights Reserved

Library of Congress Cataloging-in-Publication Data
Smith, John Charles, 1956–
Title: Imperialism in the twenty-first century : globalization,
   super-exploitation, and capitalism's final crisis / John Smith.
Description: New York : Monthly Review Press, [2016] | Includes
   bibliographical references and index.
Identifiers: LCCN 2015046537 (print) | LCCN 2015050017 (ebook) | ISBN
   9781583675779 (pbk.) | ISBN 9781583675786 (hardcover) | ISBN
9781583675793
   (trade) | ISBN 9781583675809 (institutional)
Subjects: LCSH: Capitalism—Poltical aspects. | Neoliberalism. |
   International trade. | Globalization—Economic aspects. |
   Imperialism—Economic aspects.
Classification: LCC HB501 .S636155 2016 (print) | LCC HB501 (ebook) |
DDC
   330.12/2—dc23
LC record available at http://lccn.loc.gov/2015046537

Monthly Review Press
146 West 29th Street, Suite 6W
New York, New York 10001
monthlyreview.org

Typeset in Minion Pro

5 4 3 2 1

Contents

LIST OF FIGURES AND TABLES

Per Capita GDP (PPP$*) by Nation

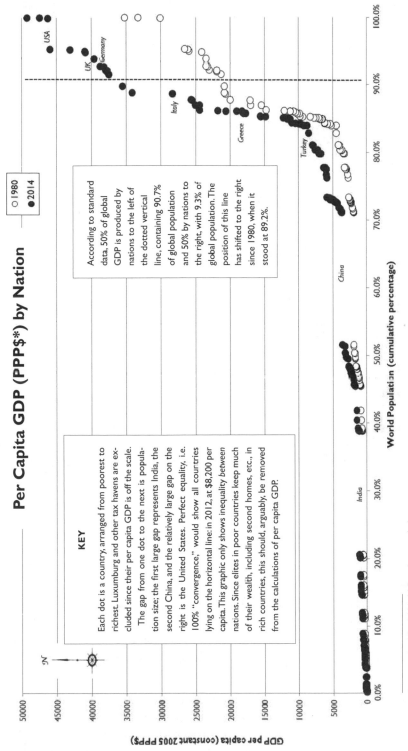

KEY

Each dot is a country, arranged from poorest to richest. Luxumburg and other tax havens are excluded since their per capita GDP is off the scale.

The gap from one dot to the next is population size; the first large gap represents India, the second China, and the relatively large gap on the right is the United States. Perfect equality, i.e. 100% "convergence," would show all countries lying on the horizontal line: in 2012, at $8,200 per capita. This graphic only shows inequality between nations. Since elites in poor countries keep much of their wealth, including second homes, etc., in rich countries, this should, arguably, be removed from the calculations of per capita GDP.

According to standard data, 50% of global GDP is produced by nations to the left of the dotted vertical line, containing 90.7% of global population and 50% by nations to the right, with 9.3% of global population. The position of this line has shifted to the right since 1980, when it stood at 89.2%.

○ 1980
● 2014

GDP per capita (constant 2005 PPP$)

World Population (cumulative percentage)

Source: World Bank, World Development Indicators.
*Purchasing Power Parity.

Instead of the conservative motto, "a fair day's wage for a fair day's work!" . . . the revolutionary watchword, "abolition of the wages system!"[1]

1

The Global Commodity

The collapse of Rana Plaza, an eight-story building housing several textile factories, a bank, and some shops in an industrial district north of Dhaka, Bangladesh's capital, on 24 April 2013, killing 1,133 garment workers and wounding 2,500, was one of the worst workplace disasters in recorded history.[2] This disaster, and garment workers' grief, rage, and demands for justice, stirred feelings of sympathy and solidarity from working people around the world—and a frantic damage-limitation exercise by the giant corporations that rely on Bangladeshi factories for their products yet deny any responsibility for the atrocious wages, living, and working conditions of those who produce all their stuff. Adding to the sense of outrage felt by many is the fact that, the day before, cracks had opened up in the building's structure and an initial inspection resulted in its evacuation and a recommendation that it remain closed. Next morning a bank and shops on the ground floor obeyed this advice, but thousands of garment workers were ordered back to work on pain of dismissal. When generators illegally installed on the top floor were started up the building collapsed. Jyrki Raina, general secretary of IndustriALL, an international union federation, called it "mass industrial slaughter."

The screams of thousands trapped and crushed as concrete and machinery cascaded down upon them unleashed a full-spectrum shockwave, amplified by the anguished howl of millions around the world. The calamity made instant headline news. Consumers of clothes made in Bangladesh's garment factories were confronted by their palpable connection to the people whose hands made their clothes, and about their miserable existence on this earth. Like an intense x-ray beam, the shockwave from Rana Plaza lit up the internal structure of the global economy, throwing into sharp relief a fundamental fact about global capitalism that is normally kept out of sight and mind: its good health rests on extreme rates of exploitation of workers in the low-wage countries where production of consumer goods and intermediate inputs has been relocated. The attention of the world was drawn in particular to Bangladesh's poverty wages—the lowest factory wages of any major exporter in the world, even after a 77 percent pay increase in November 2013; to its death-trap factories—just five months earlier a fire at nearby Tazreen Fashions killed 112 workers, who were trapped behind barred windows and locked doors while working long into the night; to the violent suppression of union rights—union activists are routinely blacklisted, beaten up, and subject to arbitrary arrest; and to the incestuous relations between factory owners, politicians, and police chiefs in Bangladesh—no employer in Bangladesh's garment industry has ever been convicted of an infringement of health and safety laws.[3] What makes all of it particularly relevant to this study is that the garment industry is "the quintessential example of a buyer-driven commodity chain . . . [where] global buyers determine what is to be produced, where, by whom, and at what price."[4] As such, Bangladesh's garment industry distils the export-oriented industrialization strategy pursued by capitalist governments across the Global South. As British Trades Union Congress General Secretary Frances O'Grady said in response to the Ran Plaza disaster, "This appalling loss of life proves that, in the global race to the bottom on working conditions, the finishing line is Bangladesh."[5]

The starvation wages, death-trap factories, and fetid slums in Bangladesh are representative of the conditions endured by hundreds of millions of working people throughout the Global South, the source of surplus value sustaining profits and feeding unsustainable overconsumption in imperialist countries. The people of Bangladesh are also in the front line of another calamitous consequence of capitalism's reckless exploitation of living labor and nature: "climate change," more accurately described as *the capitalist destruction of nature*. Most of Bangladesh is low-lying, and as sea levels rise and monsoons become more energetic, farmland is being increasingly inundated with salt water, accelerating migration into the cities. As a result Bangladesh's capital city, Dhaka, whose population has doubled in the last twenty years and is already one of the largest and most densely populated cities in the world, is growing by more than 600,000 people each year.[6] Over-extraction of fresh water is depleting Dhaka's aquifers and, worse still, exposing them to contamination with seawater. To cap it all, Dhaka sits atop an active earthquake zone. Seismologists warn that a Richter 7.5 earthquake would reduce Dhaka to rubble and 80,000 buildings could go the same way as Rana Plaza. The predicted scale of destruction is that high because, surrounded by marshland, much of Dhaka's chaotic, unplanned expansion has been vertical rather than horizontal, typically with the same standard of construction that was exhibited at Rana Plaza.[7] None of these negative consequences of capitalist development figure in calculations of Bangladesh's GDP, yet they are real, and are borne by its workers and farmers and by its natural environment. They pay the price, but who profits? How much do the proceeds of their exploitation fuel capitalist development in Bangladesh, and how much of it feeds capitalist accumulation in imperialist countries?

Many commentators have drawn an analogy between the Tazreen and Rana Plaza disasters and notorious disasters in the United States and Europe more than a century ago, arguing that by catalyzing concerted action to tackle underlying causes these recent tragedies could force Bangladesh's garment factory bosses to finally clean up their act. Thus Amy Kazmin, writing in the *Financial Times*, argued:

Across the globe, industrial disasters have proved effective catalysts for change. New York City's 1911 Triangle Shirtwaist Fire, in which 146 garment workers— mostly women—were killed in part because fire exits were locked, helped spur the growth of the International Ladies' Garment Workers' Union, which successfully fought for better conditions for factory workers, including safety. Many now say that the Rana Plaza disaster—which came five months after a fire at another Bangladeshi factory, Tazreen Fashions, killed 112 people— could start to force similar change.[8]

There is no doubt that the Rana Plaza disaster will spur the struggle to unionize Bangladesh's garment industry. But the *FT* journalist forgets two things. The response of garment employers to the rise of the ILGWU was to move production to non-union states in the U.S. South, and, eventually, out of the United States altogether, to countries like Bangladesh. Today, just 2 percent of the clothing worn in the United States is actually made there. Peter Custers points out the other weakness in the naïve liberal view expressed by Amy Kazmin:

It is necessary . . . to be aware of structural differences between nineteenth-century British industries and those in contemporary

Bangladesh. For, unlike owners of the former, Bangladeshi garment owners are at the lower end of an international chain of subcontract relations, extending from production units in Bangladesh, via intermediaries, to retail trading companies in the countries of the North. . . . Garment production has been relocated to, and re-relocated within, the Third World, in order to tap cheap sources of wage labor. While local entrepreneurs obtain a part of the surplus value created, they do not get the major share. Thus, whereas the extraction of surplus value is organized by Bangladeshi owners, its fruits are overwhelmingly reaped by companies in the North.[9]

The collapse of Rana Plaza not only shone a light on the pitiless and extreme exploitation of Bangladeshi workers. It also lit up the hidden structure of the global capitalist economy, revealing the extent to which the capital-labor relation has become a relation between Northern capital and Southern labor. The garment industry was the first industrial sector to shift production to low-wage countries, yet power and profits remain firmly in the grip of firms in imperialist countries. This reality is very different from the fantasies projected by neoliberalism's apologists. Few informed observers would dispute that Primark (JCPenney in the United States), Walmart, M&S, and other major UK and U.S. retailers profit from the exploitation of Bangladeshi garment workers. Why else have they raced to outsource the production of their clothes to the lowest of low-wage countries? A moment's thought reveals other beneficiaries: the commercial capitalists who own the buildings leased by these retailers, the myriad companies providing them with advertising, security, and other services; and also governments, which tax their profits and their employees' wages and collect the VAT on every sale. Yet, according to trade and financial data, *not one penny* of U.S., European, and Japanese firms' profits or governments' tax revenues derive from the sweated labor of the workers who made their goods. The huge markups on production costs instead appear as "value-added" in the UK and other countries where these goods are consumed, with the perverse result that each item of clothing expands the GDP of the country where it is consumed by far more than that of the country where it is produced.[10] Only an economist could think there is nothing wrong about this!

All data and experience, *except for economic data*, point to a significant contribution to the profits of Primark, Walmart, and other Western firms by the workers who work long, hard, and for low wages to produce their commodities. Yet trade, GDP, and financial flow data show no trace of any such contribution; instead, the bulk of the value realized in the sale of these commodities and all of the profits reaped by the retail giants appear to originate in the country where they are consumed. Exploring and resolving this conundrum is a central task of this book. Our first step is to examine the social, economic, and political relations between workers and employers that are woven into the fabric of each article of apparel produced in low-wage countries like Bangladesh and sold in shopping malls across the imperialist world, where more than 80 percent of garments made in Bangladesh are sold. This will then be augmented by a forensic examination of two other representative "global commodities": the Apple iPhone and the cup of coffee.

THE T-SHIRT

In *The China Price,* Tony Norfield recounts the story of a T-shirt made in Bangladesh and sold in Germany for €4.95 by the Swedish retailer Hennes & Mauritz (H&M).[11] H&M pays the Bangladeshi manufacturer €1.35 for each T-shirt, 28 percent of the final sale price, 40¢ of which covers the cost of 400g of cotton raw material imported from the United States; shipping to Hamburg adds another 6¢ per shirt. Thus €0.95 of the final sale price remains in Bangladesh, to be shared between the factory owner, the workers, the suppliers of inputs and services and the Bangladeshi government, expanding Bangladesh's GDP by this amount. The remaining €3.54 counts toward the GDP of Germany, the country where the T-shirt is consumed, and is broken down as follows: €2.05 provides for the costs and profits of German transporters, wholesalers, retailers, advertisers, etc. (some of which will revert to the state through various taxes); H&M makes 60¢ profit per shirt; the German state captures 79¢ of the sale price through VAT at 19 percent; 16¢ covers sundry "other items." Thus, in Norfield's words, "a large chunk of the revenue from the selling price goes to the state in taxes and to a wide range of workers, executives, landlords, and businesses in Germany. The cheap T-shirts, and a wide range of other imported goods, are both affordable for consumers and an important source of income for the state and for all the people in the richer countries."

The central point Norfield is making cannot be emphasized enough, because so many liberals and socialists in imperialist countries try very hard to put it out of their minds. H&M makes handsome profits, to be sure, but these are dwarfed by the state's take, once taxes on wages and profits of H&M and suppliers of services to it are added to its VAT receipts. In 2013, the tariffs charged by the U.S. government on its apparel imports from Bangladesh alone exceeded the total wages received by the workers who made these goods. The state uses this money, as we know, to finance foreign wars, health care, and Social Security, and even returns a few pennies to the poor countries in the form of "foreign aid." As Tony Norfield argues, low wages in Bangladesh help explain "why the richer countries can have lots of shop assistants, delivery drivers, managers and administrators, accountants, advertising executives, a wide range of welfare payments and much else besides."[12] His blunt conclusion: "Wage rates in Bangladesh are particularly low, but even the multiples of these seen in other poor countries point to the same conclusion: oppression of workers in the poorer countries is a direct economic benefit for the mass of people in the richer countries."

In Norfield's account the Bangladeshi factory makes 125,000 shirts per day, of which half are sold to H&M, the rest to other Western retailers. A worker at the factory earns €1.36 per day, for 10–12 hours, producing 250 T-shirts per hour, or 18 T-shirts for each euro cent paid in wages. Her factory is one of 5,000 garment factories in Bangladesh employing 4 million people, 85 percent of whom are women. According to the ILO, the average wage of female "machine operators and assemblers" is 73 percent of their male counterparts.[13] Despite the massive influx of women into garment factories, female participation in the labor force in Bangladesh as a whole remains one of the lowest in the world. In 2010, 33.9 percent of working-age women were employed, compared with 79.2 per cent of working-age men.

As noted above, factory wages in Bangladesh are the lowest in the world. An investigation by a UK parliamentary committee into conditions in Bangladesh's garment industry following the Rana Plaza disaster reported that "Bangladesh's comparative advantage, its sole asset value, is cheap labor and its correspondingly low unit costs."[14] An in-depth report by leading U.S.-based management consultancy McKinsey & Co. into the growth of Bangladeshi apparel exports included an extensive survey of the outsourcing behavior of U.S. retailers, reporting that Bangladesh "competitive price level is clearly the prime advantage—all CPOs [chief purchasing officers] participating in the study named price attractiveness as the first and foremost reason for purchasing in Bangladesh."[15] The price that CPOs find so attractive, of course, is the price of labor-power, but McKinsey & Co., not wishing to offend the sensibilities of their big-business clients, make no mention of low wages anywhere in their study. For months following the Rana Plaza disaster, Bangladesh's Ready-made

Garments (RMG) industry was hit by waves of strikes and demonstrations centering on the demand for wage increases (or payment of wages due), the right to form unions, and the enforcement of widely ignored health and safety legislation. The Bangladeshi government, many of whose top officials are factory owners, responded in the same way to previous upsurges in 2006, 2010, and 2012—with violent repression, using the regular police, the *ansars* (village-based militias), and the "antiterrorist" Rapid Action Battalion—in addition to the Industrial Police, formed in the midst of the 2010 strike wave, whose sole task is to police garment districts and repress workers' protests. Its 2,900 officers contrast with the grand total of 51 inspectors who, at the time of the Rana Plaza disaster, were charged with enforcing health and safety, minimum age and minimum wage laws in all of Bangladesh's 200,000 workshops and factories, including 5,000 in the garment sector.[16]

Nevertheless, with worker militancy growing and with the glare of world attention upon them, in November 2013 the government conceded a 77 percent increase in the minimum wage. This was a significant victory, but far short of the 170 percent wage increase the workers demanded and for which they continue to struggle. It leaves their wages a long way below all estimates of what is needed to feed, clothe, and house their families. According to the Asia Floor Wage Alliance, an alliance of Asian trade unions and activist groups such as the Clean Clothes Campaign, the new basic wage is barely one-fifth of what is necessary to nourish, house, and clothe a garment worker, one adult, and two child dependents.[17] The 2013 wage hike was the first increase since 2010, and since then inflation has raised overall prices by 28 percent, and basic necessities like food and cooking oil by much more.

Low wages make big markups possible. In this example, the total markup on the production cost of the "fast fashion" T-shirt is 152 percent. Much higher markups are to be found on more expensive products; one notorious example being the replica football shirt, "a big money-spinner with 80 percent of those sold in the UK made in the Far East for around £5. The factory then sends them on to the sportswear companies at around a 50 percent markup. They in turn mark them up by another 100 percent and sell them to the retailers for around £14. The retailers add their own markup of at least 150 percent to bring the price tag up to the recommended retail price of at least £35. That's 700 percent more than the manufacture cost."[18] Another analyst estimates that a Bangladesh-made KP MacLane polo shirt, retailing in the United States for $175, generates a cool 718 percent markup on its cost of production,

and a Hermès polo shirt retailing at $455 boasts a markup in excess of
1800 percent.[19] These eye-watering markups contrast with the wafer-thin
margins left to Bangladeshi suppliers. Writing in the *Wall Street Journal*,
Rubana Huq, owner of a garment factory in Bangladesh, claims to make
12.5¢ on each shirt, whose cost of production is $6.62, a markup of 2 per-
cent.[20] This Bangladeshi factory owner is hardly a disinterested party and
her claims must be taken with a pinch of salt, but ruthless price-gouging
by global buyers is an incontrovertible fact, as a report by British parliamentarians recognized: "In the buyer-driven supply chain margins are
thin and the fear of undercutting is strong. As such the purchasing practices of brands can incentivise violations of health and safety through
undisclosed subcontracting, excessive working hours, and unauthorized
factory expansions."[21]

Eloquent testimony to the pressures focused on supplier firms by
TNCs was provided by factory owner Ali Ahmad, speaking after 289
garment workers were burned to death in a factory fire in Karachi in
September 2012:

> You have strikes, load shedding [power outages], local mafias charg-
> ing you turf protection money—you name it. . . . Plus you have
> ruthless buyers sitting in the U.S. who don't care what you do, as long
> as you do it on time. . . . We take a hit every time we're late. That
> means lost margins. That means we do what we need to do to make
> our orders, fast. This factory owner may have been working extra
> shifts just for that purpose.[22]

According to John Pickles, a leading authority on the global apparel
industry, so successful have global buyers been in forcing down wages
that they have recently shifted their attention elsewhere: "Marginal gains
from squeezing labor costs have been reduced significantly in recent
years. When wage levels were driven below subsistence costs, and could
not be driven any further down, buyers and suppliers sought out savings
in other areas of the value chain (input costs, transaction costs, logistics,
coordination costs, demand management, etc.)."[23] The result is intensifying pressure on suppliers to slash overheads, ignore health and safety
legislation, to impose forced overtime, and to subcontract work to other
factories lower down in the pecking order, where working conditions
are typically even worse than in the first-tier suppliers, or, as UNCTAD's
World Investment Report 2013 put it: "In labor-intensive sectors (such
as textiles and garments) where global buyers can exercise bargaining

power to reduce costs, this pressure often results in lower wages. . . . In addition to downward pressure on wages, the drive for reduced costs often results in significant occupational safety and health violations."[24]

The "global buyers" can, however, count on some academic witnesses to protect them against charges of culpability. "Factory owners face huge losses if they cannot complete an order and stiff financial penalties if they do not complete it on time," reported a major study by Sarah Labowitz and Dorothée Baumann-Pauly for New York's Stern School of Business.[25] Yet this report blames low wages and lethal workplaces on Bangladeshi government corruption, intermittent power supplies, overpopulation— anything but the conscious and deliberate policies of multinational corporations. Abandoning even the pretense of objectivity, Labowitz and Baumann-Pauly state at the outset that their study "is written in the context of . . . a shared desire for higher standards.... It starts from the premise that the garment sector has greatly benefited the people and the economy of Bangladesh . . . [and] that business can and does work for the good of society. We support the goal of business to create value while emphasizing high standards for human rights performance."[26] This fawning tone contrasts with the harsh rebuke handed down by the authors to "the government of Bangladesh [which] lacks the political will, the technical capacity, and the resources necessary to protect the basic rights of its workers. Bangladesh ranks at or near the bottom across all measures of good governance, including civil justice, regulatory enforcement, and absence of corruption."[27]

Also jumping to the defense of big business is Professor Jagdish Bhagwati of Columbia University, considered to be among the foremost theorists of international trade and who confesses to feeling miffed that he is yet to be awarded the Nobel Prize for economics.[28] "Since the factories were locally owned and operated, the blame surely belonged to their owners and managers, not to their clients any more than to those of us who purchased the garments at home or abroad."[29] For such a brilliant theory, he clearly deserves *something*!

WELL BEFORE THE RANA PLAZA DISASTER, Bangladesh's dismal record of factory fires and building collapses had provoked intense discussions between NGOs, international union federations IndustriAll and UNI Global Union, and representatives of Western clothing giants. Within two weeks of the building collapse the parties announced the "Accord on Fire and Building Safety in Bangladesh," whose centerpiece is the formation of a new factory inspectorate overseen by a Steering

Committee, chaired by the International Labor Organization, made up of three representatives from international unions and three from international companies.[30] Several months of lobbying of U.S. and European retail giants resulted in the endorsement of the Accord by over forty leading brands, with GAP and Walmart being notable exceptions. The parties to the Accord agreed to make "all reasonable efforts to ensure that an initial inspection of each factory covered by this Agreement shall be carried out within the first two years," and promised the publication of safety reports, remediation, and safety training. Supplier companies are required to form health and safety committees made up of managers and workers, the latter to be selected by unions or by "democratic election" where no union is present. Touted as "legally binding," the Accord only envisages penalties—that is, loss of orders—against supplier companies. The whole program is to be financed by the Western "brands," through a subscription related to the size of their business in the country.

As we have seen, the fundamental driving force of the race to the bottom and its attendant ills—starvation wages, rickety buildings, atrocious living conditions—is price-gouging by leading firms. How does the Accord address this? Section 22 responds to complaints by factory owners that relentless pressure from international retailers to cut production costs forces them to cut corners: "In order to induce factories to comply with upgrade and remediation requirements of the program, participating brands and retailers will negotiate commercial terms with their suppliers which ensure that it is financially feasible for the factories to maintain safe workplaces and comply with upgrade and remediation requirements instituted by the Safety Inspector." Nobody and no administrative body is tasked with implementing or monitoring this clause. It can only be activated by a factory owner who believes s/he is not receiving "commercial terms" from a global buyer and decides to arraign the global buyer before the Accord's Steering Committee. Should either party disagree with the Steering Committee's ruling, they may submit the dispute to legally binding arbitration. To protect the factory owner from the threat of cancellation of orders, the Accord obliges buying firms to maintain existing contracts for two years. But legal safeguards do not change the extreme power asymmetry—fear of reprisals from their own buyers and blacklisting by others mean factory owners will hesitate to take this path. And the Accord's mechanisms involve international union representatives in giving their assent to "commercial terms" that do not provide for garment workers to be paid a living wage.

SUSCEPTIBILITY TO FIRE AND COLLAPSE are far from the only building safety issues in Bangladesh. Most deaths and injuries in the year following the Rana Plaza disaster resulted from stampedes sparked by the outbreak of small fires, revealing the lack of exits and stairwells.[31] Despite Bangladesh's sweltering climate, where temperatures often reach into the mid-90s and humidity is high year-round, lack of ventilation, often compounded by chemical vapors from dyes and other inputs, are among the unhealthy and unsafe working conditions not covered by the "Accord on Fire and Building Safety." Nor is there any mention in the Accord of excessive and forced overtime, a key health and safety issue; nor are supplier factories required to allow trade unions to organize— despite shop-floor union organization being the most important line of defense against dangerous working practices. Nevertheless, Jyrki Raina described the Accord as "historic"; Philip Jennings, General Secretary of UNI, defined it as a "turning point" that marked "the end of the race to the bottom in the global supply chain"; and a joint press release from IndustriALL and UNI generously described their multinational partners as "the most progressive global fashion brands."[32]

After Rana Plaza, Jyrki Raina pledged to "use the global muscle of IndustriALL to create sustainable conditions for garment workers, with the right to join a union, with living wages, and safe and healthy working conditions." Yet unions in Western Europe and North America outsourced the organization of protests to anti-sweatshop activists and campaigning charities and did nothing to mobilize their members in solidarity. Unions in North America added their names to an "international day of action to end deathtraps" in June 2013, but there is no evidence of any serious effort to build this action. Instead, their reflex has been to act in partnership with imperialist governments and international brands. The UK trade union Unite and North America's United Steelworkers, both of which are affiliated to IndustriALL, issued a joint statement a few days after the Rana Plaza disaster urging the U.S. and European governments "to immediately suspend Bangladesh's market access under the Generalized System of Preferences" and "to enact laws . . . that would ban the importation of goods produced under sweatshop conditions."[33] The Generalized System of Preferences (GSP) allows tariff-free imports into North America and Europe from the "Least Developed Countries." In the United States, union officials successfully petitioned the U.S. government to rescind Bangladesh's tariff-free access to the U.S. market, inducing President Barack Obama to piously declare to the U.S. Congress on June 27, 2013, that Bangladesh "is now taking steps to afford internationally recognized worker rights." Richard Trumka, president of the AFL-CIO, welcomed the decision, declaring, "The decision to suspend trade benefits sends an important message to our trading partners. . . . Countries that tolerate dangerous—and even deadly—working conditions and deny basic workers' rights, especially the right to freedom of association, will risk losing preferential access to the U.S. market."[34]

This move was largely symbolic—because of protectionist pressure from U.S. employers and union officials, less than 1 percent of imports from Bangladesh enter the United States free of tariffs. Until Obama rescinded even this, the biggest beneficiary was tobacco, followed by plastic bags, golf equipment, and hotel crockery. In 2013, the U.S. government received $809.5 million in customs duties on $4.9 billion of garment exports from Bangladesh, an average tariff of 16.5 percent.[35] The average wage of the 4 million workers in Bangladesh's RMG industry in the year of the Rana Plaza disaster, before the November 2013 increase, was $780 per year, for a total wage bill of $3.1bn.[36] The United States imports 22 percent of Bangladesh's apparel exports, so it can be estimated that 22 percent of $3.1bn, or $690m, was paid in wages to the workers who produced goods destined for the United States. In other words, the tariffs charged in 2013 by the U.S. government on its apparel imports from Bangladesh alone exceeded the total wages received by the workers who made these goods. And this punitive protectionist policy is carried out at the behest of union officials who claim to be concerned about the plight of Bangladeshi workers!

The protectionist policies supported by union officials in imperialist countries are roundly opposed by Bangladeshi trade unions and labor activists and for this reason are not promoted by IndustriALL or UNI, which include Bangladeshi trade union affiliates. Dr. Supachai Panitchpakdi, Secretary-General of UNCTAD (United Nations Conference on Trade and Development), denounced calls for punitive tariffs as a "a serious threat to the rule-based global trading system," adding that, instead of penalizing Bangladeshi employers and workers in the name of "labor rights," importing countries "must look at the business practices of their retail and wholesale industry because the problem with global value chains is the way they are exploiting the sweatshops in poor countries which are providing cheap labor."[37]

These issues are not new. Union officials and social-democratic politicians in imperialist countries have long sought to protect their workers from "unfair competition" from workers in poor countries, hiding behind feigned concern for human rights in oppressed nations. Their hypocrisy was exposed by Palash Baral, a representative of UBINIG (Policy Research for Development Alternatives), a Bangladeshi NGO, in remarks to a seminar in London organized by the UK campaigning charity War on Want in the mid-1990s:

> The issues of "labor standards" and "workers rights" have been raised out of no concern for our workers, neither do they constitute any concern for human rights. They are neo-protectionist slogans and reflect attempts by the ruling class of the North to smokescreen the real cause of the economic crisis the North is going through. . . . The World Bank and IMF create the conditions for "social dumping" . . . [then] some NGOs as well as some trade unions propose to "civilise" us . . . by twisting our arms when we come to sell our products to their markets. They have nothing to say against the World Bank, no complaints about Structural Adjustment and no attempt to understand the transnationals and their behaviour . . . if one is really serious about labor standards and workers' rights, then one should join hands with the workers of Bangladesh.[38]

THE iPHONE

In contrast to the humble T-shirt, iPhones and laptops are technologically complex commodities. Their dazzling sophistication and iconic brand status can too easily blind the observer to the exploitative and imperialist character of the social and economic relations they embody. Nevertheless, the same fundamental relationships that can be seen in the simple article of apparel are also visible in the latest high-tech gadgetry. The same question that we have asked of the T-shirt hanging from your shoulders could also be asked of the smartphone in your trouser pocket, or indeed of any other global commodity; that is, any other product of globalized production processes. The question we have asked of the T-shirt can also be asked of the iPhone: what contribution do the 1.23 million workers employed by Foxconn International in Shenzhen, China, who assemble Dell's laptops and Apple's iPhones—and the tens of millions of other workers in low-wage countries around the world who produce cheap intermediate inputs and consumer goods for Western markets—make to the profits of Dell, Apple, and other leading Western firms? Or to the income and profits of the service companies that provide their premises, retail their goods, etc.? According to GDP, trade, and financial flow statistics, and to mainstream economic theory, *none whatsoever.* Apple does not own the Chinese, Malaysian, and other production facilities that manufacture and assemble its products. In contrast to the in-house, foreign direct investment relationship that used to typify transnational corporations, no annual flow of repatriated profits is generated by Apple's "arm's length" suppliers. Just as with the T-shirt, the standard interpretation of data on production and trade assumes that the slice of the iPhone's final selling price captured by each U.S., Chinese, and other national firm is identical to the "value-added" that each contributed. They reveal no sign of any cross-border profit flows or value transfers affecting the distribution of profits to Apple and its various suppliers. The only part of Apple's profits that appear to origi-nate in China are those resulting from the sale of its products in that country. As in the case of the T-shirt made in Bangladesh, so with the latest electronic gadget: the flow of wealth from Chinese and other low-wage workers sustaining the profits and prosperity of Northern firms and nations is rendered invisible in economic data and in the brains of the economists.

APPLE'S PRODUCTS, AND THOSE OF DELL, Motorola, and other U.S., European, South Korean, and Japanese companies—an esti-mated 40 percent of the world's consumer electronics, according to the *New York Times*—are assembled by FoxConn, the major subsidiary of Taiwan-based Hon Hai Precision Industries.[39] Its complex of fourteen factories at Shenzhen in southern China became famous both for its sheer size and for the fourteen suicides among its workers in 2010—and for the management's ham-fisted attempts to show its concern, by erect-ing nets to catch workers jumping from dormitory windows. FoxConn's Shenzhen workforce peaked that year at around 430,000 workers and was then scaled back in favor of plants elsewhere in China. Most of these are young migrant workers whose right to reside in the city is depen-dent on their employment, who have no access to municipally provided health and education services, and who cannot bring their families to live with them. In 2013, according to Chinese government figures, 260 million workers were officially defined as residents of their rural places of origin, denying them legal rights and access to a wide range of benefits in the cities where they now live and work.[40] This is the *hukou* system, through which the CCP government has sought to control the influx of labor from the countryside and to create a cheap captive labor force for TNCs and their suppliers. *Hukou* is a source of deep social divisions and tensions, as the regime promises its reform but resists growing demands for its abolition.

Citing a 2012 survey of "ten factories producing Apple products in China, including a Foxconn plant," Marty Hart-Landsberg reports:

> Low wages compel workers to accept long overtime hours. Most of the factories pay a basic salary equal to the minimum wage stipulated by the local law (around $200/month), so low that workers have to work long hours to support themselves. . . . The average overtime in most of the factories was between 100 and 130 hours per month, and between 150 and 180 hours per month during peak production season, well above China's legal limits. In most factories, workers generally work 11 hours every day, including weekends and holidays during peak seasons. Normally they can only take a day off every month, or in the peak seasons may go several months without a day off. [41]

In one of the studies cited by Hart-Lansberg, Pun Ngai and Jenny Chan gathered testimonies from workers at Foxconn's Shenzhen factories that provide many insights into the brutal labor regime that is part of the hidden price for Apple's super profits and Western consumers' access to the latest high-tech gadgets:

> No admittance except on business—every Foxconn factory building and dormitory has security checkpoints with guards standing by 24 hours a day. In order to enter the shop floor, workers must pass through layers of electronic gates and inspection systems. Our interviewees repeatedly expressed the feeling that the entry access system made them feel as if working at Foxconn is to totally lose one's freedom.... While getting ready to start work on the production line, management will ask the workers: "How are you?" Workers must respond by shouting in unison, "Good! Very good! Very, very good!" This militaristic drilling is said to train workers as disciplined laborers. . . . Workers recalled how they were punished when they talked on the line, failed to keep up with the high speed of work, and made mistakes in work procedures. [42]

Not only does the length of the workday and the workweek test the limits of human endurance, workers are forced to work with great intensity throughout their long hours:

"We can't stop work for a minute. We're even faster than machines."
A young woman worker added, "Wearing gloves would eat into
efficiency, we have a huge workload every day and wearing gloves
would influence efficiency. . . . " On an assembly line in the Shenzhen
Longhua plant, a worker described her work to precise seconds: "I
take a motherboard from the line, scan the logo, put it in an anti-
static-electricity bag, stick on a label, and place it on the line. Each of
these tasks takes two seconds. Every ten seconds I finish five tasks."

THESE TESTIMONIES REMIND US THAT ultra-low wages are not
the only factor attracting profit-hungry Western firms to newly industrializing countries. As in the case of Bangladesh's garment industry,
they are also attracted by the flexibility of the workers, the absence of
independent unions, the relative ease with which they can be forced to
submit to working days as long as those described by Marx and Engels in
mid-nineteenth-century England, and the intensity with which they can
work. Charles Duhigg and Keith Bradsher, in a widely quoted *New York
Times* study, provide a vivid illustration of this:

> One former executive described how [Apple] relied upon a Chinese
> factory to revamp iPhone manufacturing just weeks before the device
> was due on shelves. Apple had redesigned the iPhone's screen at the
> last minute, forcing an assembly line overhaul. New screens began
> arriving at the plant near midnight. A foreman immediately roused
> 8,000 workers inside the company's dormitories, according to the
> executive. Each employee was given a biscuit and a cup of tea, guided
> to a workstation and within half an hour started a 12-hour shift fit-
> ting glass screens into beveled frames. Within 96 hours, the plant was
> producing over 10,000 iPhones a day.[43]

Terry Gou, chairman of Hon Hai, FoxConn's parent company, provoked a storm of criticism in January 2012 with his remark, during a visit
to Taipei zoo, that "as human beings are also animals, to manage one million animals gives me a headache," following this up with a request to the
zookeeper for advice on how best to manage his "animals." *Want China
Times* commented, "Gou's words could have been chosen more carefully.
. . . At its huge plants in China . . . working and living conditions are such
that many of its Chinese employees might well agree that they are treated
like animals."[44]

IT IS WORTH PAUSING AT THIS POINT to see how the ideologues of neoliberalism justify the brutal labor regimes fostered by the policies they have designed and promoted. Jagdish Bhagwati argues that TNCs provide job opportunities to eager workers at higher rates of pay than alternative jobs and therefore cannot be said to be exploiting anyone: "If the wages received are actually higher than those available in alternative jobs, even if low according to the critics . . . surely it seems odd to say that the multinationals are exploiting the workers they are hiring!"[45] Such charges seem absurd to him because, whatever the level of wages that prevail within a country, if they are market-determined then that is what these workers are worth, and TNCs paying slightly more cannot be accused of exploitation. Whether or not these wages meet the worker's minimum biological needs, and how hard or long s/he has to work to earn that wage, is irrelevant. Moreover, "By adding to the demand for labor in the host countries, multinationals are also overwhelmingly likely to improve wages all round, thus improving the incomes of workers in these countries."[46] Yet, as we shall explore in chapters 4 and 5, nowhere, not even in China, have jobs generated by export-oriented industrialization kept pace with the growth of the labor force, greatly limiting these alleged beneficial effects.

In a similarly cavalier manner, Bhagwati dismisses charges that there is any problem with hazardous working conditions and violations of labor law in poor countries—or, if there is, none that multinational companies should take responsibility for:

> It is highly unlikely that multinational firms would violate domestic regulatory laws, which generally are not particularly demanding. Since the laws are often not burdensome in poor countries, it is hard to find evidence that violations are taking place in an egregious, even substantial fashion. . . . Sweatshops are typically small-scale workshops, not multinationals. If the subcontractors who supply parts to the multinationals, for example, are tiny enterprises, it is possible that they, like local entrepreneurs, violate legislation from time to time. But since the problem lies with the lack of effective enforcement in the host country, do we hold multinationals accountable for anything that they buy from these countries, even if it is not produced directly by the multinationals?[47]

The reality Bhagwati so blithely dismisses is succinctly summarized by UNCTAD:

Buyer-driven GVCs [Global Value Chains] are typically focused on reduced sourcing costs, and . . . this means significant downward pressure on labor costs and environmental management costs. Some suppliers are achieving reduced labor costs through violations of national and international labor standards and human rights laws. Practices such as forced labor, child labor, failure to pay minimum wage and illegal overtime work are typical challenges in a number of industries. In addition to downward pressure on wages, the drive for reduced costs often results in significant occupational safety and health violations. . . . Downward pricing pressure has created economic incentives for violating environmental regulations and industry best practices, leading to the increased release of disease-causing pollutants and climate change–related emissions. Cutting costs by engaging in negative social and environmental practices is a particularly acute trend in developing countries.[48]

Bhagwati even uses a feminist argument to defend his beloved multi-national corporations, and was one of the few to spring to the industries' defense after the Rana Plaza disaster. Casting around for evidence of the "liberating effect [on] young girls in Bangladesh" of employment in garment factories, he quotes a study on girls' adolescence in developing countries:

Unmarried girls employed in these garment factories may endure onerous working conditions, but they also experience pride in their earnings, maintain a higher standard of dress than their unemployed counterparts and, most significantly, develop an identity apart from being a child or wife. . . . Legitimate income-generating work could transform the nature of girls' adolescent experience. It could provide them with a degree of autonomy, self-respect, and freedom from tra-ditional gender work.[49]

This is, to say the least, shallow and one-sided. It casually dismisses the conclusions of decades of feminist-inspired research into "the ways in which apparently modern factory organization drew on, and indeed actively promoted, cultural norms of femininity which helped to legiti-mate employers' 'super-exploitation' of their predominantly female workforce."[50] It forgets that TNCs and their suppliers hire "young unmar-ried girls" in order to profit from their oppression, not to liberate them from it; and it follows from Bhagwati's own theories of self-interested, profit-maximizing behavior that employers and politicians, who in Bangladesh are often the same people, have every interest in maintaining the double oppression of women—from which they benefit directly, through even lower wages, and indirectly, by entrenching gender divisions among workers. To this end they counter the potentially liberating effect of female factory employment by using every weapon at hand to perpetuate female submissiveness—including endemic violence, humiliation, and sexual abuse of women workers by male overseers, non-enforcement of laws on maternity leave and childcare, and the use of definitions of "skill" to downgrade women's labor. [51] This is not to mention the broader ideological offensive, in which promotion of obscurantist religious ideology, which in Bangladesh takes the form of Islamic fundamentalism, is aimed at preventing women workers from seeing themselves, and from being seen by others, as workers rather than housewives, as full and equal members of society rather than as possessions and appendages of present or future husbands.

The enormous influx of women into factory labor, even in countries like Bangladesh where they have traditionally been confined within the home, will be analyzed in more detail in a later chapter; so too the relation between capitalist exploitation of waged labor and women's oppression and their performance of unpaid domestic labor.

THE APPLE IPHONE AND RELATED PRODUCTS are prototypical global commodities, the result of the choreography of an immense diversity of concrete labors of workers in five continents. Contained within each hand-held device are the social relations of contemporary global capitalism.

Research on the Apple iPod published in 2007 by Greg Linden, Jason Dedrick, and Kenneth Kraemer is particularly valuable because it does something not attempted in the more recent studies cited here. These researchers attempt to quantify the living labor directly involved in the design, production, transportation, and sale of this Apple product, and also report the vastly different wages received by these diverse groups of workers.[52]

In 2006, the 30GB Apple iPod retailed at $299, while the total cost of production, performed entirely overseas, was $144.40, giving a gross profit margin of 52 percent. What Linden et al. call gross profits, the other $154.60, is divided among Apple, its retailers and distributors, and—through taxes on sales, profits, and wages—the U.S. government. All of this, 52 percent of the final sale price, is counted as value-added generated within the United States and contributes toward U.S. GDP. Linden et al. found that "the iPod and its components accounted for about 41,000 jobs worldwide in 2006, of which about 27,000 were outside the U.S. and 14,000 in the U.S. The offshore jobs are mostly in low-wage manufacturing, while the jobs in the U.S. are more evenly divided between high-wage engineers and managers and lower-wage retail and non-professional workers."[53]

Just thirty of the 13,920 U.S. workers were production workers (receiving, on average, $47,640 per year), 7,789 were "retail and other non-professional" workers (average wages, $25,580 per year), and 6,101 were "professional" workers, that is, managers and engineers involved in research and development. The latter category captured more than two-thirds of the total U.S. wage bill, receiving, on average, $85,000 per annum. Meanwhile, 12,250 Chinese production workers received $1,540 per annum, or $30 per week—just 6 percent of the average wages of U.S. workers in retail, 3.2 percent of the wages of U.S. production workers, and 1.8 percent of the salaries of U.S. professional workers.[54] The number of workers employed in iPod-related activities was similar in the United States and China, yet the total U.S. wage bill was $719m and the total Chinese wage bill was $19m.

A study published by the Asian Development Bank (ADB) in 2010 reported on the first version of Apple's next big product, revealing an even more spectacular markup: "iPhones were introduced to the U.S. market in 2007 to large fanfare, selling an estimated 3 million units in the U.S. in 2007, 5.3 million in 2008, and 11.3 million in 2009." The total manufacturing cost of each iPhone was $178.96 and sold for $500, yielding a gross profit of 64 percent to be shared between Apple, its North American suppliers and distributors, and the U.S. government, all appearing as value-added generated within the United States. The main focus of the ADB study was the effect of iPhone production on the U.S.-China trade deficit, finding that "most of the export value and the deficit due to the iPhone are attributed to imported parts and components from third countries. . . . Chinese workers . . . contribute only US$6.50 to each iPhone, about 3.6 percent of the total manufacturing cost."[55] Thus, more than 96 percent of the export value of the iPhone is composed of re-exported components manufactured elsewhere, all of which counts toward China's exports but none counts toward China's GDP.[56] The authors do not investigate in detail how these gross profits are shared between Apple, suppliers of services, and the U.S. government, but they can hardly avoid commenting on their spectacular size: "If the market were fiercely competitive, the expected profit margin would be much lower. . . . Surging sales and the high profit margin suggest that . . . Apple maintains a relative monopoly position. . . . It is the profit maximization behavior of Apple rather than competition that pushes Apple to have all iPhones assembled in the PRC." [57]

This leads the ADB researchers to imagine a scenario in which Apple moved iPhone assembly to the United States. They assume U.S. wages to be ten times higher than in China and that these hypothetical U.S. assembly workers would work as intensely as the real ones do at FoxConn, calculating that "if iPhones were assembled in the U.S. the total assembly cost would rise to US$65 and would still leave a 50 percent profit margin for Apple." [58] They finish with an appeal to Apple to show some "corporate social responsibility" by "[g]iving up a small portion of profits and sharing them with low skilled U.S. workers" and re-shore iPhone assembly to the United States. [59] The researchers do not consider Apple's "corporate social responsibility" to the Chinese workers who are paid a pittance for their labor and who would be made redundant if Apple were to follow the ADB's advice. And it should be noted that whether the profit margin is 64 percent or 50 percent, it is not just "Apple's profit"—Apple must share this markup with its service suppliers and the U.S. government.

The first version of the iPhone was also the first-ever smartphone, so Apple's initial markup might be thought of, in part at least, as a reflection of its unique status. [60] Since then Samsung, HTC, Nokia, and other producers have launched their own smartphones—indeed, in the first quarter of 2014 Apple's share of the global smartphone market had fallen to just 15 percent by units sold, half Samsung's share. "Apple remains strong in the premium smartphone segment, but a lack of presence in the entry-level category continues to cost it lost volumes in fast-growing emerging markets such as Latin America," said one industry analyst. [61] Yet, seven years after the launch of the first iPhone, Apple has broadly succeeded in maintaining these exorbitant markups. According to a report by UBS researchers published in September 2013, the production cost of a 16GB iPhone 5C was $156, rising to $213 for a 16GB iPhone 5S, while the retail price for each unlocked handset is $549 and $649 respectively, yielding gross profit margins of 61 percent and 67 percent. [62] Nevertheless, according to the *Financial Times* Lex column, "Phones, even Apple's, are becoming commoditised. Apple is selling more phones, but making less money: each iPhone went for an average $41 less than in the previous quarter as cheaper older models spearheaded an emerging markets push." [63]

IT IS PARTICULARLY INSTRUCTIVE TO COMPARE Apple's profits and share price with those of its principal supplier. In the year to May 2013 Hon Hai made $10.7bn in profits (on sales of $132.1bn), which works out as $8,685 for each of its 1,232,000 employees, compared to Apple's $41.7bn profits (on sales of $164.7bn), or $572,800 profit for each of its 72,800 employees (47,000 of whom are in the United States). In May 2013, Hon Hai's share price valued the company at $32.1bn; while Apple, with not a factory to its name, was valued at $416.6bn.[64] Since overtaking Exxon in 2011, Apple has reigned supreme as the world's most valuable company. During that year Apple's earning growth was large enough to cancel out the decline in the earnings of all other U.S. companies, thereby providing crucial support to the U.S. economy as it struggled to emerge from the post-Lehman crash.[65] Further boosting its share price, it has accumulated a huge cash stockpile—standing at $146.8bn at the beginning of 2014, despite returning billions of dollars to shareholders in a share buy-back scheme—that it has no productive use for.[66]

Meanwhile, in what one study called a "paradox of assembler misery and brand wealth," Hon Hai's profits and share price have been caught in the pincers of rising Chinese wages, conceded in the face of mounting worker militancy, and by increasingly onerous contractual requirements, as the growing sophistication of Apple's and other firms' products increase the time required for assembly.[67] While Apple's share price has risen more than tenfold since 2005, over the same period Hon Hai's share price slumped by more than 80 percent. The *Financial Times* reported in August 2011 that "costs per employee [are] up by exactly one-third, year-on-year, to just under U.S.$2,900. The total staff bill was $272m: almost double gross profit. . . . Rising wages on the mainland helped to drive the consolidated operating margin of the world's largest contract manufacturer of electronic devices . . . from 4–5 percent 10 years ago to a 1–2 percent range now."[68]

The company is seeking cheaper labor and reduced dependence on the increasingly restive Shenzhen workforce, and as *FT* columnist Robin Kwong reports, "Hon Hai . . . has invested heavily in shifting production from China's coastal areas to further inland and is in the process of increasing automation at its factories. As a result, Hon Hai last year saw its already-thin margins shrink even further."[69] FoxConn, which in 2013 reportedly relied on iPods and iPhones for at least 40 percent of its revenue, has moved its iPhone 5 assembly to Zhengzhou in northern China, where 100 assembly lines, each with three shifts of 600 workers working around the clock and exclusively occupied in iPhone assembly, churn

out 500,000 handsets every day.[70] Along with thousands more employed
in the production of metal casings and ancillary staff, a total of 300,000
workers are dedicated to meeting Apple's iPhone orders. Apple's dependence on Hon Hai is a vulnerability as well as a source of revenues and
profits; industry analysts report in April 2014 that Apple is set to dilute
its dependence on FoxConn and outsource part of the production of the
iPhone 6 to another Taiwan-based electronics contract manufacturer,
Pegatron, which to this end is building a giant factory near Shanghai.

The combination of sharply rising wages, heavy capital spending, and
relentless cost-cutting by Apple is bad enough, but worst of all is the
chronic sickness into which Hon Hai's and China's principal export markets have fallen. Kwong concludes, "it is not hard to see why the last thing
Gou needs now, after building all those inland factories, is a slowdown
in demand."[71]

THE CUP OF COFFEE

Our picture is completed by the addition of a third iconic global commodity—the cup of coffee. Perhaps you have one clasped in your hand—don't
spill any on your T-shirt or your smartphone as you read this! Coffee is
unique among major internationally traded agricultural commodities in
that none of it, apart from small quantities grown in Hawaii, is grown
in imperialist countries, and for this reason it has not been subject to
trade-distorting agricultural subsidies such as those affecting cotton and
sugar. Yet the world's coffee farmers have fared as badly if not worse than
other primary commodity producers. Most of the world's coffee is grown
on small family farms, providing employment worldwide to 25 million
coffee farmers and their families, while two U.S. and two European firms,
Sara Lee and Kraft, Nestlé and Procter & Gamble, dominate the global
coffee trade.

In common with other global commodities, the portion of the final
price of a bag or a cup of coffee that is counted as value-added within the
coffee-drinking countries has steadily risen over time. According to the
International Coffee Organization, the markup on the world market price
of coffee for nine imperialist nations that account for more than two-
thirds of global imports averaged 235 percent between 1975 and 1989,
382 percent between 1990 and 1999, and 429 percent between 2000 and
2009.[72] As this report points out, these impressive figures significantly
underestimate both the magnitude of the markup and also the pace of its
increase, since it is based on the assumption that all imported coffee is

sold to consumers at market prices, whereas an increasing percentage of coffee consumption takes place in local cafés, where the markup is considerably higher. How much higher can be estimated by considering that a barista typically obtains 60 shots of espresso per pound bag of coffee, that is, approximately 15¢ per shot. Adding another 15¢ for milk, sugar, and a disposable cup, the $3 retail price represents a 900 percent markup over the cost of its ingredients.[73]

It is notable that the trend toward ever-higher markups has continued whether the world market price of coffee is rising or falling. The period between 1975 and 1989 was marked by increasing overproduction and falling world prices, despite the operation of the International Coffee Agreement, established in 1962, which attempted to protect both producers and consumers from wild fluctuations in coffee prices through a complex system of quotas and the use of buffer stocks. Driven by ideological opposition to interference in free markets, the coffee-swilling nations torpedoed the agreement in 1989. The 1990 to 1999 period duly saw wild fluctuations in the world market price of coffee, which finished the decade even lower than it started, reaching rock bottom in 2002, 83 percent below its 1980 level. In 2002, coffee exporters earned a total of $5.5bn, to be shared among export companies, governments, and an estimated 125 million coffee farmers and their families. Ignoring the slice taken by exporters and governments, this works out to $44 per person per year, way below the $1.25/day that the World Bank defines as "extreme poverty." Oxfam reported that "there has never been such a dramatic collapse in the coffee market," and urged immediate action to mitigate the devastating effects on coffee producers and coffee-producing nations, pleas that were completely ignored.[74] During the first decade of the new millennium coffee prices recovered from their historic lows, tripling in value by the decade's end, yet the markup in the imperialist nations and therefore the contribution of coffee to their GDPs continued to rise. By 2010 coffee had been swept up in the "commodities supercycle," fueled by increasing demand in China and other new consumers and also by speculative financial flows driven by ultra-low interest rates in the main imperialist economies. Having tripled between 2002 and 2010, in a matter of months the market price of coffee doubled again, reaching a thirty-four-year high in March 2011, only to fall 60 percent by November 2013 as speculators took their profits. An unprecedented drought in Brazil, the world's biggest producer, provoked an 85 percent rise in the world market price in the first four months of 2014, amid accumulating evidence that capitalism-induced climate change is already wreaking havoc on tropical agriculture and ecosystems. These wild gyrations have terrible consequences for coffee producers, but they create immense opportunities for speculation and profiteering for imperialist coffee monopolies and financial speculators.

The real human cost of the imperialist-dominated global coffee market cannot be grasped by mere statistics, however. The destruction of the International Coffee Agreement in 1989 played a crucial but almost completely unacknowledged role in the creation of the conditions for genocide in Rwanda. This poor African nation relied almost exclusively on coffee for its export earnings. As the world market price of coffee plummeted so did the Rwandan economy, bringing famine, hyperinflation, and government collapse down on the heads of the Rwandan people. When the Rwandan government begged the IMF for emergency assistance, the latter duly responded with a stingy loan and a savage structural adjustment program that only intensified the misery and insecurity of the Rwandan people.[75] Isaac Kamola, in the aptly named *The Global Coffee Economy and the Production of Genocide in Rwanda,* adds that "these economic stresses created the conditions in which state-owned enterprises went bankrupt, health and education services collapsed, child malnutrition surged and malaria cases increased by 21 percent."[76] Michel Chossudovsky, in *The Globalization of Poverty,* comments that "no sensitivity or concern was expressed [by the IMF] as to the likely political and social repercussions of economic shock therapy applied to a country on the brink of civil war. . . . The deliberate manipulation of market forces destroyed economic activity and people's livelihood, fuelled unemployment and created a situation of generalized famine and social despair."[77] Apart from these and a few other exceptions, it is shocking the degree to which the causal role played by the destruction of the International Coffee Agreement and the IMF's imposition of brutal austerity in Rwanda's genocide has been ignored, both in the copious Western media coverage of the terrible events of 1994 and in the academic literature generated by it.

Coffee differs from the T-shirt and the iPhone in one important respect: unlike the other members of this profane trinity, coffee does not arrive in the consuming nations as a finished good, already bagged and labeled and ready for sale. Part of the gross value-added captured by coffee retailers within the imperialist countries production therefore corresponds to the roasting and grinding of the dry cherries, and also, in the case of coffee consumed in cafés, the production labor of the barista. Yet this does not change the overall picture. Roasting and grinding coffee beans, in contrast to their cultivation, is not labor-intensive, one reason why the imperialist monopolies that dominate the global coffee economy have not been tempted to outsource this production task. Another reason is to ensure that monopoly power remains concentrated in their hands: the big markups and juiciest profits are in the processing of the raw beans, unlike in the clothing industry, where the big markups are obtained from the retailing of finished garments, or smartphones, where Apple's fat profits arise from patented technology as well as branding and retailing. Those who cultivate and harvest the coffee receive less than 3 percent of its final retail price.[78] In 2009, according to the International Coffee Organization, the roasting, marketing, and sale of coffee added $31bn to the GDP of the nine most important coffee-importing nations, more than twice as much as all coffee-producing nations earned from growing and exporting it—and, as noted above, this does not include the value-added captured by cafés and restaurants.

Just as, according to the economists and accountants, not one cent of Apple's profits comes from Chinese workers and just as H&M's bottom line owes nothing to super-exploited Bangladeshi workers, so do all of Starbucks' and London-based Caffè Nero's profits appear to arise from their own marketing, branding, and retailing genius, and not a penny can be traced to the impoverished coffee farmers who hand-pick the fresh cherries. In all of our three archetypical global commodities, gross profits, that is, the difference between their cost of production and their retail price, are far in excess of 50 percent, flattering not only Northern firms' profits but also their nations' GDP.[79]

Squeezing wages allows markups to increase. Thus UNCTAD reports that "clothing, footwear, textiles, furniture, miscellaneous manufacturers (which includes toys) and chemicals all experienced import price declines (relative to U.S. consumer prices) over two decades of more than 1 percent per year on average, or 40 percent over the period 1986–2006."[80]

THIS CHAPTER'S INVESTIGATION INTO THE SOCIAL relations embodied in three global commodities yields some important paradoxes and anomalies requiring further analysis and a series of distinct dimensions that need to be investigated separately before they can be brought together in a synthesis, a theory of the latest stage of capitalism's imperialist evolution. Together they shape the book's overall structure, and can be resolved into seven themes that will be addressed in the following sequence:

1. THE GLOBAL SHIFT OF PRODUCTION TO LOW-WAGE COUNTRIES. The T-shirt, the iPhone, and the cup of coffee are representative examples of the universe of global commodities, i.e., the products of global value chains and globalized production networks. Chapters 2 and 3 turn the telescope around, so to speak, and survey the transformation and global shift of production that these archetypical commodities are representative of. Chapter 2, "Outsourcing, or the Globalization of Production," analyzes neoliberal globalization's most important transformation: the globalization of production processes, discovering its antecedents, its proportions, its qualities, its dynamism, and its driving force: the hunger of Northern capitalists for low-wage labor corralled in Southern nations. Chapter 3, "The Two Forms of the Outsourcing Relationship," continues the study of global outsourcing by analyzing three aspects of particular importance: the differences and similarities between the two forms of the outsourcing relationship—"in-house" and the increasingly favored "arm's length" relations with an independent supplier; the peculiar structure of world trade, in which firms in low-wage nations compete with each other in export markets, as do firms in imperialist nations, but competition between firms in imperialist and low-wage nations is by and large absent, their relationship is complementary, not competitive; and the divergence between the low-wage nations' increasing share of manufacturing trade and the much less impressive growth in their share of global manufacturing value-added.

2. CONDITIONS IN LABOR MARKETS ARE AT LEAST AS IMPORTANT AS CONDITIONS IN PRODUCT AND CAPITAL MARKETS. This first chapter has highlighted the critical importance of conditions in labor markets, as well as product and financial markets, to any understanding of the forces shaping the global political economy. Chapter 4, "Southern Labor: Peripheral No Longer," examines the economic and social conditions that determine the terms on which Southern workers can sell their labor-power, paying particular attention to the massive structural unemployment and underemployment in low-wage nations and to the violent suppression of the free movement of working people across the borders between imperialist and low-wage countries, arguing that this lies at the root of the vast wage differentials. The role of these characteristic features of so-called development in the promotion of informal, flexible, and precarious labor regimes is analyzed, and the chapter concludes by studying the intersection of patriarchy, class, and imperialism that gives rise to another striking feature of the global transformation of production, one

that is highlighted in particular by Bangladesh's ready-made garment industry: the massive influx of women into wage labor in general and manufacturing production in particular.

3. GLOBAL WAGE DIFFERENTIALS AND THE MYTH OF CONVERGENCE. As chapter 1 has revealed—and as chapters 2 and 3 will confirm—capitalists' lust for ultra-cheap labor-power is a fundamental determinant of the global shift of production. Chapter 5, "Global Wage Trends in the Neoliberal Era," attempts to bring global wage trends into focus, singling out three aspects for special attention: international wage differentials, growing in-country wage inequality, and the accelerating decline in labor's share of national income. Along the way, the accuracy and reliability of data on wages is questioned and found wanting, especially in low-wage countries. Calculation of real wages paid in domestic currency requires their conversion into "purchasing power parity"—adjusted dollars—thereby correcting for the failure of market exchange rates to equalize the purchasing power of "hard" and "soft" currencies. Since this adjustment is large and affects all international comparisons of wages, living standards and much else, it will be examined in some detail.

4. WAGES AND PRODUCTIVITY—GLARING PARADOXES THAT MAINSTREAM AND HETERODOX ECONOMIC THEORY CANNOT EXPLAIN. Chapter 6, "The Purchasing Power Anomaly and the Productivity Paradox," marks a transition from the analysis of empirical data that preoccupies the first five chapters to the theoretical development and critique presented in chapters 7 to 9. Chapter 6 begins by asking why the purchasing power anomaly exists, discovering that two recurring themes of this book are centrally implicated: international differences in labor productivity (as conventionally defined and measured) and restrictions on the free international mobility of workers. As we discovered in chapter 1 and is further discussed in chapters 2 and 3, supposed international differences in labor productivity are used by mainstream economists and neoliberal apologists to explain and justify global wage differentials. This standard view, an ideological belief with little basis in empirical data, gives rise to a series of paradoxes and absurdities, for instance that the "productivity" of Bangladeshi garment workers is a tiny fraction of the European and North American workers who place the finished goods on shop shelves. Despite its central importance to neoliberal ideology, the "wage reflects productivity" argument has never been systematically criticized by heterodox and Marxist critics of neoliberalism.

Examination of mainstream theories claiming to explain the purchasing power anomaly adds a further set of paradoxes and absurdities to this list. The remainder of chapter 6 identifies the source of the problem: the failure of ruling economic theory to distinguish between use-value and exchange-value, a distinction that is the very foundation of Karl Marx's theory of value. Thus the necessity for a reengagement with this theory is derived from analysis of empirical data and from the failure of mainstream economic theory to explain its key findings.

5. WAGE DIFFERENTIALS AND DIFFERENCES IN THE RATE OF EXPLOITATION. The most important fact revealed by our analysis of three global commodities is the centrality of vast international wage differences in driving and shaping the global transformation of production during the neoliberal era. Chapters 2–6 analyze different dimensions of this, creating the basis for the development of a theoretical concept of it in chapters 7 and 8, in which international wage differentials are seen as a surface manifestation and distorted reflection of international differences in the degree of exploitation. Chapter 7, "Global Labor Arbitrage: Key Driver of the Globalization of Production," considers attempts by mainstream economists to understand the significance of wage-driven production outsourcing. Finding these to be, at best, purely descriptive, we turn to contemporary Marxist scholarship, and find this, with few but important exceptions, to be astonishingly indifferent to and accepting of bourgeois economists' argument that international wage differentials merely reflect international differences in labor productivity. The remainder of chapter 7 continues the quest for a concept of international differences in the rate of exploitation by visiting the debate on "dependency" that accompanied the anticolonial national liberation movements of the 1960s and 1970s, while chapter 8, "Imperialism and the Law of Value," completes the quest by testing the ability of Marx's theory of value, as presented in *Capital*'s three volumes, to explain the ancient and modern reality of super-exploitation.

6. HOW IMPERIALIST EXPLOITATION IS OBSCURED BY CONVENTIONAL INTERPRETATIONS OF ECONOMIC DATA. Chapter 9, "The GDP Illusion," explains one of the most striking paradoxes revealed in the analysis in chapter 1 of the global commodity: commodities produced mostly or entirely in low-wage countries and consumed mostly or entirely in imperialist countries expand the GDP of the nations where they are consumed by far more than the GDP of the nations where they

are produced. The source of this optical illusion is found in a fallacy that is at the heart of mainstream bourgeois economic theory and its heterodox variants: the tautological conflation of the value generated in production of a commodity with the price realized by its sale.

7. THE ORIGIN, NATURE, AND TRAJECTORY OF THE GLOBAL ECO-NOMIC CRISIS—WHY THE "FINANCIAL CRISIS" IS ROOTED IN CAPITALIST PRODUCTION. The first nine chapters of this book analyze the defining transformation of the neoliberal era, namely the outsourcing and global shift of production. Chapter 10, "All Roads Lead into the Crisis," shows why this transformation, itself a response to the system-threatening crisis of the 1970s, prepared the ground for the reappearance of systemic crisis in 2007. Contrary to the economists' cozy consensus, this concluding chapter argues that this is a financial crisis in form only, and that no understanding of the origin, nature, and trajectory of the global economic crisis is possible unless it is seen as the inevitable result of explosive contradictions at the heart of globalized capitalist production. The chapter concludes by arguing that the current crisis is the most profound in the two centuries of capitalism's existence—and this is before we include, as we must, the added dimension of climate change, a euphemism for the capitalist destruction of nature. A decades-long economic depression, increasingly punctuated by wars and revolutions, is now unavoidable. There are two possible outcomes: either humanity resumes the transition to socialism inaugurated by the Russian Revolution one century ago, or it will descend into barbarism.

2

Outsourcing, or the Globalization of Production

How the capital-labor relation has evolved during the neoliberal era is the subject of this book. Chapter 1 zoomed in on three representative global commodities; this chapter turns the telescope around, presenting a historical and panoramic view of the global transformation of production and of the producers, the global working class. The purpose of this and the next chapter is to develop a rich, sharply focused concept of the globalization of production. To develop tools needed for analysis of this phenomenon, we will critically examine standard definitions of "production," "industry," and "services."

ANTECEDENTS OF GLOBAL OUTSOURCING

In order to oppose their workers, the employers either bring in workers from abroad or else transfer manufacture to countries where there is a cheap labor force. Given this state of affairs, if the working class wishes to continue its struggle with some chance of success, the national organisations must become international. Let every worker give serious consideration to this new aspect of the problem.[1]
      —KARL MARX, 1867, Address of the General Council to
         the Lausanne Congress of the Second International

The wildfire of outsourcing spread during the past three decades is the continuation, on a vastly expanded scale, of capital's eternal quest for new sources of cheaper, readily exploitable labor-power. What began as a trickle in mid-nineteenth-century Europe and became a steady stream in North America in the early twentieth century had, by the end of that century, become a flood tide, described by Kate Bronfenbrenner and Stephanie Luce as "a systematic pattern of firm restructuring that is moving jobs from union to non-union facilities within the country, as well as to non-union facilities in other countries."[2] Antecedents of modern wage-arbitrage–driven outsourcing of production can be found in diverse branches of the nineteenth-century economy. Clothing and textiles, which played an important role in all stages of capitalist development, provide many early examples of the wage-arbitrage–driven production outsourcing that Karl Marx warned about 150 years ago.

The story of jute, the "golden fiber" native to Bangladesh and used for sacking and canvas sheets, contains important elements and features that foreshadow modern low-wage-seeking production. In the early nineteenth century, industrialists in Dundee worked out how to modify their linen- and flax-spinning machinery to process jute, spelling the demise of India's hand-spinning industry. By 1860, Dundee's sixty jute mills employed some 50,000 mostly female workers, many of them Irish migrants who had fled the Great Famine to find work in what was a notoriously low-paid sector of the economy. They were nevertheless more expensive than Indian workers, prompting Dundee's jute barons to shift production to Bengal. Chhabilendra Roul reports that the first mechanized jute spinning mill in India was established in 1855 on the banks of the Hoogli River near Kolkata by a George Auckland, an Englishman, "with machinery imported from John Kerr of Douglas Foundry, then the leading machine manufacturer for flax machinery in Dundee."[3] By the first decade of the twentieth century the bulk of production had shifted to India, yet remained in the possession of Scottish jute barons, who successfully blocked the entry of Indian capitalists and who went on to provide a billion sandbags for Britain's trenches in the First World War.[4]

IN *LINKED LABOR HISTORIES*, A STUDY of the co-evolution of the labor movements in New England and Colombia since the late 1900s, Aviva Chomsky argues that modern outsourcing "continues a pattern begun by the earliest industry in the country, the textile industry, a century earlier,[5] and recounts how flight "from strong trade unions and toward cheap labor" saw New England textile mills pioneer international production outsourcing in the Americas, relocating first to North Carolina in the first decades of the twentieth century, then to Puerto Rico in the 1930s, and to Colombia and beyond in the decades since the Second World War.

The absence of international borders aided capital mobility in North America, where, as Gary Gereffi recounts, by the early twentieth century "many industries . . . began to move to the US South in search of abundant natural resources and cheaper labor, frequently in 'right to work' states that made it difficult to establish labor unions. The same forces behind the impetus to shift production to low-cost regions within the United States eventually led US manufacturers across national borders."[6]

Global outsourcing of manufacturing production began in earnest in the 1960s and 1970s, with the exodus of production jobs in shoes, clothing, toys, and electronic assembly to low-wage countries, providing a new generation of commercial capitalists such as Tesco, Walmart, and Carrefour with the battering rams and trebuchets that helped them to end the reign of the "manufacturer's recommended retail price" and established the supremacy of commercial capital in consumer goods markets. As U.S. labor historian Nelson Lichtenstein has observed:

> For more than a century, from roughly 1880 to 1980, the manufacturing enterprise stood at the center of the U.S. economy's production/distribution nexus. . . . Today, however, the retailers stand at the apex of the world's supply chains. . . . The dramatic growth in the power of the American retail sector began in the 1960s and 1970s when Sears, K-Mart and some U.S. apparel makers/distributors began to take advantage of the cheap labor and growing sophistication of the light manufacturers in the offshore Asian tigers, especially Hong Kong, Taiwan and South Korea.[7]

Unable any longer to dictate prices to its distributors, the shift in power toward commercial capital increased pressure on the producer monopolies to ax agreements with their labor unions and to de-unionize and "flexibilize" their domestic labor force—and follow the trail blazed by the retail giants and outsource their labor-intensive production processes to low-wage countries. This involved both a redistribution of profits from industrial to commercial capitalists and the distribution of some of outsourcing's bounty to increasingly wide sections of the working class through falling prices of consumer goods.

From the early 1960s, while the emerging retail giants were pioneering the outsourcing of toys, clothing, and other consumption goods, prominent electronics firms such as Cisco, Sun Microsystems, and AT&T were unleashing what was soon to become a torrent of outsourcing by high-tech industry. Its driver was not the domestic battle with commercial capital but competition between U.S. and Japanese corporations. Until manufacturers learned how to print electronic circuits, circuit-board manufacture was exceedingly labor-intensive; its outsourcing to Taiwan and South Korea helped U.S. electronics firms to cut production costs and gave a mighty impulse to export-oriented industrialization in what became known as "newly industrializing countries."[10] The electronics and other high-tech industries have been at the forefront of the out-sourcing wave. As an UNCTAD study found, "Strikingly, the growth rates of exports from developing countries exceed those of world exports by a higher margin the greater is the skill and technology intensity of the product category. . . . However, this does not signify a rapid and sustained technological upgrading in the exports of developing countries." Far from it—"The involvement of developing countries is usually limited to the labor-intensive stages in the production process."[11]

The high-water mark of production outsourcing occurred, not coincidentally, in the period leading up to the outbreak of global crisis in 2007, or as UNCTAD put it, "Since around 2000, global trade and FDI have both grown exponentially, significantly outpacing global GDP growth, reflecting the rapid expansion of international production in TNC-coordinated networks."[12] Mainstream and radical explanations of the root causes of the global crisis have focused almost exclusively on ballooning debt, the derivatives explosion, and the financial feeding frenzy that preceded its outbreak, but have given scant attention to the accompanying transformation and global shift of production. Kate Bronfenbrenner and Stephanie Luce estimate that each year from 1992 to 2001 between 70,000 and 100,000 production jobs "from ICT to high-end manufacturing of industrial machinery and electronics components to low-wage manufacturing in food processing and textiles" shifted from the United States to Mexico and China.[13] This sharply accelerated at the start of the new millennium, when "the total number of jobs leaving the U.S. for countries in Asia and Latin America increased from 204,000 in 2001 to as much as 406,000 in 2004."[14] Epitomizing this epochal shift was the decision by the iconic "made in the U.S." brand Levi Strauss, which in the 1960s operated sixty-three factories across the United States, to sack 800 workers at its last U.S. factory in 2004 and move production to Mexico and China.[15]

Outsourcing and Migration

Aviva Chomsky makes a crucial connection: "Most accounts treat immigration and capital flight separately. My approach insists that they are most fruitfully studied together, as aspects of the same phenomenon of economic restructuring."[16] She adds that "capital flight [which here means

---

Note on Trade Statistics

Conventional trade statistics double-count imported inputs—for example, Bangladesh's earnings from garment exports include the cost of the imported textiles that Bangladeshi garment workers fashion into clothes. As the share of intermediate inputs in total trade increases this distortion has grown ever larger. Statisticians at WTO and the OECD have forged new analytical tools and datasets capable of measuring, sector by sector, how much of a given country's exports were actually generated in that country. Results from this enormous labor are presented in UNCTAD's 2013 *World Investment Report,* which estimates that "today, some 28 percent of gross exports consist of value added that is first imported by countries only to be incorporated in products or services that are then exported again. Some $5 trillion of the $19 trillion in global gross exports (in 2010 figures) is double counted."[8]

Illustrating this, China's export performance is not quite so spectacular when full account is made of its export-processing regime, which allows imports for processing and re-export to enter duty-free. This trade accounts for more than half of China's exports, and is mostly conducted by U.S., European, Taiwanese, and South Korean TNCs. Van Assche et al. found that in 2005 processed imports made up 90 percent of the value of China's high-tech exports, compared to 50 percent in the medium-high-tech category and 30 percent in the low-tech category. In other words, the greater the sophistication of the goods being exported, the smaller the fraction of the export value actually added in China. Correcting for this distortion, China's share of world trade in 2005 was 4.9 percent, more than a third lower than the 7.7 percent reported by World Bank and IMF data. Van Assche et al. comment, "China has turned into a global assembly platform that sources its processing inputs from its East Asian neighbors while sending its final goods to high-income countries. Since China is often only responsible for the final assembly of its export products, this puts into question China's responsibility for the growing U.S. trade deficit."[9]

---

outsourcing] was one of the main reasons the textile industry remained one of the least organized in the early to mid-twentieth century, and it was one of the main reasons for the decline of unions in all industries at the end of the century."[17] At the beginning of the neoliberal era, Jeffrey Henderson and Robin Cohen made the same connection: "While some fractions of metropolitan capital have taken flight to low-wage areas, partly in response to the class struggles of metropolitan workers, less mobile sections of Western capital have enormously increased their reliance on imported migrant labor to cheapen the labor process and lower the costs of the reproduction of labor in the advanced countries."[18]

Bangladesh provides a vivid example of how, during the neoliberal era, outsourcing and migration have become two aspects of the same wage-differential–driven transformation of global production. Speaking of 1980s and 1990s Bangladesh, Tasneem Siddiqui reported that "the continuous outflow of people of working-age . . . has played a major role in keeping the unemployment rate stable."[19] It has also become a crucial source of income for poor households. According to the International Organization for Migration, 5.4 million Bangladeshis worked overseas in 2012, more than half of them in India, around a million in Saudi Arabia, with the rest spread between other countries in the Middle East, Western Europe, North America, and Australasia. They sent $14bn from their wages to their families back home, equivalent to 11 percent of its GDP. In the same year, Bangladesh received $19bn for its garment exports, 80 percent of Bangladesh's total exports, $4bn of which was paid out in wages to some 3 million RMG workers. Gross exports earnings includes the cost of imported cotton and other fabrics, typically 25 percent of the production cost, thus remittances from Bangladeshis working abroad approximately equalled total net earnings from garment exports. According to the World Bank, in 2013 each of Britain's 210,000 Bangladeshi migrant workers remitted an average of $4,058, three times the annual wages of his (most Bangladeshi migrant workers are male) wife, sister, or daughter working in a garment factory back home. Why export-oriented industrialization has not provided enough jobs to absorb the growth of the workforce, obliging so many to migrate in search of work, will be considered in chapter 4.

Outsourcing and the Reproduction of Labor-Power in Imperialist Nations

Neoliberal globalization has transformed the production of all commodities, *including labor-power*, as more and more of the manufactured consumer goods that reproduce labor-power in imperialist countries are produced by super-exploited workers in low-wage nations. The globalization of production processes impacts workers in imperialist nations in two fundamental ways. Outsourcing enables capitalists to replace higher-paid domestic labor with low-wage Southern labor, exposing workers in imperialist nations to direct competition with similarly skilled but much lower paid workers in Southern nations, while falling prices of clothing, food, and other articles of mass consumption protects consumption levels from falling wages and magnifies the effect of wage increases. The IMF's *World Economic Outlook 2007* attempted to weigh these two effects, concluding: "Although the labor share [of GDP] went down, globalization of labor as manifested in cheaper imports in advanced economies has increased the 'size of the pie' to be shared among all citizens, resulting in a net gain in total workers' compensation in real terms."[20] In other words, cost savings resulting from outsourcing are shared with workers in imperialist countries. This is both an economic imperative and a conscious strategy of the employing class and their political representatives that is crucial to maintaining domestic class peace. Wage repression at home, rather than abroad, would reduce demand and unleash latent recessionary forces. Competition in markets for workers' consumer goods forces some of the cost reductions resulting from greater use of low-wage labor to be passed on to them.

Perhaps the most in-depth research into this effect was conducted by two Chicago professors, Christian Broda and John Romalis, who established a "concordance" between two giant databases, one tracking the quantities and price movements between 1994 and 2005 of hundreds of thousands of different goods consumed by 55,000 U.S. households, the other of imports classified into 16,800 different product categories. Their central conclusion: "While the expansion of trade with low wage countries triggers a fall in relative wages for the unskilled in the United States, it also leads to a fall in the price of goods that are heavily consumed by the poor. We show that this beneficial price effect can potentially more than offset the standard negative relative wage effect." They calculate that China by itself accounted for four-fifths of the total inflation-lowering effect of cheap imports, its share of total U.S. imports having risen during the decade from 6 to 17 percent, and that "the rise of Chinese trade . . . alone can offset around a third of the rise in official inequality we have seen over this period."[21]

The conclusion to be drawn from this brief survey is that the globalization of the production of intermediate inputs and final goods on the one hand and the globalization of the production of labor-power on the other are two dimensions of the outsourcing phenomenon. They produce contradictory effects and interact in complex ways. They must be studied both separately and together. The increasingly global character of the social relations of production and the increasing interdependence between workers in different countries and continents objectively strengthens the international working class and hastens its emergence as a class "for itself" as well as "in itself," struggling to establish its supremacy; yet, to counter this, capitalists increasingly lean on and utilize imperialist divisions to practice divide-and-rule, to force workers in imperialist countries into increasingly direct competition with workers in low-wage countries, while using the cheap imports produced by super-exploited Southern labor to encourage selfishness and consumerism and to undermine solidarity.

THE GLOBALIZATION OF PRODUCTION PROCESSES

In the early stages of the Industrial Revolution, before the widespread introduction of power machinery, the various stages in the processing of raw materials into final goods typically took place within a single factory, often supported by armies of homeworkers working up raw materials for final processing. Waves of mechanization over the next hundred years spurred concentration and specialization, fostering the growth within national borders of more complex production networks. For most of these two centuries international trade consisted of raw materials and final goods. Neoliberal globalization, by extending the links in the chain of production and value-creation across national borders, has profoundly transformed this picture. As William Milberg noted in a study for the ILO, "Because of the globalization of production, industrialization today is different from the final goods, export-led process of just 20 years ago."[22] The big difference, "the defining manifestation of globalized production," no less, is "the rise in intermediate goods in overall international trade, whether it is done within firms as a result of foreign direct investment or through arm's length subcontracting." This does not mean, however, that outsourcing can be reduced to trade in the intermediate inputs—our concept must also include the export of finished goods from low-wage countries to firms and consumers in imperialist countries.

 Mainstream theory has ill equipped International Financial Institutions such as the IMF and World Bank to conceptualize and

measure the outsourcing phenomenon. As late as 2007 the IMF estimated that "offshoring intensity," defined as the "share of offshored
inputs in gross output," has "increased only moderately since the early
1980s. The share of offshored inputs in gross output ranges from 12
percent in the Netherlands to about 2–3 percent in the United States
and Japan."[23] Yet this definition omits the export of intermediate inputs
to low-wage nations for final assembly. It also excludes finished goods
destined for use as inputs by Northern firms, including computers and
other electronic goods, and it excludes finished goods destined for consumption by workers.[24] According to the IMF's definition, none of the
three global commodities I examined in chapter 1 would count toward
the offshoring intensity of the nations whose firms and citizens supply
final demand. The result is an absurdly low estimate of the extent and
pace of the globalization of production processes. Particularly risible
is the IMF's estimate of the offshoring intensity of Japanese manufacturing. Japan's signature form of outsourcing is known as "triangular
trade," in which "Japanese firms headquartered in Japan produce certain
high-tech parts in Japan, ship them to factories in East Asian nations
for labor-intensive stages of production including assembly and then
ship the final products to Western markets or back to Japan."[25] This pattern evolved after the 1985 Plaza Accord, when Japanese manufacturers
responded to sharply declining competitiveness resulting from appreciation of the yen by offshoring labor-intensive production processes
to neighboring low-wage countries,[26] often referred to as the "hollow-
ing out" of Japanese industry. Yet the IMF calculates Japan's offshoring
intensity to be a negligible 2–3 percent.

Another defect of the IMF's approach is that it takes no account of
where these imported inputs come from. It discovers a more or less
stable ratio of imported inputs to total inputs, but this conceals a big
swing toward lower-cost suppliers in low-wage countries. Three OECD
researchers reported that "while intermediate imports into the OECD
as a whole from China and the ASEAN have risen sharply (as a share of
total manufacturing imports), this has been offset by reductions in intermediate imports from other countries"—"other countries" being other
rich nations in the OECD.[27] The U.S. auto industry, which imports more
than 25 percent of its inputs, more than any other industrial sector, provides a clear example of this.[28] The OECD's Trade in Value Added (TiVA)
database reveals that in 1995 the U.S. auto industry imported four times
as much automotive value-added from Canada as from Mexico, just
10 percent more in 2005, and by 2009, the latest year for which data

is available, Mexico had overtaken Canada to become the source of 48 percent more automotive value-added than the United States' northern neighbor—a striking indication of how the global economic crisis has accelerated the southward shift of production.[29] The shift would be even more pronounced but for the odd behavior of non-U.S. auto companies that have set themselves up in the United States to win a share of the U.S. market. As a study for the World Bank noted, "Political sensitivity . . . explains why Japanese, German, and Korean automakers in North America have not concentrated their production in Mexico, despite lower operating costs and a free trade agreement with the United States," while the United States' own auto giants, who are evidently less patriotic than U.S. consumers, relocate more and more of their production to the other side of the Rio Grande.[30]

An alternative and widely used way to estimate the magnitude of outsourcing is to measure the share of intra-firm trade in overall international trade. This is the antithesis of the IMF's approach, since it captures both intermediate inputs and finished goods, but it has no place for the increasingly important arm's-length relations between Northern firms and their Southern suppliers.[31] Peter Dicken comments that "unfortunately there are no comprehensive and reliable statistics on intra-firm trade. The ballpark figure is that approximately one-third of total world trade is intra-firm although . . . that could well be a substantial underestimate."[32] Princeton economists Gene Grossman and Esteban Rossi-Hansberg are more helpful, reporting that, "in 2005, related party [i.e. intra-firm] trade accounted for 47 percent of U.S. imports. . . . This fraction has risen only modestly since 1992, when it was already 45 percent."[33] This modest rise, however, conceals a dramatic reorientation of this trade toward low-wage economies: "Imports from related parties [i.e. subsidiaries] accounted for 27 percent of total U.S. imports from Korea in 1992, and 11 percent of total U.S. imports from China. By 2005, these figures had risen to 58 percent and 26 percent, respectively."

Reviewing these attempts to quantify production outsourcing, William Milberg has pointed out that "most attempts to measure the magnitude of the phenomenon of vertical disintegration have captured only parts of the process. Some analysts focus on intra-firm imports and others on the import of intermediate goods whether these are intra-firm or arm's-length."[34] However, the total outsourcing picture *is* captured by one set of comprehensive and readily available data—*manufactured exports from low-wage nations to imperialist nations as a whole.* Milberg and Winkler, in a study of the impact of the crisis on global production networks, explain the simple, powerful logic behind this approach:

> Standard offshoring measures capture only trade inputs . . . [yet] much of the import activity in global supply chains is in fully finished goods. In fact, the purpose of corporate offshoring, whether at arm's length or through foreign subsidiaries, is precisely to allow the corporation to focus on its "core competence," while leaving other aspects of the process, *often including production*, to others. Many "manufacturing" firms now do not manufacture anything at all. They provide product and brand design, marketing, supply chain logistics, and financial management services. Thus, an alternative proxy for offshoring may simply be imports from developing countries.[35]

According to this broad measure of goods offshoring, "developing-country imports constitute over half of total imports by Japan (68 percent) and the United States (54 percent), while the European countries range from 23 percent in the United Kingdom to only 13 percent in Denmark."[36] This must be qualified in two ways. First, imports of raw materials and foodstuffs from developing countries reflect the traditional, pre-neoliberal pattern of North–South trade, and do not in general correspond to cheap labor-seeking outsourcing. Second, a small but significant fraction of developing nations' manufactured exports arise not from outsourcing relationships controlled by imperialist leading firms but from home-grown industrial development. Brazil's aerospace industry and China's solar panel and wind-turbine industries are examples of this. But, as we shall see in more detail in the next chapter that discusses the structure of world trade, these higher value-added exports form a small part of overall South–North trade. With these caveats, then, we can agree with Milberg and Winkler and regard *manufactured imports by imperialist countries from low-wage countries as a whole* to be a composite of diverse outsourcing and offshoring relationships, manifested in different types of global value chains. Developing countries' share of imperialist nations' manufactured imports have rocketed since 1980, more than tripling their share of a cake that itself quadrupled in the subsequent three decades. In a study published by UNCTAD in 2013, Rashmi Banga found that 67 percent of the total value-added generated in global value chains is captured by firms based in rich nations.[37]

Transnational corporations, the majority of which are headquartered in imperialist countries and owned by capitalists resident in those countries, are the supreme drivers of the globalization of production. Their connection with production processes in low-wage countries takes two basic forms: an "in-house" relation between the parent company and its overseas subsidiary, as in FDI, or an "arm's-length" relation with formally independent suppliers—an important distinction that will be examined in the next chapter. Its diverse forms, problems of definition, and non-availability of data mean that obtaining a precise measurement of the magnitude of outsourcing is fraught with difficulties. Nevertheless, UNCTAD estimates that "about 80 percent of global trade (in terms of gross exports) is linked to the international production networks of TNCs."[38] The extent of this transformation is indicated by UNCTAD's 2013 *World Investment Report*, which estimates that "about 60 percent of global trade . . . consists of trade in intermediate goods and services that are incorporated at various stages in the production process of goods and services for final consumption."[39]

In conclusion, South-North (S-N) export of manufactured goods as a whole must be thought of not so much as trade but as an expression of the globalization of production, and this in turn must be seen not as a technical rearrangement of machinery and other inputs, but as an evolution of a social relation, namely the relation of exploitation between capital and labor. International competition between firms to increase profits, market share, and shareholder value continues, but the fate of each worker is no longer tied to the fortunes of her/his employer; on the contrary, the employers that survive are those who most aggressively substitute their own employees with cheaper foreign labor.

The production process can be thought of as a sequence or choreography of tasks, of different concrete labors, in which "task" means a production task; as the *labor expended in the production of commodities*, "industry" is where this takes place. A striking feature of neoliberal globalization of production is the outsourcing of *individual segments and links* of production processes, leading analysts to talk of the fragmentation of production, or "slicing up the value chain," as Paul Krugman described it in a much-commented-upon article.[40] The old conception of North-South trade of raw materials for finished goods sorely needs updating. Baldwin's notion of "task trading" captures a change in the nature of global competition, "which used to be primarily between firms and sectors in different nations, [but] now occurs between individual workers performing similar tasks in different nations."[41] This manifests an evolution of the capital-labor relation, which increasingly takes the form of a relation between Northern capital and Southern labor. Before the transformations of the neoliberal era, when competition consisted of firms producing different final goods, the relative wages and security of employment of workers in imperialist countries was dependent on their employer's defense of market share and conditioned by the threat of redundancy resulting from the introduction of labor-saving technology. Before the neoliberal era the more successful and dominant the TNC, the greater the number of direct employees it concentrated in domestic factories. "Task trading" signifies that employers now have an alternative way of making their employees redundant, an alternative way of cutting production costs, by outsourcing individual tasks, that is, jobs, to where wages are significantly lower. Now the successful TNC is the one that has outsourced production to low-wage countries and does as little as possible itself. Apple has replaced GM in terms of market capitalization by going much further down the road that GM itself is traveling. Competition between workers is therefore sharpening and becoming more direct, and is less and less a simple function of their firm's competitiveness.

EXPORT-ORIENTED INDUSTRIALIZATION: WIDELY SPREAD OR NARROWLY CONCENTRATED?

For nearly half a century, export-oriented industrialization has been the only capitalist option for poor countries without abundant natural resources.[42] Yet it is a widely held view that the growth in the Southern industrial proletariat is highly concentrated in a small number of Southern nations, namely China, "the supplier of choice in virtually all labor-intensive global value chains,"[43] and a handful of others. Ajit Ghose, a senior economist at the ILO, argues that "what appears to be a change in the pattern of North-South trade is in essence a change in the pattern of trade between industrialized countries and a group of 24 developing countries. . . . The rest of the developing world, in contrast, remained overwhelmingly dependent on export of primary commodities."[44] "The rest," comprising more than 107 developing countries, "face global exclusion in the sense that they became increasingly insignificant players in the global marketplace."[45] Yet the 24 countries that Ghose reports have "shift[ed] their export base from primary commodities to manufactures" include eight of the ten most populous Southern nations, home to 76 percent of the total population of the global South. Of the ten most populous Southern nations, only Nigeria receives more from primary commodity exports than from manufactures.[46] In addition, many other smaller nations have made a brave effort to reorient their economies to the export of manufactures and play host to manufacturing enclaves, also known as export processing zones, which exert a powerful and distorting influence on their national economies.

The southward shift of production during the neoliberal era is strikingly portrayed in Figures 2.1, 2.2, and 2.3. The solid line in Figure 2.1 shows that Southern nations' share of global exports of manufactured goods began its steady rise in the late 1960s. Its ascent steepened in the second half of the 1970s, rising from around 5 percent in the pre-globalization period to 30 percent by the first decade of the twenty-first century. Figure 2.2 decomposes this trace to shows the share of developing nations in Europe, Japan, and the United States' manufactured imports. The traces for Japan and the United States show a dramatic increase in their manufactured imports from low-wage countries, rising from around 10 to 45 percent in the case of the United States and to nearly 60 percent in the case of Japan, results that make IMF estimates of Japan's static outsourcing intensity reported above appear ridiculous.[47]

The second trace in Figure 2.1 (broken line) shows that the share of manufactured goods in developing nations' total exports commenced its astonishing ascent around 1980, increasing from 20 percent in that year to more than 60 percent in barely one decade. It then stabilized at this much higher level and, from the early 2000s, sloped downward, reflecting buoyant primary commodity prices and deteriorating manufacturing terms of trade. Figure 2.3 (page 54) decomposes this into different regions, revealing the widespread yet uneven character of the shift from the export of raw materials and foodstuffs to manufactured goods. If the different regions were disaggregated into individual countries we would find, as Ghose argues, that many small nations have not followed this pattern of development, yet the overall picture is clear.[48]

China's rise is depicted in the trace for East Asia and Pacific, of which it is by far the largest component. There is other interesting detail in the graph—for example, manufactured exports as a share of total exports from South Asia, which includes India, Pakistan, Bangladesh, and Sri Lanka, was high even in 1980. Africa's trace (data only from 1996) shows the continent has not made the transition to export-oriented industrialization—on the contrary, its domestic light industries have been ravaged by competition from China and other Asian countries. And the trace for the Middle East, for which manufactures make the smallest contribution to overall exports, is explained by the weight of oil in the regions' total exports—its low score is therefore a sign of abundant wealth (which is not, of course, shared evenly between different Middle Eastern countries), and not, as in Africa's case, a sign of poverty.

FIGURE 2.1: Developing Economies' Trade in Manufactures

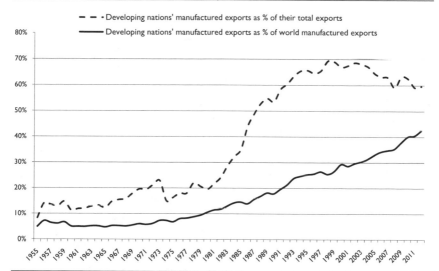

Source: UNCTAD Handbook of Statistics.

FIGURE 2.2: Developing Nations' Share of Developed Nations' Manufactured Imports

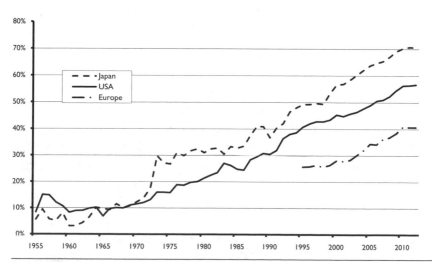

Source: UNCTAD, Handbook of Statistics Archive: Network of exports by region and commodity group, historical series (available at http://stats.unctad.org/handbook/ReportFolders/ReportFolders.aspx).

FIGURE 2.3: Manufactured Exports as a Percent of Merchandise Exports, by Region

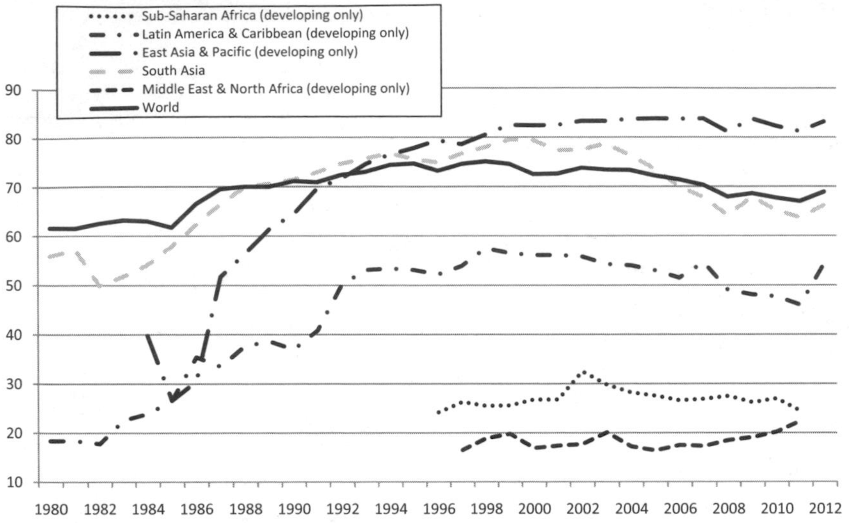

Source: World Bank, World Development Indicators, July 2015.

Export-Processing Zones (EPZs)

The proliferation of EPZs, now found in more than 130 countries, provides further evidence that though industrial development in the global South may be unevenly distributed it is nevertheless very widespread. It also adds more detail to our account of the insatiable appetite of imperialist TNCs for ultra-flexible, low-waged employment in which all their needs are laid out on a carpet and "the burden of the cyclical nature of demand is placed on workers."[49]

According to the World Bank, an export-processing zone is "an industrial estate, usually a fenced-in area of 10 to 300 hectares, that specializes in manufacturing for export. It offers firms free trade conditions and a liberal regulatory environment."[50] EPZs exhibit the following characteristics: "duty-free imports of raw and intermediate inputs and capital goods . . . red tape is streamlined . . . labor laws are often more flexible than . . . in the domestic market . . . generous, long-term tax concessions . . . infrastructure more advanced than in other parts of the country. . . . Utility and rental subsidies are common."[51] A long list, yet it is strangely incomplete—"flexible labor laws" is a euphemism for almost universal hostility to trade unions; the predilection of investors in EPZs for female labor is not mentioned—invariably, the large majority of the workforce are women (see chapter 4 for more on this), and neither is the most important factor of all, indeed the EPZs' *raison d'être*—low wages.

EPZs in their various forms have played and continue to play a key role in the competitive race for export-oriented industrialization. Not only are they now found in a large majority of Southern nations, their classic features have become generalized: neoliberal globalization has gone a long way toward turning the whole of the global South into a vast export processing zone. As William Milberg comments, "The distinction between EPZ and non-EPZ activity has diminished in many countries as liberalization policies have expanded in the WTO and regional trade agreements." [52] Yet far from declining in significance, EPZs have experienced accelerating growth—the numbers employed in them nearly tripled between 1997 and 2006, the latest year for which there are statistics, when 63 million workers were employed in EPZs located in 132 countries. Milberg's study of EPZ reports figures for a selection of economies, revealing that in 2006 EPZs were responsible for 75 percent or more of export earnings in Kenya, Malaysia, Madagascar, Vietnam, Dominican Republic, and Bangladesh, while Philippines, Mexico, Haiti, and Morocco earned 50 to 60 percent of exports from their EPZs. Between regions, however, significant disparities persist. The ILO's Employment in EPZs database reports that Asia's 900+ zones employed 53 million workers, 40 million of them in China and 3.25 million in Bangladesh. Another 10 million workers were employed in EPZs elsewhere in the world, 5 million in Mexico and Central America, with another million or so in each of Africa, the Middle East, and Central Europe. South America lags, with half a million employed in EPZs.

Although China remains the most important host, EPZs have been growing faster still in other low-wage countries: 80 percent of EPZ employment was accounted for by China in 1997, falling to 63 percent in 2005–6.[53] After China, the largest EPZ employer is Bangladesh, with 3.25 million employees in 2005–6.

Since their inception, EPZs have been the focus of intense controversy, and were singled out by scholars and activists influenced by the New International Division of Labor school as the epitome of unbridled exploitation of low-wage labor by TNCs.[54] In a survey for the ILO published in 2007, Milberg concludes that "despite the presence of EPZs— for over 30 years in some cases—there are very few cases where EPZs have played an important role in accomplishing . . . direct developmental goals,"[55] and UNCTAD warned in 2004 that manufacturing EPZs were reproducing colonial forms of "enclave-led growth" in which "a relatively rich commodity-exporting sector, well connected to roads, ports and supported by ancillary services, exist side by side with large undeveloped hinterlands where the majority of the population live."[56]

The general failure of EPZs to stimulate economic development outside of the zones, typically importing all inputs except labor and paying little or no taxes to host governments, has aroused further controversy. EPZs have also received much criticism because the export subsidies and other trade-distorting emoluments dangled by host governments to lure outsourcing TNCs confound efforts by the World Trade Organization to create a "level playing field." Given the controversy surrounding EPZs and their paltry contribution to the economic and social development of their hosts, the question arises, why are they continuing to proliferate? The answer is that, having signed up to the IMF/World Bank–promoted strategy of export-oriented industrialization, EPZs provide governments in low-wage countries with a way to attract inward FDI and connect to global value chains. In addition, what "may be the most important political factor," according to Milberg, is that "governments find the employment creation in EPZs to be essential for absorbing excess labor."[57]

SERVICES AND THE GLOBALIZATION OF PRODUCTION

Until around the turn of the millennium, outsourcing was associated with labor-intensive links or "tasks" in the manufacture of commodities. This took place on a massive scale, despite the significant costs and delays involved in transporting commodities over long distances. The eruption of this into "services," in particular any service that can be delivered instantaneously to a computer screen with zero transportation costs, has only become a practical possibility for most firms since the late 1990s. Richard Freeman's prediction that "if the work is digital—which covers perhaps 10 percent of employment in the United States [around 14 million workers]—it can and eventually will be offshored to low-wage highly educated workers in developing countries," was widely reported in the U.S. news media.[58] So too an article in *Foreign Affairs* in 2006 by Alan Blinder, an eminent economics professor at Princeton University, titled "Offshoring: The Next Industrial Revolution?," which warned "we have so far barely seen the tip of the offshoring iceberg, the eventual dimensions of which may be staggering."[59] Suddenly a layer of professional, middle-class workers began to feel the cold breath of global competition. As Gary Gereffi remarked, "While low-cost offshore production had been displacing U.S. factory and farm jobs for decades, the idea that middle-class office work and many high-paying professions were now subject to international competition came as something of a shock."[60] Under the subheading "This time it's personal," Blinder concluded, "Many people blithely assume that the critical labor-market distinction is, and will remain, between highly educated (or highly skilled) people and less-educated (or less-skilled) people. . . . The critical divide in the future may instead be between those types of work that are easily deliverable through a wire . . . and those that are not."[61]

Services made up 75 percent of the GDP of "high-income countries" in 2013, but only 22 percent of their gross exports,[62] but this understates their contribution because services also form part of the value added of exported manufactured goods. "While the share of services in gross exports worldwide is only about 20 percent," reports UNCTAD, "almost half (46 percent) of value added in exports is contributed by service-sector activities, as most manufacturing exports require services for their production."[63]

Clearly, a concept of the globalization of production that concentrates exclusively on manufacturing and ignores so-called services would be seriously deficient. Mainstream conceptions of industry and services classify economic activities according to the physical properties of their output, and therefore of the specific nature of the tasks, of the concrete labors, that generate it. Services are conventionally defined as weightless, intangible commodities; they cannot be stored and transported and therefore must be consumed in situ and at the moment of their production, as in the case, for instance, of a haircut or a bus journey. Thus, according to *The Economist*, services are "products of economic activity that you can't drop on your foot."[64]

Yet tangibility is not firm enough to serve as the criterion for dividing industry from services. In the first place, the delivery of the intangible service invariably also involves the consumption of a tangible product of "industry," as in the scissors used to cut hair or the bus used to transport its passengers. A musical performance cannot be touched, but it does touch the human eardrum by means of a tangible perturbation of the air. Telecommunications are also classified as a service: as with a musical performance, a telephone conversation is consumed at the moment of its delivery and cannot be stored for later use.[65] Yet this, too, involves a physical, tangible alteration of matter. Even transportation, also classified as a service, involves a change in the physical location of a product if not in its physical characteristics.

In contrast to the crude physicalist definition, what is critical from a Marxist perspective is not the nature of the specific labor but the social relations of its employment—whether it is employed in the production of commodities or as a personal service, and, if the former, whether the labor is performed in production or in circulation. To develop a valid, concrete and useful concept of the distinction between industry and services it is therefore necessary to consider the distinction between the production of commodities and their circulation.

The Production and Circulation of Commodities

The simplest form of market relation is barter. A barter trade, in which one commodity (for example, a pair of trousers) is exchanged directly for another (for example, a sack of flour), can be expressed by the expression C–C. Assuming equal exchange, C, representing the exchange-value of the commodity, is the same on both sides of the formula. The exchange-value of a commodity is determined not by the subjective desires of the buyers and sellers, as both orthodox and heterodox economic theory maintains,[66] but by how much effort it took to make it. If, for example, it takes twice as long to produce a pair of trousers as a sack of flour, then the equilibrium exchange-value of a pair of trousers would be two sacks of flour.

As market relations expand, one commodity becomes the money commodity (usually gold), against which all other commodities are measured. Here, again assuming equal exchange, the formula now becomes C–M–C. In this case, market participants sell something they don't need in order to buy something they do. Money (M) now intermediates between trouser-sellers and flour-sellers, thanks to which they do not need to meet face-to-face.

Unlike simple commodity producers, who sell in order to buy, merchants buy in order to sell. Their aim is not to acquire something they need, but to acquire money. Their starting and end points begin not with C, but with M. They buy some commodities and then sell them for a higher price. The formula now becomes M–C–M' where the apostrophe signifies that s/he ends up with more money then s/he started with; in other words M'>M. For this to be so, at least one of these transactions (M–C or C–M') must be an *unequal* exchange, a violation of the law of value, in which the merchant takes advantage of surfeits or shortages which cause prices to move away from values.

John Maynard Keynes, who boasted of his ignorance of Marx's economic theories, commented that:

real exchange relations . . . bear some resemblance to a pregnant observation by Karl Marx. . . . He pointed out that the nature of production in the actual world is not, as economists seem often to suppose, a case of C–M–C', i.e. of exchanging commodity (or effort) for money in order to obtain another commodity (or effort). This may be the standpoint of the private consumer. But it is not the attitude of business, which is a case of M–C–M', i.e. of parting with money for commodity (or effort) in order to obtain more money."[67]

However, in one crucial respect, this garbles Marx's concept. M–C–M', as we have seen, describes the behavior of the merchant, who buys and sells C, commodities, in order to increase M, his money, but not the behavior of the capitalist. Whereas small commodity producers sell in order to buy, and merchants buy in order to sell, capitalists buy in order to *make*. The merchant does not physically alter the commodity that has come into her/his possession (s/he does not in any way produce it). Mercantile capitalism is a primitive form, in which capitalists have yet to separate the producer from the means of production and take possession of the production process. This distinction between simple commodity production and capitalist production, which Keynes omits from his reference to Marx, requires a fundamental modification of the formula expressing the circuit of commodities, which now becomes M–C–C'–M'. Here the merchant has turned into a capitalist. M–C is now the purchase not of commodities for resale, but of "factors of production": labor-power, means of production, and raw materials. C–C' is the production process, in which living labor replaces C, its own value and that of materials, etc., used up in production, and generates a surplus value (the difference between C and C'). The time spent by living labor producing this surplus value Marx called surplus labor. This surplus labor is the source and substance not only of profit in all its forms, but of capital itself, which is nothing but accumulated surplus labor. Marx commented, "The production process [C–C'] appears simply as an unavoidable middle term, a necessary evil for the purpose of money-making."[68]

In this schema, value production takes place only in C–C'; the other two links, M–C and C'–M', encompass the *circulation* of these values, the exchange of titles of ownership. Whether or not a task or link in a value chain is productive of value depends not on the specific nature of this particular task or link, but where in the circuit of capital it is situated. This forms the foundation for Marx's theory of productive and non-productive labor.

Productive and Non-Productive Labor

As with our earlier discussion of different ways to measure the magnitude of outsourcing, what is of fundamental importance is not the physical properties of the commodities being produced but the social relations of their production. And more important than the largely spurious distinction between services and industry is another that is often confused with it—the one between productive and non-productive labor. As Anwar Shaikh and E. Ahmet Tonak have pointed out, "The very term 'services' conflates a vital distinction between production and nonproduction labor."[69] This question is of great relevance to our investigation into labor productivity and the "GDP illusion," and to the development of a theory of the imperialist form of the value relation. Its introduction at this point is necessary in order to liberate our concepts of industry and services from the vulgar physicalist approach that dominates mainstream conceptions and has contaminated Marxist approaches.[70]

Marxist value theory maintains that economic activities that are not integral but contingent to the production process, for example banking and finance, police and security services, government bureaucracies and so forth, make no net addition to social wealth; they therefore produce no value and should instead be regarded as nonproduction activities, *as forms of social consumption* of values produced elsewhere. Nonproduction activities also include security, administration, advertising—activities that may be no less necessary than production activities but do not in themselves add to social wealth and should instead be regarded as forms of social consumption. Commerce, too, pertains to the circulation of commodities, and therefore consumes value but does not produce any. As Marx explains:

> Since the merchant, being simply an agent of circulation, produces neither value nor surplus-value . . . the commercial workers whom he employs in these same functions cannot possibly create surplus-value for him directly. . . . Commercial capital's relationship to surplus-value is different from that of industrial capital. The latter produces surplus-value by directly appropriating the unpaid labor of others. The former appropriates a portion of surplus-value by getting it transferred from industrial capital to itself.[71]

Marx's rejection of a crude physicalist conception of value is perhaps nowhere clearer than in his attitude to transportation, where "the purpose of the labor is not at all to alter the form of the thing, but only its position."[72] Provided this transportation is socially necessary, the productive labor of the transport worker is materialized as the enhanced exchange value of the commodity that has been transported, yet the physical properties of the commodity show no trace of this. But this is not necessarily the case, as Shaikh and Tonak point out:

> It is important to understand that not all transportation constitutes production activity. . . . Suppose our oranges are produced in California to be sold in New York, but are stored in New Jersey because of cheaper warehouse facilities. . . . The loop through New Jersey has no (positive) effect on the useful properties of the orange as an object of consumption [thus] this loop is internal to the distribution system. It [is] therefore . . . a nonproduction activity.[73]

We therefore need to radically redefine what we mean by industry and services. For Marx, industry is the application of human labor to harness or alter natural forces and resources in order to satisfy human needs. From this perspective, agriculture, and much of what is counted as services, are all "industry." Agriculture differs from manufacturing industry in that the productivity of agricultural labor is determined by the inherent fecundity of soil and climate as well as the efficient application of technology, and is similar to the case of extractive industries. These natural monopolies give rise to differential profits, and provide the point of departure for Marx's theory of rent developed in *Capital,* vol. 3.[74] Though of necessity we have no choice but to work with the categories of bourgeois economic theory and the statistical data based on them, the theoretical concept of industry informing this study includes all that is encompassed by the standard International Labour Organization (ILO) classification of industry and agriculture, and also includes many production tasks conventionally counted as services.

Services in low-wage countries comprise a very different mix of ingredients than in imperialist countries. Financial services and other non-productive, rent-seeking activities that have come to dominate the "financialized" economies of the imperialist nations have a much smaller weight in the economies of the Global South (and are themselves increasingly dominated by Northern financial TNCs). With the exception of tourism, services as a whole make a proportionately smaller contribution to the exports and GDP of Southern nations than of the imperialist countries. But by far the biggest difference is that in the South the services sector encompasses—and is almost everywhere dominated by—the informal economy where people scratch out a subsistence by providing ultra-cheap services to the formal economy.

Finally, data on services trade are much less reliable than data on trade in minerals and agricultural and manufactured goods. In contrast to merchandise trade, most services trade does not pass through customs and is not subject to import tariffs. For this and other reasons, data on the outsourcing of services is vitiated by under-reporting and dubious accounting practices.[75]

THE MAINSTREAM ECONOMISTS' TAUTOLOGICAL equation of value with value added not only makes exploitation disappear, it also obliterates the classical distinction between productive and non-productive labor. If every price is by definition a value, then any activity that results in a sale is by definition productive. "To the practical economist . . . if it is sold, or could be sold, then it is defined as production. Thus—within orthodox accounts—commodity traders, private guards, and even private armies are all deemed to be producers of social output, because someone is paying for their services." [76]

A distinction between productive and non-productive labor exists in all modes of production and is not specific to commodity exchange in general, let alone to capitalism. What is specific to capitalism is that this distinction is veiled by universal commodification, and by the capitalists' new criterion for productivity, *profitability*.

It may be asked, *are not these non-productive activities providing "common goods" necessary for the reproduction of society?* Shaikh and Tonak provide a cogent response: "To say that these labors indirectly result in the creation of this wealth is only another way of saying that they are necessary. Consumption also indirectly results in production, as production indirectly results in consumption. But this hardly obviates the need for distinguishing between the two."[77] To see the veracity of this argument, consider an economy made up of laborers and security guards.[78] The laborers produce all of the goods that both they and the security guards need to live on; the security guards provide a "common good," security. It is plain that the higher the ratio of security guards to laborers, all other things being equal, the lower the total product, and it is therefore logical to regard this economic activity as unproductive labor, a form of social consumption. Once this distinction is established for one category of economic activity, the door is opened for more additions to the list. Suppose, for instance, our imaginary community finds it necessary to allocate part of its social labor to weighing and recording the output of the production workers, and that the only available means of doing this is to carve the data into stone tablets, a slow process requiring many hours of labor. Their labor is non-productive in exactly the same way as it is of the security guards. These stones do not add to social wealth, they are merely representations of the wealth created by production labor. Were a technological advance to replace chisel and stone with pen and paper, much of this nonproduction labor could be released for production, thereby increasing total social wealth, or redeployed as security guards, resulting in no change to social wealth. Designation of security and administrative functions as nonproduction activities does not at all imply that they are unnecessary—in our simple model, both the security guards and the stone-carvers perform necessary functions.

In this simple model, as in reality, the social wealth that is consumed by the nonproduction laborers derives from the *surplus labor* of the production laborers, that is, the labor they perform in excess of what is required to replace their own consumption, what Marx calls *necessary labor*. Just as with the distinction between productive and non-productive labor, the division of the working day or week into surplus labor time and necessary labor time exists in all modes of production—for example, serfs working three days on the manor lord's land and three days on their own. In its capitalist form, surplus labor results from extending the workday beyond the time needed to replace the value of the basket of goods for which they exchange their wage—what Karl Marx called *necessary labor time*. In the Marxist framework, the ratio of surplus labor to necessary labor, or "the rate of surplus value" is synonymous with the rate of exploitation.

It might be asked: If workers in finance, advertising, security, etc., produce no value, how can they be exploited? So long as workers are obliged to work for longer than the labor-time needed to produce their basket of consumption goods, they are exploited. This is independent of the specific way their labor is employed and of whether they are employed in production, circulation, or administration. For present purposes, we can assume that all these workers endure the (nationally prevailing) rate of exploitation in common with production labor.

Nonproduction sectors are sustained by part of the surplus value extracted in production; the values consumed by them subtract from what is available for realization as profit in all its forms. The rate of surplus value can be ramped up, for instance by holding down wages, and yet the rate of profit may still decline. The more that social labor is employed non-productively, in commerce, finance, security, legal services, etc.—exactly what has been happening on an accelerated scale in the imperialist economies during the neoliberal era—the greater the downward pressure on profits and the greater the imperative to compensate for this by intensifying the exploitation of productively employed workers. The growing weight of services in imperialist economies is therefore as much the cause of the outsourcing pressure as it is the consequence of it.

Services and the Productivity Paradox

This brief survey of the role of services in the outsourcing of production concludes by summarizing the paradoxical effects of services outsourcing on measures of labor productivity in industry. First, we must note that many service tasks are inherently labor-intensive and cannot easily be mechanized, resulting in what appears to be stagnant or even falling levels of labor productivity in the service sector. Thus Katharine Abraham, a leading authority in the field of national accounts, reports that, in the United States,

> labor productivity in the services industries . . . actually declined over the two decades from 1977 through 1997. . . . Among the individual service industries showing declines in labor productivity were educational services and health services, as well as auto repair, legal services and personal services. Construction was another problem industry, with the implied labor productivity falling by 1 percent per year over the entire 20-year period.[79]

In contrast, "the rate of productivity growth in U.S. manufacturing increased in the mid-1990s, greatly outpacing that in the services sector and accounting for most of the overall productivity growth in the U.S. economy,"[80] releasing labor for redeployment to service jobs or to the reservoir of unemployed, resulting in a relative decline in manufacturing's contribution to GDP and in an even faster decline in manufacturing employment as a share of total employment.[81] This points to the first of a series of paradoxes that we must note for further study: the more rapidly that labor productivity advances in industry, the more important industry becomes in sustaining the rest of the economy and society. But at the same time, this means the more rapidly industry's share of GDP and of total employment *diminishes*, an effect that gives rise to all kinds of nonsense about "post-industrial society."

But the paradoxes arising from the tendency of productivity in industry to advance faster than in services do not stop here. Intensification of the labor process through brutal speed-ups and the introduction of labor-saving technology have undoubtedly made their contribution to productivity advances in industry, but some of the apparent increase in labor productivity in manufacturing is due to firms in this sector externalizing service tasks. When an industrial firm contracts out labor-intensive services such as cleaning, catering, etc., the productivity of its remaining employees increases, according to the conventional and most widely used measure of productivity. This occurs even if nothing about their work may have changed, and is the simple result of the firm's unchanged output now being divided by a smaller workforce. The trend in this direction accounts for a part of industry's rise in productivity and exaggerates the decline of industry's reported share of the total workforce. If an industrial firm contracts out service provision to a firm that employs cheap labor *in another country* the apparent gains in productivity in the industrial firm's productivity are even larger, since labor has not only been outsourced, its price has been slashed, reducing the cost of this input and therefore boosting the numerator in the formula for productivity (the firm's value added) while reducing the denominator, the size of the directly employed workforce. As Susan Houseman found, "Services offshoring, which is likely to be significantly underestimated and associated with significant labor cost savings, accounts for a surprisingly large share of recent manufacturing multifactor productivity growth."[82] Thus, she argues, "to the extent that offshoring is an important source of measured productivity growth in the economy, productivity statistics will, in part, be capturing cost savings or gains to trade but not improvements in the output of American labor."[83] Houseman believes this solves "one of the great puzzles of the American economy in recent years . . . the fact that large productivity gains have not broadly benefited workers in the form of higher wages . . . productivity improvements that result from offshoring may largely measure cost savings, not improvements to output per hour worked by American labor."[84] The important point here is that Houseman's argument applies just as much to the outsourcing of low value-added production tasks as it does to the outsourcing of services.

Three years before Houseman published her paper, Morgan Stanley economist Stephen Roach made the same point: "In the case of the United States . . . offshore outsourcing of jobs [is] the functional equivalent of 'imported productivity,' as the global labor arbitrage substitutes foreign labor content for domestic labor input. In my view, that could well go a long way in explaining the latest chapter of America's fabled productivity saga."[85] Where Houseman and Roach are wrong is in thinking that this solves the "productivity paradox," which they narrowly define as the divergence between wages and productivity in U.S. industry, thereby calling into question something that is an article of faith for these bourgeois economists, namely the direct relation between wages and productivity. On the contrary, the paradoxical effects of outsourcing on measures of productivity are merely superficial and relatively trivial consequences of the profoundly contradictory nature of labor productivity in capitalist society, which can be defined *either* as the physical quantity of useful goods (use-value, in Marxist parlance) created by workers in a given time *or* as the quantity of money they generate for their employer. In different ways, each chapter of this book tries to cast empirical and theoretical light on this most important of questions, and it will be given special attention in chapter 6.

TO SUMMARIZE THE FINDINGS OF THIS CHAPTER, export-oriented industrialization is extremely widespread throughout the Global South. It is just as true that this industrialization is extremely uneven, and is highly concentrated in some countries and some regions within those countries. The Global South has made significant progress in implementing the export-oriented industrialization strategy urged on them by imperialist governments, international financial institutions (IFIs}, and mainstream academics. The large majority of the roughly five billion inhabitants of the Global South now live in countries where manufacturing exports—mainly to the imperialist economies—form more than a half of their total exports.

Outsourcing has been a conscious strategy of capitalists, a powerful weapon against union organization, repressing wages and intensifying exploitation of workers at home, and has led above all to a huge expansion in the employment of workers in low-wage countries. The wage gradient between imperialist and developing nations also generates migration of low-wage workers in the opposite direction. Outsourcing and migration should therefore be seen as aspects of the same process, driven by the efforts of capitalists to profit from divisions among workers and from the huge wage differentials these divisions give rise to.

It is widely insinuated that if large parts of the Global South remain mired in extreme poverty it is because of the failure of many Southern economies to successfully integrate into world markets, "integration" meaning that if they have no natural resources, they must export more manufactured goods. Evidence presented in this chapter, and in chapters to come, indicates that, with few exceptions, those poor nations that have found success in reconfiguring their economies in line with neoliberal prescriptions have succeeded only in joining a race to the bottom.

3

The Two Forms of the
Outsourcing Relationship

Production outsourcing takes two basic forms: foreign direct investment (FDI), where the production process is moved overseas but kept in-house, and arm's-length outsourcing, when a firm outsources part or all of the production process to an independent supplier, independent in the sense that the "lead firm" owns none of it even though it may control its activities in many ways. Yet, according to the conventional definition, transnational corporations are "enterprises comprising parent enterprises and their foreign affiliates,"[1] in other words, enterprises that indulge in FDI. According to this definition Tesco and Walmart only count as TNCs to the extent that they operate retail outlets in other countries—Walmart's 2.1 million global workforce (up from 2,600 in 1971) does not include any of the workers who produce the goods that fill its shelves.[2] Until the first decade of the twenty-first century, both mainstream and Marxist analysts tended, as William Milberg observed, "to see globalization through a foreign direct investment lens. Like the proverbial drunk who searches for his lost keys under the streetlight only because that is where he can see best, economists have overemphasized the relevance of foreign direct investment."[3] The rapid growth of arm's-length outsourcing has made this approach increasingly anachronistic, and has also stimulated the rise of value-chain analysis and related approaches that see in-house FDI and arm's-length contractual relations as two different types of links comprising global value chains. Similar considerations have led many analysts to propose a fundamental change to the definition of transnational corporation, which, instead of denoting a firm with wholly or partly owned subsidiaries in other countries, should be redefined as "a firm that has the power to coordinate and control operations in more than one country, even if it does not own them."[4]

UNCTAD's *World Investment Report 2011* is a watershed in research into arm's-length, contractual relationships, defining these as

> a cross-border nonequity mode of TNC operation [in which] a TNC externalizes part of its operations to a host-country-based partner firm in which it has no ownership stake, while maintaining a level of control over the operation by contractually specifying the way it is to be conducted. . . . the defining feature of cross-border NEMs, as a form of governance of a TNC's global value chain, is *control over a host-country business entity by means other than equity holdings.*[5]

The differences and commonality between these two forms of outsourcing can be seen with the help of a thought experiment. A TNC can, and often does, convert a direct in-house relation with a subsidiary into an arm's-length relation with an independent supplier simply by signing some legal documents, erecting new signage, opening up a new bank account—without making any changes to the work regimes or to the labor processes, or to the price of inputs, or to the profits realized upon the sale of the output. The actual process of production and value creation/extraction would then be identical in every respect. Nothing would change except titles of ownership. Yet surface appearances would show a profound change: a visible South-North flow of repatriated profits from subsidiary to HQ would vanish without trace, even if the new arrangement turned out to be more effective in squeezing production costs and boosting the HQ's profits. As we saw in the case of the three global commodities in chapter 1, in the arm's-length relationship *all* of the lead firm's profits appear to arise as a result of its own value-added activities in the countries where the commodities are consumed, while their suppliers and the super-exploited workers employed by them make no contribution whatsoever.

This chapter examines these two forms of the outsourcing relationship, first separately and then together, in order to further enrich our concept of the globalization of production, and in order to identify questions and paradoxes that both mainstream and heterodox approaches cannot explain.

FOREIGN DIRECT INVESTMENT

According to the internationally accepted UN definition, "FDI is made to establish a lasting interest in or effective management control over an enterprise in another country. . . . As a guideline, the IMF suggests that investments should account for at least 10 percent of voting stock to be counted as FDI."[6] However, the contrast between portfolio and FDI investment is not as clear-cut as this excerpt from the standard UN definition of FDI suggests. As Ricardo Hausmann and Eduardo Fernández-Arias note, "FDI is not bolted down, machines are. If a foreigner buys a machine and gives it as a capital contribution (FDI) to a local company, the machine may be bolted down. But the company's treasurer can use the machine as collateral to get a local bank loan and take money out of the country."[7] This is not the only way that financial imperatives can override the production relation—retained profits may be reinvested in domestic government debt or other financial assets; alternatively, repatriated profits may exceed the affiliate's earnings, signifying disinvestment.

FDI can be categorized into four different types according to the motive of the investor. "Efficiency-seeking" FDI is neoliberalism's paradigmatic form—efficiency means cutting costs, in particular the cost of labor—and is the prime concern of this study. "Market-seeking" FDI was the dominant form in the years before neoliberal globalization, when protectionist barriers obliged TNCs to move production close to markets, and it is still important, as in the example of Japanese- and European-owned car plants in the United States. In contrast to efficiency-seeking FDI, market-seeking FDI typically does not involve the fragmentation of production processes but their replication in the host country. Since the most important markets for final goods are in the imperialist nations, market-seeking FDI is dominated by cross-border investments between imperialist countries—or, as a study by three UNCTAD economists put it, "Trade based on horizontal international production sharing occurs mainly between developed countries."[8]

"Resource-seeking" FDI refers primarily to foreign investment in the extractive industries (hydrocarbons and minerals), but natural resources can include foodstuffs, ingredients of cosmetics, and much else. When these are not merely harvested or extracted but have first to be cultivated, they are regarded as agricultural products, not natural resources. Agriculture and natural resource extraction have important features in common: FDI in these sectors is primarily determined by the location of mineral, hydrocarbon deposits, and the like, or of fertile tracts of land, in contrast to efficiency-seeking production outsourcing, whose location is primarily determined by the location of pools of cheap, super-exploitable labor. To resource-seeking FDI the availability of low-wage labor is an added bonus. The shift from in-house to arm's-length production arrangements is much less evident in extractive industries, because the collection of rents from rich deposits of ore or oil are much easier to protect when the lead firm directly owns the resources and the means of their extraction. The two forms of TNC exploitation of low-wage labor seen in manufacturing industry—in-house and arm's length—are also evident in agriculture. Nestlé's 800,000 contract farmers display many similarities to the arm's-length relations in manufacturing value chains; while, in contrast, plantation capitalism in old and new forms correspond to FDI, in that they involve direct ownership of capital in the low-wage economy. Finally, "technology-seeking" FDI seeks access to scientific or technological knowledge available in the host location. This is rarely an important motive for FDI flows into poor countries.

Until the first decade of the new millennium, it was a widespread, almost universal view that FDI in developing nations was of peripheral importance to rich-nation TNCs. Thus David Held, the social democratic visionary, argued that "the vast majority of . . . FDI flows originate within, and move among, OECD countries."[9] Kavaljit Singh, writing from a radical-reformist perspective representative of many NGO critics of globalization, concurs: "The bulk of global FDI inflows move largely within the developed world. . . . This situation could be aptly described as investment by a developed country TNC in another developed country. The U.S. and the EU . . . continue to be the major recipients of FDI inflows."[10] Sam Ashman and Alex Callinicos, writing in the Marxist journal *Historical Materialism*, similarly conclude that "the transnational corporations that dominate global capitalism tend to concentrate their investment (and trade) in the advanced economies. . . . Capital continues largely to shun the Global South."[11] Chris Harman, like Ashman and Callinicos, a partisan of the "International Socialist Tradition," draws out the big implication of this: if N-S FDI is so weak, so too must N-S exploitation be: "Whatever may have been the case a century ago, it makes no sense to see the advanced countries as 'parasitic,' living off the former colonial world. . . . The centres of exploitation, as indicated by the FDI figures, are where industry already exists."[12] Alex Callinicos, writing in 2009, similarly argued that data on FDI flows "are indicative of the judgments of relative profitability made by those controlling internationally mobile capital: these continue massively to favour the advanced economies,"[13] flatly contradicting the finding of UNCTAD's 2008 *World Investment Report* that TNC profits "are increasingly generated in developing countries rather than in developed countries."[14]

The massive pre-crisis surge of outsourcing to low-wage countries, a trend that the global crisis has only intensified, has finally demolished this consensus view—in 2013 FDI flows to developing countries surpassed those to developed countries for the first time.[15] But this consensus view was false even when Held et al. enunciated their words. The biggest problem with peering through an FDI lens is that arm's-length outsourcing is rendered invisible, but even before we bring this into the picture, a cursory examination of the relevant UNCTAD data is sufficient to refute the Eurocentric consensus and demonstrate that in fact the opposite is true, that *Northern capital is increasingly dependent on exploiting low-wage labor.*

As soon as we look beneath the headline UNCTAD data on gross FDI stocks and flows and examine their composition, a different picture begins to emerge. Headline data on total FDI flows, on which the "capital is shunning the Global South" thesis rests, are misleading for three reasons. First, they take no account of the extent to which FDI flows between imperialist countries are puffed up by non-productive investments in finance and business services. Between 2001 and 2012, developing economies received $464bn in such flows, compared to $609bn flowing into developed countries, and in the most recent years reported, from 2010 to 2012, manufacturing FDI flows into developing countries reached $151bn, surpassing the $145bn received by developed countries.[16] On the other hand, between 2001 and 2012 inward FDI in "Finance" and "Business Activities" in imperialist countries totalled $1.37 trillion in these years, more than twice the inward flow of manufacturing FDI into these countries, compared to $509bn in "Finance" and "Business Activities" FDI into developing countries.

Second, a much greater proportion of FDI flows between imperialist countries is made up of mergers and acquisitions (M&A), that is, FDI that transfers ownership of an existing firm, as opposed to "greenfield" FDI, that is, investment in new production facilities. M&A FDI reflects the *accelerating concentration of capital*, a process superbly documented in chapter 4 of *The Endless Crisis* by John Bellamy Foster and Robert McChesney, and is fundamentally different from the disintegration of production processes and their dispersal to low-wage countries, which are most clearly reflected in data on greenfield FDI. In 2007, for example, developed economies received 89 percent of the $1.64 trillion in M&A

FDI, more than half of which (51.4 percent, to be exact) occurred in financial services. In that same year, total FDI flows were $1.83 trillion. Though differences in the way these figures are collated means they are not directly comparable, they starkly highlight the overwhelming weight of M&As in overall FDI flows on the eve of the crisis. M&A have markedly declined since the pre-crisis feeding frenzy, but the pattern persists— between 2008 and 2013, M&A formed 45 percent of total inward FDI flows into imperialist countries and just 14 percent of flows into developing countries. On the other hand, developing nations received 69 percent of total greenfield FDI between 2008 and 2013, accentuating a pattern that was clearly established in the five years before the outbreak of the global economic crisis—between 2003 and 2007, developing nations attracted 59 percent of global greenfield FDI flows.[17] Overall, between 2003 and 2014 developing nations were the destination for $5.9 trillion in greenfield FDI, compared to $3.3tr in developed nations As Alexander Lehmann reported in a 2002 IMF working paper, "FDI in the developing world is predominantly in the form of so-called greenfield investment, rather than through the acquisitions of existing enterprises."[18]

Third, and perhaps most important of all, much of what is counted as FDI flows between imperialist countries are investments in firms *that have relocated some or all of their production processes to low-wage nations.* To illustrate this, the 2005 restructuring of the world's second-largest oil company, Royal Dutch Shell, increased the UK's inward FDI by $100bn, causing it to leap above the United States to become that year's prime destination for FDI. Yet, wherever they may book their sales and their profits, the great majority of the 98 countries hosting Shell affiliates (second only to Deutsche Post AG with majority-owned affiliates in 111 countries) are in Latin America, Africa, Central Asia, and the Middle East.[19]

The dangers of looking no further than headline figures on N-S FDI are highlighted by a cursory examination of the M&A data cited above. In conventional accounting, the merger or acquisition of one European, North American, or Japanese firm with or by another is regarded as an unambiguous instance of North-North FDI. A brief examination of the three largest M&A deals in 2007—which, like all but seven of the fifty largest M&A deals in that year, were between firms in imperialist nations—shows why such a reading of the data is simplistic and misleading. The largest cross-border M&A deal in 2007 was the ill-fated acquisition of the Dutch bank ABN-AMRO by the Royal Bank of Scotland for $98.2bn. Banks circulate titles to wealth, skimming off some of it for themselves, but produce none of it. In a multitude of ways—through their loans and investments, participation in hedge funds and futures markets, handling of flight capital, etc., and indirectly through the TNCs they finance—their tentacles are coiled around the Global South. Second on the list of the largest M&A deals in 2007 was the mining and packaging giant Alcan, purchased from its Canadian owners by the UK's Rio Tinto. Alcan employs 65,000 workers in 61 countries, 28 percent of them outside of Europe and North America.[20] Number three was the acquisition of the Spanish-owned utilities giant Endesa SA by a group of Italian investors for $26.4bn. In that year, Endesa operated affiliates in Spain, Portugal, Italy, and France, and also in Morocco, Chile, Argentina, Colombia, Peru, Brazil, Central America, and the Caribbean. In 2007, it earned 18 percent, or €471m, of its operating profits from its business in Latin America and the Caribbean.[21] Continuing down the list the picture becomes ever clearer. Every time a company or group of investors acquires or merges with a TNC headquartered in another imperialist country, counted as North-North FDI by the UNCTAD statisticians, they are likely to be buying into an entity with assets and activities spread on both sides of the North-South divide. No such ambiguity exists in the case of North-South FDI, since FDI originating from Southern nations is not only a small fraction of the FDI, but the bulk of it is in other emerging economies—UNCTAD reports that "FDI from developing economies has grown significantly over the last decade and now constitutes over a third of global flows. . . . [However,] most developing-economy investment tends to occur within each economy's immediate geographic region."[22] Despite this recent rise of FDI by Southern TNCs, in 2014 79 percent of the $25.9 trillion global stock of FDI was owned by TNCs headquartered in imperialist countries.[23]

The overwhelming weight of M&As in N-N FDI flows in the years before the onset of global economic crisis reflects a process of concentration and monopoly-formation among TNCs, in the financial sector and in all industrial sectors, proceeding in parallel to the shift of production processes to low-wage economies. These diverse phenomena are all lumped together as FDI. William Milberg is among those who have drawn attention to this dual process: "The global wave of merger and acquisition activity constituted a consolidation of the oligopoly position of lead firms who, in the process, focused their efforts on 'core competence' and outsourced other activities."[24] Gary Gereffi has also pointed to these "two dramatic changes in the structure of the global economy. The first is a historic shift in the location of production, particularly in manufacturing, from the developed to the developing world. . . . The second is a change in the organization of the international economy. The global economy is increasingly concentrated at the top and fragmented at the bottom, both in terms of countries and firms."[25]

FDI statistics thus merge three very different trends: the concentration of imperialist banks and finance capital; a process of concentration among Northern industrial and commercial capitals, many of them lead firms in value chains in which the actual production is performed by workers for distant Southern suppliers; and a process of disintegration of production processes and their dispersal to Southern nations in the quest for super-exploitable labor.

TNC Employment, North and South

UNCTAD's 2007 *World Investment Report* boasts a particular focus on the employment effects of foreign direct investment. Yet even here the amount of information is meager, providing data on total TNC employment in only a handful of developing countries. The most interesting and relevant part of this study was an analysis of the employment effects of foreign direct investment by U.S. TNCs. It reported that, in 2003, 9.8 workers were employed for each $1 million of FDI stock owned by U.S. TNCs in the manufacturing sector in developed countries, whereas the same stock of FDI in developing countries employed 23.8 workers, or 2.4 times as many.[26] As a result, a stock of $281bn in U.S. manufacturing FDI in developed countries employed 2.76 million workers, while a stock of $88bn in developing countries employed 2.1 million workers. The same quantity of investment in extractive industries (mining, quarrying, and petroleum) employs a much smaller number: 1.3 workers in developed countries per $1 million of FDI, compared to 2.5 workers in developing countries. To complete the picture, each $1 million invested in services leads to the employment of 2.1 workers in developed countries and 2.3 workers in developing countries.

However, this data underestimates TNC employment, since UNCTAD does not count temporary, casual, and subcontracted workers as employees, yet U.S. TNCs have led the way in casualizing Southern labor, as in the case of Coca-Cola, considered below. Counting all of these employees, it is reasonable to conclude that TNCs headquartered in the United States employ more workers in low wage countries than they do domestically, and, by extension, the same is true of TNCs headquartered in Europe and Japan.[27]

The Profits of FDI

Qualitative differences between N-N FDI and N-S FDI mean they cannot be simplistically compared. Flows of investment and repatriated profit between the United States, Europe, and Japan are symmetrical inasmuch as they invest in one another. In striking contrast, cross-border investments between the Global South and the Triad nations are extremely asymmetric: S-N FDI is negligible in comparison to N-S FDI. UNCTAD reported in 2008 that "the large gap between TNCs from the developed and developing groups remains. For instance, the total foreign assets of the top 50 TNCs from developing economies in 2005 amounted roughly to the amount of foreign assets of General Electric, the largest TNC in the world."[28] In consequence, direct investment and profits flow in both directions between the United States, Europe, and Japan, but between these nations and the Global South *the flow has been and continues to be overwhelmingly one-way*. As the accumulated stock of FDI in the South has increased, so the return flow of profits has grown into a mighty torrent, which, as Figure 3.1 shows, are now of a similar magnitude to new N-S FDI flows. A particularly striking feature of Figure 3.1 is the steepness of the increase of both FDI flows and profits in the early years of the millennium, consistent with evidence cited elsewhere on the acceleration of outsourcing following the bursting of the dot-com bubble at the beginning of the new millennium.

According to UNCTAD's 2008 *World Investment Report*, the world's TNCs earned $1,130bn in 2007 in profits from their foreign subsidiaries, 406,967 of which are located in developing economies and 259,942 in developed economies.[29] The report provided no breakdown or detailed analysis of FDI profits by firm, sector or country, except for "Annex Table B.14," which reports that in 2005, the most recent year for which data is available, U.S. TNCs earned $549bn in profits from what it elsewhere reports to be their $2.05 trillion stock of direct investments. Japan, the only other country to report profits from FDI, earned $87bn.

This UNCTAD table with just two entries exemplifies the scanty information on global profit flows in data provided by public bodies. Furthermore, there are many reasons to question the accuracy of the sparse data. FDI income has three components: repatriated profits, retained profits, and interest payments on loans extended to the affiliate by the parent company, but "many countries fail to report reinvested earnings, and the definition of long-term loans differs among countries."[30]

FIGURE 3.1: North-South Flows of FDI and Profits ($bn)

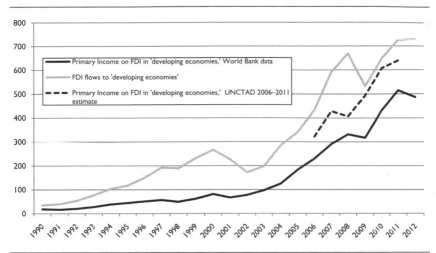

Source: FDI flows from UNCTAD (available at http://unctadstat.unctad.org/)

Alexander Lehmann, in a rare IMF working paper on the subject of corporate profits, says, "In practice, only few emerging markets adhere to these standards."[31] So poor were the data published by his employer, the IMF, Lehmann turned instead to the U.S. Department of Commerce and its data on FDI by U.S. firms, from which he concluded that the rate of return on FDI in developing countries in the 1995–98 period was at least twice as high as was reported by the IMF. He adds: "The estimates for the return on foreign direct investment suggest that profitability is widely underestimated. U.S. data show returns on total foreign direct investment in emerging markets in the order of 15 to 20 percent. An additional three percent on invested capital [is] paid to parent companies for royalties, license fees and other services."[32]

Twelve years on (Lehmann's paper was published in 2002), neither the IMF, UNCTAD, or any other IFI has shed any further light on this murky and decidedly non-trivial matter—no further working papers, no studies, no "FDI profits" theme for any of the annual reports, no revision of the data discredited by Lehmann, no attempt to publish new, more credible data. Instead, some dubious estimates with minimal information about how they were compiled and none about how the problems identified in Lehmann's paper have been addressed. However, what UNCTAD does report is interesting. Its 2013 *World Investment Report* informs us, "While the global average rate of return on FDI for 2006–2011 was 7.0 percent, the average inward rate for developed economies was 5.1 percent. In contrast, the average rates for developing and transition economies were 9.2 percent and 12.9 percent, respectively."[33] In other words, the rate of return on FDI was twice as high in developing countries as in imperialist countries.

UNCTAD publishes no tabular data on income from FDI, even though FDI is central to its remit. This it leaves to the World Bank, which manages the "Primary Income on FDI" database, whose data is presented in Figure 3.1. For the reasons cited by Lehmann and others discussed here, this surely significantly underestimates the true flow of profits from FDI in developing countries. The figures it provides for the 1995–98 period suggest a rate of return of around 4 percent, just one-fifth of the rate of return discovered by Lehmann for this same period.

Lehmann pointed in particular to a general failure by national authorities to collect data on reinvested income, that is, FDI profits that are not repatriated but used to finance an expansion of the TNC's affiliate. The *World Investment Report* of 2013 reported that around 40 percent of FDI profits in developing countries is retained in the host country, but "not all of this is turned into capital expenditure; the challenge for host governments is how to channel retained earnings into productive investment."[34] This alludes to the fact that not all retained earnings are reinvested in the affiliate that generated this income. The TNC may use these funds to invest in domestic government debt, in portfolio investments, in domestic stock markets, or any other legal or illegal activity that it thinks will be profitable, yet there is no publicly available information on the extent to which TNCs use their foreign subsidiaries as financial conduits rather than production facilities.

Declared profits also ignore underreporting, transfer pricing, and other widespread practices of dubious legality. Jennifer Nordin and Raymond Baker, a leading authority on "the countless forms of financial chicanery . . . prevalent in international business,"[35] reported in the *Financial Times* that

> over the past four decades or so, a structure has been perfected that facilitates illegal cross-border financial transactions. . . . Many multinational companies and international banks regularly use this structure, which functions by ignoring or skirting customs, tax, financial and money laundering laws. The result is nothing less than the legitimisation of illegality. . . . By our estimate, it moves some $500bn a year illegally out of developing and transitional economies into Western coffers.[36]

The profits that firms repatriate from their foreign subsidiaries are very much smaller than the surplus value extracted from its employees in these low-wage nations. We saw in chapter 1 that this surplus value is shared among many capitals in the imperialist economies, and a large chunk of it is captured by their states. And leaving aside firms' concealment of their actual profits, profit as such is what remains of surplus value after the subtraction of many unproductive yet necessary activities (necessary from the perspective of capitalists seeking to crystallize their profits, if not from the perspective of society as a whole), all of which consume surplus value extracted from exploited workers. Zero profits, or even large losses, are therefore quite compatible with major flows of surplus value and high rates of exploitation. The profits that are so imperfectly and partially described in statistics therefore suffer from much more fundamental problems than poor coverage and technical deficiencies, considerable as they are.

ARM'S-LENGTH OUTSOURCING

In contrast to FDI, where the production process and associated revevues are offshored but kept in-house, an outsourcing firm may choose to contract out some or all of production to an independent supplier while retaining effective control over both the final product and the process of its production. According to Gene Grossman and fellow Princeton economists, "It does not matter much whether the firm opens a subsidiary in a foreign country and employs workers there to undertake certain tasks within its corporate boundaries, or whether it contracts with a foreign purveyor under an outsourcing arrangement. . . . In either case the effects on production, wages and prices will be roughly the same."[37] The Princeton professors neglect to mention the effect of outsourcing on profits—which is odd, since the maximization of profits is the whole point of the exercise. But what's really odd is that, despite the fact that FDI generates a flow of repatriated profits while an arm's-length relation does not, multinational corporations increasingly favor arm's-length relationships over FDI. As Gary Gereffi points out, "While companies regularly decide whether they wish to produce goods and services 'in-house' or buy them from outside vendors, the tendency in recent years has shifted in the direction of 'buy.'"[38] Timothy Sturgeon, another leading researcher into global value chains, also "detect[s] a shift in the organization of global production toward external networks."[39] William Milberg concurs: "Despite the stunning increase in the transnational activity of

large firms ... such firms find it increasingly desirable to outsource internationally in an arm's length rather than non-arm's length (intra-firm)
relation."[40]

China provides an eloquent illustration of this. Grossman and Rossi-
Hansberg report that intra-firm trade, as a proportion of total U.S.
imports from China, rose from 11 percent in 1992 to 26 percent in 2005.[41]
But in 1992, following the relaxation of restrictions on inward FDI in
1991, the doors were only beginning to open to U.S. TNCs; since then
they have built a giant exporting platform almost from scratch, resulting
in annual imports into the United States from U.S.-owned TNC subsidiaries in China leaping from $3bn to $63bn, a thirty-fold increase that
is exaggerated by the exceedingly low initial level. On the other hand,
imports from independent suppliers in China increased "only" nine-
fold, from $22bn to $180bn.[42] Thus, while China-U.S. intra-firm trade
increased its share from a tiny base, arm's-length outsourcing by U.S.
companies in China greatly increased its absolute lead over direct U.S.
investments in that country, accounting, on the eve of the global crisis,
for three-quarters of total China-U.S. trade.

The Mysteries of Outsourcing

Milberg's recognition of outsourcing's growing preponderance leads
him to rhetorically ask, "Why should arm's-length outsourcing be of
increasing importance in a world where transnational corporations
play such a large role? . . . Why should cost reductions be increasingly
prevalent externally rather than within firms?"[43] He answers, "The
growing tendency toward externalization implies that the return on
external outsourcing—implied by the cost reduction it brings to the
buyer firm—must exceed that on internal vertical operations. . . . These
cost savings constitute rents accruing abroad in the same sense that
internal profit generation does for a multinational enterprise."[44] This is
a crucial insight, yet it poses a perplexing puzzle. As the three global
commodities discussed in chapter 1 illustrate, "rents accruing abroad"
appear, in company and national accounts, to accrue instead from the
domestic design, branding, and marketing activities of the lead firm.
We will return to this puzzle a few pages hence, but first we'll consider
some reasons why the arm's-length relationship might be increasingly
favored over FDI.

One reason why arm's-length outsourcing may be more profitable than FDI is that, as Martin Wolf notes, "transnational companies

pay more—and treat their workers better—than local companies do."[45] Citing "detailed econometric evaluation" that takes into account "the educational levels of employees, plant size, location, and capital- and energy-intensity . . . the premium is 12 percent for 'blue collar' workers and about 22 percent for the 'white-collar' workers."[46] Jagdish Bhagwati also reports that TNCs "pay an average wage that exceeds the going rate, mostly up to 10 percent and exceeding it in some cases."[47] Writing in *The Economist*, Clive Crook gives much higher estimates: he claims that wages in the affiliates of TNCs in "middle-income countries" are 80 percent higher than those paid by local employers, and in "low-income countries" their wages are 100 percent higher.[48] Thus one reason why TNCs increasingly prefer to externalize their operations is that forcing outsourced producers into intense competition with one another is a more effective way of driving down wages and intensifying labor than doing so in-house through appointed managers.

A further incentive to "deverticalize"—that is, to move from a vertical parent-subsidiary relationship to a horizontal contractual relation between formally equal partners—is that arm's length also means "hands clean"—the outsourcing firm externalizes not only commercial risk and low value-added production processes, it also externalizes direct responsibility for pollution, poverty wages, and suppression of trade unions. One notorious example is Coca-Cola's operations in Colombia, the hub of its Latin American soft drinks empire, where the food workers' union, SINALTRAINAL, accuses company management of colluding with death squads who have assassinated nine union members and leaders since 1990 and forced many others into exile. "Eighty percent of the Coca-Cola workforce is now composed of non-union, temporary workers, and wages for these individuals are only a quarter of those earned by their unionized counterparts. . . . Coca-Cola is in fact a stridently anti-union company, and the destruction of SINALTRAINAL, as well as the capacity to drive wages into the ground, is one of the primary goals of the extra-judicial violence directed against workers."[49] Coca-Cola's Atlanta-based international directors wash their hands of any responsibility either for the poverty wages paid to their workers or for the violent repression of their efforts to remedy this, on the grounds that its Colombian bottling plants are independent companies operating under a franchise, enabling it to make the legally precise claim that "Coca-Cola does not own or operate any bottling plants in Colombia."[50] Mark Thomas, an investigative journalist, commented that this is the "Coca-Cola system," operating as an entity but claiming no legal lines of accountability to the Coca-Cola Company. . . . The case here is similar to that of Gap and Nike in the 90s . . . [who] outsourced their production to factories in the developing world that operated sweatshop conditions. It was not Nike or Gap that forced the workers to do long hours for poor pay, it was the contractors.[51]

The "Coca-Cola system" not only distances TNCs from direct responsibility for super-exploitation, pollution, etc., during normal times, they don't have to take responsibility for imposing mass layoffs during times of crisis. Though the arm's-length relationship may have political or public relations benefits, the bottom line is its effect on TNC profits and asset values. A third reason is that arms's-length relationships also allow TNCs to offload many of the costs and risks associated with cyclical fluctuations in demand and with much larger disruptions in world markets, as exemplified by the whiplash effect felt in the lowest rungs of global value chains following the collapse of Lehman Brothers in 2008. As UNCTAD reports, "Jobs in labor-intensive NEMs [Non-Equity Modes] are highly sensitive to the business cycle in GVCs [Global Value Chains], and can be shed quickly at times of economic downturn."[52]

Finally, not only does the arm's-length relationship not generate any S-N flows of repatriated profits, it does not involve any N-S capital flows, enabling Northern firms to divert investment funds into what Silver et al. call "financial intermediation and speculation."[53] In other words, the increased profits delivered by outsourcing are not invested in production either at home or as FDI, and can be entirely devoted to leveraging asset values, through share buyback schemes and generous dividend payments, or invested in financial markets in order to reap speculative profits, thereby feeding the financialization of the imperialist economies.

In sum, it is possible to identify four major reasons why outsourcing firms might favor an arm's-length relationship with their low-wage suppliers: 1) foreign investors find it necessary to pay higher wages than domestic employers, limiting the desired reduction in costs; 2) arm's-length means hands clean; 3) transference of risk; 4) avoidance of FDI in favor of what UNCTAD calls a "non-equity mode" releases funds for investment in financial markets or to finance acquisitions and share buybacks (two ways in which the fragmentation of production can accelerate the concentration of capital).[54]

The puzzle posed by Milberg's insight that a large portion of the profits of firms in imperialist countries (he does not call them this) is accrued in distant production processes can be restated as follows. The foreign direct investments of northern TNCs generate a gigantic S-N flow of repatriated profits, but in complete contrast, between Southern firms and Northern lead firms there is, in the data on financial flows, neither sign nor shadow of any S-N profit flows or value transfers. Furthermore, the various subterfuges indulged in by transnational corporations to conceal part of this flow from tax authorities (transfer pricing, under-invoicing, etc.) are not available in arm's-length relationships. These are large benefits to forgo—yet TNCs increasingly find the arm's-length relationship to be more profitable than in-house FDI. Does the fact that the S-N flow of value and profit is invisible mean that this flow doesn't exist? If not, what becomes of the profit-flows that are visible in the case of an in-house relationship but completely disappear when this is replaced by an outsourcing relationship?

This is the question left unanswered by Milberg, Gereffi, etc., a conundrum that cannot be resolved without breaking free of the neo-classical framework, which presumes markets to be the "ultimate arbiter of value" and price to be its ideal measure,[55] precluding the possibility of hidden flows or transfers of values between capitals prior to their condensation as prices. This calls to mind the physical phenomenon known as sublimation—when the application of heat to a visible solid turns it into a flow of invisible vapor, only for it to rematerialize as a visible solid at a different relocation. Similarly, the flow of value from Southern producers to Northern capitalists is invisible—that is, there's no sign of it in standard data on global capital and commodity flows. According to the bourgeois economists, if it's not visible it doesn't exist; and since value can only appear in the form of price, this, to positivist economics, is its measure.[56] This, the central premise of neoclassical economics, crassly precludes the possibility that value is transferred or redistributed between capitals in order to achieve equilibrium prices that equalize profits. Conversely, to recognize the existence of such flows is to dislodge the keystone of the ruling economic theory, causing the entire edifice to collapse. Renaming "profit' as "rent," as do Milberg, Kaplinsky, Gereffi, and others studying this phenomenon, does not clarify this question. In fact, it blurs the important distinction between profit and rent.[57] Milberg's notion of "rents accruing abroad" implies that the South-North flow continues; and simply calling it rent says nothing about a really interesting implication of this. These "rents accruing abroad" appear in the GDP—the gross domestic product—of the importing nation—even though they were "accrued abroad." The solution of this paradox, which we have been hinting at so far, will be presented in chapter 9, "The GDP Illusion."

THE STRUCTURE OF WORLD TRADE

A most striking feature of the imperialist world economy is that, as we have seen, *Northern firms do not compete with Southern firms, they compete with other Northern firms*, including to see who can most rapidly and effectively outsource production to low-wage countries. Meanwhile, Southern nations fiercely compete with one another to pimp their cheap labor to Northern "lead firms." We therefore have N-N competition, and we have cutthroat S-S competition, *but no N-S competition*—that is, between firms, if not between workers. Of course, important exceptions can be identified and qualifications can be made, but the overall pattern is clear: Apple competes with Samsung and Nokia, but not with FoxConn, Taiwan Semiconductor Manufacturing Company (TSMC), and its other suppliers. Similarly, British Home Stores (BHS) and Marks & Spencer (M&S) compete with each other but not with their Bangladeshi suppliers, and the same goes for Tesco, General Motors, or any other TNC sourcing its final goods or intermediate inputs from suppliers in low-wage countries. The lead firms' relationship with their suppliers is therefore complementary, not competitive, even if it is highly unequal. This important point was underlined by Richard Herd, head of the China division at the Organisation for Economic Co-operation and Development (OECD), who noted that "at the moment, China is not a threat to Japan's core industries"; on the contrary, outsourcing labor-intensive production tasks to China has given many Japanese firms "a new lease on life . . . if you look at Chinese exports and Japanese exports they are not competing, they are complementary."[58]

The complementary relation between Japanese and Chinese firms can be applied to relations between firms in imperialist and oppressed nations in general. China's manufacturing industry is no more a threat to the supremacy of U.S. TNCs than are the *maquiladoras* along the U.S.-Mexican border. Not only do the headline figures that show a huge deficit in trade with China actually reflect the importation of intermediate inputs produced in Japan, Malaysia, South Korea, and elsewhere, a great deal of it results directly from the decision of U.S. firms to move their production to take advantage of low Chinese wages. There cannot be anything more absurd nor more disingenuous than the nationalist-protectionist hoopla over the U.S. trade deficit with China!

The same is true of Europe's TNCs. As Ari Van Assche, Chang Hong, and Veerle Slootmaekers explain in a study of EU-Chinese trade, "Europe's importers and retailers . . . increasingly rely on cheap inputs and goods from Asia. . . . EU companies are now also producing in low-cost countries, and not simply importing inputs."[59] Far from being locked in competition with China, "the possibility of offshoring the more labor-intensive production and assembly activities to China provides an opportunity to our own companies to survive and grow in an increasingly competitive environment,"[60] and they conclude, "Our direct competitors in the tasks in which we have a comparative advantage are not located in China, but continue to be the usual suspects: the United States, Western Europe and a handful of High-Income East Asian economies." [61]

Competition between firms in imperialist and developing countries does exist. Even in the garment sector, where the global shift of production to low-wage countries is most advanced, low-end producers have not entirely disappeared from imperialist countries and residual competition with firms in low-wage countries persists. Competition between firms on both sides of the global divide is much more intense in branches and sectors where the global shift is still under way, as in the automobile industry. Finally, great significance must be attached to rising competition between imperialist firms and firms in China, South Korea, and Taiwan and elsewhere that are beginning to directly compete with them in strategic and/or higher value-added products. A prime example of the latter is China's rapid rise to dominance of solar panel and wind turbine production; another is the rise of Chinese civil engineering behemoths now regularly undercutting their European and North American rivals in tenders for railway, port, and power station construction; companies such as HTC, Samsung, and Xiaomi are challenging Apple's supremacy in smartphone production. The pharmaceutical industry is another important terrain of competition, with firms based in imperialist countries with Indian firms like Cipla and Ranbaxy challenging the supremacy of the West's "big pharma." This is an important trend, a real exception to the dominant pattern of trade established during the era of neoliberal globalization, and is part of the evidence that, in some sectors at least, the grip of imperialist capital is being loosened by Southern competitors

Nevertheless, despite these and other high-profile examples of N-S competition, the overwhelmingly dominant form of interaction between firms in imperialist and low-wage economies is synergetic and complementary. The general absence of head-to-head competition between firms on opposite sides of the N-S divide is brought into sharp focus by the "complexity index" developed by Arnelyn Abdon, Marife Bacate, Jesus Felipe, and Utsav Kumar at the Asian Development Bank and by Harvard's Ricardo Hausmann and César Hidalgo. This approach classifies both national economies and individual commodities according to their complexity, "complex economies" being "those that can weave vast quantities of relevant knowledge together, across large networks of people, to generate a diverse mix of knowledge-intensive products," while complex products, for example, "medical imaging devices or jet engines, embed large amounts of knowledge and are the results of very large networks of people and organizations. By contrast, wood logs or coffee embed much less knowledge, and the networks required to support these operations do not need to be as large."[62]

The "Index of Complexity"

To explain the idea of complexity, Abdon et al. use the simile of a Lego bucket to represent a country and various kinds of Lego pieces to represent the capabilities available in the country:

> The different Lego models that we can build (i.e., different products) depend on the kind, diversity, and exclusiveness of the Lego pieces that we have in a bucket. . . . A Lego bucket that contains pieces that can only build a bicycle most likely does not contain the pieces to create an airplane model. However, a Lego bucket that contains pieces that can build an airplane model may also have the necessary pieces needed to build a bicycle model. . . . Hence, determining the complexity of an economy by looking at the products it produces amounts to determining the "diversity and exclusivity" of the pieces in a Lego bucket by simply looking at the Lego models it can build.[63]

Hausmann and Hidalgo provide a useful illustration of the number-crunching methodology used to generate their Index of Complexity:

> Consider the case of Singapore and Pakistan. The population of Pakistan is 34 times larger than that of Singapore. At market prices their GDPs are similar since Singapore is 38 times richer than Pakistan in per capita terms. . . . They both export a similar number of different products, about 133. How can products tell us about the conspicuous differences in the level of development that exist between these two countries? Pakistan exports products that are on

TABLE 3.1: Total Exports, by Product Complexity
Percent of total exports in each Product Complexity Level (1 = highest; 6 = lowest)

	1	2	3	4	5	6
Japan	40	19	22	11	7	2
Germany	40	25	16	11	6	4
USA	28	22	23	13	9	5
France	26	22	22	16	8	6
Singapore	15	14	38	11	4	18
Korea	18	19	34	14	8	8
Malaysia	5	15	38	15	7	20
India	8	10	8	10	30	34
China	6	16	22	19	15	23
Thailand	7	10	32	16	11	24
Philippines	3	7	50	20	7	13
Indonesia	3	5	13	15	15	49
Vietnam	2	3	4	8	14.	67
Pakistan	1	2	2	4	12	78

Source: Table 6 in Arnelyn Abdon, Marife Bacate, Jesus Felipe and Utsav Kumar, *Product Complexity and Economic Development, Levy Economics Institute Working Paper No. 616* (2010).

average exported by 28 other countries (placing Pakistan in the 60th percentile of countries in terms of the average ubiquity of their products), while Singapore exports products that are exported on average by 17 other countries (1st percentile). Moreover, the products that Singapore exports are exported by highly diversified countries, while those that Pakistan exports are exported by poorly diversified countries. Our mathematical approach exploits these second, third and higher order differences to create measures that approximate the amount of productive knowledge held in each of these countries.[64]

"Diversity" is here defined as the number of products that a country exports with "revealed comparative advantage," that is, where their share of the global market in that good is greater than their share of global population, the idea being that countries specialize in what they do best, thereby exploiting their comparative advantage, and this is revealed in the composition of their exports.

One deficiency of complexity theory is that unavailability of data prevents its extension to trade in services. More serious, in the context of the present discussion, is that, in the words of World Bank researchers, "The technological sophistication and competitive stature of an exporter's industrial base can be exaggerated when exports are used as a measure of industrial capability."[65] Thus China's complexity score will be exaggerated by its export of iPhones and other electronic goods that are assembled, but not manufactured, in that country. Complexity theorists are aware of this problem, but their remedy is ineffective: "Countries may also export things they do not make. To circumvent this issue we require that countries export a fair share of the products we connect them to."[66] "Fair share" means when the share of a given commodity in a country's total exports is greater than the global share of this commodity in global exports as a whole, that is, when its revealed comparative advantage (RCA) is greater than one—but iPhones, etc., will all pass this test and thus lead to an overestimation of China's complexity score .

Abdon et al.'s Complexity Ranking lists 124 nations according to the complexity of their exports (see Table 3.2), while Hausmann and Hidalgo generate an Economic Complexity Index comprising 128 countries. Both present a broadly similar picture rich with fascinating details. In Abdon et al.'s ranking, all of the ten most complex nations are imperialist nations. In Hausmann and Hidalgo's table Singapore, Slovenia, and the Czech Republic make it into the top ten most economically complex nations. Norway, Australia, and New Zealand, also members of this exclusive club, appear much further down among a slew of middle-income Southern nations, their position depressed by the large share of primary commodities in their exports. Also notable is the lowly position of Greece and Portugal, the two countries most battered by the Eurozone crisis, indicating that these nations directly compete not with core Eurozone countries, but with China and other low-wage nations.[67] Pakistan, Sri Lanka, Bangladesh, and Cambodia, four countries whose exports consist mostly of garments, languish at the bottom of the table among the poorest nations on earth.

There is a broad consensus among economists and policy makers that the loss of competitiveness by peripheral countries in the Eurozone vis-à-vis Germany and other core countries is at the heart of the forces tearing Europe apart. Unable to restore their competitiveness through currency devaluation, their only option is savage cuts in nominal wages, including that part of it received in the form of social benefits. Contemplating the divergence between German and Mediterranean productivity, *Financial Times* journalist Samuel Brittan commented that "even the Greek colonels, Franco, Mussolini or Salazar would have been hard put to reduce nominal wages on the scale required."[68] But this broad consensus rests on a false premise—that Germany is Greece's, Spain's, etc., principal rival. As Jesus Felipe and Utsav Kumar have pointed out:

Ireland, Spain, Portugal, and Greece do not compete directly with Germany in many products that they export and hence comparing their aggregate unit labor costs and drawing conclusions is probably misleading. . . . German exports are concentrated in the most com plex products of the complexity scale . . . in the case of Greece and Portugal, their exports are concentrated in the least-complex groups. . . . Their export shares (by complexity groups) are similar to those

TABLE 3.2: Complexity Ranking

1.	Japan	32.	Saudi Arabia	63.	Algeria	94.	Ecuador
2.	Germany	33.	New Zealand	64.	Macedonia	95.	Togo
3.	Sweden	34.	Armenia	65.	Iran	96.	Chad
4.	Switzerland	35.	Argentina	66.	Senegal	97.	Syria
5.	Finland	36.	South Africa	67.	Libya	98.	Viet Nam
6.	USA	37.	Croatia	68.	C.A.R.	99.	Nicaragua
7.	UK	38.	Malaysia	69.	Moldova	100.	Morocco
8.	Austria	39.	Sierra Leone	70.	Niger	101.	Pakistan
9.	Belgium	40.	Australia	71.	Uzbekistan	102.	Honduras
10.	France	41.	Latvia	72.	Egypt	103.	Côte d□Ivre
11.	Ireland	42.	Kazakhstan	73.	Burundi	104.	Tanzania
12.	Netherlands	43.	Venezuela	74.	Philippines	105.	Mozambi□ue
13.	Czech Rep.	44.	Lithuania	75.	Panama	106.	Benin
14.	Canada	45.	Bosnia	76.	Indonesia	107.	□amen
15.	Denmark	46.	Chile	77.	Tunisia	108.	Sri Lanka
16.	Norway	47.	Bulgaria	78.	Jamaica	109.	Turkmenistan
17.	Slovenia	48.	Romania	79.	Kenya	110.	Ethiopia
18.	Russia	49.	India	80.	Guatemala	111.	Cameroon
19.	Singapore	50.	China	81.	Peru	112.	Ghana
20.	Israel	51.	Greece	82.	Albania	113.	Sudan
21.	South Korea	52.	Portugal	83.	Dominican R.	114.	Malawi
22.	Slovakia	53.	Uruguay	84.	Uganda	115.	Angola
23.	Italy	54.	Azerbaijan	85.	El Salvador	116.	Madagascar
24.	Hungary	55.	Lebanon	86.	Zambia	117.	Bangladesh
25.	Ukraine	56.	Hong Kong	87.	Rwanda	118.	Guinea
26.	Poland	57.	Jordan	88.	Burkina Faso	119.	Laos
27.	Spain	58.	Colombia	89.	Nepal	120.	Congo
28.	Mexico	59.	Thailand	90.	Mali	121.	Haiti
29.	Belarus	60.	Turkey	91.	Bolivia	122.	Nigeria
30.	Brazil	61.	Kyrgyzstan	92.	Tajikistan	123.	Papua NG
31.	Georgia	62.	Costa Rica	93.	Paraguay	124.	Cambodia

Source: Appendix C in Arnelyn Abdon, Marife Bacate, Jesus Felipe, and Utsav Kumar, *Product Complexity and Economic Development, Levy Economics Institute Working Paper No. 616* (2010).

of China. If China were the correct comparator, then perhaps the situation of the European countries would be significantly worse. We believe that this is where the real problem of the peripheral countries lies. . . . The problem is that they are stuck at middle levels of technology and they are caught in a trap. Reducing wages would not solve the problem. [69]

The European Union is a club of imperialist nations, part of the united front with other imperialist powers against so-called emerging nations, and which during the neoliberal era has considerably deepened its exploitative and parasitic relation with the Global South. Spain, Portugal, and Greece are minor imperialist nations whose economies, banking systems, political structures, and military forces are an integral part of Europe and whose history is of marauding, oppressor nations. The short list of core nations, Fred Halliday reminds us, has "remained the same for a century and a half, with the single addition of Japan."[70] But now at least one of them—Greece—is threatened with ejection from this club, and finds itself increasingly in competition with China and other low-wage countries, a competition that it is unable to win because of its much higher wages and its lack of a technological edge.

The Index of Complexity suggests that a Grexit from the EU would merely formalize its demotion from this imperialist club. In 1978, Greece's complexity index was 0.64, the lowest in Western Europe. By 2008 this had collapsed to 0.21, on a par with China, as can be seen from Greece's ranking in Table 3.2. In contrast, the indices of Portugal and Spain which in 1978 stood at 0.85 and 1.05 respectively, have suffered a much gentler decline, to 0.70 and 0.93.[71] In other words, though Europe's core nations have a complementary relation with Chinese firms, using them in the competitive battle against each other and with those in Japan and North America, Greek firms increasingly find themselves in direct competition with Chinese firms. It is no surprise to find Greece in the relegation zone. Relegation, that is, from the club of imperialist nations. Consumption levels are declining rapidly, but ejection from the Eurozone will very likely result in Greece's precipitous collapse. Bourgeois democracy would be unlikely to survive such an eventuality, with the return of military dictatorship a distinct medium-term possibility. Should Greek workers show signs of challenging Greece's capitalist rulers for power, fascist violence will be mobilized against them, opening the possibility of a fully fledged fascist government taking power on the mainland of Europe.

Asymmetric Market Structures: Monopolistic "Lead Firms" in the North, Cutthroat Competition in the South

The Index of Complexity, whose most striking feature, according to Abdon et al., is that "richer countries are the major exporters of the more complex products while the poorer countries are the major exporters of the less complex products,"[72] reveals with remarkable clarity the extent to which poor countries, and therefore firms in poor countries, do not compete with firms in rich countries. The enormous significance of this for the operation of the law of value in the contemporary global economy will be considered in chapter 8. The aim of this and the preceding chapter is to to identify and analyze the most important empirically observable features of the outsourcing relationship, in particular the fact that, in the words of UNCTAD economists, "developing country exports tend to be increasingly concentrated in . . . labor-intensive production processes." This raises the "risk that the simultaneous drive in a great number of developing countries . . . to export such dynamic products may cause the benefits of any increased volume of exports to be more than offset by losses due to lower export prices.[73] In other words, what has become known as "the race to the bottom."

William Cline was one of the first to warn of the danger that "first mover" advantage would not be available to latecomers:

> Other developing countries would be . . . ill-advised to expect free-market policies to yield the same results that were achieved by the East Asian economies, which took advantage of the open economy strategy before the export field became crowded by competition from other developing countries, and did so when the world economy was in a phase of prolonged buoyancy. . . . Elevator salesmen must attach a warning label that their product is safe only if not overloaded with too many passengers at one time: advocates of the East Asian model would do well to attach a similar caveat to their prescription.[74]

The success of the "first movers," especially South Korea, Taiwan, and Singapore (often termed the Newly Industrializing Countries), seemed to show the path for other poor and underdeveloped to follow, but, as Raphael Kaplinsky and many others have noted, "the so-called gains from outward-oriented manufacturing may reflect a fallacy of composition. In other words, it may make sense for an individual country such as China to expand massively its exports of manufactures, but if the same path is

adopted by all low-income economies, everyone will lose."[75] Kaplinsky
bleakly concludes that for every winner there will inevitably be many
losers, and that firms occupying lower links in the chain can only escape
the race to the bottom if they succeed in erecting some form of barrier to
competition, that is, some degree of monopoly. "When barriers to entry
are eroded . . . the best option may be to vacate the chain altogether" and
find something else to do.[76]

Intense competition between Southern producers, combined with
what Kaplinsky has called a "fierce oligopsony"[77] of global buyers, drains
wealth from Southern producers and supports profits and asset values
of firms in imperialist countries. Gary Gereffi identifies the root cause
of these unequal outcomes to lie in "the fundamental asymmetry in the
organisation of the global economy between more and less developed
nations. To a great extent, the concentrated higher-value-added portion
of the value chain is located in developed countries, while the lower-
value-added portion of the value chain is in developing economies."[78]
Robert Feenstra and Gordon Hanson, two other leading lights of value-
chain research, give a similar description of asymmetry:

> The asymmetry of market structures in global production networks,
> with oligopoly firms in lead positions and competition among first-
> and certainly second-tier suppliers, has meant intense pressure on
> suppliers who, in seeking to maintain markups, must keep wages low
> and resist improvements in labor standards that might lead to a shift
> . . . to another firm or country.[79]

The acknowledgment by these researchers that the promised level playing field is in fact steeply sloping leads them to pessimistic conclusions.
In particular, Southern suppliers "have no rents to share with employees,
and can survive only if wages are kept at a minimum. The increased use
of sweatshop labor today, which has come with the rise in arm's-length
outsourcing, can be seen as tied to global production sharing."[80]

There is a high degree of unanimity among these researchers about
the pernicious combination of oligopolistic global buyers and unbridled
competition among Southern producers. They accurately describe some
important facts in plain view about the unequal relations between the
Northern and Southern links of the value chains, but their explanatory
power is limited, because, in line with the value-chain literature in general, "asymmetry in market structures in global production networks"
includes product and capital markets in its gaze, but ignores the role

of asymmetry in labor market structures, including the suppression of labor mobility, the vast reserve army of unemployed workers, repressive labor regimes, etc., in determining the distribution of value added. To explain anything about real relationships and actual outcomes—super-profits, swollen asset values, and high(er) wages at one end of the chain; sweatshops and starvation wages at the other—our concept of asymmetry must be extended far beyond product market structures to include all asymmetries of wealth and power.

UPGRADING, OR "MOVING UP THE VALUE CHAIN"

Export-oriented industrialization was presented as the route out of the impoverishment resulting from dependence on the export of primary commodities suffering chronically declining terms of trade vis-à-vis manufactured goods. However, as UNCTAD reported in 1999:

> Terms-of-trade losses are no longer confined to commodity export-ers. Many manufactures exported by developing countries are now beginning to behave more like primary commodities as a growing number of countries simultaneously attempt to raise their exports in the relatively stagnant and protected markets of industrial countries. For example, the prices of manufactures exported by developing countries fell relative to those exported by the European Union by 2.2 percent per annum from 1979 to 1994.[81]

Three years later, UNCTAD delivered a damning verdict on the results of two decades of export-oriented industrialization: "Of the economies examined here, none of those which pursued rapid liberalization of trade and investment over the past two decades achieved a significant increase in its share in world manufacturing income, although some of them experienced a rapid growth in manufacturing exports."[82] Faced with this harsh reality, "upgrading," which means capturing a bigger share of the total value of the finished commodity by moving into higher value-added activities, has become the mantra of development economics, or as Milberg and Winkler put it, "Economic development has increasingly become synonymous with 'economic upgrading' within global production networks."[83] In other words, adoption of the export-oriented industrialization strategy is an insufficient condition for the attainment of development. But if overcrowding has stranded the EOI elevator in the basement, the upgrading elevator, which has a much smaller capacity, suffers even bigger problems. Before we examine the evidence for this and consider its implications, we should note the major problem that the upgrading imperative poses for mainstream economic theory: upgrading contradicts dominant models of international trade, which stress that, rather than trying to do things that they presently cannot do, countries should concentrate on what they are able to do best and employ the resources they are most generously endowed with, that is, they should exercise their "comparative advantage." Milberg and Winkler add,

> The general perspective of upgrading is anathema to traditional theories of trade based on comparative advantage. The notion of economic upgrading is largely about gaining competitiveness in higher value-added processes, a strategy that may conflict with the dictates of the principle of comparative advantage in which an "optimal" pattern of trade may call for countries remaining specialized in low value-added goods.[84]

The implication is that "traditional theories of trade", that is, the modern variants of the theory of comparative advantage that occupy a sacrosanct place in mainstream economic theory, are useless as a guide to nations seeking development. (Mainstream trade theory will be discussed in later chapters.) Milberg and Winkler propose that "absolute upgrading" occurs when "value added per worker engaged" rises faster than the value of exports; "weak upgrading" when it rises, but more slowly than exports, and if value added per worker rose less than a quarter as fast as exports, no upgrading is taking place. The logic of this approach is that there are two possible conditions that might cause the value of exports to rise faster than domestic value added per worker: a rise in the import composition of those exports, or an increase in the size of the workforce producing them. In the first case, the shrinking domestic contribution to the value of exports is symptomatic of race-to-the-bottom competition; in the second case the developing country is doing more of the same thing but with diminishing returns. In their sample of thirty developing countries drawn from three continents, not one achieved absolute upgrading and just nine of the thirty countries experienced "weak upgrading."[85]

Milberg and Winkler see this as "a contemporary version of the Prebisch-Singer dilemma,"[86] in other words, a repetition of the deteriorating terms of trade suffered by the South's traditional primary exports over much of the twentieth century, now as then blighting hopes of development and depriving producers of the fruits of their labor.[87] Thus they argue that "the export-led growth strategy adopted by most developing countries following the debt crisis in the 1980s (in place of the previous strategy of import substitution industrialization) has suffered from a 'fallacy of composition' problem. . . . The result can be a disproportionately small rise in value added, implying minimal economic upgrading."[88] Their conclusions are apt, as is their tinge of scorn for the failure of analysts to challenge the hyperbole and false promises of the proponents of neoliberal reforms: "There is a need for a theory of 'downgrading.' Our cross-country results are consistent with many findings that most countries and sectors are not experiencing upgrading by acceptable definitions. Since these instances predominate, it would be useful to theorize this rather than simply label them as instances where upgrading does not occur."[89] A "theory of downgrading," that is, a new version of dependency theory, is precisely what the present work is seeking to develop.

SLOW GROWTH IN THE SOUTH'S SHARE OF GLOBAL MANUFACTURING VALUE ADDED

Manufacturing value added (MVA) is often only a small fraction of the value of Southern manufactured exports and has been growing much more slowly than employment, trade, or just about any other measure of globalization.[90] Had the IMF used this measure in place of gross exports, instead of reporting the dynamic growth of the globally integrated Southern workforce, it would have had the embarrassing task of explaining why this growth has been so lackluster.

The long-running decline in MVA's share of GDP in imperialist nations is widely interpreted to mean a corresponding decline in the importance of manufacturing production, giving rise to notions of a transition to a "post-industrial society" or a "knowledge economy," notions that are Eurocentric in that industry hasn't diminished, it has moved, out of sight and out of mind, and reflect the petit-bourgeois social milieu of their proponents, far distant from the sphere of production. Industry's real contribution to GDP is far greater than the statistics appear to show, since it is the source of the value consumed by non-productive sectors of the economy and misread as their contribution to GDP. Indeed, once we dispense with crude physicalist definitions of industry and services, and reclassify so-called service tasks intrinsic to the production process as "industry," *industry is then, by definition, the source of all value, and therefore of all value added, in an economy.*

Two factors account for the apparent decline of industry's contribution to GDP: the substitution of workers by machines resulting in the rising productivity of industrial labor, and the substitution of higher-paid domestic workers with low-wage workers in poor countries. The latter is analyzed in depth in this book. Considering by itself the effect of the introduction of labor-saving technology, advancing productivity means industry supports an ever-more complex society with fewer workers—yet this shows up in standard economic data as a decline in industry's importance, leading to the simplistic and misleading notion that we now live in a "post-industrial society."

The World Bank's World Development Indicators provide data on MVA growth (for 1990 and 2002) and on growth in export of manufactures (for 1990 and 2004) for 55 low- and middle-income nations and 16 high-income' nations.[91] Manufactured exports from the 55 low-wage nations increased by 329 percent between 1990 and 2004 (434 percent if China is included), while their combined MVA grew by just 46.3 percent.[92] During this decade and a half of intense globalization, the 16 high-income nations increased their exports of manufactures by 127.4 percent, while their combined MVA grew by 14.2 percent, and by just 1 percent if the United States is omitted—the United States' 40.6 percent growth in MVA accounted for nearly all of the MVA growth of high-income nations, boosting its share of all 71 nations' MVA from 29 percent to 34 percent.

AS THE PORTION OF GDP CONTRIBUTED by manufacturing has declined in imperialist economies so it has increased in many Southern nations, yet the leap in the South's share of global manufacturing trade is not reflected in its share of global MVA, which has increased by a much smaller amount.[93] The continuing global shift in production is indicated by WDI data reporting that between 1996 and 2005 high-income nations' share in global MVA declined from 80 percent to 74 percent, with the share of low- and middle-income nations rising from 20 percent to 26 percent. Given the qualitative advances in the globalization of production this is, to some extent, to be expected. It also reflects the shrinking share of the value of the final product that is captured by the Southern producer. Thus, in 1990, the MVA of the 55 low- and middle-income nations was 1.8 times the value of its exports of manufactures; by 2002 this had fallen sharply, to 0.6. This major decline has three main components: the demise of ISI-protected industry, increased imported value-added content of exports, and deteriorating terms of trade (falls in relative prices) of manufactured exports.

Mexico offers the most extreme example of booming manufactured exports and bombing MVA. Boosted by membership of the NAFTA free trade area with the United States and Canada and by the collapse of the peso in 1994, which made Mexican labor even cheaper, between 1990 and 1998 Mexico's manufactured exports increased nearly tenfold, yet total value-added in its manufacturing sector increased by barely 50 percent and its share of world MVA actually fell. High-income nations present a mirror image: their ratio of MVA to manufactured exports doubled, from par in 1990 to 2.0 in 2002. As UNCTAD has pointed out, "in relative terms, industrial countries appear to be trading less but earning more in manufacturing activity."[94]

Despite the enormous increase in the global south's manufactured exports from 1980 onwards, the rate of growth of MVA in these nations slowed down compared to the pre-.globalization period. Figure 3.2 compares the growth of MVA during the first two decades of export-oriented industrialization with the previous crisis-ridden decade of import substitution industrialization in four Latin American nations and six Asian nations at the forefront of the EOI stampede. Remarkably, only Chile saw an improvement in MVA growth.

FIGURE 3.2: Annual Growth in Manufacturing Value-Added Percent for Selected Developing Nations

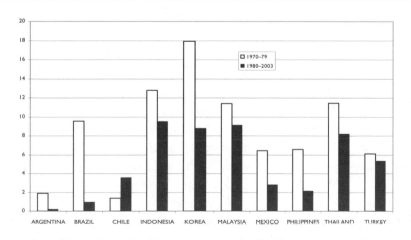

Source: Özlem Onaran: *The Effect of Neoliberal Globalization on Labor's Share in Developing Countries,* Table 1, p. 31, http://www.univie.ac.at/ie/alt/files/lva/artikel.pdf.

Prior to the neoliberal era, Southern MVA growth exceeded manufactured exports by a wide margin, signifying that manufacturing was
oriented to satisfying domestic needs. As we saw in chapter 2 (Figures
2.2–2.4), the transition to neoliberalism was marked by an astonishing increase in Southern manufactured exports, with major but much
slower growth in MVA, signifying that more and more of the value of
the South's exports are made up of imported inputs.[95] The consequence,
that "developing countries have greatly expanded their share of global
manufacturers' exports while seeing their share of global value added
in manufacturing rise by proportionally much less,"[96] dashed hopes that
export-oriented manufacturing provides the path to prosperity.

The pronounced tendency of the MVA of emerging nations to decline
relative to the value of their manufactured exports, a strong indication
of the existence of a race to the bottom among Southern manufactures-
exporting nations, is revealed in Figure 3.3, which shows the ratio of
MVA to manufactured exports between 1980 and 2007.

Figures 3.3 and 3.4 reveal a contrast between the early globalization
period of 1980–1995 and the late globalization period from 1995 to the
onset of the global financial crisis in 2007. Close inspection reveals that
the sharp divergence between MVA and manufactures-exports growth
rates began in the early 1990s and accelerated in the early 2000s.

An outstanding feature of the entire postwar period is the relative
decline of manufacturing as a contributor to the GDP of the dominant
nations and to global GDP. In the United States, for example, the major
imperialist country where it has held up best, manufacturing industry
accounted for 65 percent of GDP and 38 percent of employment in 1939,
falling to 54 percent of GDP and 28 percent of employment by 1979, and
to 43 percent of GDP and 17 percent of employment by 2004.[97]

IN CONCLUSION, COPIOUS EVIDENCE has been amassed that outsourcing, otherwise known as export-oriented industrialization, is not
a path to development or to convergence with developed countries. On
the contrary, extreme power asymmetries and race-to-the-bottom competition results in much of the proceeds of this expanded exploitation
of low-wage labor being captured by imperialist firms and imperialist
states. The global shift of production has fuelled the development of
imperialist countries at least as much as it has fostered development
in the supposedly developing countries, who are also left to deal with
the hidden costs of development—the damage to the environment and
workers' health.

FIGURE 3.3: MVA vs. Manufactured Exports, 1980–2007

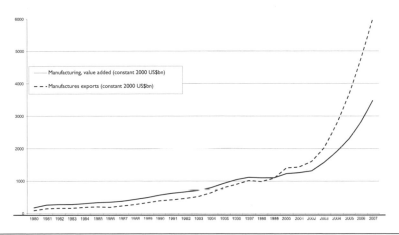

Source: World Development Indicators (September 2009, available at http://esds80.mcc.ac.uk/wds_wb).

FIGURE 3.4: MVA Growth and Export Growth, Selected Nations

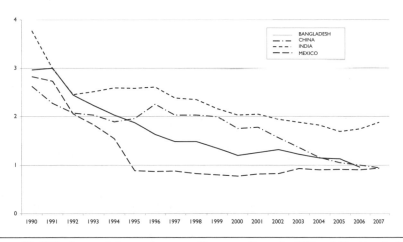

Source: World Development Indicators, three-year rolling average (September 2009, available at http://esds80. mcc.ac.uk/wds_wb).

The study of the economic processes of global outsourcing conducted in this and the preceding chapter focused on commodity and
capital markets, yet a central finding of chapter 1's study of three global
commodities is that conditions in the labor market—which include
imperialist borders, the "planet of slums," informalization, chronic and
massive unemployment and under-employment, and gender dynamics,

or the so-called "feminization" of labor—are at least as important as conditions in commodity and capital markets. Accordingly, our attention now shifts to the conditions in which workers in low-wage countries are forced to sell their labor-power. In doing so it makes these hundreds of millions of women and men visible, brings them into our consciousness, places their contribution to global wealth, their agency and their place in history at the center of this enquiry, and aids discovery of the real questions about the world that analysis and theory must answer.

4

Southern Labor, Peripheral No Longer

A striking feature of contemporary globalization is that a very large and growing proportion of the workforce in many global value chains is now located in developing economies. In a phrase, the centre of gravity of much of the world's industrial production has shifted from the North to the South of the global economy.

—GARY GEREFFI

The momentous, continuing and indeed accelerating shift in the center of gravity of capitalist production examined in the past two chapters has its counterpart in a similarly momentous transformation of the global working class.[1] So far we have discussed labor processes, the instruments of labor, the products of labor; we have considered the behavior and motivations of those who come into possession of this living labor by paying wages. Now we turn to analyzing the working class itself.

Figure 4.1 (p. 103) shows the growth of the global industrial workforce between 1950 and 2010 in "more developed regions" and "less developed regions." In 2010, 79 percent, or 541 million, of the world's industrial workers lived in "less developed regions," up from 34 percent in 1950 and 53 percent in 1980, compared to the 145 million industrial workers, or 21 percent of the total, who in 2010 lived in the imperialist countries.[2] For workers in manufacturing industry this shift is more dramatic still, since in low-wage countries manufacturing forms a much higher proportion of total industrial employment than in the imperialist economies, and therefore, as John Bellamy Foster, Robert W. McChesney, and R. Jamil Jonna point out, "The broad category of 'industrial employment' systematically understates the extent to which the world share of manufacturing has grown in developing countries," citing figures for the United States and China showing these ratios to be 58.1 percent and 75.2 percent respectively.[3] Extrapolating these two ratios to "more developed" and "less developed" countries as a whole, 83 percent of the world's manufacturing workforce lives and works in the nations of the Global South.

This quantitative growth is an indication of a qualitative transformation: the industrial workers of the Global South have not only become more numerous, they have become very much more integrated into the global economy, greatly magnifying their economic importance and social weight. The IMF has attempted to capture this qualitative change with its "export-weighted global workforce," constructed by multiplying the numerical growth of the workforce by the increasing degree to which they produce for the global market rather than the domestic market, as is indicated by the growing ratio of exports to GDP. Since Southern-manufactured exports grew more than twice as fast as GDP during the quarter-century leading up to the outbreak of the global crisis in 2007, the IMF reckons that the "effective global workforce" quadrupled in size between 1980 and 2003.[4] On the other hand, in the imperialist nations, while the proletarians (those who live by selling their labor-power) have increased their already overwhelming predominance within the economically active population, the industrial working class has declined both absolutely and relatively.

In absolute terms, and as a share of the global industrial proletariat, the South's industrial workforce has seen spectacular growth since 1980, yet its share of the South's total workforce has been much more modest, rising from 14.5 percent in 1980, to 16.1 percent in 1990, to 19.1 percent in 2000, to 23.1 percent in 2010 (by comparison, industry's share of employment in imperialist nations declined from 37.1 percent in 1980, to 33.2 percent in 1990, to 27.2 percent in 2000, to 22.5 percent in 2010).[5]

Between 1980 and 2000, only in the United States did the industrial working class avoid an absolute decline, reflecting the much greater success of U.S. employers in holding down wages, intensifying labor, and recruiting large numbers of low-wage migrant workers. But a sharp corner was turned at the end of the 1990s. One outcome of the "Asian contagion," the waves of bankruptcies and currency devaluations that swept through Thailand, Indonesia, Malaysia, South Korea, and other

FIGURE 4.1: Global Industrial Workforce

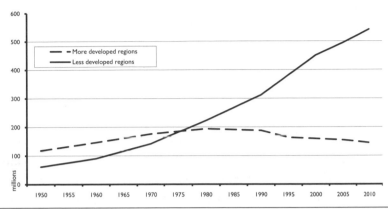

Sources: 1950–1990: ILO, Population and Economically Active Population, 2004; 1995–2005: ILO, 2007, *Key Indicators of the Labor Market* (KILM, 5th ed., chap. 4, Box 4B http://www.oitcinterfor.org/public/english/region/ampro/cinterfor/news/key_ind.htm); 2010: KILM 6th ed. Box 4B. To generate this graph, ILO/KILM data on the percentage of the workforce employed in "industry" in more and less developed regions was applied to data on the economically active population in these two regions. The 2010 data for more developed nations' industrial workforce includes ILO estimate of recession-induced decline of 9.5m industrial jobs.
Note: The 2004 ILO publication is no longer available from ILO's website. After 2004, data on world employment by sector is contained in annex tables in annual editions of the ILO's Global Employment Trends, http://laborsta.ilo.org/.

Asian economies in 1997, was to substantially cut the cost of labor in these countries. This, and the rise of China, helped stimulate a big outsourcing surge; between 2000 and 2010, industrial employment in the United States fell by 12 million to 29.6 million, now comprising 16.7 percent of the employed population, down from 23.2 percent in 2000.[6] Manufacturing employment fared worse: 19.6 million were employed in this sector in mid-1979, the highest level in history, falling to 17.3 million by 2000, before tumbling by 37 percent to 11.5 million by 2010. The anemic economic recovery since then saw U.S. manufacturing employment climb to 12.3 million by 2015.[7]

Meanwhile, agricultural employment in the Global South has declined to 48 percent of its EAP, down from 73 percent in 1960, and from "approximately one-third" to just 4 percent of EAP in developed countries. Yet the ILO reports: "Despite the declining share of agricultural workers in total employment, the absolute numbers of those engaged in agriculture are still rising, most notably in South Asia, East Asia, and sub-Saharan Africa."[8]

As noted above, despite the rapidly growing numerical preponderance of Southern industrial workers in the global industrial proletariat, between 1995 and 2005 their share of total Southern employment grew

modestly, from 19.4 percent to 20.2 percent. With the partial and temporary exception of China—a special case because of the one-child
policy that reduced births by an estimated 200 million since its introduction in 1979 and because of its extraordinarily rapid GDP growth
since then—no economy has grown fast enough to provide jobs to the
legions of young people entering the labor market and the rural exodus
to swollen cities in search of work. Even at the zenith of export-oriented
industrialization the ILO reported that "in the late twentieth century,
manufacturing ceased being a major sector of employment growth,
except in East and Southeast Asia."[9] Senior ILO economist Nomaan
Majid expanded on this, pointing out that "manufacturing is not the most
important sector of employment growth. . . . The commerce sector . . .
is the main employment growth sector in both low- and middle-income
groups. . . . [This] shows that the expectation on manufacturing leading
employment growth is unwarranted."[10] As it does so often, Bangladesh
provides an extreme case, where the structure of the labor market "is
characterized by a very high rate of labor force growth (8 percent per
annum), low employment growth rate and declining absorption in the
industrial manufacturing sector. . . . The decline in the relative share of
agricultural employment is not matched by increase in manufacturing
employment."[11]

The relative stagnation in Southern industrial employment (relative,
that is, to the growing pool of labor) continued into the first five years
of the new millennium. As the ILO commented in 2006, "Despite robust
economic growth . . . the global economy is failing to deliver enough
new jobs for those entering the job markets."[12] Thus, even in those
unprecedented and not-to-be-repeated years, the Southern capitalist
economies fell far short of being able to absorb the growing workforce.
The result—massive structural unemployment, misery and destitution
for an immense multitude, and an enormous downward pressure on
wages for those able to find work.

THIS CHAPTER HAS TWO PARTS. The first considers how the imperialist division of the world into oppressed and oppressor nations has
shaped the global working class, central to which is the violent suppression of international labor mobility. Just as the infamous pass-laws
epitomized apartheid in South Africa, so do immigration controls form
the lynchpin of an apartheid-like global economic system that systematically denies citizenship and basic human rights to the workers of
the South and which, as in apartheid-era South Africa, is a necessary

condition for their super-exploitation. The second part of the chapter is concerned with the dynamics of this process of class formation, resolved into three distinct dimensions: the relative weight of wage-labor vis-à-vis self-employment; formal employment vis-à-vis employment in the informal economy; and "gender," that is, the intersection of class exploitation and women's oppression, and why this resulted in the massive incorporation of women into the Southern workforce.

THE SUPPRESSION OF FREE LABOR MOBILITY AND THE MAKING OF THE SOUTH

The proclaimed free movement of capital and commodities must also be applied to that which must be above all else: human beings. No more bloodstained walls like the one being constructed along the American-Mexican border, which costs hundreds of lives each year. The persecution of immigrants must cease! Xenophobia must end, not solidarity! [13]

—FIDEL CASTRO, Durban, 2 September 1998

A facile analogy between the modernization processes taking place in the Global South since the Second World War and the nineteenth-century development of capitalism in Europe and North America is central to capitalist ideology in both its liberal and neoliberal variants. Convergence between developing and developed nations was both the premise and the prediction of Walter Rostow's paradigm-setting *The Stages of Economic Growth: A Non-Communist Manifesto*, which argued that developing countries would naturally pass through the same stages of development as did Europe and North America a century earlier, from agrarian societies to industrialized societies, eventually attaining development and convergence with developed countries. Sixty-five years on, and only Taiwan and South Korea have risen from the ranks of developing nations, and the global crisis will test how secure is their grip on the higher rungs of the development ladder. Rostow's seminal work helped to turn this deterministic and Eurocentric notion into the intellectual foundation both for the mainstream academic theories of development and for the policies promoted by imperialist governments and international financial institutions (IFIs) from the 1960s until now.

Rostow argued that Europe's takeoff resulted from internal processes:

All that lies behind the breakup of the Middle Ages is relevant to the creation of the preconditions for takeoff in Western Europe. Among the Western European states, Britain, favored by geography, natural resources, trading possibilities, social and political structure, was the first to develop fully the preconditions for takeoff. The more general case in modern history, however, saw the stage of preconditions arise not endogenously but from some external intrusion by more advanced societies.[14]

But is it true that Britain and Europe's "takeoff" was due to endogenous factors alone, as Rostow asserts? Marx had a different view: "The veiled slavery of the wage laborers in Europe needed the unqualified slavery of the New World as its pedestal. . . . The treasures captured outside of Europe by undisguised looting, enslavement and murder flowed back to the mother-country and were turned into capital there."[15]

Rostow presents the more recent external shocks triggering modernization processes in "traditional societies" as benign and progressive. In continuation of the earlier quote, he says: "These invasions—literal or figurative—shocked the traditional society and began or hastened its undoing; but they also set in motion ideas and sentiments which initiated the process by which a modern alternative to the traditional society was constructed out of the old culture."

But did the "invasions" of ideas, commodities, missionaries, and soldiers from "advanced societies" play a beneficient, progressive role, or did they create obstacles to progress? "Politically, the building of an effective centralized national state—on the basis of coalitions touched with a new nationalism, in opposition to the traditional landed regional interests, the colonial power, or both, was a decisive aspect of the preconditions period; and it was, almost universally, a necessary condition for takeoff." But corrupt, kleptocratic elites often violently resisted change, and elites in the advanced nations—and states under their control—often colluded with them, out of desire to continue plundering natural resources and exploiting cheap labor, or for fear of independent nation-states pursuing their own interests and making their own friends, or to crush rebellious subject populations, and often all three.

Rostow was well aware of this: "In . . . a setting of political and social confusion, before the takeoff is achieved and consolidated politically and socially as well as economically . . . the seizure of power by Communist conspiracy is easiest; and it is in such a setting that a centralized dictatorship may supply an essential technical precondition for takeoff and a sustained drive to maturity."[16] In practice, the impulse to develop and modernize thus took the form of civil wars and wars of national liberation, in which struggle against old and new forms of colonialism and neocolonialism meshed with struggles to overthrow domestic elites who were too afraid of their subject peoples to dare to mobilize their energies in a push for modernization and development. This, not Soviet expansionism, explains why the struggle for modernization often took the form of socialist revolution—for example, in China, Cuba, Vietnam. The pro-Moscow Communist parties often played a deeply ambiguous or even counterrevolutionary role in these struggles.

It is no surprise, therefore, that the development promoted by the United States and its allied Western democracies following the Second World War so often included the installation of "centralized dictatorships."

This modernization thesis dovetailed with the dominant neo-classical economic theories of international trade, in particular the Hecksher-Ohlin-Samuelson (HOS) variant of David Ricardo's theory of comparative advantage.[17] HOS theory predicts a tendency toward equalization of factor prices between rich and poor countries, one of these factors being wages.

This combination of economic and political obstacles, both internal and external, and the vast social forces set in motion, involving tens and hundreds of millions of people, created the context for the emergence of radical critiques of the modernization paradigm, collectively known as "dependency theory." This is why the debate between "modernization" vs. "dependency" took the form of a debate between capitalist, social-democratic, and socialist paths of development. (This will be reviewed in chapter 7.)

Rostow's vision of modernization was elite-led. Its agents are entrepreneurs, supported by an efficient, technocratic state. It was natural, inevitable, and desirable that inequalities should increase in the early stages of development, as elites accumulate large profits before reinvesting them to obtain even larger profits for themselves and, as a by-product, development for the country. The role of the state is to provide a secure environment, infrastructure, and the rule of law, which means protection of property and enforcement of contracts.

In the dominant modernization paradigm development is elite-led, and is best served by a competent technocratic state that preserves its autonomy from the elite in order to better serve elite interests, which are assumed to be in alignment with national interests. This paradigm implicitly or explicitly regards authoritarian regimes able to suppress resistance to austerity, low wages, privatization, etc., as necessary, at least in the early stages of development. As Rostow argued in *The Stages of*

Economic Growth, "A centralized dictatorship may supply an essential technical precondition for takeoff and a sustained drive to maturity." Fulfilling Rostow's vision, military dictatorship was, until recently at least, the prevalent form of political rule in Latin America, Africa, and much of Asia.

A FATAL FLAW IN THE "STAGES" theory of development and the convergence hypothesis, one that more or less invalidates it, is that the very processes that produced modern, developed, prosperous capitalism in Europe and North America also produced backwardness, under-development, and poverty in the Global South. While workers were leaving nineteenth-century Europe in droves for the New World, rampant European imperialism resulted in the "forcible incorporation into the world market of the great subsistence peasantries of Asia and Africa," entailing "the famine deaths of millions and the uprooting of tens of millions more from traditional tenures." The real parallel between the second half of the nineteenth century in Europe and the second half of the twentieth century in the Global South is therefore very different. To quote Mike Davis: "The brutal tectonics of neoliberal globalization since 1978 are analogous to the catastrophic processes that shaped a 'Third World' in the first place."[18]

The accelerated spread of capitalist social relations among Southern nations during the neoliberal era has been far more effective in dissolving traditional economies and ties to the land than in absorbing into wage labor those made destitute by this process. The rural exodus and growth of the urban workforce is analogous to what happened in Europe a century earlier, but there are important differences, the most far-reaching and significant of which is that the free movement of workers across borders and oceans that characterized the nineteenth century became subject to increasing restrictions.

Between 1850 and 1920—a time when, according to ILO economist Deepak Nayyar, "there were no restrictions on the mobility of people across national boundaries—passports were seldom needed and immigrants were granted citizenship with ease"—about 70 million people emigrated from Europe, 36 million of them to the United States, 6.6 million to Canada, 5.7 million to Argentina, and 5.6 million to Brazil, settling on land cleared by the genocide of indigenous civilizations.[19] The total migratory flow was equivalent to more than a sixth—17 percent—of the 408 million people living in Europe in 1900. This mass emigration to the Americas and Australasia mitigated the growth of pauperism and the reserve army of labor in Europe. According to Ajit Ghose, another senior ILO economist, "For several European countries, emigration was large and sustained enough to make growth rates of population and labor force insignificant or negative for years."[20] If the same proportion had emigrated from the Global South since the Second World War as left Europe between 1850 and 1920, 800 million people would have moved north,[21] expanding the total population of the more developed countries by 70 percent. Instead, "a negligible 0.8 percent of the workforce of the developing world has migrated to work in industrial countries,"[22] one-twentieth of the fraction of Europe's population that emigrated in the earlier period. As Ghose remarks, "It is quite clear that, for most of the developing countries, international migration is of no help in coping with the major labor market problem—that of surplus unskilled or low-skilled labor."[23]

The contrast between the two periods is all the more striking when we consider reasons why much larger migration flows in the late twentieth century than a hundred years earlier could have been expected, including the huge increase in wage differentials and disparity in living conditions between source and destination countries, the greater ease and safety of travel, the vastly improved possibilities of maintaining contact with families and communities back home and of financially supporting them through remittances, and of eventual return.

The contrast could not be starker—or of greater significance to understanding the shaping of the modern global political economy: "The European urban-industrial revolutions were incapable of absorbing the entire supply of displaced rural labor . . . but mass emigration . . . provided a dynamic safety valve that prevented the rise of mega-Dublins and super-Napleses. . . . Today, by contrast, surplus labor faces unprecedented barriers to emigration to rich countries."[24] Because of these barriers, "the majority of migrants move from one developing country to another rather than from a developing country to a developed one."[25] South-North migration was negligible before the Second World War, and, *relative to the potential migrant population*, it has remained negligible. As Deepak Nayyar points out, "Between the late 1940s to the early 1970s, there [was] a limited amount of labor migration from developing nations to the industrialized world. Since then, however, international migration has slowed to a trickle because of draconian immigration laws or restrictive consular practices,"[26] flatly contradicting widespread perceptions in imperialist countries, fanned by xenophobic politicians and mass media, of an explosive growth in their numbers.

The true picture is more nuanced than the one portrayed by Nayyar. The United Nations Department of Economic and Social Affairs reports that, in 2013, a total of 64.2 million migrants from Southern nations lived in imperialist nations,[27] more than double the 28.6 million who had migrated north by 1990. The International Organization for Migration (IoM) estimates that around half of Southern-born migrants are employed, one twentieth of the imperialist nations' total workforce,[28] and it further estimates that 40 percent of them work in industry, compared to 25 percent of the indigenous workforce—which means that approximately 9 percent of the 145 million industrial workers in imperialist countries were born in oppressed nations. The IoM also reckons they are three times more likely to work in agriculture, 10 percent of whom do so, compared to 3 percent of the indigenous workforce.[29]

During the 1990s the United States was much more open to Southern immigration than other imperialist nations—during this decade they increased by 70 percent, compared to a 26 percent increase in Europe.[30] This much larger inflow of super-exploitable Southern labor partly explains the United States' relative economic dynamism vis-à-vis Europe during this decade. The 2000–2013 period, however, presents an opposite picture—Southern-born migrants in Europe increased by 65 percent, compared to a 39 percent increase in the United States, and, if the surge in migration during this period from Central Europe is included, this rises to 71 percent, while the increase in the United States falls to 37 percent.

Japan has been and continues to be the most restrictive of all in its admission of migrant labor. As Table 4.1 reports, in 2013 Japan was home to 2.3 million migrants from oppressed nations, mostly from elsewhere in Asian nations. Assuming that half of these were employed, they formed 1.8 percent of Japan's total workforce of 65 million, much lower than in the United States or EU.[32] The IoM's 2003 *World Migration Report* provides an interesting detail: in 2001, 142,000 immigrants entered Japan with work visas. Of these, 117,839 (71,678 of them Filipinas) were classified as "entertainers," "which includes actors, singers, and professional athletes. However, some of the entertainers are actually recruited to work in the sex industry." [33] Nevertheless, migrant labor has become increasingly important to Japanese manufacturing industry: "Rather than provide stable employment, factories hire temporary workers—often Chinese or Brazilians on short-term visas—who get low pay and poor conditions. Japan has not just moved factories to cheap labor, it has also brought cheap labor to the factories."[34]

TABLE 4.1: Migrants in Imperialist Countries, by Countries of Origin (millions)[31]

	SOURCE NATIONS											
	World			Imperialist Nations			Former COMECON countries (central Europe central Asia)			Global South		
HOST	1990	2000	2013	1990	2000	2013	1990	2000	2013	1990	2000	2013
Europe	24.5	32.6	50.1	10.2	11.2	13.5	3.2	7.3	13.5	11.1	14.0	23.2
U.S.	23.3	34.8	45.8	5.0	4.7	4.4	1.8	2.2	2.5	16.5	27.9	38.8
Japan	1.1	1.7	2.4	0.1	0.1	0.2	0.0	0.0	0.0	1.0	1.6	2.3

Source: United Nations, Trends in International Migrant Stock: Migrants by Destination and Origin, POP/DB/MIG/Stock/Rev.2013.
Europe comprises Belgium, Channel Islands, Cyprus, Denmark, Faeroe Islands, Finland, France, Germany, Gibraltar, Greece, Iceland, Ireland, Isle of Man, Italy, Liechtenstein, Luxembourg, Malta, Monaco, Netherlands, Norway, Portugal, San Marino, Spain, Sweden, Switzerland, UK. The column heading "imperialist nations" includes all the above, plus Australia, Canada, Israel, Japan, New Zealand, and the United States.

For highly skilled workers the picture is very different. In the first place, a high proportion of the South's highly skilled workers have joined the "brain drain" and have taken advantage of what, to them, is an open door into the rich nations. The OECD (Organization for Economic Cooperation and Development), a club of mostly rich nations, reports that "for virtually all countries of origin, the emigration rate of the highly skilled exceeds the total emigration rate"; in 2010, one in every nine Africa-born graduates lived in OECD nations, compared to one in thirteen for Latin America and the Caribbean and one in thirty for Asia. Some African nations endure emigration rates of the highly skilled that are more than twenty times the emigration rates of their citizenry as a whole. Among African nations and small island nations in 2010, for example, 46 percent of skilled Jamaicans lived in OECD countries, 43 percent of skilled Zimbabweans, and 41 percent of those born in Mauritius. Guyana topped the list, with close to 90 percent of its graduates living in OECD countries. In contrast, non-OECD countries with large populations, such as Brazil, China, India, and Russia, experience emigration rates below 3.5 percent.[35] As Ghose comments, "For certain countries . . . the brain drain seems to be of truly astonishing magnitudes."[36] Perhaps its most nefarious effects can be seen in health care systems depleted by emigration, as exemplified by the Royal Africa Society's headline-grabbing report in 2005 that more doctors from Malawi were working in Birmingham in the UK than in Malawi itself.[37] A 2013 study of the exodus of African doctors to the United States revealed the startling scale of the medical brain-drain, finding that

the physician brain drain from SSA [sub-Saharan Africa] to the
US began in earnest in the mid-1980s and accelerated in the 1990s
during the implementation years of the SAPs [Structural Adjustment
Programs] imposed by . . . the International Monetary Fund (IMF)
and the World Bank, [whose] conditionalities included . . . deep
cuts to basic public sector health care services; imposition of fees
for health care provision and education; near obliteration of health
research budgets; extended freezes in public sector hiring, including
public education and public health sectors; unprecedented pauper-
ization of academic and public health sector staff; increases of social
inequalities and economic vulnerability; and the mushrooming of
international non-governmental organizations, often with minimal
accountability to the local authorities.[38]

Illustrating this, the study cites WHO estimates that between 1995
and 2004 Tanzania lost 78.3 percent of its doctors through emigration,
decreasing its physician density of 4.1 per 100,000 people to 0.69 per
100,000 people. In the United States, the corresponding figure is 250
doctors per 100,000 people.[39]

So, while the migration of low-skilled workers has made a trifling
impact on the South's vast labor surplus, the migration of highly skilled
workers has damaged the South's health and education services and its
quest for sovereignty and social development. To retain these workers,
poor nations must offer wages comparable to those paid in high-wage
countries—an important source of increasing wage inequality in poor
nations, as we shall discuss in the next chapter.

Instead of emigrating, the South's surplus population has congre-
gated in the "planet of slums," as documented by Mike Davis in his book
of that name, where hundreds of millions of people live in destitution
surpassing the worst horrors of Victorian England that were described
by Engels in 1845. They form part of the permanent and massive reserve
army of labor, the rest dispersed in conditions of great misery in rural
villages and homesteads. The spectacular growth of urban slums is testimony to the profundity of the rural crisis—despite their squalor and
danger, still people flock in from the countryside. As Mike Davis points
out, "Third World urbanization . . . continued its breakneck pace . . .
in spite of falling real wages, soaring prices, and skyrocketing urban
unemployment. This perverse urban bloom surprised most experts and
contradicted orthodox economic models that predicted that [migration
from the countryside] . . . would slow or even reverse."[40]

Hundreds of millions of residents of urban slums and the impoverished countryside are supported by remittances from family members
working in the imperialist nations. The World Bank estimates that
remittances flowing to developing countries reached $440bn in 2010
(from $132bn in 2000),[41] around ten times larger than total N-S devel-
opment aid, much of which is anything but; and it is three times larger
than the total annual income of the world's poorest one billion people.[42]
It is also stunning evidence of migrants' frugality and the strength of
their family connections—these remittances are out of low, often sub-
minimum, wages, and they must replace the high costs of the voyage,
often scraped together out of family savings and sales of assets, before
they can yield a net income. The potential for increased labor mobility to make an immediate and major impact on extreme poverty in the
Global South—and the hypocrisy of those who talk about development
while clamping down on immigration—was underlined by former
World Bank economist Dani Rodrik:

> Imagine that the negotiators who recently met in Doha to hammer
> out an agenda for world trade talks . . . really meant it when they
> said the new round would be . . . designed to bring maximum ben-
> efit to poor countries. What would they have focused on? Increasing
> market access . . . ? Reform of the agricultural regime in Europe . . . ?
> Intellectual property rights . . . ? The answer is none of the above.
> . . . The biggest bang by far . . . was not even on the agenda at Doha:
> relaxing restrictions on the international movement of workers. . . .
> Nothing else comes close to the magnitude of economic benefits that
> this would generate.[43]

The Growth of the Southern Workforce and Its Proletarianization

The world's "economically active population" (EAP) grew from 1.9 billion in 1980 to 3.1 billion in 2006, a 63 percent increase.[44] Almost all
of this numerical growth has occurred in the "emerging nations," now
home to 84 percent of the global workforce,[45] 1.6 billion of whom worked
for wages, the other one billion are small farmers and a multitude of
people working in the infinitely variegated "informal economy."

In Figure 4.2 (next page) "more developed regions" include North
America, Japan, Europe, Australia and New Zealand, and "less devel-
oped regions" comprise "all regions of Africa, Latin America and the
Caribbean, Asia (excluding Japan), Melanesia, Micronesia and Polynesia."

FIGURE 4.2: Global Economically Active Population (EAP)

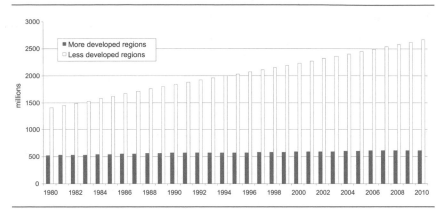

Source: ILO/Laborsta: EAPEP (Economically Active Population Estimates and Projections). "More developed regions" include Northern America, Japan, Europe, Australia and New Zealand; and "less developed regions" comprise all regions of Africa, Latin America and the Caribbean, Asia (excluding Japan), Melanesia, Micronesia, and Polynesia.

Over the past three decades the proletarians of the Global South not only have become more numerous, they have become much more integrated into the global economy. The 63 percent quantitative growth in the global EAP therefore significantly understates the qualitative increase in the role and weight of the South's waged workers. Harvard's Richard Freeman attracted much media attention in 2005 with his assertion that the global workforce had doubled in size in just fifteen years: "In the 1980s and 1990s, workers from China, India and the former Soviet bloc [entered] the global labor pool. Of course, these workers had existed before then. The difference, though, was that their economies suddenly joined the global system of production and consumption."[46] As a result, 1.47 billion workers had been added to the global labor pool, "effectively doubling the size of the world's now connected workforce." The IMF went even further, asserting that what it calls the "export-weighted global labor force" quadrupled in size between 1980 and 2003.[47]

The absolute and relative (to the workforce in the imperialist nations) growth of the Southern workforce is a striking feature of the neoliberal globalization period, but it only tells part of the story. Examination of how the composition of this global labor pool has evolved, between the employed and the self-employed, reveals other features of fundamental importance.

Between 1980 and 2005 the proportion of wage and salaried workers in total EAP in what Laborsta calls the developed nations steadily rose,

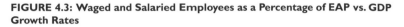

FIGURE 4.3: Waged and Salaried Employees as a Percentage of EAP vs. GDP Growth Rates

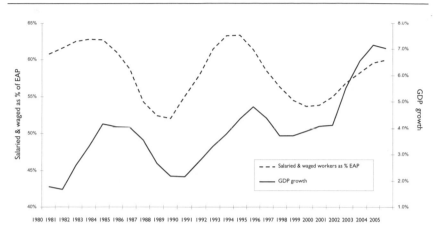

Source: Employment status for 111 "developing nations" from Laborsta *Key Indicators of the Labour Market* (KILM) 5th ed.; GDP growth rates are calculated from World Development Indicators data for GDP of low- and middle-income countries in constant 2000 USD.

from 83 to 88 percent (in 2005, around 500 million people), indicating an ever-deeper proletarianization in these countries. The counterpart to this is a decline in self-employment, including a continuing shrinkage in the number of small family farmers.

Figure 4.3 compares the rate of GDP growth with the proportion of the economically active population who work for a wage or a salary. Both sets of data are smoothed, showing a three-year rolling average. They reveal that the ratio of wage labor to total EAP has followed a cyclical pattern, its share fluctuating between 50 and 65 percent of total EAP, waxing and waning in line with changes in the pace of GDP growth. This figure contains a great deal of information when we consider other facts; for example, the big decline of wage labor's share of total employment in emerging nations between 1982 and 1988 coincided with the worst years of the Third World debt crisis, and the gains made in the subsequent five years were reversed by another period of slower growth and economic crises. Beyond these cyclical peaks and troughs, no secular trend in the ratio of wage labor to total EAP in Southern nations over the 1980 to 2005 period can be detected, in contrast to its steady ascent in the imperialist countries (not shown). Nevertheless, a constant share of a rapidly growing workforce means an absolute rise in the numbers of Southern wage workers and a big change in the composition of the global proletariat.

The persistently high proportion of self-employed workers within the South's EAP casts doubt on the ILO's confident assertion in its *Global Wage Report,* that between 1995 and 2007 "paid employment appears to be growing everywhere (with the exception of Latin America) and has been expanding particularly rapidly in East Asia. . . . This suggests that, over time, wages will become an ever more important dimension of total employment-related income."[48]

Figure 4.3 also provides evidence for a different and much less complacent conclusion than that reached by the ILO economists. The apparent correlation between economic growth and the share of waged labor in total EAP indicated in the graph suggests that a higher share of wage labor in total EAP is a sign of growing prosperity and that a lower share is a sign of increased misery, part of the evidence against the argument of those who glorify self-employment, notably the Peruvian economist Hernando de Soto, who believes the teeming microentre-preneurs in Third World cities, "possess[ing] talent, enthusiasm, and an astonishing ability to wring a profit out of practically nothing," are "not the problem but the solution."[49]

THE INFORMAL ECONOMY: CAPITALISM'S "RELATIVE SURPLUS POPULATION"

In a 2002 report, *Decent Work and the Informal Economy,* the ILO reported:

> Contrary to earlier predictions, the informal economy has been growing rapidly in almost every corner of the globe, including indus-trialized countries—it can no longer be considered a temporary or residual phenomenon. The bulk of new employment in recent years, particularly in developing and transition countries, has been in the informal economy.[50]

The informal sector was first defined by the ILO in 1972 as compris-ing all activities that "are unrecognized, unrecorded, unprotected or unregulated by public authorities." [51] "Informal sector" was abandoned in favor of "informal economy"; the former term misleadingly implied a separate sector connected to the "formal sector" only at its bound-ary. In *Women and Men in the Informal Economy, a Statistical Picture,* the ILO explained some ways the formal and informal economies are intertwined:

Most segments of the informal economy have direct or indirect production, trade or service links with the formal economy. There are the women forced to work from their homes under subcontracting arrangements because the employer will not hire them under more secure work arrangements, the workers in a sweatshop producing garments for lead firms on the other side of the world, the street vendors selling on commission for formal firms, or even the janitor who cleans the offices of formal firms under a subcontracting arrangement.[52]

By definition, the informal economy is unregulated by the state—there's no taxation, workplace inspection, etc. Informal workers are highly vulnerable. "They are not recognized under the law and therefore receive little or no legal or social protection and are unable to enforce contracts or have security of property rights. They are rarely able to organize for effective representation and have little or no voice to make their work recognized and protected. They are excluded from or have limited access to public infrastructure and benefits."[53]

The state is not absent; it has regressed to a more primitive form, reduced to its core competencies: coercion and parasitism. For want of a state able to enforce laws and contracts, capitalists and petty entrepreneurs must rely on custom, and on their own muscle and firepower, to protect what's theirs. The informal economy stimulates state corruption, replacing taxation with bribery and protection money and the rule of law with collaboration between the police and gang leaders to maintain control over slum neighborhoods and give protection to market monopolies. Business elites and state authorities in Southern nations actively foster and promote the expansion of the informal economy, in tandem with their efforts to informalize and flexibilize the formal economy. Alessandra Mezzadri's finding, in her study of the textile and garment industry in India, could be applied across sectors and across borders. The "capitalist State . . . has been a very active agency in . . . a broader process of informalization of labor which condemns Indian working classes to precarious and vulnerable working conditions."[54]

It is far from the case that wage labor corresponds to the formal economy, self-employment to the informal economy. Much, in some countries most, of wage labor is performed in the informal economy. According to a 2002 ILO survey, informal employment as a percentage of total non-agricultural employment ranged from 51 percent in Latin America and North Africa (40 percent of these being waged workers) to 65 percent in Asia (41 percent of whom are waged) and 72 percent in sub-Saharan Africa, or 81 percent if South Africa is excluded (30 percent of whom are waged).[55] Within this, India is an extreme case, with 83 percent of its employed population active in the informal economy, 48 percent of these working for a wage.[56] As Mike Davis points out, "Altogether, the global informal working class (overlapping with but non-identical to the slum population) is about one billion strong, making it the fastest-growing, and most unprecedented, social class on earth."[57]

Table 4.2 shows the result of an ILO investigation into informal employment around the world. Its enormous proportions leap to the eye—an absolute majority of the economically active population of every region, with the exception of North Africa, were informally employed. These data are likely to underestimate the full extent of informal employment, since "few developing countries collect data that would enable estimations of the numbers of people who, for example, have casual jobs that do not amount to be being fully employed but are above the threshold for unemployment."[58] This is confirmed by a study of subcontracting in Sri Lanka by Swarna Jayaweera, who reports, "[w]hat has emerged . . . is the relative invisibility of these sub-contracted workers in international subcontracting chains in the labor market . . . It is apparent that the incidence of subcontracting is much higher than reported in macro, sectoral, and regional studies."[59] Martha Chen, Jennifer Sebstad, and Lesley O'Connell, in their investigation of the growth of homeworking, note, "[i]f the magnitude of women's invisible paid work, particularly homebased remunerative work, were to be fully counted, both the share of women and the share of informal workers in the work force would increase."[60]

Informalization and Social Retrogression

What Stephanie Barrientos, Naila Kabeer, and Naomi Hossain have termed "the march of modernization" is, for so many, a mirage. What *is* on the march is informalization—growing insecurity and corrosion of social and communal solidarity. The "continuum . . . between formal and informal work in global production"[61] is becoming ever more continuous. As Henry Bernstein has commented, "We observe virtually everywhere today and especially in the 'Global South' that the boundaries between the active and reserve armies of labor become ever more fluid."[62] And the flow is faster and faster in one direction. SIDA, the Swedish International Development Agency, reported in 2004 that "all segments

TABLE 4.2: Informal Employment

Average for 1994–2000	Informal Employment as a Percent of Non-agricultural Employment			Waged Employment as a Percent of Non-agricultural Informal Employment		
	ALL	WOMEN	MEN	ALL	WOMEN	MEN
NORTH AFRICA	**48**	**43**	**49**	**38**	**28**	**40**
Egypt	55	46	57	50	33	53
SUB-SAHARAN AFRICA	**72**	**84**	**63**	**30**	**29**	**30**
Benin	93	97	87	5	2	9
Kenya	72	83	59	58	67	44
South Africa	51	58	44	75	73	77
LATIN AMERICA	**51**	**58**	**48**	**40**	**42**	**39**
Bolivia	63	74	55	19	9	29
Brazil	60	67	55	59	68	50
Colombia	38	44	34	62	64	60
Honduras	58	65	74	28	23	35
Mexico	55	55	54	46	47	45
ASIA	**65**	**65**	**65**	**41**	**37**	**45**
India	83	86	83	48	43	49
Indonesia	78	77	78	37	30	41
Philippines	72	73	71	52	37	64

Source: ILO, 2002, *Women and Men in the Informal Economy, a Statistical Picture,* tables 2.1 and 2.2. http://www.wiego.org/publications/women and men in the informal economy.pdf.

of the informal workforce—self-employed, casual, sub-contract, temporary and part-time workers and microentrepreneurs . . . appear to be growing,"[63] and the "main reason for this growth appears to be that the formal labor markets have not been able to generate sufficient amounts of jobs."[64]

During the era of neoliberal globalization spontaneous economic forces, World Bank "structural adjustment" policies dictated by the imperialist powers, and the employers' worldwide anti-labor offensive have spurred a process of informalization of the formal economy, exemplified by the spread of temporary contracts and more generally by labor's heightened insecurity and precarity. There is overwhelming evidence that "self-employment, casual labor markets, and subcontracting rather than union contracts appear to be a defining characteristic of recent economic trends,"[65] contradicting the prediction of Rostow, Lewis, and others that the march of progress would see the steady diminution of the informal economy and its absorption into the formal economy.[66] Like so much else of the tattered "convergence hypothesis," this turns out to have been so much wishful thinking. Alejandro Portes and Kelly Hoffman, speaking of Latin America, confirm this verdict: "A shrinking formal working class and a stagnant or rising informal proletariat negate predictions about the capacity of the new economic model to absorb labor and reduce poverty." [67] What William Robinson has called the "transition from a regime of Fordist to flexible employment relations"[68] has had particularly acute effects in Latin America. Robinson cites data showing that in 1950, 69.2 percent of Latin America's urban workers worked in the formal economy; this was barely unchanged in 1970, when it stood at 70.2 percent. But by 1985 the formal economy only employed 53.1 percent of urban workers, falling to 45.7 percent by 1992, and to just 42.1 percent by 1998.[69]

Chen et al. noted, "The informal sector, particularly small-scale enterprises, accounts for a larger share of output and employment than anyone ever dreamed of in the 1950s and 1960s."[70] Mike Davis reinforces this observation: "Among researchers, there is a base consensus that the 1980s crisis—during which informal-sector employment grew two to five times faster than formal-sector jobs—has inverted their relative structural positions, establishing informal survivalism as the new primary mode of livelihood in a majority of Third World cities."[71] This is what modernization means for a majority of the world's people.

Thus, what is truly modern is not universal progress toward prosperity and the rule of law but an accelerating descent into informality and precariousness. This trajectory was already well established before the financial blowout that began in August 2007. The reality that capitalist progress is bringing to the peoples of the Global South is that "instead of upward mobility, there is seemingly only a down staircase by which redundant formal-sector workers and sacked public employees descend into the black economy."[72] And not just in the Global South. This retrogression has also been gathering pace in imperialist countries, and has received a mighty boost since 2007.

The growth of the informal economy did not merely coincide with the onset of neoliberal globalization, it was produced by it. It was given a mighty boost by the wrenching transition from import protection and state regulation to the new neoliberal laissez-faire export-oriented regime. As the ILO stated, "It is now widely acknowledged that the stabilization and structural adjustment policies of the 1980s and 1990s, which in many countries resulted in growing poverty, unemployment and underemployment, contributed to the spread of the informal economy."[73] These traumas were far from being "teething troubles"; the growth of the informal economy has proved to be not a transient effect of transition from protectionism and state regulation but a defining feature of neo-liberal capitalist development in the Global South, as the ILO explained:

> As part of cost-cutting measures and efforts to enhance competi-tiveness, firms are increasingly operating with a small core of wage employees with regular terms and conditions (formal employment) . . . and a growing periphery of "non-standard" or "atypical" and often informal workers in different types of workplaces scattered over different locations. These measures often include outsourcing or subcontracting and a shift away from regular employment relation-ships to more flexible and informal employment relationships.[74]

This explicit recognition that capitalist development is promoting a big expansion of the informal economy is accompanied by a lame attempt to sing from the same hymn book as the World Bank and IMF: "It is the failure or inability of countries to participate in globalization processes (whether because of their own domestic policies or because of international barriers), rather than globalization per se, that contributes to preventing these countries from benefiting from trade, investments and technology."[75]

Flexibilization

In pursuit of "flexibilization and informalization of production and employment relationships," the ILO argues that "more and more firms, instead of using a full-time, regular workforce based in a single, large registered factory or workplace, are . . . reorganizing work by forming more flexible and specialized production units, some of which remain unregistered and informal . . . scattered over different locations and sometimes different countries . . . and the final producer is an often own-account worker in a micro-enterprise or a homeworker in a developing or transition country."[76]

Flexibility and informality are closely related qualities. Conditions of informal labor allow capitalists to reduce costs and increase flexibility, including through forced overtime, extended lay-offs and an absence of regulations and legal protection. Together, flexibility and informality allow capitalists to transfer risks and the costs of adjustment to changes in demand onto their workers. Barrientos et al. point to the "increasing emphasis on 'flexibility' in the manufacturing industry," whose aim is "to enable shorter production runs, facilitate rapid shifts between different products and product specifications for different markets, and to do so at ever lower costs."[77] The authors observe that "flexible employment allows producers to vary their employment levels on a constant basis. It is normal in many sectors to lay off workers on rainy days, or to vary (compulsory) overtime so that workers have no advance notice of the hours they will be expected to work."[78]

Flexibilization is a conscious goal of capitalists; judged by the frequency of "labor reforms" in IMF and World Bank policy prescriptions it is the remedy for all known economic ills. It is one reason why the informalization of labor and the growth of the informal economy is neither accidental nor unintended. It is one of neoliberal globalization's most essential features. Just as the exploitation of low-wage labor is the essential driving force influencing Northern firms' outsourcing decisions, so the informalization of labor is key to achieving the goal of flexible production. Barrientos et al. clearly recognize this: "Some of [the desired] flexibility has been achieved through technological changes. . . . Some . . . through more decentralized forms of management. . . . Most importantly, however, it has been achieved through forms of employment that are temporary, part-time, casual or contract-based."[79]

But what is the driving force behind the "cost-cutting measures and efforts to enhance competitiveness"? For analysis to advance beyond description, this driving force—Northern capital's insatiable desire to extract super-profits from low-wage labor—must be explicitly identified or else the social nature of this phenomenon will be mystified, presented as a force of nature.

The Informal Economy and Capitalism's Relative Surplus Population

The most devastating effects of capitalism's production of a relative surplus population is in the Third World. Official unemployment rates, while themselves very high, conceal the true enormity of the numbers of human beings who live on the knife-edge of existence without any way to make a living. . . . These dispossessed toilers are both peasants who would pour back to the countryside in their millions if arable land and cheap credit were available to them, but at the same time are unemployed workers in the growing ranks of capitalism's relative surplus population.[80]

"Relative surplus population" was Karl Marx's term for a specific feature of capitalist social relations, the outcome of the "capitalist law of population," whose discovery he considered to be one of his most important findings in *Capital*: capitalism's tendency to generate what he called a surplus population. There are two aspects to this. One is capitalism's dissolution of the traditional rural economy: "As soon as capitalist production takes possession of agriculture, and in proportion to the extent to which it does so, the demand for a rural working population falls absolutely. . . . Part of the agricultural population is therefore constantly on the point of passing over into an urban or manufacturing proletariat."[81] The destruction of precapitalist social formations is only one reason why the relative surplus population is increasing in every nation of the Global South. Capitalism not only creates a surplus population at the frontiers of its collision with pre-capitalist social formations, but, according to Marx,

> capitalist accumulation itself constantly produces . . . in direct relation with its own energy and extent, a relatively redundant working population, i.e. a population which is superfluous to capital's average requirements for its own valorisation and is therefore a surplus population. . . . The working population therefore produces both the accumulation of capital and the means by which it is itself made relatively superfluous; and it does this to an extent which is always increasing. This is a law of population peculiar to the capitalist mode of production.[82]

Bangladesh provides a vivid illustration of what this means for millions of people across the Global South. Active and large-scale participation in global value chains has failed to prevent a major expansion of Bangladesh's relative surplus population. An ILO survey of the Bangladeshi labor market found that "the percentage of workers in informal employment . . . increased from 76.2 percent in 1999–00 to 87.5 percent in 2010."[83] Within this, the double oppression of women workers is evident: 92.3 percent of women workers were informally employed in 2010, compared to 85.5 percent of men.

The integration of the Global South into the imperialist world economy since the Second World War and especially since 1980 brings together both of these trends, the dispossession of small farmers and other small producers on the one hand, and the substitution of wage labor by machinery on the other. TNCs and domestic capitalists not only exploit low-wage labor, they can do so with advanced production processes that absorb far less living labor than those available to nineteenth-century European capitalists. As the ILO recognized, "For developing countries . . . manufacturing is unlikely to absorb much of their increased labor supply as unskilled, strongly labor-intensive, technological options become less viable on global markets."[84]

Today's vast and growing informal economy corresponds to the relative surplus population analyzed by Marx in *Capital* 140 years ago. But it, along with capitalism, has enormously evolved since then. The relative surplus population played a key role in the development of nineteenth-century capitalism and it has played a key role in the development of late twentieth-century imperialism. Now the reserve army of labor, a part of the relative surplus population, is global, shaped by the violent suppression of the right of working people in oppressed nations to cross the same borders as the wealth that they, in combination with nature, produce. The result: an inexhaustible supply of labor at subsistence rates of pay for TNCs to exploit at their leisure.

THE FEMINIZATION OF LABOR AND THE
PROLETARIANIZATION OF WOMEN

Export-led industrialization has been strongly female-intensive, with no developing country having increased manufacturing exports without greater recourse to women workers.[85]

The massive incorporation of young women into wage labor has been a striking feature of export-oriented industrialization. The changing gender composition of the workforce is particularly marked in manufacturing industry. A report by the United Nations, the *World Survey on the Role of Women in Development*, declared: "Among the newly industrializing countries . . . none of [them] has increased its exports of manufactures without recourse to women workers. It is by now considered a stylized fact that industrialization in the context of globalization is as much female-led as it is export-led."[86] Guy Standing concurs: "All countries that have successfully industrialized have done so only by mobilizing large numbers of (low-paid) women workers."[87] Barrientos et al. add that "in almost every region, women's employment has increased faster than that of men,"[88] as a result of which "women now represent more than one-third of the manufacturing labor force in developing countries and nearly a half in some Asian countries. The greatest increases over the past twenty years have occurred in countries which have adopted export-oriented strategies."[89] The preference of foreign investors for female labor is particularly marked in export processing zones, where "women make up the majority of workers in the vast majority of zones, reaching up to 90 percent in some of them."[90]

The huge expansion of female factory employment that is so characteristic of the neoliberal era was an important change from the ISI era, the era of import substitution industrialization that preceded it, when employment in protected national industries was largely male, yet ISI was the anomaly: in previous waves of industrialization in nineteenth-century Europe, large numbers of factory workers were female, and in some sectors, especially textiles and apparel, they often formed the majority.[91]

A Perfect Fit

During the 1980s and 1990s, the terms of trade for the South's traditional exports remorselessly declined. UNCTAD reported that "between 1980 and 2003, the price of food . . . declined by 73.3 percent; agricultural raw materials prices fell by 60.7 percent; and the price of minerals, ores and metals declined by 59.5 percent. By the first half of 2003, the price of coffee had lost 83 percent of its 1980 value."[92] In a study of the influx of rural Malaysian women into export-oriented factories, Lie Merete and Ragnhild Lund show how the resulting rural crisis spurred the influx of young peasant women into the factories: "As a consequence of decreasing prices of agricultural products in the world market, the community was in a difficult situation, and young daughters felt a strong obligation to contribute in various ways . . . [creating] a perfect fit between the needs of the company for young female labor and the needs of the local population for cash income and employment for the young generation."[93]

The supply of female factory labor has been forthcoming in the most diverse cultures and societies, including those where patriarchal oppression confines women to the home. Razavi et al. note that "the shift towards female factory employment has occurred both in countries with a history of relatively high . . . [and] low female labor force participation."[94] In their study of rural Malaysia, Merete and Lund report "the most peculiar of the local change processes we have observed is that a

formerly most protected group, namely young women, have been the
spearheads in the process of transformation of the local community."[95]
Laetitia Cairoli, whose research included work on the assembly lines
of a Moroccan garment factory, reported that "the entrance of females,
en masse, into the garment factories of Fez contrasts vividly with local
ideals of appropriate female behavior."[96]

Persistent, profound poverty, and the desire of women to escape from
stultifying and oppressive domestic servitude, explains why millions of
poor women have sought employment with multinational corporations
and their local suppliers. A survey of female employment in Pakistan
by Saba Gul Khattak reports that in Pakistan "women are joining the
workforce due to worsening economic conditions. Their economic contribution to the household is crucial for survival."[97] Shahra Razavi and
Jessica Vivian report that "women employed in the manufacturing sector
in Morocco and Bangladesh prefer this work to the other employment
options available to them," despite, in Bangladesh, "extremely long hours
. . . often from 8 a.m. until 10 p.m., six days a week," and their average
age is 16.6 years.[98]

National governments have vied with each other to offer up cheap
labor to TNCs and their suppliers, or as Barbara Ehrenreich and Annette
Fuentes put it, "The relationship between many Third World governments and the multinational corporations is not very different from the
relationship between a pimp and his customers. The governments adver-
tise their women, sell them, and keep them in line. . . . But there are
other parties to the growing international traffic in women—such as the
United Nations Industrial Development Organisation (UNIDO) and the
United States government itself."[99]

SO MUCH FOR THE SUPPLY OF CHEAP female labor. What about the
demand for it, or as Maria Mies asked, "What is it that makes Third World
women more attractive as workers to international capital than men?"[100]
Academic researchers and others widely cite the perceived cheapness,
flexibility, docility, and dexterity of female labor. Barrientos et al. found
that "the most widely shared features of women's manufacturing employment across the developing world are longer hours of work and lower
wages than men."[101] The ILO reports that "evidence from developing
economies . . . has shown that the liberalization of trade and investment
has led to wider gender pay gaps," a divergence that might be explained
by "women's weaker ability to negotiate terms and conditions of employment. . . . Women . . . are still overwhelmingly segregated in occupations

that tend to be at the lower end of the wage scale."[102] According to Stephanie Seguino, "Those Asian economies with the widest wage gaps between men and women grew most rapidly."[103]

South Korea, one of the fastest-growing Asian economies during this period, had the world's highest gender pay gap: in 1980, women's wages were just 44.5 percent of men's.[104] Women's resistance to low pay and long hours became the spearhead of the mass movement against the U.S.-backed military dictatorship of General Chung Hee Park and blazed the trail for the massive labor struggles of the 1980s. In her study of this important episode in labor history, Kim Mikyoung comments that "one of the ironies of South Korea's 'economic miracle' was the co-existence of phenomenal growth and women's labor resistance. Women initiated labor strikes at a time when labor activism was severely repressed, and this behavior was always in sharp contrast to male workers' overall labor inactivity during the 1970s."[105]

What is it about Third World women that makes them cheaper, more flexible and less prone to offer resistance than men? In Maria Mies's opinion, it is because "the strategy of integrating women's work into development . . . defines Third World women *not as workers, but as housewives* . . . [and] all the work women do—whether in the formal or informal sectors—is *supplementary work*, the income as supplementary income to that of the so-called main 'breadwinner,' the husband. The economic logic of this *housewifization* is a tremendous reduction of labor costs." This "is not an accidental side-effect of the new IDL [International Division of Labor], but a necessary condition for its smooth functioning."[106] But the more that women gain employment as workers, the more they come to identify themselves as workers, and to demand equality with male workers—potentially negating the main reason for capitalists' special interest in them. To counter this, the expansion of female employment in industry is often accompanied by an ideological offensive aimed at reinforcing women's second-class status and social divisions between men and women within and outside the workforce.

Guy Standing argued that not only is the global workforce becoming more female, labor has become feminized in another sense: TNCs and states and local employers use gender divisions, and the perceived acquiescence of young female workers to the low pay, long hours, and temporary employment contracts typical of TNC-led industrialization, to impose these inferior conditions on all workers, men included. As Standing said, "The types of employment and labor force involvement traditionally associated with women—insecure, low-paid, irregular, etc.—have been spreading relative to the type of employment tradition-ally associated with men—regular, unionized, stable."[107]

Once this degradation of the conditions of labor is accomplished, a lessening of the incentives for TNCs to hire female labor and a partial "de-feminization" of the manufacturing workforce can often be observed. As William Rau and Robert Wazienski reported, "Initially . . . factory jobs are typed as women's work and provide employment for mostly young, unmarried women. However, as the factory system spreads . . . many of these jobs are reallocated to men."[108] This trend has continued into the twenty-first century: UNCTAD reported in its 2013 *World Investment Report* that "the relative dynamism of female employment growth tends to decrease as countries move up the value chain."[109]

According to Barrientos et al., this was first observed in the manu-facturing industry in Japan, where the proportion of women workers in the manufacturing workforce fell from 36 percent in 1960 to 26 percent in 1990, and was followed by a similar trend in South Korea,[110] where fierce labor militancy by women lost them favor. Another distinctive example of de-feminization is provided by the *maquiladoras*, assembly plants strung along the U.S.-Mexican border that "boomed in the 1980s with employment growing at 20 percent annually from 1982–89."[111] Low pay and retrograde conditions at first deterred male employment, and the large majority of those on the assembly lines were female. Once these retrograde conditions were firmly entrenched and had become the new standard, increasing numbers of male workers began to enter the maqui-ladora workforce: "Young working-class men in the northern Mexican border regions were being socialized into becoming docile labor, as the absence of unions and workforce discipline came to be accepted by the working class: it then became possible for the industry to hire young, inexperienced and docile men."[112] And so the *maquiladora* workforce moved from 85 percent female in the earliest years to 64 percent in 1988, down to 41 percent by 1999. Yet this de-feminization is only relative; the number of women working in *maquiladoras* continued to increase: total employment in these factories increased from 100,000 (75 percent women) in the early 1980s to 750,000 (41 percent women) by the end of the 1990s. Since then they have struggled to survive in the face of keen competition from lower-cost Asian workers, many of them female, too.

Women workers are even more likely than male workers to be trapped in the informal economy and denied the most minimal legal rights and protections. According to the ILO, in Latin America and Africa women are significantly more likely to be employed in the informal economy than men, whereas in Asia the reported gender balance is much more equal. The outlier is North Africa, where female informal employment is low because female employment of any sort beyond the home is low. The persistence of gender discrimination within the workforce and within the labor process can also be seen in the export processing zones. In the conclusion to their review of the evolution of EPZs over the past half-century, Mayumi Murayama and Nobuko Yokota discover that "a conspicuously common feature across time and space is that women have constituted the core of the labor force within the EPZs," and they ask "whether the problems for female workers have changed since the time when they were the pathfinders,"[113] problems including discrimination in hiring, wages, benefits, and career development; lack of accommodation and child-care facilities; forced overtime and irregular working hours; dismissal on becoming pregnant and absence of maternity leave; and sexual harassment and exposure to violence while commuting to and from work. They conclude that "although there may have been improvements in certain areas of concern . . . it seems that the basic problems remain unchanged," indicating "either an alarming absence of serious initiatives . . . or an alarming degree of negligence."[114]

Gender Pay Gap—As Wide as Ever

An ILO study concluded in 2006: "Across nearly all occupations [women] still do not get equal pay for work of equal value or balanced benefits that would ensure equality with men . . . they are still overwhelmingly segregated in occupations that tend to be at the lower end of the wage scale."[115] The overall gender pay gap continues to widen in most developing countries, the result of two trends: a small narrowing of within-country pay differentials between unskilled men and women, but this is more than cancelled by a sharp increase in the gap between skilled and unskilled wages, and men are disproportionately represented in higher-skilled jobs.[116] Marva Corley, Yves Perardel, and Kalina Popova, in an important empirical survey of wage differentials within and between countries, reported that "the gap in wages and earnings between men and women remains entrenched in many countries. In the EU Member States the gender gap in pay was 15 percent in 2003. In many countries in Asia and the Middle East and North Africa, the gap was upwards of 40 percent in some sectors."[117] The ILO's *Global Wages Report 2008–9* reports that "the wage gap is still wide and is closing only very slowly," adding, "In about 80 percent of the countries for which data are available the gender pay gap has narrowed. However, the size of change is small, and in some cases negligible . . . the reduction in the gender pay gap has clearly been disappointing in the light of recent developments, namely women's educational achievements, the progressive closing of the gender gap in work experience and the favourable economic context."[118]

Feminism and Class Analysis

Feminist writers and researchers have done a great service in opening up the dimension of gender in the analysis of world political economy in general and into globalization in particular. But a focus on the gender dimension of industrialization can become a limitation if it is not integrated with a class perspective. For instance, Barrientos et al. conclude that "the most widely shared features of women's manufacturing employment across the developing world are longer hours of work and lower wages than men,"[119] yet the most widely shared feature of all is the one they share with their male co-workers: they are exploited by capitalists who strive to maximize profits and drive down the value of labor-power of all workers, including by using sexual divisions and patriarchal oppression to divide and weaken those driven by poverty onto the assembly lines. Since TNCs are motivated by "extract[ing] product from low-wage workers"[120] and employ women for no other reason, to focus on gender while disregarding capitalist exploitation, seeing this as the natural order of things, something outside the scope of critical analysis, tends to gloss over the antagonistic nature of the social phenomenon they are attempting to investigate. Thus Merete and Lund et al. discover "a perfect fit between the needs of the company for young female labor and the needs of the local population for cash income and employment for the young generation."[121] They conclude: "The motives for relocation were far more complex than the search for cheap labor. This does not mean that we undervalue the importance of low labor costs. However . . . these motives must be considered in relation to a range of other matters. It is the sum of these factors rather than any single one that counts."[122]

Without recognizing the exploitative, antagonistic nature of the capital-labor relation, it is impossible to understand why capitalists have an interest in maintaining gender segregation and discrimination. Without this, the persistence of gender discrimination in the workforce appears to be irrational and inexplicable. Thus ILO researcher Ricard Anker argued, "What could be a more important source of labor market inefficiency than the extensive segmentation of male and female work-ers?"[123] Zafiris Tzannatos bemoans the loss of output implied by the persistence and prevalence of gender discrimination in labor markets, arguing that "better use of women's potential in the market results in greater efficiency at the macro level."[124] Restrictions on the free move-ment of labor and the persistence of racial and national discrimination also result in sub-optimal economic outcomes. No mainstream econo-mist could dispute this, yet this is the one area of economic life in which theory is not allowed to inform practice.

The interaction of class and gender is more effectively captured by Mary-Alice Waters, who wrote: "Since the beginning of the Industrial Revolution in the 18th century, capitalist expansion and the lash of com-petition have dictated the incorporation of larger and larger numbers of women into the labor force. This is so because capital always seeks to incorporate into the workforce large numbers of workers in oppressed social categories (in this case women), the value of whose labor power under capitalism is less than that of others. This is a key way in which the employers drive down the overall average value of labor power by heightening competition among workers for jobs."[125]

Waters, speaking specifically about the changes in the United States since the Second World War, further argues:

> The development of capitalism . . . creates real and ultimately insolu-ble contradictions for the exploiting class. The capitalists' increasing purchase of women's capacities as wage laborers inevitably brings in its wake greater economic independence for women. It contributes to further disintegration of the family, and expands the need for house-hold appliances and prepared foods. . . . These factors, in turn, tend to raise the value of women's labor power, to raise the wages they can command in the labor market.[126]

However, this process takes place in very different conditions in oppressed nations. Wages are so low in the oppressed nations in part because the costs of social reproduction are borne by the extended family and the wider informal economy. As Rakhi Sehgal has argued, "Capital may be attracted to communities that are primarily based on the logic of reciprocity and therefore most likely to assume the burdens of social reproduction of the labor force as part of their cultural prac-tice. This is perhaps the real savings that capital reaps when seeking out 'cheap labor.'"[127]

IN THIS CHAPTER WE HAVE BEGUN the identification and analysis of the most important and relevant features of the transformation of Southern labor during the era of neoliberal globalization. One of the findings is that there isn't the slightest sign of the clearing of labor markets, which would allow the marginalist thesis—that wages are determined by productivity—to satisfy even its own criteria. The wages paid to workers in the South are affected by factors that have no bearing on or relevance to the productivity of these workers when at work, factors arising from conditions in the labor market and more general social structures and relations affecting the reproduction of labor-power, including the suppression of the free international movement of labor and the emergence of a vast relative surplus population in the Global South. This knocks a large hole in the tottering edifice of mainstream economics. In the next chapter, which surveys the trajectory of Southern wages in the neoliberal era, we will continue the process of demolition of prevailing theories and the construction of a new one.

5

Global Wage Trends in the Neoliberal Era

G iven their central role in driving and shaping the globalization of production, the wide international wage differentials between developed and developing nations demand special attention. The cheapness of labor power in oppressed nations is not the only factor propelling production outsourcing. Other factors include the substantial differences in non-wage costs between different countries, for example, land and energy resources—but this only means that capitalists exploit both living labor and nature. More than any other type of data, data on wages must be treated with great caution: the survey data they are based on often covers only the formal sector; governments and employers have many reasons and many opportunities to embroider the facts; and there are huge problems of data coverage and comparability.

Perhaps the biggest problem of all in determining the magnitude and trajectory of global wage differentials is that wages paid in national currencies must be converted into a common currency if they are to be compared. Using market exchange rates for such comparisons results in a major distortion, since a unit of national currency in a poor country will buy more at home than if it was turned into dollars and spent in the United States or another developed country. Conversely, as visitors from rich countries to poor countries know to their delight, their dollars, euros, pounds, and yen command greater purchasing power when converted into the national currency of a poor country and spent there. For example, the distortion inherent in the market exchange rate between Bangladesh's national currency, the taka, and the United States dollar, means that in 2013 just $0.32 converted into takas buys in Dhaka what a whole dollar purchases in New York, according to data supplied by the IMF's World Economic Outlook database. The smaller a nation's per capita GDP, the greater the deviation tends to be of its currency from purchasing power parity with the dollar.

This distortion matters if we wish to compare the real purchasing power of wages in different countries, but it is of no consequence to TNCs eyeing possible locations in low-wage countries, since, as the Bureau of Labor Statistics puts it, wages "converted into U.S. dollars at prevailing commercial market currency exchange rates . . . are appropriate measures for comparing levels of employer labor costs."[1] As a rule, the larger the development gap between a given country and the United States (whose dollar is used as the reference currency) the bigger the distortion. The result is that when adjustments are made for purchasing power parity (PPP) to allow comparison of real wages, N-S wage differentials are, depending on the country, reduced to around half of what is reported by market exchange rates. Since we have no choice but to view the world with the help of PPP-adjusted statistics, it is important to be aware of their shortcomings.

The first two sections of this chapter investigate these important issues in more detail, critically evaluating the reliability and probity of the statistics on global wage differentials, on the way revealing much about the conditions confronted by workers in low-wage nations. The third section analyzes an outstandingly important feature of the neoliberal era: on both sides of the North-South divide, *labor's share of national income* has been steadily declining throughout the neoliberal era; this decline has accelerated since the turn of the millennium, and it is declining even faster in emerging nations than in rich nations, from a much lower level. The fourth section considers another issue of fundamental importance, that data on average wages ignore the fact that *wage inequality* is growing rapidly in most rich countries and even faster in most poor countries, obscuring the reality of stagnant and falling wages received by many average- and low-paid workers. All of the foregoing lays the groundwork for an evaluation of global wage trends in the neoliberal era, the subject of the fifth section. This is followed by an investigation into what happens to *wages in times of crisis*, a regular occurrence in low-wage nations during the neoliberal era, and its central finding—that stagnant or weakly rising wages during periods of growth typically turns into strongly falling wages when the economy contracts—is particularly relevant to the contemporary world, in which times of crisis are set to become increasingly frequent in imperialist nations as well as low-wage nations. The final section considers what all of this means for the "convergence hypothesis," the mainstream consensus that the North-South divide is eroding and that wages and living standards in the developing nations are converging with those in the North.

POOR QUALITY OF DATA ON GLOBAL WAGES

Global data on wages have been collected since 1924 by the ILO's "October Inquiry," an annual questionnaire requesting detailed information from national governments on the prevailing wage rates for different occupations in their countries. The coverage has increased from 18 occupations in 15 countries in its first survey in 1924 to 161 occupations in 171 countries in 2008. However, the October Inquiry is notorious for missing data and for the poor quality, inconsistency, and incompatibility of the data that it receives, especially from developing countries: as the ILO notes, "In developing countries . . . wage statistics are often scarce. This is because wage statistics are not only among the most complex statistics but also require substantial resources and infrastructure for their collection."[2] The problem is getting worse: 71 countries returned data on wages for "at least one" occupation in 1985, 43 countries did so in 2002, and in 2008 only 26 countries filed any data in response to the ILO's request.[3] Sturgeon et al.'s warning, made in connection with research into value added, applies equally to wages: "Resources for data collection and the political will required to burden private sector respondents with surveys are declining in many countries."[4]

Another important limitation is that data supplied by national government to the ILO "is often based on a narrow subset of paid employees in the formal economy or in urban areas."[5] As Nomaan Majid has pointed out, "Statistics on wage rates generally, and quite understandably, cover organised parts of economies. Therefore in developing economies they tend to exclude unorganised sections of the labor force where the bulk of poor workers exist."[6] In addition to their paucity and selection bias, the ILO reports that "the vast majority of the Inquiry statistics are non-comparable"—countries use different definitions for the same occupation; wages may or may not include non-wage benefits such as employer contributions to national insurance; wages may be reported before taxes or after and per hour, day, week, or month. And all, of course, in national currencies whose real purchasing power fluctuates according to domestic inflation, around a point that in any case does not establish purchasing power parity between different currencies. The result, says the ILO, is that "data from the October Inquiry are seldom used."[7]

Thanks to the efforts of Richard Freeman and Remco Oostendorp, who created a cleaned-up and harmonized version of the October Inquiry's raw statistics, and of other analysts and economists working for the ILO and the international agencies, a dynamic picture of global wage disparities and trends has begun to emerge.[8] The ILO's *Global Wage Report*, first published in November 2008 with new editions appearing every two years, marks a big stride forward in the production of useful information on wage levels and trends around the world. The *Global Wage Report 2012–13* claims to draw on "information for 94.3 percent of the world's employees who together account for approximately 97.7 percent of the world's wage bill."[9] Given the major shortcomings in wage statistics listed above this claim is open to question: "information *for* 94.3 percent of the world's employees" is not the same as information *on* them—the ILO analysts have made much use of extrapolation and interpolation to create the impression of comprehensive coverage. How accurate they are is another question, since they are vitiated by all of the defects and biases discussed in this chapter.

PURCHASING POWER PARITY PITFALLS

Production of the PPP conversion indices used to convert national currencies into PPP dollars requires the collection of vast amounts of raw data and statistical techniques of great complexity, responsibility for which is borne by the United Nations Statistical Commission's International Comparison Program (ICP).[10] As the OECD's (Organization for Economic Cooperation and Development) *Methodological Manual on Purchasing Power Parities* explains, this means constructing different baskets of goods for each country, reflecting "differences in tastes, cultures, climates, price structures, product availability and income levels," so that each nation's basket should "provide equivalent satisfaction or utility,"[11] a heroic task when the countries to be compared are as dissimilar as Norway and Rwanda. The ICP also makes estimates and adjustments for urban-rural price differences, seasonal variations in prices and government subsidies for essential commodities, though the last of these are nowadays far less prevalent, having been frowned on as "market distorting" by the IMF and World Bank. A glimpse of the complexity of this task can be seen in the Asian Development Bank's report on its contribution to the 2005 global benchmarking: "Precisely specifying the price-determining characteristics of products often required expert knowledge specific to the products in each particular field. For example, knowledge of milling processes and the different types of outputs produced was needed in the area of cereals."[12]

Leaving aside the errors and distortions that arise from incomplete or inaccurate data collection (not to mention the manipulation of this data by national governments attempting to conceal the prevalence of illegally low wages or to massage politically sensitive data on the rate of inflation, poverty levels, etc.), there are three pitfalls that plague the production of purchasing power parity indices. These are sporadic benchmarking; substitution bias—deviation from the standard basket caused by changing consumer behavior; and the myth of the "average basket"—the deviation between the goods consumed by the mythical average citizen and what is actually consumed by workers, farmers, and small producers.

Infrequent Benchmarking

The ICP benchmarks its data, product categories, and methodologies every five to ten years (most recently in 2011, though the results were not published until 2013; previous benchmarking years were in 2005 and 1996). Data for intervening years are obtained by extrapolation, using reported domestic inflation rates and changes in market exchange rates. The 2005 benchmarking, in which the ICP implemented many methodological refinements, caused startlingly large changes to estimates of real (PPP-adjusted) GDP per capita, showing how far and how quickly the ICP's projections can depart from reality. For Asia-Pacific nations, real per capita GDP in 2005 was 30 percent lower than the pre-benchmark value, with China's per capita GDP turning out to be 39 percent lower and India's 38 percent lower than previous estimates, while countries in Africa and Latin America saw large swings in both directions.[13] The sharp downward revisions of Indian and Chinese per capita GDP made the world look much more unequal than before, and caused estimates of the number of people living below the World Bank's poverty line to jump upward by 400 million. The 2011 benchmarking resulted in revisions of a similar magnitude—but in the opposite direction, at a stroke reducing estimates of the number of extremely poor people from 1.2 billion to less than 600 million people. These wild gyrations have damaged the credibility of widely touted estimates of those living in global poverty levels, or, as Gargee Ghosh, director of Development Policy for the Bill and Melinda Gates Foundation said of the 2011 revisions, "What this has really highlighted to me is the sense of false precision with which we operate in development."[14]

Substitution Bias

Substitution bias occurs when consumers increase consumption of goods that are becoming relatively cheaper, changing the relative weights of these goods in the actual basket, though their weights in the standard basket used to calculate PPP conversion indices remains unaltered until the next benchmarking exercise comes around. The resulting increase in consumption is misinterpreted as an increase in purchasing power, thus overstating the income level in the country whose currency is being converted. This can become a big problem because data are collected only periodically and the bias can accumulate from one year to the next.

The ICP is fully aware of this: "Extrapolating one benchmark year value to another benchmark year . . . will fail to capture any changes . . . which may result from changes in relative prices and interplay of supply and demand of complementary and substitute products. This is a well-known effect in international comparisons and it could lead to significant differences over a short period of time."[15] Despite such warnings, the existence of this bias is routinely ignored by journalists and social scientists commenting on global inequality. Yet, as research by Robert Ackland, Steve Dowrick, and Benoit Freyens demonstrates, substitution bias dramatically affects calculations of the number of people living in poverty. They report that, correcting for this bias, estimates of the number of people in the world surviving on less than $2 per day increases by 29 percent, and the number in extreme poverty (less than $1 per day) increases by an astonishing 44 percent, with the biggest jump in East and South Asia, results that indicate "there is significant bunching of the population in East and South Asia just above the $1/day poverty line."[16]

A related but distinct distortion arises from the simplifying assumption of what economists call "homotheticity"—the assumption that an x-percent increase or decrease in income will result in an equal rise or fall in the consumption of a given good. In the economists' lexicon, this means that the "income elasticity of demand" equals 1, thus preserving the relative weights of items in the consumption basket when income rises or falls. Nicholas Oulton has shown that this procedure significantly diminishes the real gap in living standards between rich and poor countries, citing the example of the poorest nation in the world, the Democratic Republic of the Congo (DRC). The World Bank's PPP index, which incorporates the assumption of homotheticity, indicates that real average per capita GDP in the United States is 236 times higher than in the DRC; relaxing this assumption shows that this underestimates the true income gap by up to 35 percent (depending on which model is used to correct for this).[17]

The Myth of the Standard Basket

An even more serious distortion arises from the discrepancy between the actual contents of the meager basket of goods consumed by low-wage workers and those in the standard consumption basket of the mythical average citizen used to calculate the PPP index. To illustrate, the ICP reports that "under the beef heading in the list of goods and services collected in Africa, prices are collected for filet mignon among other products."[18] More generally, as the ICP notes, poor people "spend a much larger share of their budgets on food, and they spend very little on housing and essentially nothing at all on air travel or on financial services."[19] Expanding on this, the ICP explains that

> in the absence of poverty-specific PPPs, the common practice is to use PPPs for aggregate consumption. This has two limitations. First, the PPPs are based on prices of consumption items for all countries in the comparison. Consequently, the PPP estimates for developing countries are unduly influenced by the consumption baskets and spending habits of their developed counterparts. Second, the PPPs are derived using national average expenditure weights. Therefore, goods that are important to the poor and comprise a large part of their expenditure carry proportionally less weight.[20]

Efforts to produce poverty-specific PPPs (PPPPs) have yet to bear fruit. It is astonishing that World Bank estimates of those living in extreme poverty ignore the ICP's warning that "PPPs offer comparisons across economies, not across the rich and poor within economies"[21] and continue to calculate poverty rates using PPP indices that are not designed for this purpose. It is worth recalling at this point where the insultingly low extreme poverty threshold of $1.25 per day comes from. The threshold for extreme poverty was set by the World Bank in 1990

at $1.00 per day, justified then and since on the grounds that this level
is close to an average of the national poverty lines set by governments
in the poorest countries. Its subsequent increase to $1.25 per day does
not mean that the World Bank became slightly more softhearted—it
was raised to take into account the erosion in the value of the dollar
due to inflation in the United States: $1.25 in 2005 equalled $1.00 a day
in 1996.[22] It should also be remembered that this $1.25 is adjusted for
purchasing power parity—in other words, the expenditure of extremely
poor people, *at market exchange rates*, is typically 50¢ per day or less.[23]
Martin Ravallion, the senior World Bank economist who proposed the
$1/day global poverty line in 1990, explains that "the original '$1 a day'
line was a typical line amongst low-income countries in the data available at the time of the 1990 WDR [World Development Report]. This is
acknowledged to be a frugal line; naturally richer countries have higher
national poverty lines." [24] In other words, national poverty lines set by
corrupt and despotic elites in poor countries were adopted by the World
Bank and turned into an international poverty line, *for use in poor countries but not rich ones*, a procedure justified by Ravallion, on the grounds
that, in continuation, "one could hardly argue that the people in the
world who are poor by the standards of the poorest countries are not in
fact poor. This gives the global poverty line a salience in focusing on the
world's poorest that a higher line would not have." It is hard to imagine a
more specious argument. Why didn't the World Bank make an effort to
determine the composition of the minimum basket of goods necessary
to provide people with a nutritious diet, shelter, and access to health and
education, calculate its monetary value, and turn this into the international poverty line?[25] We can guess the answer.

The biggest difference between the standard basket and the workers'
basket is the amount spent on food, which consumes a much larger fraction of the incomes of working people than they do of elites. The very
sharp increases in food and fuel prices beginning in 2002 (see Figure
5.1) signify that current PPP indices significantly exaggerate the real
purchasing power exercised by low-wage workers in both rich and poor
countries. The ILO reports that "in advanced economies (Denmark, the
Netherlands and Switzerland), food expenditure is less than 20 percent
of total expenditure, but . . . is more than 60 percent in many developing
countries . . . and all these are national averages which obscure intra-na-
tional inequality."[26]

FIGURE 5.1: The Soaring Price of Food, 2000–2012 (Food Price Index: International Price of Major Food Commodities)

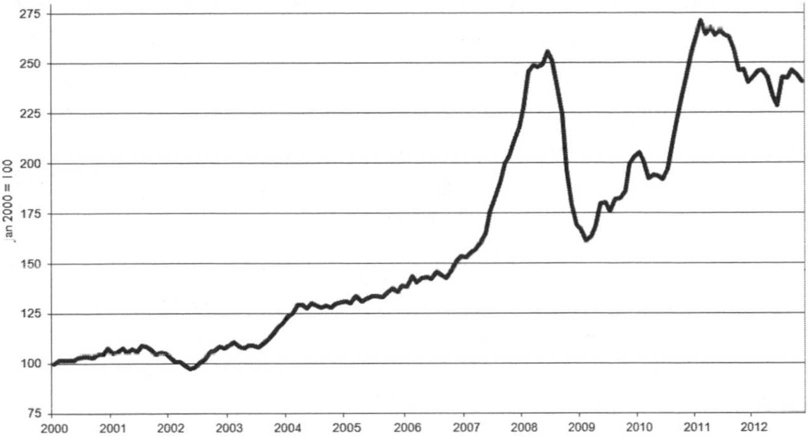

Source: http://www.fao.org/fileadmin/templates/worldfood/Reports_and_docs/Food_price_indices_data.xls.

THE PURCHASING POWER ANOMALY AND THE NORTH-SOUTH DIVIDE

As we have seen, when a dollar, or a pound, a yen, a euro, a Swedish krona, or a Swiss franc—in a word, a unit of hard currency—is converted into the national currency of just about any Southern nation, it will buy more goods and services in that country than it would at home. To correct for this distortion, wages denominated in local currency must be converted into a common *numeraire* currency, almost always based on the domestic purchasing power of the U.S. dollar, the PPP$.[27] The big discrepancy in the purchasing power of hard and soft currencies violates the Purchasing Power Parity (PPP) hypothesis, first advanced by Gustav Cassel in the 1920s,[28] which predicted that the exchange rate between any two currencies will tend toward an equilibrium that equalizes the prices of similar goods and services between nations (or what is the same thing, that it equalizes the purchasing power of the two currencies).

When PPP measures began to be widely used, a common reaction among Marxists and radical critics of neoliberalism was to suspect the motives behind them and ignore their rationality. This is not so surprising, since the use of PPP exchange rates diminishes international disparities between wages and per capita GDP (which, of course, remain extremely large), and there is good reason to question the motives of the international institutions responsible for this shift. The only significant attempt from anywhere in the broadly defined Marxist tradition to theorize the purchasing power anomaly has been made by Alan Freeman, who notes that "the concept of Purchasing Power Parity [has] made a rapid journey from the unrecognized work of a coterie of enthusiasts to a near-universal standard," charging that "the marriage of political expediency and unrequited expertise . . . proved a potent antidote to professional caution. PPP statistics, in a nutshell, made globalization look good. More specifically, they made the World Bank and the IMF look good."[29] But Freeman overstates his case—the purchasing power anomaly *is* a major distortion and—if we wish to compare wages and poverty rates between countries—PPP$ are necessary to correct it. The same goes for his argument that using PPP$ to measure GDP is inappropriate, since they are "a consumption standard of price, systematically understating the importance of production costs for the Third World."[30] They are, in fact, a weighted average of PPP conversion indices for household consumption, government investment, and private sector fixed capital formation, these being the three different ways a nation spends its income (the World Bank provides two sets of PPP conversion indices, for GDP and for private consumption, the latter being calculated only from the prices of consumer goods). The really important point he makes is that the cost of intermediate inputs used up in production are invisible in the broader PPP index, for which firms in poor nations generally have to pay more than their counterparts in rich countries. This matters because "successful attainment in the sphere of consumption in fact depends on prior success in production."[31]

Figure 5.2 shows the correlation between the size of the purchasing power anomaly and per capita GDP as it stood in 2015, for 171 countries arranged along the x-axis from poorest to richest. All imperialist nations show a purchasing power anomaly close to or greater than 1.0, indicating broad purchasing power parity between their currencies, while currency markets significantly undervalue the national currencies of the vast majority of developing nations, most of them by 50 percent or more.

The PPP anomaly grows or shrinks according to changes in the rate of inflation in the United States (since this affects the purchasing power of the dollar); the rate of inflation in the country whose data is being converted into dollars; and changes in this currency's actual rate of exchange with the dollar. Thus if, over a given period of time, the rate of inflation within, say, Bangladesh, is 10 percent higher than in the United States, and the taka's rate of exchange depreciates by 10 percent, the foreign visitor would not notice any change in her/his purchasing power. Inflation and currency appreciation therefore have an identical effect

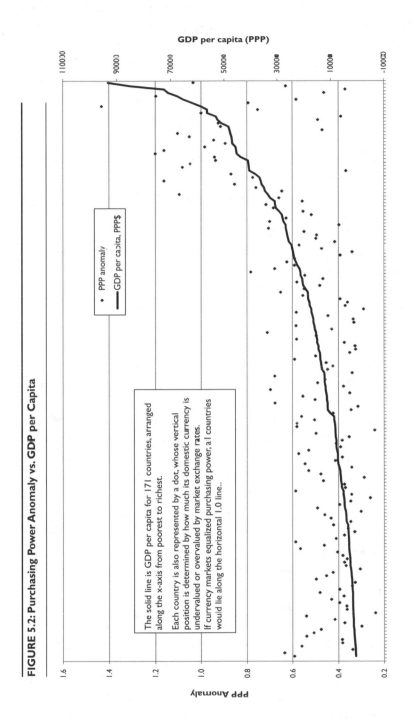

FIGURE 5.2: Purchasing Power Anomaly vs. GDP per Capita

GDP per capita (PPP)

PPP anomaly
GDP per capita, PPP$

The solid line is GDP per capita for 171 countries, arranged along the x-axis from poorest to richest.

Each country is also represented by a dot, whose vertical position is determined by how much its domestic currency is undervalued or overvalued by market exchange rates.

If currency markets equalized purchasing power, all countries would lie along the horizontal 1.0 line...

PPP Anomaly

Source: World Bank, World Economic Output Database, 2015.

on the purchasing power of visitors, but they have very different effects
on the domestic population—high domestic inflation presses down on
consumption levels within the affected country, while currency appreciation, by cheapening imported goods, raises consumption levels.

Further complicating the picture, the size of the PPP anomaly
is affected by the vagaries of the dollar. A change in the taka's rate
of exchange with the dollar might reflect a rise or fall in the value of
Bangladesh's currency against all other countries or a rise or fall in the
value of the dollar against all other countries. This problem can be evaded
by using a weighted basket of hard currencies as the *numeraire*, instead
of the dollar, thereby showing the undervaluation of the domestic currency vis-à-vis the currencies of the imperialist economies as a whole.
There is a strong argument for this, but the argument against it is stronger still: most international trade takes place in dollars, most external
debt is denominated in dollars, and PPP indices calculated against the
dollar are most widely used.

Figure 5.3 shows how the average purchasing power anomaly has
evolved since 1980 for the 152 nations classified by the IMF as "developing" or "emerging," weighted for GDP.[32] This graph tells the story
of the neoliberal era. Its steep rise from 1980 and 1986 reflected the
currency collapses and imploding economies that swept the South following the "Volcker shock" in October 1979,[33] whereas the decline over
the half-decade from 1987 to 1996 shows the effects of the raging inflation that afflicted many oppressed nations and caused price differences
between their domestic market and the United States to narrow—and
also the fall in the value of the dollar following the 1985 Plaza Accord,
when the other members of the G-5 (France, Germany, the United
Kingdom, and Japan) acquiesced to U.S. demands and helped engineer
a fall in the dollar's value, thereby restoring the competitiveness of U.S.
industry and rescuing the United States from recession. Between 1990
and 2002 the renewed ascent of the purchasing power anomaly correlates
with another wave of economic crises in the South, while the steep and
prolonged decline from 2002 to 2011 reflects the appreciation of many
soft currencies that resulted from high rates of growth buoyed by high
primary commodity prices, a major surge of production outsourcing,
and soaring flows of FDI and short-term "portfolio" investments from
imperialist countries seeking higher rates of return than those available
at home.

Figure 5.3's most startling feature is the huge extent of the purchasing
power anomaly, which since 1982 has only once dipped below 2.0 and in

FIGURE 5.3: The Purchasing Power Anomaly, Developing Nations, 1980–2015

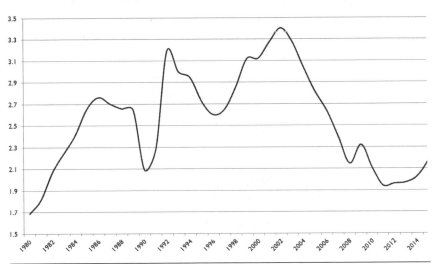

Source: World Bank, World Economic Output Database, 2015

2002 reached the extraordinarily high level of 3.4, meaning that in that year a dollar purchased 3.4 times more goods and services in the average developing nation than in the United States, and even after this major decline the anomaly only briefly breached 2.0. And yet these decades of globalization are supposedly defined by the integration of markets and the elimination of such distortions! Why this did not happen will be explored in the next chapter.

FALLING LABOR SHARE OF GDP

Several factors have contributed to the rise in profit margins. The most important is a decline in labor's share of national income.

—GOLDMAN SACHS[34]

All income can be divided into income to labor, that is, money wages and the "social wage" and income to capital, that is, profit streams from financial assets of all kinds. This reflects the capitalist form of the division of the social product, and of society itself, between two antagonistic social classes: those who produce and those who live off the producers.[35] The proportion in which aggregate income is divided between labor and capital provides the basis for an important metric: *labor's share of national income*.[36] Its continuous decline in both rich and poor countries is one of the most outstanding features of the neoliberal era, and accounts for much of the global trend toward ever-increasing social inequality.

The standard measure of labor's share used by the U.S. Bureau of Labor Statistics (BLS), the OECD, the ILO, and the IMF is the ratio of total employees' compensation (pre-tax wages and salaries plus employers' national insurance and other social contributions) to total national income. Wages are recorded pre-tax because it is assumed that workers receive benefits in exchange for, and equal in value to, the taxes they pay to the state. In other words, the state, by definition, *adds no value*—a clear sign of the ideological bias built into the foundation of bourgeois economics. Indirect taxes, insofar as they are paid out of labor income, automatically count toward labor's share. As a result, most of the fraction of GDP that accrues to the state is counted toward labor's share, even that part of it spent servicing sovereign debt, waging foreign wars, or tooling up police to attack picket lines. It is therefore no surprise that "increasing government spending is associated with an increase in labor shares, for both rich and poor countries."[37] During the decades of harsh "structural adjustment," however, most poor countries were not increasing government spending, they were slashing it, and so labor's share in "poor countries have also been negatively affected by . . . the fall in government spending."[38] Including the bulk of government spending in labor's share of GDP does at least capture the entire social wage—the transfer payments, health and education provision, and other social services that in imperialist countries typically account for 70 percent or more of state expenditure (and a much smaller proportion of a much smaller amount elsewhere).[39]

Income to Capital Masquerading as Income to Labor

One factor causing labor's share of income to be overestimated and the steepness of its decline to be underestimated are the super-wages, bonuses, stock options, and other benefits paid to employers and managers that are falsely counted as labor income. [40] The £2.7 million lump sum and £703,000 annual pension (later reduced to £342,500) received by Royal Bank of Scotland chief executive Sir Fred Goodwin upon his retirement in January 2009 is counted toward labor's share of GDP. This payoff became notorious a few weeks later, when the UK government covered £24 billion losses by his bank, the largest loss in UK corporate history. Anne Krueger, former World Bank chief economist, provided another striking example, in a 2002 paper titled "Measuring Labor's

Share": "If the owner of the Chicago Bulls, Jerry Reinsdorf, were to pay [basketball star] Michael Jordan an additional $20 million, and reduce his own salary by an equivalent amount, labor's share would be unchanged because both are counted as employees of the Bulls."[41] Luckily for Jordan he didn't have to rely on Reinsdorf's generosity. In 1998 Nike paid him $45 million in "wages" for appearing in their advertisements, enough to pay the annual wages of around 30,000 of the Indonesian workers in factories producing Nike's shoes—and this also counted toward labor's share.

Another distortion arises from the method of accounting for the income received by self-employed workers and by family members. The convention is to split this into two parts, income to capital and income to labor. The IMF bravely assumes that these "categories of workers earn the same average wage as employees,"[42] a procedure also followed by the BLS,[43] and is especially problematic when applied to low-wage nations where a much higher proportion of the economically active population is counted as self-employed, subsisting on an income that is often a small fraction of the paltry wages paid to those employed.

In a revealing study, Michael Elsby, Bart Hobijn, and Ayşegül Şahın report that in the United States—and, by implication elsewhere in other imperialist countries—this arbitrary treatment of self-employed income seriously impairs calculations of the decline of labor's share. Elsby et al.'s research is especially important because they reveal how headline figures on labor's share of national income (or of GDP, which amounts to the same thing), which are already dramatic enough, greatly underestimate the true extent of its decline. In the United States the "rise in inequality is even more striking for proprietors' income than it is for payroll income. In 1948 the bottom 90 percent of employees earned 75 percent of payroll compensation. By 2010 this had declined to 54 percent. For entrepreneurial income, however, this fraction plummeted from 42 percent in 1948 to 14 percent in 2010."[44] To exclude distortions arising from this Elsby et al. focus on the "payroll share," that is, the total labor compensation received by waged workers. Self-employed workers and proprietors comprise just 6.8 percent of the economically active population—in the United States, waged workers as a proportion of the economically active population increased from 90.6 percent in 1980 to 93.2 percent in 2011.[45] They obtain startling results. A decline of 3.9 percent in the share of national income of all employees becomes a 10 percent decline when the highest-paid 1 percent of employees are excluded and a 14 percent decline when the highest-paid 10 percent are excluded—in other words, the lowest 90 percent of wage earners (84 percent of the United States' total economically active population) earned 42 percent of the total payroll in 1980 and just 28 percent in 2011—Thus the share of national income received by the bottom 90 percent of U.S. employees has declined not by 3.9 percent (the headline figure), but by a staggering 33 percent.[46] Another extremely important finding of Elsby et al.'s research is that, as the neoliberal era ground on, so the decline of labor's share accelerated, declining by twice as much between 2000 and 2011 as in the previous two decades.

According to the ILO's *World of Work Report 2011*, since the early 1990s the "share of domestic income that goes to labor . . . declined in nearly three-quarters of the 69 countries with available information," as Figure 5.4 illustrates.[47] The decline is generally more pronounced in emerging and developing countries than in advanced ones.[48] The declines in labor's share in emerging and developing economies were very steep—falling in Asia by around 20 percent between 1994 and 2010; moreover, "The pace of the decline accelerated in . . . recent years, with the wage share falling more than 11 percentage points between 2002 and 2006. In China, the wage share declined by close to 10 percentage points since 2000."[49] Africa's toilers saw their share of national income decline by 15 percent in the two decades from 1990, again "with most of this decline—10 percentage points—taking place since 2000. The decline is even more spectacular in North Africa, where the wage share fell by more than 30 percentage points since 2000."[50] The lowest decline occurred in Latin America, where it fell by 10 percent since 1993, most of this before 2000. Slower decline since then reflects the redistributive policies targetting extreme poverty rolled out by Latin America's left-wing governments—and copied by right-wing governments fearful of social upheaval. Meanwhile "the wage share among advanced economies has been trending downward since 1975. The fall, however, has occurred at a much more moderate pace than among emerging and developing economies—falling roughly 9 percentage points since 1980."[51]

The falls reported by the ILO take no account of sharply increasing inequality between skilled/professional and unskilled workers or of income to capital masquerading as income to labor. These effects are likely to be at least as large as that reported above by Elsby et al. for the United States—in which case the true extent of the fall in labor's share is likely to have been several times greater than the already vertiginous falls reported by the ILO. Truly, the workers of the world "stand outcast and starving 'mid the wonders we have made"![52]

FIGURE 5.4: Share of World Labor Income in World Gross Output, 1980–2011

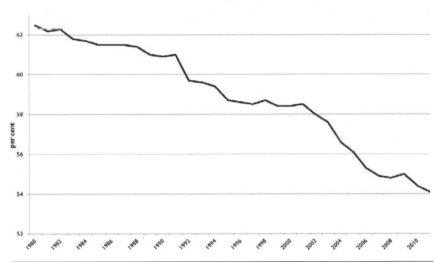

Source: UNCTAD, Trade and Development Report, 2013: "Adjusting to the Changing Dynamics of the World Economy," figure 1.4.

Labor's Share in Oppressed Nations

Figure 5.4 confirms the findings of NBER economist Anne Harrison, one of the first to ask, "How has globalization affected the relative share of income going to capital and labor?"[53] Harrison investigated what happened to labor's share of national income between 1960 and 1996 in two groups of rich and poor countries, more than one hundred countries in all, and found "enormous declines in labor's share in the poorest 20 percent of countries, and significant increases in labor's share in the top 20 percent of all countries."[54] In rich nations, labor's share of GDP rose by 0.2 percent per year between 1960 and 1993 before declining by 0.4 percent per year between 1993 and 1996.[55] The 1960–93 period spans the onset of the neoliberal era at the end of the 1970s, before which labor's share was gently rising. As the ILO stated, in its *Global Wage Report 2008-9*, "Studies using long-term series data from European countries indicate that the wage share appears to have peaked around the mid-1970s and has declined at an accelerating pace since then."[56] Measuring the decline against its average over an arbitrarily selected period instead of from its high point results in a serious underestimation of the true extent of the decline. Nevertheless, she concludes that "in Europe, the change is enormous: labor's share of aggregate income has declined as much as ten percentage points of GDP. In the United States, the trend is still discernable but much smaller: labor's share in national income has declined by several percentage points."[57]

In its first and only detailed examination of the impact of globalization on real wages and labor's share, in the April 2007 edition of its *World Economic Outlook*, the IMF also reported "a clear decline since the early 1980s across the advanced economies . . . a reversal of the rise in labor shares that took place in the 1970s, especially in Europe and Japan."[58] But the IMF said that "due to data availability reasons" their study was "limited to advanced OECD economies."[59] This is a feeble excuse. Lack of data didn't stop Ann Harrison or other researchers cited here from establishing as a fact that, throughout the last three decades of neoliberal globalization, labor's share of GDP has tended to decline even faster in the Global South than in the developed nations, or prevent senior ILO economist Nomaan Majid from discovering that median real wages in developed countries during the 1990s were 36.2 percent higher than in the 1980s while the increase in developing countries was just 6.12 percent, despite the fact that "real GDP per capita growth has been similar across developing and developed economies."[60] As we shall see, a major factor in this North-South divergence is the tendency of wages to collapse in times of crisis—and these were crisis decades for much of the Global South. Since these findings knock a big hole in the IMF's claims that neoliberal capitalism is leading billions out of poverty and to convergence between developed and developing countries, it is not hard to see a clear motive for the IMF's reticence.

One remarkable aspect of Figure 5.4's graph is its depiction of *global* labor's share of a *global* product. This is a welcome change: labor's share of GDP is invariably conceived of and measured as labor's share of national GDP. The globalization of production signifies that the process of wealth creation has become qualitatively more international; conceptualizing the division of income between capital and labor as relative shares of a *global* product would seem more appropriate than ever. But even when there is an attempt to depict a global trend, as in Figure 5.4 (as also in the study by Karabarbounis and Neiman cited below), this is only ever conceived of as an average or aggregate of national trends and does not imply their agreement with the argument developed here, that the global division of value is determinant, deciding the size of the slice to be shared between classes in each nation, and that a significant part of the national income shared between classes in imperialist nations is actually produced by workers and farmers in the low-wage nations. Instead, they remain trapped by "methodological nationalism"—the unquestioning assumption that the nation-state or national economy is the basic unit of analysis characterizes both mainstream and heterodox economics and bourgeois social science in general.

Labor's falling share poses a difficult question for mainstream economists because it contradicts what was long considered an established fact, at least for developed capitalist nations: that labor's share of GDP is constant. This "fact" is often attributed to Nicholas Kaldor, who argued in a 1957 paper that "the share of wages and the share of profits in the national income has shown a remarkable constancy in 'developed' capitalist economies"; this is so because "real wages . . . rise automatically at the same rate as the productivity of labor, so that distributive shares remain constant through time."[61] "Productivity of labor" here means value added per worker, which, when combined with labor cost per worker, yields the capitalists' preferred measure of productivity and the standard measure of competitiveness: unit labor cost, that is, the cost of the labor required to produce an additional unit of output. Reducing ULC and increasing competitiveness is a central aim of employers and governments alike, and this is achieved when the productivity of labor rises faster than the wage paid to labor, or when it falls slower. Jesus Felipe, a researcher at the Asian Development Bank, has made the extremely important point that *unit labor cost is just a different way of expressing labor's share of GDP*, or, in his words, "in standard analyses, an economy is deemed more competitive the lower its ULC is. The flip side of this line of reasoning is that an economy is more competitive the lower its labor share is, *ceteris paribus*. Hence, a great deal of policies to lower ULCs are, effectively, policies to lower the share of labor in income."[62] In a paper with Utsav Kumar, Jesus Felipe adds, "Unit labor costs calculated with aggregate data are no more than the economy's labor share in total output multiplied by a price effect."[63] Closer examination of unit labor cost in chapter 6 will reveal more about the contradictory nature of labor productivity under capitalism and the failure of mainstream economics to resolve it.

Why Is Labor's Share Falling?

Nothing could be less mysterious or surprising than the fall in labor's share of income in the neoliberal era. This dramatic trend reflects the change in the balance of class forces to the detriment of the producers of wealth resulting from neoliberalism, the economic/political counter-revolution that eviscerated labor unions, drove the informalization and flexibilization of labor, mobilized armies of police and soldiers to restrict the international mobility of workers as it removed obstacles to the inter-national mobility of capital. A long-running controversy continues to rage among bourgeois economists over whether this is due to global-ization or to technological advances that reduce demand for labor and/or the cost of capital investment goods. The debate has centered on the degree to which globalization has repressed wages and widened wage differentials within imperialist countries, especially within the United States, and has been shaped in part by the need to counter protection-ist pressure from workers and employers exposed to competition. The debate has largely ignored the effects on workers in low-wage countries where, regardless of the effects of globalization, standard development theory predicts that a rise in inequality is an inevitable and necessary accompaniment of the early stages of development. The ILO has sum-marized the opposing views as follows:

> It has been considered that technical progress has been responsible for the decline in wages relative to profits. This is the explanation apparently favoured by the IMF. Our own statistical analysis suggests that globalization may also have played a part . . . the intensification of competition—particularly the presence of large low-wage export-ers in the market for labor-intensive products—has worked as a wage moderation factor.[64]

In fact, the IMF and ILO were not so far apart: in the survey of labor and globalization included in the 2007 *World Economic Outlook*, the IMF stated: "Both labor globalization and technological progress have acted to reduce the labor share, with the impact of technological pro-gress being somewhat larger."[65] Yet technology versus trade is a false dichotomy; qualitative analysis reveals how inseparably intertwined and mutually reinforcing they are. ICT (Information and Communication Technology), for example, has not only made possible vast labor-saving within the imperialist economies, it has played a key role in facilitat-ing the integration of markets and the fragmentation of production and its shift to various locations around the world. The ICT sector has itself pioneered production outsourcing to low-wage countries, and the cheapening of ICT and other investment goods is itself in large measure the result of low-wage outsourcing.

A prominent study by Loukas Karabarbounis and Brent Neiman also found that "the global labor share has declined significantly since the early 1980s, with the decline occurring within the large majority of countries and industries."[66] They also provide a representative example of a typical mainstream argument that the cause of this decline is technological advance, not globalization, and this not only explains the decline of labor's share but justifies it, too. They argue that within each industry "productivity of capital" is rising faster than the productivity of labor, and this is because of "a global decline in the relative price of investment goods of about 25 percent,"[67] above all of ICT equipment, "induc[ing] firms to substitute away from labor and toward capital to such an extent that it drives down the labor share."[68] Not only their argument, but the data on which it stands, are spurious.[69] The supposed 25 percent decline in the relative price of investment is greatly exaggerated by their use of U.S. government data that has been subject to highly dubious "hedonic adjustments"; for example, the price of a computer is considered to have fallen even if it stays the same but its speed doubles or the resolution of its screen is improved. Hedonic prices affect around 20 percent of the total output measured in North American and European GDP.[70]

Derived from the Greek word for pleasure, "hedonic" adjustments of prices aim to account for changes in the quality or performance of commodities such as cars, cameras, and computers, qualities that may be highly subjective and difficult if not impossible to quantify. Since the 1996 report by the Boskin Commission, a group of experts tasked by the U.S. government to advise on how changes in the quality of commodities should be reflected in calculations of GDP and inflation, such adjustments have become standard for an increasing range of commodities in the United States, resulting in reduced estimates of inflation and magnifying estimates of real wages, productivity, and GDP.[71] From the standpoint of Marxist value theory, this methodology rests on a crass confusion between a change in the *use-value* of a commodity with a change in its *exchange value*, allowing bourgeois economists to misinterpret increased productivity of labor—that is, the increase in the quantity and utility of the objects created by a given quantity of labor-power—as an increase in the productivity of capital.

Having discovered a correlation between the "pervasive decline" in the relative prices of capital goods and falling labor shares of income, Karabarbounis and Neiman's next step is to assume that the former causes the latter, and, in a manner typical of neoclassical economists, conceal their contentious assumptions and arbitrary procedures under a thick mat of complex algebra. Their literature review entirely excludes value-chain analysis and other heterodox schools as well as the extensive literature supporting the view that the decline in labor's share is rooted in globalization and the global shift of production, which is only mentioned in order to peremptorily dismiss it: "The prominence of the within-industry component . . . rules out otherwise plausible stories related to the increasing trade integration of China or globalization more generally."[72]

In contrast to this casual dismissal of alternative explanations, Elsby et al. go to considerable efforts to test the validity of Karabarbounis and Neiman's argument before rejecting it and advancing their own alternative explanation. Their most compelling reason for rejecting it is that, far from witnessing an increase in the rate of investment in capital goods, neoliberal globalization has seen it collapse—in favor of outsourcing production to low-wage countries. Thus they argue that "the acceleration of the decline in the labor share over the last decade was not accompanied by an acceleration in investment-specific technological change. On the contrary, investment-specific technological change slowed down during the latter period."[73] *Indeed,* "There is in fact a weak *negative* relationship between the change in equipment prices and payroll shares across industries. This is the opposite of what one would expect if capital deepening due to the decline in price of equipment were the driving force of the decline in the payroll share."[74] Instead, they find that "declines in payroll shares are more severe in industries that face larger increases in competitive pressures from imports,"[75] and that "increases in the import exposure of U.S. businesses can account for 3.3 percentage points of the 3.9 percentage point decline in the U.S. payroll share over the past quarter-century."[76] UNCTAD reinforces this verdict: "The tendency of companies to seek profit gains from exploiting wage differentials, rather than through innovation and investment, has produced limited dynamic benefits for the rest of society. In other words, the presumed transmission of higher profits to higher gross fixed capital formation has not materialized."[77]

To conclude this section, the ILO found that countries with high trade-union density experience a slower decline in labor's share, but a decline nonetheless: "In countries where collective bargaining covered more than 30 percent of employees, any additional 1 percent of economic growth was accompanied by a 0.87 percent growth in wages, compared with only 0.65 percent wage growth in countries with lower coverage . . . our analysis shows that collective bargaining contributed to lower overall wage inequality."[78] But there is a price to pay: union organization might result in a larger share, but of a smaller pie, as the ILO's Nomaan Majid has found: "In developing economies . . . greater bargaining rights in parts of the organized economy may . . . constitute investment disincentives," resulting in lower GDP growth and therefore a "depressing impact on the wages of all workers taken together. This finding seems to be valid in both the developing and the developed economies."[79] The conclusion that workers and their trade unions should draw from this is that the fall in labor's share that is so characteristic of the neoliberal era was not dreamed up by devilish capitalist politicians, nor is it merely the result of a particular type of capitalism that can be changed like a suit of clothes. It is the result of systemic contradictions, and the efforts of capitalists and their captive governments to resolve them by increasing their exploitation of living labor and nature. This trend cannot be resisted without challenging capitalism itself. So long as trade unions restrict themselves to seeking to protect workers' conditions within capitalism, they will not only fail, they will become part of the problem, as the logic of protectionism and nationalism leads to xenophobia, the construction of razor-wire borders to keep migrant workers out, and ultimately to fascism and the destruction of independent union organizations.

GROWING WAGE INEQUALITY

Not only is labor's share of income declining, this share is itself being distributed ever more unequally. Along with the falling labor share, growing wage inequality within nations is another outstanding feature of global wage trends during the neoliberal era, and this is so even after we exclude income to capital masquerading as income to labor—the super-wages and pseudo-wages paid to CEOs, celebrities, etc. The ILO's *Global Wage Report*, 2008–9, called this "one of the most important developments in recent years," and it has occurred in many countries, "irrespective of their national income levels."[80] As we have shown above in relation to the United States, sharply rising wage inequality is enough on its own to substantially change the picture conjured by data on global trends in average wages. Corley et al. find abundant evidence of rising wage inequality: "Since the 1980s, evidence from cross-country studies has shown the existence of rising inequality in wages and earnings. In many high- and low/middle-income countries, the wages of high-skilled workers have increased, while those of low-skilled workers have grown relatively more slowly, fallen or remained stagnant. . . . In the United States, real earnings of low-wage workers have fallen while the earnings of high-wage workers have grown significantly. In Latin America and much of Asia, the same scenario exists."[81] The scenario, however, is not quite the same: according to the ILO, "On average, wage inequality is higher in countries with a lower GDP per capita." [82] Freeman and Oostendorp also find that the poorer the country the higher the wage inequality, a fact already "well known from more limited country comparisons."[83]

Alan Freeman points to an important factor causing wage differentials to rise—wages are pulled in different directions by the ever more strenuous suppression of the international mobility of unskilled workers and the "brain drain," whereby skilled workers are enticed to migrate to high-wage countries: "A country that fails to pay global rates . . . will find its skilled workforce systematically evaporating to the places in the world that are content to pay for it, and whose objections to immigration mysteriously evaporate confronted with a skilled workforce whose education they never had to pay for."[84] Yet global competition pushing up wages of some skilled workers in low-wage countries is not the main cause of widening wage differentials: detailed analysis by the ILO indicates that this increasing trend is being driven above all by falling wages of the lowest-paid workers, in contrast to rich countries where the driver is the increasing wages of the highest paid. These two groups of nations represent two distinctly "different types of increase in wage inequality. In the first—the 'collapsing bottom'—wage inequality grows because of a deterioration in the lowest wages. The second—the 'flying top'—is the opposite case, where top wage earnings are increasing faster than in other wage groups." The report identifies a third type, "where both changes are taking place simultaneously, which results in a 'polarization' of wage earnings."[85] Comparing the years 1995–2000 with the years 2001–6, the report found that "developed countries such as the United Kingdom and the United States mainly fall into the category of 'flying top' wages, with the exception of Germany, which falls into the category of 'collapsing bottom' wages . . . countries from developing regions are predominantly close to the scenario of 'collapsing bottom' wages . . . [that is,] growing inequality between the median and lowest wages."[86]

Their findings confirm the different trajectories followed by real wages in imperialist nations and in the Global South, a fundamental cause of which is the weight in the latter of the relative surplus population desperate for work. As Corley et al. put it, rising wage inequality "may be due to the surplus of labor in developing economies, whereby the initial impact from globalization (and growth) may be to bring previously underemployed or unemployed people into the formal labor market," although the "initial impact" has turned out to be remarkably enduring.[87]

FIGURE 5.5: Output/Worker—Developed and Developing Countries

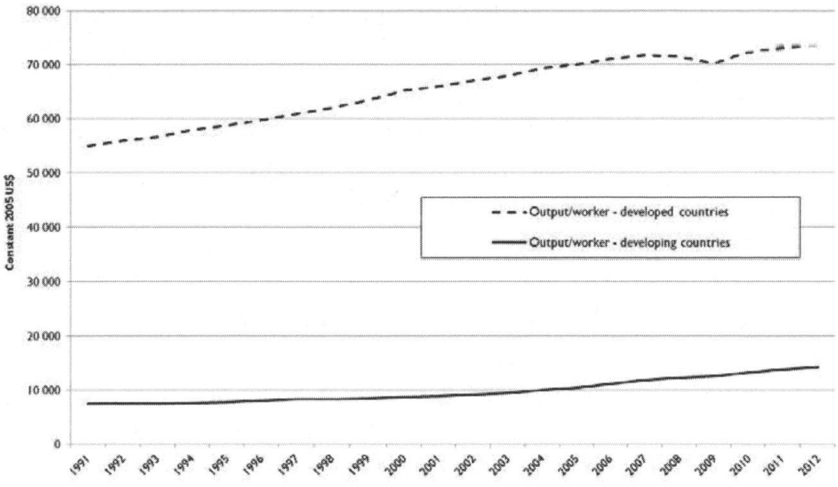

Source: *Key Indicators of the Labour Market* (KILM), 8th edition, Tables R4 and R8.

GLOBAL WAGE TRENDS IN THE NEOLIBERAL ERA

Emphasis on relative wages can lead to a one-sided view. For example, if the average wage in a poor country rose by 100 percent, from $1,000 to $2,000 per annum, and in a rich country by 20 percent, from $10,000 to $12,000, the ratio of rich to poor country wages would fall from 10:1 to 6:1—in other words, relative inequality would decline, yet the absolute difference between them would increase, from $9,000 to $10,000.

This effect is illustrated in Figure 5.5. Unfortunately, data limitations discussed at the beginning of this chapter impede the construction of a similar graph showing the trajectory of average wages in these two groups of nations, but since wages are correlated with value added per worker (the ILO calls this "output per worker"), the latter can serve as a useful proxy for the former, with the caveat that since wage growth has lagged growth in output per worker in both imperialist and low-wage nations—reflected in falling labor shares of national income—the gradient of wage growth in both sets of nations would be significantly gentler than the traces shown. Data on output/worker are also vitiated by the inclusion of the "output" supposedly generated by "workers" such as hedge fund traders and basketball stars, just as the inclusion of high-paid elites exaggerates average income growth. Bearing this in mind, between 1991 and 2011 output per worker in developed nations rose from $54,800 to $73,600, measured in constant 2005 dollars, a 34 percent increase over the 22 years, while output per worker in developing countries rose from $7,460 to $14,220, a 91 percent increase. A glance at Figure 5.4 is enough to show that though these trends might satisfy the mathematical definition of convergence, reality continues to be defined by absolute divergence. Robert Wade comments, "The whole discussion about inequality misleads by considering only relative incomes. Absolute income gaps between the West and the rest are widening even in the case of the fast growing countries like China and India. . . . No one disputes this, but it is treated as a fact of no significance."[88]

Over the course of the neoliberal era, it is indisputable that absolute wage differentials between imperialist and developing nations have increased. Assessing the evolution of relative wages is much more difficult, since average wages take no account of sharply increased wage dispersal between high- and low-skilled occupations and for other reasons discussed earlier in this chapter. One way to get around this is to consider international wage differentials *within* occupations. One of the few attempts to investigate this was Freeman and Oostendorp's, who surveyed wages during early and late periods of globalization (1983–89 and 1992–99) for 137 occupations across 135 countries. The key result of their research: "Inequality of wages across countries in the same occupation increased over this period despite globalization, which should have reduced the inequality."[89]

Textile workers' wages are among the most readily available of global wage data, and their growth serves as a strong indication of what is happening to wages in other industrial sectors. Figure 5.6 and Table 5.1 present data on gross wages for textile production workers in 32 countries.[90] Werner International, a management consultancy, reports that U.S. textile wages in 2008 stood at $17.41 per hour, substantially below the $32.78 per hour reported by the U.S. Bureau of Labor Statistics for manufacturing workers as a whole. Werner finds no sign in the textile and clothing sector of convergence in wages between rich and poor countries. On the contrary—as their 2012 report concludes, "The wage gap between developed and developing countries is increasing and the range from the lowest hourly cost to the highest hourly cost is showing an ever increasing expansion."[91] This finding was confirmed by *Global Wage Trends for Apparel Workers*, a report by the Worker Rights Consortium, which found that "over the past decade . . . apparel manufacturing in most leading garment-exporting nations has delivered diminishing returns for its workers. Research conducted . . . on 15 of the world's leading apparel-exporting countries found that between 2001 and 2011,

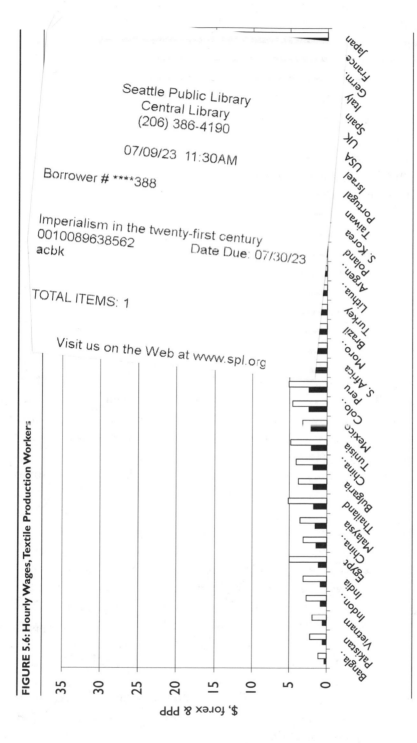

FIGURE 5.6: Hourly Wages, Textile Production Workers

Source: Werner International, "Primary Textiles Labor Cost Comparisons, 2008," http://texnet.ilgstudios.net/files/2009/08/Werner_International_-_Labor_Cost_Study_2008.pdf.

Seattle Public Library
Central Library
(206) 386-4190

07/09/23 11:30AM

Borrower # ****388

Imperialism in the twenty-first century
0010089638562
acbk   Date Due: 07/30/23

TOTAL ITEMS: 1

Visit us on the Web at www.spl.org

wages for garment workers in the majority of these countries fell in real terms."[92] They found that in five of the top ten sources of U.S. apparel imports—Bangladesh, Mexico, Honduras, Cambodia, and El Salvador— garment workers' wages declined in real terms between 2001 and 2011 by an average of 4.6 percent. Real wages also fell over this period in Guatemala, the Philippines, and Thailand. Garment workers in Mexico, the Dominican Republic, and Cambodia saw the biggest declines, with real wages in these countries falling by 28.9 percent, 23.74 percent, and 19.2 percent respectively. Real wages rose in four of the top ten export- ers—in China by 124 percent, Indonesia by 38.4 percent, Vietnam by 39.7 percent, Peru by 17.1 percent and India by 13 percent.

Evidence presented in this section indicates the persistence of very high wage differentials; suggests convergence in the wages received by skilled workers but not in the wages received by unskilled workers; and reveals a very high degree of wage dispersion within and between economic sectors. Comparing trends during 2001 to 2007 with ear- lier periods, across 83 countries comprising about 70 percent of the world's population, the ILO observed that "wage growth has tended to slow down in the majority of countries for which data are availa- ble"—despite the Global South experiencing the strongest and most sustained period of GDP growth of the entire neoliberal globalization period.[93] The ILO explains that "the difference is rather modest,"[94] but the fact that we have not seen any reflection in Southern wages of the vaunted boom-time for the Global South is an eloquent indication of the underlying dynamics.

There is enormous variation between and within regions: in some countries, particularly in Latin America, wage levels have not recovered from their destruction during economic crises in the 1980s and 1990s; in others, real wages received by workers in the South's export-oriented manufacturing industry are subject to enormous downward pressure, as we have seen in the case of textile and apparel workers. China, where real wages have grown (thanks, in part, to labor shortages arising from the one-child policy as well as to China's exceptionally rapid growth), weighs heavily in the global data but are exaggerated by the inclusion of super- wages paid to highly-skilled labor, managers, etc., the exclusion of the wages of migrant workers and the failure to properly measure the value of the social wage—the "iron rice bowl"—that has been jettisoned in that country's attempted transition to capitalism. Decelerating growth, huge overcapacity, and asset bubbles waiting to burst suggest that what goes up could very soon come down.

TABLE 5.1: Hourly Wages, Textile Production Workers, 2008

	Hourly wage $	Ratio of U.S. wage to national wage (Forex)	Hourly wage PPP$	Ratio of U.S. wage to national wage (PPP)
Bangladesh	0.31	56.2	1.08	16.2
Pakistan	0.56	31.1	2.21	7.9
Vietnam	0.57	30.5	1.92	9.1
Indonesia	0.83	21.0	2.72	6.4
India	0.85	20.5	3.12	5.6
Egypt	1.12	15.5	4.98	3.5
China Inland	1.44	12.1	3.14	5.6
Malaysia	1.57	11.1	3.56	4.9
Thailand	1.8	9.7	5.13	3.4
Bulgaria	1.85	9.4	3.79	4.6
China Coastal	1.88	9.3	4.09	4.3
Tunisia	2.12	8.2	4.84	3.6
Mexico	2.17	8.0	3.24	5.4
Colombia	2.45	7.1	4.58	3.8
Peru	2.45	7.1	5.07	3.4
S. Africa	2.58	6.7	5.29	3.3
Morocco	2.89	6.0	5.94	2.9
Brazil	3.41	5.1	5.07	3.4
Turkey	4.27	4.1	6.24	2.8
Lithuania	4.28	4.1	5.95	2.9
Argentina	4.48	3.9	6.75	2.6
Poland	4.81	3.6	6.24	2.8
S. Korea	6.31	2.8	8.85	2.0
Taiwan	7.89	2.2	8.66	2.0
Portugal	9.45	1.8	9.94	1.8
Israel	11.31	1.5	10.49	1.7
USA	17.41	1.0	17.41	1.0
UK	17.7	1.0	14.79	1.2
Spain	18.39	0.9	17.43	1.0
Italy	22.31	0.8	19.31	0.9
Germany	25.42	0.7	21.38	0.8
France	30.39	0.6	23.52	0.7
Japan	30.81	0.6	27.25	0.6

Source□□erner International Management Consultants□2008 PPP indices from □orld Bank□□orld □d□opment Indicators.
□ote □forex□ signifies co□ersion of wages paid in national currencies into dollars at actual market exchange rates.

WAGES IN TIMES OF CRISIS

Wrenching crises in dozens of nations provided the emergency shock conditions in which Southern governments were brought to heel, trade unions broken, and labor protection swept away, breaking resistance to casualization and downwardly mobile wages. A significant finding reported in the ILO's *Global Wage Report* 2008–9 is the steepness of the decline in real wages during times of crisis, when "wages tend to become overly responsive and fall faster than GDP."[95] Thus "wage elasticity to GDP," the amount by which wages rise or fall for each 1 percent increase or decrease in GDP per capita, for 83 developed and developing nations between 1995 and 2006 was just 0.65 during periods of positive GDP growth (that is, for each 1 percent rise in per capita GDP, real wages rose by 0.65 percent) but leapt to 1.55 during periods of negative GDP growth (that is, for each 1 percent decline in per capita GDP, real wages declined by more than 1½ percent). This supports Harrison's finding that "exchange rate crises in poor countries lead to declining labor shares, suggesting that labor pays disproportionately the price when there are large swings in exchange rates."[96] In a survey of ten "major developing countries," Özlem Onaran also found that "the crises of the post-1990s have had a clear and long-lasting effect in all countries. The percentage decrease in the wage share by far exceeds the rate of decline in economic activity."[97] Furthermore, sharp falls in real wages during times of crisis disproportionately affect low-paid workers, resulting in increased wage inequality.[98]

Confirming this verdict, the ILO reported in 2008 that "in many of the countries that suffered from an economic crisis in the late 1990s (in particular some South Asian and Latin American countries) real wages have not fully recovered to pre-crisis levels despite significant economic recovery over recent years."[99] These findings add to research published in 2001 by Ishac Diwan, a World Bank economist, who recorded 216 crises in developing nations between 1975 and the mid-1990s,[100] of which 67 crises provided sufficient data for analysis. In every case these crises resulted in a sharp and sometimes precipitous fall in labor's share of national income, beginning a slide that typically continued for five years. On average, "GDP per capita drop[ped] by 4.7 percent during the year of the crisis, 7.3 percent in years 2 and 3, before stabilising in year 4,"[101] and he finds that "more recent crises have tended to hurt labor more than older ones, as if the mobility of capital has increased over time . . . causing a larger share of the losses to be shifted to labor."[102]

Diwan described the "transfer of assets away from labor during the crisis period" as "staggering, which goes a long way in explaining why workers fear financial crises so much. The world average is 33.7 percent of GDP per financial crisis."[103]

The so-called Tequila Crisis—when, in a few days around Christmas 1994 Mexico's peso lost 42 percent of its value against the dollar—is an excellent example of the sort of crisis that Diwan is talking about. A *Financial Times* editorial a few months after the crash observed approvingly that "devaluations improve a country's competitive position by bringing about a reduction in real wages . . . four-fifths of pay settlements have not exceeded 7.5 percent, compared with officially forecast inflation of 42 percent this year."[104] Conditions attached by Congress to the U.S. contribution of $20bn to the $50bn rescue instructed the Mexican government to ensure that wages increased no faster than productivity, thereby locking in the huge fall in wages. Onaran reported that "in Mexico . . . the wage share has declined 29.5 percent as of 1996 compared to 1993, and indeed has still not returned to its pre-crisis level ten years after the crisis."[105] She also reports similar declines in labor's share elsewhere: in Turkey the 1994 crisis led to a "24.8 percent cumulative decline in the wage share" and another crisis in 2001 saw Turkey's wage share decline by 32.2 percent, taking two years and three years, respectively, before it began a slow recovery. In Korea, "the wage share has continued to decline for three years following the 1997 crisis, and was 21.6 percent lower in 1999 compared to 1996."[106]

Some idea of what this data means in terms of human death and suffering can be gleaned from the World Bank's estimate that "countries that suffered economic contractions of 10 percent or more between 1980 and 2004 experienced . . . more than one million excess infant deaths. Evidence suggests that growth collapses are costly for human development outcomes, as they deteriorate more quickly during growth decelerations than they improve during growth accelerations."[107]

Ishac Diwan, as we have seen, painted a bleak picture of the hammering that incomes of millions of already poor workers receive during periods of economic crisis and the slowness and partial nature of their recovery. Bleaker still is his advice to workers, that they have no choice but to meekly accept their fate: "As capital becomes more mobile, and labor more focused on reducing the occurrence of crises, cooperative behavior becomes crucial. . . . [It is] in labor's own interest to take losses when they occur." He believes that "currency devaluation and inflation are important mechanisms to reduce real wages in the short term," and advises their continued use: "Small and vulnerable economies would want to retain the ability to devalue."[108]

WAGES AND THE MYTH OF CONVERGENCE

Modernization theory, standard trade theory, leading exponents of neoliberal globalization, and the mass media all agree that international wage differentials are being eroded and are firmly set on a course to disappear as poor nations converge with rich nations. Pages could be filled with asinine hyperbole along the lines of Columbia University professor Arvind Panagariya's observation that, during the next half-century, wage differences between the United States and China and India will disappear because "the chances are excellent that India and China themselves will turn into rich countries,"[109] or PricewaterhouseCoopers' belief that convergence is certain "provided that there are no catastrophic shocks (e.g. global nuclear war, asteroid collisions, extreme global climate change, etc.) that derail the overall global economic development process on a sustained basis."[110] The ILO has added its authoritative voice to this chorus of fools:

> The process of economic convergence between developing countries and advanced economies has gathered momentum. Between 1980 and 2011, per capita income in developing countries grew, on average, by 3.3 percent per year—much faster than the 1.8 percent per capita income growth recorded in advanced economies. This process of convergence has accelerated since the early 2000s, especially since the start of the global crisis in 2007–8.[111]

No sooner had the ILO published its report (2014) than the global economic crisis finally caught up with low-wage countries. The reversal of the commodities super-cycle, of hot money flows from imperialist countries, and other headwinds has caused emerging market growth to slow sharply, and once China is stripped out of the equation, is expected to be close to zero in 2015.[112] Once population growth is taken into account this means falling per capita GDP growth in the rest of the developing world. A cursory glance at World Bank data on per capita GDP growth is sufficient to reveal the propagandist nature of the proclaimed convergence. Per capita GDP growth for low and middle income countries, according to world development indicators, was 2.7 percent for the entire neoliberal era (not the 3.3 percent reported in the above

TABLE 5.2: Real per Capita GDP Growth

	1980–2000	2001–2011	1980–2011
Low- and middle-income countries	1.70%	4.60%	2.70%
High-income countries	2.20%	1.10%	1.80%

Source: World Development Indicators, GDP per capita in constant 2005 USD.

quote), nearly 1 percent faster than the 1.8 percent experienced by developed nations. But, as the table above shows, the higher rate of growth in developing nations trumpeted by the ILO as a feature of the entire neoliberal period is entirely due to much faster growth in those nations during the first decade of the new millennium. In contrast, during the first two decades of neoliberalism, per capita GDP growth in developing nations significantly lagged growth in rich countries—in other words, the gap increased relatively as well as absolutely. Furthermore, the most recent decade has also seen a vertiginous collapse in labor's share of national income in those countries, amplified by sharply rising wage dispersal. When these and other factors discussed in this chapter are taken into account, there is not much left of the ILO's claim that convergence has accelerated.

The improved growth of developing nations during the most recent decade, whose benefits have been disproportionately captured by capitalists, middle-class layers, and skilled workers, was made possible by the confluence of three factors: a particularly intense and broad-based outsourcing surge during the decade leading up to the onset of global crisis, the increased flow of capital driven south by ultra-low interest rates in the imperialist economies, and the "commodities supercycle"—a period of rising food and raw material prices beginning in 2002 that was fueled, in large part, by China's rapidly growing demand. Each of these are time-limited and are unlikely to endure: investment flows are fickle and have gone into reverse, sagging consumer markets in imperialist economies imply overproduction and an intensification of race-to-the-bottom competition among their suppliers, and China's breakneck growth has been fed by a huge expansion of debt, much of it used to finance unproductive investments, with the result that China's leaders are battling to avoid a "hard landing."

THIS CHAPTER HAS EXAMINED ONE of the most striking features of the past three decades—the sharp decline in labor's share of GDP on both sides of the North-South divide. Whether or not real wages have increased at all depends on where in the Global South you live; virtually nowhere are wages rising as fast as GDP. The chapter also examined the tendentious methodology used by official bodies to estimate labor's share of GDP, which perversely include super-wages and bonuses paid to bankers and bosses and the cost of the war in Afghanistan. It reported some of the reasons why official data on average wages should be treated with great caution, especially the poor quality of raw data, the biases that affect its probity, and the increased wage inequality within nations that mask important trends behind average figures. Finally, evidence was cited here of the extreme vulnerability of real wages and labor's share of GDP in times of crisis, whose frequency and intensity in Southern nations is set to increase as spreading economic depression blocks the road of export-oriented industrialization. The cozy convergence consensus is blind to the reality of workers in both developing and developed countries. They face an accelerated deterioration of living and working conditions, heightened insecurity, attacks on wages, job security, and (where they exist) social services. Capitalism is increasingly unable to satisfy the minimum social needs of large sections of the working population in imperialist nations and of the great majority of the working population of developing nations.

6

The Purchasing Power Anomaly and the Productivity Paradox

In the early 1990s, the World Bank and IMF started using PPP exchange rates—hypothetical exchange rates that equalize the prices of goods and services between economies—to enable international comparisons of wages, output, per capita GDP, spending on health. The size of the required adjustment to market exchange rates is substantial, and a great deal rests on the validity and accuracy of the purchasing power parity (PPP) conversion. Quite simply, without PPP exchange rates we would have no measuring stick with which to compare GDP, real wages, and consumption levels between different nations. The previous chapter examined some of the main sources of inaccuracy, bias, and distortion in the use of PPP exchange rates to measure the real incomes of workers and poor people. In this chapter we examine why the purchasing power anomaly exists in the first place, discovering that the key factors—restrictions on the free movement of labor across borders and wide variations in the rate of exploitation resulting from the high degree of autonomy of wages from productivity—are also key conditions for the rise of global labor arbitrage.

WHY DO MARKET EXCHANGE RATES UNDERVALUE "SOFT" CURRENCIES?

How to correct for the purchasing power anomaly is an unavoidably complex practical question. Of a different order entirely is the question: *Why* does the purchasing power anomaly exist between hard-currency and soft-currency nations? The ubiquity and persistence of this anomaly indicates that it cannot be explained by contingent or episodic causes such as protectionism, movements of hot money, government deficits and so forth, and that its causes must be sought in structural characteristics concerning the way in which Southern nations are inserted into the global economy. As we shall see, investigation of the purchasing power anomaly provides persuasive reasons to question the mainstream doctrine that international wage differentials are mere reflections of international differences in labor productivity, and it sheds light on the complex interaction between national and international economies, important for our goal of developing a concrete concept of the global labor-capital relation.

Reviewing "an enormous and ever growing empirical literature on PPP,"[1] Kenneth Rogoff noted in 1996 that "for many years researchers found it difficult to . . . prove that there was any convergence toward PPP in the long run. . . . [This] was something of an embarrassment. Every reasonable theoretical model suggests that there should be at least some temporary component to PPP deviations."[2] Wider and more detailed data coverage and the arrival of faster computers and more powerful statistical techniques have combined to spare the economists' blushes. As Rogoff remarked, "At long last, a number of recent studies have weighed in with fairly persuasive evidence that real exchange rates . . . tend toward purchasing power parity in the very long run."[3] More than a decade later and more of the picture has come into focus—and it is not kind to the PPP hypothesis.

Even between hard currencies, PPP is a feeble force. Robert Blecker notes that "relative PPP is routinely violated. . . . There are some exceptional cases in which PPP appears to hold . . . at least for [a] few major currencies . . . over extremely long time horizons."[4] Kenneth Rogoff asks, "How can one reconcile the enormous short-term volatility of real exchange rates with the extremely slow rate at which shocks appear to damp out?"[5] and calling this the "purchasing power parity puzzle."[6] To underline just how weakly the PPP hypothesis applies, Rogoff cites studies showing that "the relative prices of very similar goods across the U.S. and Canada are much more volatile than the relative prices of very different goods within either country."[7]

This, of course, is all very discomfiting to mainstream economists ideologically committed to to the "efficient market hypothesis." Whether or not the PPP hypothesis holds for exchanges between hard-currency nations, its failure in exchange rates between hard and soft currencies is undisputed. In their analysis of the long-run behavior of exchange rates of eighty developed and developing countries, Imed Drine and Christophe Rault found that what they call "strong PPP"—that is, a tendency for exchange rates to equalize price levels—was verified for OECD countries, but neither "strong" nor "weak" PPP (a tendency for the exchange rate, following a shock, to revert to a stable rate of exchange that is nevertheless displaced from purchasing power parity by unknown factors) could be validated for developing countries. Instead, they discovered "the absence of an equilibrium relationship between national prices, foreign prices and the exchange rate for developing countries, hence confirming that the PPP theory is empirically rejected. This result also confirms that PPP deviations are permanent."[8]

The North-South purchasing power anomaly is sometimes called the Penn effect, after the Penn World Table, which has gathered comparative price data from most countries in the world since 1950. This effect is inversely correlated with per-capita GDP; as Figure 5.2 (page 143) clearly shows, the poorer the nation, the bigger the gap. Mainstream neoclassical economics advances two chief explanations for this anomaly, the Balassa-Samuelson hypothesis,[9] which hinges on differences in labor productivity between rich and poor countries; and an alternative model, proposed by Jagdish Bhagwati, Irving Kravis, Richard Lipsey, and others, which claims to circumvent differences in labor productivity and accounts for the anomaly as the consequence of differences in "factor endowments," that is, the relative abundance of capital and labor in the two countries. Since their arguments are tautological, they arrive at the same conclusion. In the former approach, the relative productivity of labor and capital determines the demand for these two factors and, in conjunction with their supply, determines their equilibrium (market-clearing) prices. In the second approach, different factor endowments affect the supply and demand in markets for labor and capital, determining marginal productivities, so arriving at the other's starting point.

According to both approaches, the purchasing power anomaly arises because of the low wages of workers providing services (for example, a bus journey or a haircut), resulting in the prices of these services being typically much lower in, say, Bangladesh than in Belgium.[10] But equilibrium exchange rates do equalize the prices of internationally tradable goods—in other words, they assume that strong PPP holds in the tradable goods sector. Service sector wages are low in Bangladesh because wage levels in the service sector are determined by wage levels in the tradable goods sector. This occurs because labor is intersectorally mobile but not internationally mobile; in other words, workers can freely move between the tradable and non-tradable sectors within nations, equalizing wages between them, but cannot freely move across the borders between nations, especially those between hard-currency and soft-currency nations. It therefore turns out that the suppression of the free international movement of labor, the great exception to the principle of globalization and whose cardinal importance is stressed in this book, is also at the heart of the purchasing power anomaly.

The claim that wages in Southern nations' industry and agriculture—the "tradable goods" sector—are so miserably low because the productivity of these workers is a tiny fraction of that achieved by workers in developed countries like Belgium is a core tenet of mainstream theory. The strong consensus among mainstream economists is typified by this statement from *The Economist*: "Differences in wages reflect differences in productivity. Low wages in emerging economies go hand-in-hand with low productivity."[11]

The vast productivity differences alleged to exist in the tradable goods sector do not exist in the non-tradable sector. There is much less scope for technology-driven productivity differences in the non-tradable goods sector, many services being inherently labor-intensive. It is not easy for mainstream economists to argue that low wages of bus drivers in Bangladesh "go hand-in-hand with low productivity" and keep a straight face. Indeed, if Bangladesh's buses are more crowded, they may well be more productive. However, there is no connection between markets for haircuts in Bangladesh and in Belgium, no common process of price discovery. Only if Bangladeshi barbers and bus drivers were free to offer their services in Belgium, in other words if their living labor had the same freedom to move as tradable commodities, would these two markets be connected; only this could give rise to a process of wage and price equalization. In the circumstances created by the suppression of free mobility of labor, wages between Bangladesh and Belgium can therefore, according to the Balassa-Samuelson hypothesis, be determined by relative productivities in the tradable sector.

In sum, the Balassa-Samuelson hypothesis says that the purchasing power anomaly results from the lack of correspondence between the similar levels of productivity of service workers in Belgium and Bangladesh and the vast differences in their wages. The contrary argument advanced here is that it is the oversupply of labor, not its productivity, that is the prime determinant of Southern wage levels. Wages of service providers and incomes of petty entrepreneurs are kept low not by the paltry productivity of workers in the tradable goods sector, as mainstream theory has it, but by the destitution of a large part of the working population. This is why a haircut or a bus journey in Dhaka is so much cheaper than in Amsterdam, even though a pair of scissors or a bus may cost the same in both countries, and may even have come off the same production line. Furthermore, local capitalists are not the prime beneficiaries of the super-profits generated by this expanded employment of low-wage labor. Instead, intense competition among Southern exporters leaves them with only a minor share of the proceeds, the rest passed on to their northern customers through ever-lower export prices. The purchasing power anomaly results not only or mainly from conditions in goods and Forex markets but is fundamentally the product of conditions in labor markets and in the sphere of production where this labor is put to work. The enormous growth in the relative surplus population combines with suppression of international labor mobility to exert a tremendous downward pressure on all wages and on the incomes of small producers, maintaining or widening still further the distance between real wages in the imperialist nations and in the Global South.

PPP and the Productivity Paradox

The fatal flaw at the heart of the mainstream explanation for the purchasing power anomaly is to be found in economists' conception of productivity. Labor productivity in capitalist society can be defined in two antithetical, mutually exclusive ways: in terms of its productivity of use-values and its productivity of exchange-values, or, to use the economists' terminology, "value added." The former is a universal definition of labor productivity that applies in all societies and modes of production; the latter is specific to commodity-producing societies and becomes supreme in capitalism. Capitalists and neoclassical economists are not interested in the use-value or volume definition of productivity—the rate at which living labor transforms nature to satisfy social needs. Only the value or value-added definition matters—the rate at which living labor satisfies the private needs of capitalists to make profits.

Occasionally, practical economists acknowledge the contradictory nature of productivity, as in this passage from the ILO's *World Employment Report 2004–5*:

> Productivity can be understood in terms of *value* as well as *volume*.
> For example, if for whatever reason the value of the final product

increases (an increase in its price with no increase in the cost of inputs), this in money terms is an increase in productivity. It can even be imagined that productivity could increase in volume terms, e.g. more coffee beans picked with the same number of workers, but decline in value terms through plummeting market prices, as has indeed happened in the case of coffee. Thus, higher physical productivity can result in lower earnings and incomes rather than higher ones.

The first sentence in this quote from the ILO provokes two comments. First, by *value* they mean *value added*. To the neoclassical mainstream, the two are synonymous; through a Marxist lens these are revealed to be two distinct categories, the first signifying value created, the second signifying value captured. The second is to appreciate the sheer nerve of the ILO's statement that productivity "can be understood in terms of value as well as volume." The *only* definition of value that matters to capitalists, and the only one that is ever used by governments and IFIs to measure productivity, is the value-added definition. For all practical purposes, from compiling GDP data to making investment decisions, the value-added definition of productivity is universally taken to be correct while the volume definition is discarded. In other words, the incompatible yet inseparable definitions of productivity are conflated in the neoclassical account, subordinated to a measure exclusively based on the ability to attract money in the marketplace.

In terms of its productivity of use-values, the labor of Bangladeshi barbers and bus drivers is no less productive than that of their Belgian counterparts. But when we consider the exchange-value of their product, the quantity of money with which haircuts or bus journeys in Belgium and in Bangladesh are equated, we obtain a very different result—barbers and bus drivers in Belgium produce far more value added than in Bangladesh. Both definitions are true, even though they contradict each other, even though, according to the formal logic that hobbles bourgeois economics, one of them must be false.

This allows us to see a glaring inconsistency at the heart of the Balassa-Samuelson hypothesis. It uses a value-added definition of productivity to reach its conclusion that the productivity of workers in the tradable goods sector in countries such as Bangladesh is lamentably low, and it switches to a volume definition of productivity to rationalize its perception that the productivity of Bangladeshi service workers is similar to that of their Belgian counterparts.

From within the mainstream Jagdish Bhagwati, Irving Kravis, Richard Lipsey, and others have advanced an alternative model that claims to explain the purchasing power anomaly without any reference to differences in labor productivity. Instead, the anomaly results from differences in "factor endowments."[12] The relative scarcity of capital and abundance of labor in poor countries give them a natural advantage in the production of labor-intensive services, lowering their prices relative to prices of manufactured goods. As in Balassa-Samuelson, the prices of manufactured goods are equalized through international competition, but not so the prices of services—hence the title of Bhagwati's seminal paper, "Why are services cheaper in poor countries?" They both agree that because labor is mobile between sectors but not between nations that wages in the service sector are determined by wages in the tradable goods sector, and in particular by wage levels in manufacturing industry, which provides the bulk of traded goods. They both implicitly accept that PPP holds in the traded goods sector. They both implement a comparative advantage framework that rests on two dubious premises: that all "factors of production" (labor and capital) are fully employed (known as Say's Law, after the early nineteenth century French economist Jean-Baptiste Say), and that neither capital nor labor is mobile between countries. The main difference between the two is that Bhagwati et al. seek to go "beyond the excessively limiting Ricardian framework of a single factor, labor," and introduce capital as a separate factor of production with a productivity all its own.[13]

Bhagwati et al.'s emphasis on factor endowments opens the interesting possibility that Bangladesh may be overendowed with a limitless supply of people desperate for work, and that it is this oversupply that explains why wages are so low, not the productivity of those in work. This would imply that wages are depressed far below marginal productivity, and gives rise to a notion of exploitation, since it would mean that Bangladeshi workers are not fully compensated for their product. Bhagwati et al. are rescued from this dangerous notion by their impressive faith in Say's Law, that is, that everything produced for sale will be sold, including living labor, and thus that more and more workers will be drawn into employment until, at equilibrium, workers' wages are equalized with their marginal productivities.

Investigation of the purchasing power anomaly helps to reveal the existence of two contradictory dimensions of labor productivity. In the case of industrial production, mainstream neoclassical economics is able to ignore the contradictory nature of labor productivity by ascribing value-creating powers to machines, but in labor-intensive services this is not possible. The technologies utilized by barbers and bus drivers, namely scissors and diesel engines, are similar in both countries. Things get considerably more complex when we turn to analyze the productivity of industrial workers in the two countries, whose relative capacities to produce both use-values and exchange-values are significantly affected by differences in the technologies they set in motion. But the same contradictory definition of productivity applies to the labor of industrial workers as it does to service workers.

THE PRODUCTIVITY PARADOX

> If economists were to play a game of word association, the one that would leap to mind on hearing *productivity* would be *puzzle.*
>
> —DIANE COYLE

Statistics on labor productivity, obtained by dividing the value added of a firm, industrial sector, or nation by its total workforce, are highly deceptive. Much of the alleged increase in labor productivity in the imperialist nations is an artifact resulting from the outsourcing of low value-added, labor-intensive production processes to low-wage countries. As Susan Houseman has argued, "When manufacturers outsource or offshore work, labor productivity increases directly because the outsourced or offshored labor used to produce the product is no longer employed in the manufacturing sector and hence is not counted in the denominator of the labor productivity equation."[14] This is extremely important, because "the rate of productivity growth in U.S. manufacturing increased in the mid-1990s, greatly outpacing that in the services sector and accounting for most of the overall productivity growth in the U.S. economy."[15] Thus she argues, "To the extent that offshoring is an important source of measured productivity growth in the economy, productivity statistics will, in part, be capturing cost savings or gains to trade but not improvements in the output of American labor."[16] Houseman believes this solves

> one of the great puzzles of the American economy in recent years . . . the fact that large productivity gains have not broadly benefited workers in the form of higher wages. . . . Productivity improvements that result from offshoring may largely measure cost savings, not improvements to output per hour worked by American labor.[17]

Thus, when a firm outsources labor-intensive production processes, the productivity of the workers who remain in its employment rises, even though nothing about their specific labor has changed. Outsourcing therefore has what might be called a "ventriloquist effect" on measures of productivity. But this only scratches the surface of the productivity paradox. Labor-intensive production processes are practically synonymous with low value-added production processes, yet the more labor-intensive it is, that is, the larger living labor is relative to dead labor, the greater is its contribution to value and surplus value—but much of this is captured by capital-intensive capitals, showing up as a much higher value added per worker.

Productivity, Industry, and Services

One aspect of the distinction between industry and services of great significance to our subject is that many service tasks, for example, hairdressing and bus-driving, are inherently labor-intensive and are therefore far less susceptible to productivity-enhancing capital investments than is the case in manufacturing industry. For this reason, labor productivity tends to advance much faster in industry than in services, signifying an innate tendency toward a relative decline in manufacturing employment.[18] One paradoxical result of this is that the faster that labor productivity in manufacturing industry advances relative to the economy as a whole, the more rapidly does industry's contribution to GDP decline. This differential pace of productivity advances between industry and services is known to mainstream economics as the Baumol effect (later renamed the Baumol disease), after William Baumol's seminal paper in 1967.[19] Baumol complained that within-country labor mobility between industry and services means that wage levels in the service sector are determined by those in industry, and industrial wages are in turn, according to the marginalist economic theory that Baumol promotes, equalized by market forces with the value of labor's product.[20] In other words, service-sector wages are determined not by the productivity of service-sector workers but by the productivity of workers in industry, and wage increases justified by the rising productivity of industrial workers are not justified by the stagnant productivity of services workers. Baumol illustrated his point by contrasting the enormous leap in the productivity of pencil-makers with the zero productivity growth of chamber musicians. Four musicians are required to perform a Beethoven string quartet today, the same number as two hundred years ago, yet their wages have risen along with those of the pencil-makers, whose output of pencils has leapt in quantity and very likely also in quality. The musicians' wages, therefore, violate a cardinal rule of bourgeois economics—that labor is awarded according to the value of its product.

What is a perplexing paradox from the perspective of bourgeois economics is, from the perspective of Marxist value theory, a simple puzzle. Marx counted among the greatest of his discoveries *"the twofold character of labor, according to whether it is expressed in use-value or exchange-value."*[21] To the twofold character of labor there corresponds the twofold character of the productivity of labor, the other of which is particular to commodity-producing society, of which capitalism is the highest expression. The universal definition of labor productivity, true for human society in all its stages of development, is the quantity of use-values that can be produced by a day or a week of living labor. But capitalists are not interested in pencils, or even in how long it takes to produce one; they are only interested in how much money these pencils can be exchanged for. From this flows an entirely different concept and measure of productivity: how much the firm's value added (the market value of the firm's output minus the market value of all inputs) is increased by one hour, day, or week, etc., of labor.

The utility, or use-value, of a pencil is the same today as two centuries ago (or higher, thanks to superior pencil lead and the like), yet the quantity of labor necessary to produce each one is now many magnitudes smaller. Measured in terms of use-values, there has been a colossal leap in productivity, but measured in terms of exchange-value, it is moot whether productivity has grown at all. The two definitions of labor productivity yield divergent and contradictory results. From the point of view of society as a whole, the use-value definition of productivity, that is, how many socially useful goods or services can be produced with a given amount of labor, is of supreme importance. But it is of supreme indifference to capitalists who are interested only in how much they can be sold for. The two definitions are incompatible, mutually contradictory, yet they are both true.[22] The economists' utility functions attempt to convert use-values into numbers, but they are by definition incommensurable. Just as there is no objective way of comparing the utility of a pencil with that of a string quartet, neither can the productivity of a pencil-maker be measured against that of a musician. If, for example, one million hours of the living labor of shipbuilders is required to produce one ship, and the same amount of living labor of agricultural workers results in one million boxes of strawberries, which of these workers is the most productive? The shipbuilder, because ships are so much bigger than strawberries, or the strawberry picker, because there's so many more strawberries than ships? The answer: it would be absurd to even attempt to make such comparison, since the exchange-value generated by their labor is determined by its quantity, not its particular form. As Marx pointed out, "Productivity . . . naturally ceases to have any bearing on that labor as soon as we abstract from its concrete useful form."[23] In other words, some shipbuilders may be more productive than other shipbuilders and some fruit-pickers fill boxes faster than others, but it cannot be said that shipbuilders are more or less productive than fruit-pickers.[24]

Productivity and Unit Labor Cost

Marx's concept of value is a unity of the two opposing poles of use-value and exchange-value contained in the social form we call a commodity. Corresponding with these two contradictory dimensions of value are two diametrically opposed definitions of labor, and therefore of productivity: one according to the quantity and quality of useful objects produced by this labor; the second according to the sum of the prices achieved by these useful objects when they are marketed and sold.

The universal definition of labor productivity, one that applies to human society in all its stages of development, is the quantity of use-values, the number of cars, pencils, kilos of grain, etc., it produces in a given time, which in turn is a function of labor intensity, technology, and social organization. The reign of capital superimposes upon this a new and antithetical definition: productivity is now the amount of value added that can be harvested for each unit of value paid in wages. If wages are cut and everything else remains the same, labor becomes more productive—more productive, that is, of capital, despite being no more productive of use-values. As Marx explained in *Capital*, vol. 1 :

> Looked at from the simple standpoint of the *labor process*, labor seemed *productive* if it realized itself in a *product*, or rather a commodity. From the standpoint of capitalist production we may add the qualification that labor is productive if it directly valorises capital, or creates surplus value. . . . The worker who performs *productive work* is *productive* and the work he performs is productive if it directly creates *surplus-value*, i.e. if it *valorises* capital.[25]

At this level of abstraction—leaving to one side, for instance, the distinction between productive and non-productive labor—and considering not just a single commodity but all of those against which its value is being measured, the ratio of the value of the product to the value paid as wages is nothing else and nothing less than the rate of exploitation. The meaning of productivity has therefore been eviscerated and has become nothing more and nothing less than a euphemism for exploitation: the more workers are exploited, the more productive they are:

> Capitalist production is not merely the production of commodities, it is essentially the production of surplus-value. The worker produces, not for himself, but for capital. It no longer suffices, therefore, that he should simply produce. He must produce surplus-value. That worker alone is productive who produces surplus-value for the capitalist, and thus works for the self-expansion of capital. . . . Hence the notion of a productive worker implies not merely a relation between work and useful effect, between worker and product of labor, but also a specific, social relation of production.[26]

The reigning definition of productivity, the one that really matters to capitalists, is not labor productivity, obtained by dividing the total value added by the total workforce, it is unit labor cost, obtained by dividing the total value added by the *cost* of the total workforce. Unit labor cost, the format preferred by practical economists, is the inverse of this, that is, how much labor must be purchased to obtain a one unit increase of output.[27]

Unit labor cost is premised on a value-added definition of productivity and shares all of its fallacies. According to neoclassical theory and various authorities cited here, the correlation between wages and marginal product means that ULCs in rich and poor countries are broadly the same. As Robert Blecker has noted, "Complaints about low-wage labor (sometimes referred to as the 'sweatshop labor argument') are routinely dismissed as illogical because, if trade follows comparative advantages à la Ricardo, relative wages merely track relative productivities, and therefore no country can gain an overall competitive advantage in average unit labor costs."[28]

An example of such a routine dismissal was provided by Martin Wolf, who argues in *Why Globalization Works* that "the evidence on the relationship between productivity and wages is overwhelming."[29] Yet the only evidence Wolf cites to justify his belief that workers north and south only get what they deserve is research by Stephen Golub, a U.S. economics professor who helped develop the IMF's theoretical and methodological approach to labor productivity and labor's share of GDP. Disputing Golub's claim that unit labor costs in rich and poor countries are more or less equal,[30] Larudee et al. point out:[31]

> The data—much of it gathered and published by Golub and his co-authors—simply do not support these conclusions. The available evidence indicates quite clearly that average ULCs [unit labor costs] are *not* equal across countries. Indeed, labor cost gaps among countries appear to be quite common. In some cases these gaps are quite large.

Reviewing this evidence, these researchers find that unit labor costs in low-wage countries are often less than half of those in rich countries, and provisionally conclude that "there is a correlation between GDP per capita and low ULCs; that is, ULCs in poor countries tend to be lower than ULCs in rich countries,"[32] contradicting Golub's much-cited assertion that "low wages are a symptom of low productivity, not an independent source of international competitiveness."[33] Indeed, in a staff study for the IMF co-written with Anthony Turner, Golub refutes his own theory: "To the extent that capital and intermediate goods are traded in international markets, whereas labor remains largely immobile internationally, labor costs are likely to diverge much more across countries than other costs of production, and therefore play a disproportionately important role in competitiveness."[34] The implication is that wage differences are significantly affected by coercive suppression of labor mobility—in other words, by a factor that is, on the face of it, quite independent of productivity. Yet, far from attempting to estimate the distorting effect of this extra-economic factor, Golub dismisses it with the argument that "differences in productivity explain 70–80 percent of the international variation in rates of labor compensation."[35] But even 20 to 30 percent is a big deal to those on the breadline.

So, the raw data on unit labor costs do *not* provide the "overwhelming proof" claimed by Wolf that differences in wages between high-wage and low-wage countries track differences in their productivity, even when using standard value-added data, which obscures at least as much as it reveals. Figure 6.3 displays World Bank data that shows that, in the matter of unit labor costs, as in so much else, the earth is not flat. But the case against Wolf and other proponents of mainstream orthodoxy does not stop there. There are many reasons to suspect that official data overestimates unit labor costs in developing countries, and that the discrepancies reported by Larudee et al. are much wider. In the first place, the data used to compute ULCs suffer from the biases and distortions affecting wage data investigated in the last chapter. Larudee et al. also argue that the TNCs' widespread practice of using "transfer pricing to reduce their tax liability . . . means productivity in low-wage countries is likely to be substantially understated."[36]

A final reason, on its own enough to refute the mainstream view that unit labor costs in the Global South are not substantially out of line with unit labor costs in the imperialist countries, is Wolf et al.'s implicit assumption that the productivity of workers in a TNC subsidiary operating in a low-wage economy is no different from the average productivity of workers in that country. But, as Larudee et al. emphasize, "There is abundant empirical evidence that multinational firms' productivity levels often exceed those of local firms in underdeveloped countries. . . . Firms carry a considerable share of their productivity with them."[37] In other words, TNCs can take advantage of low wages but do not need to accept prevailing productivity levels, enabling them to reap super-profits. This fact alone—that productivity is, to a considerable extent, firm-specific—fatally undermines Martin Wolf's strident assertion that "an irresistibly competitive China is a figment of the fevered imagination, since the real cost of labor will tend to remain in line with its productivity."[38] He backs this up by a reference to Golub's research—but on this specific issue Golub flatly contradicts Wolf (and his own writings of a decade before): "Given the attention focused on Chinese wages, RULC [relative unit labor costs] are a very prominent candidate for explaining China's booming exports of manufactures"[39]; and he concludes, "Our measures indicate that . . . Chinese unit labor costs in manufacturing are very low relative to a wide range of other countries."[40]

That productivity is, to a considerable extent, firm-specific fatally undermines Martin Wolf's assertion, in his 2005 book *Why Globalization Works*, that "the real cost of labor tend[s] to remain in line with its productivity."[41] Ridiculing the very idea that Chinese workers are exploited by the United States and UK firms they are directly or indirectly working for, Wolf argued, "It is right to say that transnational companies exploit their Chinese workers in the hope of making profits. It is equally right to say that Chinese workers are exploiting transnationals in the (almost universally fulfilled) hope of obtaining higher pay, better training and more opportunities."[42] In the same year, the ICFTU reported that "the

FIGURE 6.1: Labor Productivity and Labor Cost, 1995–1999

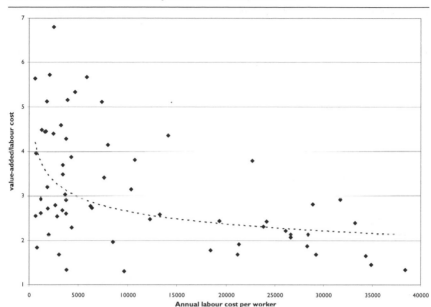

Source: World Bank, World Development Indicators 2006.

people who provide everything from T-shirts to DVD players to the world's consumers often have 60–70-hour working weeks, live in dormitories with eight to 16 people in each room, earn less than the minimum wages that go as low as $44 per month, and have unemployment as the only prospect if they should get injured in the factories."[43]

Figure 6.1 explores the relationship between value added per worker in manufacturing and labor cost per worker in manufacturing over a five-year period for the 64 countries covered by the World Bank's Data for World Development Indicators.[44] Table 6.1 (p. 183) presents this data in tabular form. Labor cost is wages plus other costs associated with employment—for example, national insurance contributions. In Figure 6.1, each marker represents a country. The x-axis is the annual labor cost per worker; the y-axis is the unit labor cost: the ratio of value-added per worker to labor cost per worker.

The wages-equals-productivity theory thus fails the test of external validity. There is a lack of correspondence between the uniform ULCs predicted by the theory and empirical evidence. However, my argument goes much further than this. The mainstream, dominant concept of productivity, which even has many Marxists in thrall, fails the test of internal validity as well. In a word, the concept of ULCs, and the methodology used to compile them, is incoherent. Unable to give expression to the living contradiction between use-value and exchange-value, mainstream theory attempts to repress it, to conflate the two definitions of value, but the tensions reappear in the form of insoluble paradoxes.

If it was true that labor is rewarded in proportion to its contribution to value added, and if the capital-labor ratio is the same in rich and poor countries we would expect the trend line shown in Figure 6.3 to be flat. To the extent that labor costs are a smaller fraction of total production costs in the capital-intensive industries typical of developed countries, one would expect value added per worker to increase faster than labor cost per worker, and therefore the value added per worker/labor cost per worker ratio would *rise* as we move along the X-axis toward countries with more expensive labor. Instead, as Figure 6.1 shows, the opposite is the case.

In light of all these considerations, the consensus view that international differentials in real wages reflect international differentials in productivity is, in Golub's own words, "an article of faith" at odds with empirical evidence. It also conflicts with reason. If unit labor costs in China, Bangladesh, and Morocco are in line with those of Belgium, Japan, and the United States, why would TNCs based in imperialist countries go to such trouble to relocate production to these low-wage countries?

Unit Labor Cost Unmasked

As discussed above, a ULC calculated for an entire national economy is nothing else than labor's share of GDP, or as Jesus Felipe and Utsav Kumar put it, "Unit labor costs calculated with aggregate data are no more than the economy's labor share in total output multiplied by a price effect." [45] In an earlier paper, Felipe explained the implication of this: "In standard analyses, an economy is deemed more competitive the lower its ULC is. The flip side of this line of reasoning is that an economy is more competitive the lower its labor share is. . . . Policies to lower ULCs are, effectively, polices to lower the share of labor in income." [46] The desired effect—increasing competitiveness by reducing unit labor costs—can be achieved by increasing productivity or by repressing wages, or by a combination of the two. Either way, whether output is increasing or not, any reduction in unit labor costs implies an increase in capital's relative share of total output.

Unit labor costs are increasingly regarded as the ultimate criterion of a firm's or nation's competitiveness, namely the Europe debate, where economists agree that whether through productivity improvements or through wage repression ULCs in Greece, Spain, and other peripheral countries must be lowered, whether or not these nations stay in the Eurozone. This exclusive focus on labor productivity, with its implication

TABLE 6.1: Value-Added vs. Labor Cost, 1995–1999

	Labor cost per worker in manufacturing	Ratio of value added to labor cost		Labor cost per worker in manufacturing	Ratio of value added to labor cost
Sri Lanka	604	5.64	Chile	5,822	5.66
Bangladesh	671	2.55	Portugal	6,237	2.77
China	729	3.96	Panama	6,351	2.73
Kenya	810	1.04	Argentina	7,338	5.11
Romania	1,190	2.93	Mexico	7,607	3.41
India	1,192	2.62	Turkey	7,958	4.14
Yemen, Rep.	1,291	4.48	South Africa	8,475	1.96
Ethiopia	1,596	4.44	Slovenia	9,632	1.30
Poland	1,714	4.46	Hong Kong	10,353	3.15
Guatemala	1,802	5.12	Korea, Rep.	10,743	3.81
Egypt	1,863	3.21	Greece	12,296	2.47
Slovakia	1,876	2.72	Iraq	13,288	2.58
Mauritius	1,973	2.14	Brazil	14,134	4.36
Jordan	2,082	5.72	New Zealand	18,419	1.78
Philippines	2,450	4.40	Spain	19,329	2.43
Colombia	2,507	6.81	Israel	21,150	1.68
Honduras	2,658	2.79	Singapore	21,317	1.91
Costa Rica	2,829	2.54	Ireland	22,681	3.79
Indonesia	3,054	1.68	United Kingdom	23,843	2.31
Paraguay	3,241	4.59	Belgium	24,132	2.43
Morocco	3,391	2.68	Australia	26,087	2.22
Zimbabwe	3,422	3.49	Sweden	26,601	2.13
Malaysia	3,429	3.69	Finland	26,615	2.07
Jamaica	3,655	3.03	Austria	28,342	1.87
Ecuador	3,738	2.61	Canada	28,424	2.14
Uruguay	3,738	4.29	United States	28,907	2.81
Hungary	3,755	2.91	Denmark	29,235	1.69
Czech Rep.	3,815	1.34	Japan	31,687	2.92
Thailand	3,868	5.16	Germany	33,226	2.40
Zambia	4,292	3.87	Netherlands	34,326	1.65
Syria	4,338	2.29	Italy	34,859	1.46
Venezuela	4,667	5.33	Norway	38,415	1.34

Source: World Development Indicators 2006.

that labor is the sole source of value added and national prosperity, seems to give a backhanded compliment to the otherwise derided labor theory of value. What's happened to capital, and its supposed contribution to value added and total output? How do the economists reconcile exclusive attention given to labor costs and labor productivity with the doctrine that labor is just one among several factors of production? Furthermore, this unblinking focus on labor contrasts with the treatment of labor cost and value added in national accounts. In the accounting identity at the heart of the National Income and Product Accounts (NIPA), total value added is by definition equal to total wages plus total profits. So—and this is the second key point advanced by Felipe and Kumar—why not apply the marginalist logic underlying ULCs to the other factor of production, and calculate unit capital costs? "Analysis of competitiveness could be equally carried out in terms of what could be defined as the *unit capital cost* (UKC) The notion of UKC shifts the burden of competitiveness onto capital, i.e., to become more competitive, capitalists have to accept lower profit rates or increase the productivity of the capital invested." [47]

From the standpoint of the ruling economic theory, the exclusion of capital from the concept of competitiveness is arbitrary and absurd. [48] But it is also highly convenient; it allows capitalists and governments to concentrate attention on how to use labor more efficiently, how to bear down on labor costs, etc., and to treat investment decisions, profits, and their distribution as private matters, unconnected with the drive to boost competitiveness and productivity.

The standard justification for the exclusive attention to ULCs is that because capital is far more internationally mobile than labor, the cost of capital varies far less between countries than the cost of labor. Thus a team of Cambridge economists explains: "From the perspective of competitiveness, we are interested in those costs . . . that differ from one country to another. . . . Clearly, a focus on labor costs neglects all other . . . costs, some of which may show important cross-country differences. However, labor costs do account for a substantial element of non-traded inputs to production." [49]

Later in their paper they underline the central point, that the cost of labor is singled out because it is a major input and because its price varies wildly between countries: "While labor costs by no means dominate the cost structure of manufacturing subsectors, they remain more important for the competitiveness of different geographical locations than this statistic might suggest, because they are *an important cost element which varies between those locations.*" [50]

Felipe and Kumar's two papers also provide insights into how unit labor costs may be understood from the perspective of Marx's theory of value. They were cited above as saying: "Unit labor costs calculated with aggregate data are no more than the economy's labor share in total output multiplied by a price effect." It was immediately followed by this: "While this is true also at the firm (product) level, the difference is that at the aggregate level, one cannot calculate unit labor costs without using an aggregate price deflator. This is not true at the product level with physical data."[51]

This price deflator is a purchasing power parity adjustment (or PPP's sector-specific close relative, the UVR or unit value ratio)[52] applied to the value of output, as academics at the University of Groningen explain:[53]

> A specific characteristic of unit labor cost measures is that the *numerator*, which reflects the labor cost component of the equation, is typically expressed in nominal terms, whereas the *denominator*, which is output or productivity, is measured in real or volume terms. This implies that, when comparing unit labor cost levels across countries, the level of wages or labor compensation is converted at the official exchange rate. . . . In contrast, output or productivity relates to a *volume* measure as it resembles a *quantity unit* of output. Hence for level comparisons output needs to be converted to a common currency using a purchasing power parity instead of the exchange rate, so that comparative output levels are adjusted for differences in relative prices across countries.[54]

So, a curious and paradoxical feature of unit labor costs is that while wages are converted into the *numeraire* currency at market exchange rates, output uses PPP- or UVR-adjusted exchange rates—yet both are necessary conditions for unit labor costs between countries to be compared. The paradox arises from the fact that the living labor that produces commodities is not itself traded across national borders—as we have discussed, the commodity labor power is internationally immobile. Furthermore, labor power is the only commodity that is not produced by capitalists—they purchase it from its owner. The capitalists are therefore only interested in the price of labor power at market exchange rates, which corresponds directly to the costs of its (re)production. On the other hand, the commodities produced by this living labor are traded across frontiers—if they weren't, there would be no point in computing their international competitiveness. As far as their value is concerned,

their competitiveness is not determined directly by their actual nation-
ally- or sectorally-specific costs of production, but by the exchange-value
they command in global markets, that is, by their average socially-nec-
essary costs of production. Use of PPP- or UVR-adjusted exchange rates
signify the conversion of the former into the latter. Finally, the academics
at GroniNgen introduce confusion when they say "output or productivity relates to a *volume* measure as it resembles a *quantity unit* of output."
No—by "output" they mean value added, and by "productivity" they
mean value added per worker, both of which are value measures, not
volume measures. Their terminology is yet another example of the inability of bourgeois economists to recognize the fundamental difference
between—and contradiction between—use-value and exchange-value,
and the two antithetical definitions of productivity corresponding to
them, as discussed earlier in this chapter.

THIS CHAPTER BEGAN WITH A CRITICAL EVALUATION of mainstream explanations for the large and persistent purchasing power
anomaly between imperialist and low-wage nations. These explanations insist, as an article of faith, that international wage differentials are
determined by international differences in the productivity of labor, a
doctrine that leaves unresolved a series of paradoxes and anomalies but
is marvelously successful in making exploitation of workers by capitalists
and of poor nations by rich nations disappear without trace. Our investigation therefore led to an interrogation of the marginalist theory of
value on which mainstream theories of productivity rest, which began to
reveal its secrets under questioning. In so doing the chapter showed the
need for a theory of value and productivity that starts from a recognition
of the "twofold character of labor, according to whether it is expressed
in use value or exchange value," the starting point for Marx's theory of
value. The necessity for reengagement with Marx's theory was thereby
established, but this must also be done critically, and no less severely, by
testing it and validating it against facts about today's imperialist world
economy not anticipated by Marx in his great work. This task will be
addressed in the next two chapters, which begin by analyzing the sin-
glemost important empirical fact uncovered in this study: global labor
arbitrage, the fundamental driving force of the globalization of production, the defining feature of the neoliberal era.

—— 7 ——

Global Labor Arbitrage: The Key Driver of the Globalization of Production

Half of the world's labour force is working in poverty, socially and economically excluded from globalization except that their meager earnings serve as a brake on the market wage for unskilled labour in developing countries. Gender and other forms of discrimination remain widespread. And while skilled workers have greater opportunities to move within and between countries in search of better rewards, their mobility is also restricted. The interaction between this emerging but highly fragmented global labour market and the increasingly open markets for products and finance is a major driver of change in the world of work.
                    —INTERNATIONAL LABOUR ORGANIZATION[1]

So far we have surveyed and analyzed a mass of empirical data on many aspects and dimensions of the transformation of production and of the producers during the era of neoliberal globalization. Along the way, we have recorded anomalies and paradoxes left unexplained by mainstream accounts and we have subjected the methodologies and conceptual underpinnings of standard statistical data to critical evaluation, thereby opening up a critique of the fundamental premises of mainstream economic theory. A mass of evidence and argument brings into question the assertions of mainstream and Euro-Marxist economists that wage differences reflect productivity differences, at least for the workers we met in chapter 1 who harvest our coffee, assemble the gadgets in our pockets, and make the T-shirts on our backs. We have seen, in fact, that their concept of productivity is itself deeply flawed. This chapter marks the transition from analysis of the separate elements to synthesis, and to the generation, in outline at least, of a value theory of imperialism. We focus first on the fundamental driver and shaper of the globalization of production—*global labor arbitrage*, or the substitution of relatively high-wage workers in imperialist countries with low-wage workers in China, Bangladesh, and other nations in the Global South.[2] The second task is to consider how global labor arbitrage may be explained in terms of the law of value.

The first section below critically evaluates the usage of global labor arbitrage by mainstream economists, and considers how modern trade theory explains this phenomenon. The second section considers how contemporary Marxist scholars most associated with theories of the new imperialism explain it, in particular Ellen Wood and David Harvey. It examines the 1960s and 1970s debate between dependency theorists and orthodox Marxists, mainly based in Europe. This is important because this was the last time that imperialism and the law of value were at the center of a wide-ranging debate, and because the debate left unanswered questions that have only grown in importance in the decades since.

GLOBAL LABOR ARBITRAGE: AN INCREASINGLY URGENT SURVIVAL TACTIC

By uprooting hundreds of millions of workers and farmers in Southern nations from their ties to the land and their jobs in protected national industries, neoliberal capitalism has accelerated the expansion of a vast pool of super-exploitable labor. Suppression of its free movement across borders has interacted with this hugely increased supply to produce a dramatic widening of international wage differentials between industrialized and developing nations, vastly exceeding price differences in all other global markets.[3] This steep wage gradient provides two different ways for Northern capitalists to increase profits: through the emigration of production to low-wage countries, or the immigration of low-wage migrant workers for exploitation at home. The IMF's *World Economic Outlook 2007*, which included a special study of labor and globalization, made the connection between outsourcing and migration quite precisely: "The global pool of labor can be accessed by advanced economies through imports and immigration," significantly observing that "trade is the more important and faster-expanding channel, in large part because immigration remains very restricted in many countries."[4]

What the IMF calls accessing the global labor pool others have dubbed global labor arbitrage (sometimes global wage arbitrage), whose essential feature, according to Stephen Roach, the economist most associated with this term, is the substitution of "high-wage workers here with like-quality, low-wage workers abroad."[5] Roach, then a senior economist at Morgan Stanley responsible for its Asian operations, argued that "a unique and powerful confluence of three mega-trends is driving the global arbitrage." These are "the maturation of offshore outsourcing platforms . . . E-based connectivity . . . [and] the new imperatives of cost control."[6] Of these, cost control—by which Roach means wages—is the most important, "the catalyst that brings the global labor arbitrage to life." The first two mega-trends, in other words, merely provide the necessary conditions for the third, profiting from ultra-low wages, to express itself. Expanding on this, Roach explains:

> In an era of excess supply, companies lack pricing leverage as never before. As such, businesses must be unrelenting in their search for new efficiencies. Not surprisingly, the primary focus of such efforts is labor, representing the bulk of production costs in the developed world; in the U.S., for example, worker compensation still makes up nearly 80% of total domestic corporate income. And that's the point: Wage rates in China and India range from 10% to 25% of those for comparable-quality workers in the U.S. and the rest of the developed world. Consequently, *offshore outsourcing that extracts product from relatively low-wage workers in the developing world has become an increasingly urgent survival tactic for companies in the developed economies.*[7]

This is a much sharper and richer description of neoliberal globalization's driving force than the one offered above by the IMF technocrats. We might ask, though, why does Roach say extracting product instead of extracting value? Capitalists, after all, are not interested in the product of labor but in the value contained in it. The answer, we suspect, is that extracting value would make it even more explicit that these low-wage workers create more wealth than they receive as wages, in other words, that they are exploited. This implication of Roach's argument cracks the very foundations of modern economic theory, which has no room for any notion of exploitation, and opens the door to Marx's critique, which is founded on recognition of a systematic divergence between the value generated by a worker and the value s/he receives in the form of a wage; the difference between the two being *surplus-value,* the source and substance of profit in all its forms.

Roach's insightful observation also begs the same question that caught our attention in chapter 3. Given that the only visible flow of profits are those repatriated from direct investments, excluding the increasingly favored arm's-length, contractual relation with independent suppliers, exactly how do companies in the developed economies extract product from low-wage workers?

That capitalist firms seek to boost profits by cutting wages is hardly a startling revelation. Workers don't need Stephen Roach to tell them this. Indeed, Roach's advice is not intended to alert workers to the challenges they face but to advise capitalists what they need to do more of. Nor is Stephen Roach alone in according primacy to the voracious appetite of capitalists for low-wage labor. Other analysts who have given currency to the term and concept of global labor arbitrage include Charles Whalen, a prominent labor economist, who has argued that "the prime motivation behind offshoring is the desire to reduce labor costs. . . . A U.S.-based factory worker hired for $21 an hour can be replaced by a Chinese factory worker who is paid 64 cents an hour,"[8] setting in motion what he called "global wage arbitrage." David Levy, another international business scholar, also recognizes that what he calls the "new wave of offshoring . . . is a much more direct form of arbitrage in international labor markets, whereby firms are able to shift work to wherever wages are lower."[9] Roach's views receive the attention given to them in this book because of their large international audience and because he goes further than most in analyzing why wage arbitrage is the force that gives life to outsourcing. Roach's emphasis on the extraction of product from low-wage workers in India, China, etc., by TNCs headquartered in developed economies contrasts with the general rule in academic and business literature—to obfuscate this most important point and treat labor as just one factor of production among others, making glancing, desultory references to wage differentials as one of a number of possible factors that influence outsourcing decisions. IBM CEO Samuel J. Palmisano gave a classic example of this in an article in *Foreign Affairs*:

> Until recently, companies generally chose to produce goods close to where they sold them. . . . Today . . . companies are investing more to change the way they supply the entire global market. . . . These

decisions are not simply a matter of offloading non-core activities, nor are they mere labor arbitrage. They are about actively managing different operations, expertise, and capabilities so as to open the enterprise up in multiple ways, allowing it to connect more intimately with partners, suppliers, and customers.[10]

Intimately! Mr. Palmisano wants his partners, suppliers, and customers to feel intimately connected to his firm, and indeed we are, but he omits to mention his firm's intimate connection with the workers who spend much of their waking lives making him rich.

UNCTAD's Inward FDI Potential Index provides an example of the obfuscation typical of IFI reports: the said index is an unweighted composite of 12 variables: GDP per capita; real GDP growth rate; exports/GDP; inward FDI; telephone lines and mobile phones per 1,000 inhabitants; commercial energy use per capita; R&D/GNI; tertiary students/population; country risk; share of world exports of natural resources, electronics and automobile components; and services. The criterion most closely related to the price of labor is GDP per capita, but this is included to indicate the size of the potential market for the firm's products, not the cost of hiring labor.[11] The price of labor is also conspicuously absent from a recent list of "factors determin[ing] a TNC's choice of host country locations" presented in UNCTAD's *World Investment Report 2013*: "economic characteristics (e.g. market size, growth potential, infrastructure, labor availability and skills), the policy framework (e.g. rules governing investment behavior, trade agreements and the intellectual property regime) and business facilitation policies (e.g. costs of doing business and investment incentives)."[12]

However, *WIR 2013* is a strange document. It is made up of two sections whose concepts clash and conclusions diverge and are evidently written by different teams of economists. The first, from which the above quote is taken, presents the standard mainstream technocratic analysis, while a second major portion of the report analyzes the growth of value chains and presents a very different picture of the motives and behavior of Northern firms:

Buyer-driven GVCs are typically focused on reduced sourcing costs, and in many labour-intensive industries this means significant downward pressure on labour costs and environmental management costs. Some suppliers are achieving reduced labour costs through violations of national and international labour standards and human rights laws. Practices such as forced labour, child labour, failure to pay minimum wage and illegal overtime work are typical challenges in a number of industries.[13]

It is refreshing to see acknowledgment of the central place of grinding down the cost of labor in the decisions and actions of capitalists, and of their readiness to inflict environmental damage, but UNCTAD's implementation of the global value-chain approach is not itself free from obfuscation:

> As a result of the rise of global production capabilities and the growth of export-oriented industries in many developing countries, combined with intensifying global competition due to the entry of major new producers and exporters (located largely in Asia), TNCs face significant pressure to reduce costs and increase productivity in their GVCs. . . . In turn, this is putting considerable pressure on both wages and working conditions. Especially in labor-intensive sectors (such as textiles and garments) where global buyers can exercise bargaining power to reduce costs, this pressure often results in lower wages.[14]

According to this, TNCs are the victim of rising global production capabilities in developing countries. But, for firms in imperialist countries seeking to cut production costs, the growing availability of low-wage workers has been a boon, not a bane. This passage makes sense only if *significant pressure* is replaced with *significant opportunity*. If the TNCs are facing significant pressure to outsource production to low-wage countries, it comes from their rivalry with other TNCs and from their shareholders' demand for dividends and capital gains.

Reducing the wage bill, not through investment in labor-saving technology or through wage cuts of domestically employed workers but through outsourcing to low-wage countries, has dramatically risen in importance during the neoliberal era. William Milberg comments:

> The irony is that precisely at the moment computerisation has led to a revolution in the mechanisation of production, the ability to outsource has reasserted the importance of the labour component of production costs. Instead of being inconsequential as the result of technological change, labor costs are now an important determinant in the production location decision.[15]

What is especially ironic is that instead of being a means to raise the productivity of labor, new technology is being used to lower its cost through outsourcing; and instead of replacing labor through the introduction of more advanced machinery, capitalists are using new technology to replace labor with cheaper labor, thereby prolonging the life of obsolete production processes while freeing up corporate income for speculation in financial assets, where much bigger profits are to be made.[16]

The general rule in mainstream literature is to downplay or, often, completely ignore the importance of capitalists' attraction to low wages in driving the outsourcing wave. Yet wage arbitrage must not only be added to the lists of major and minor factors affecting outsourcing decisions, it must be singled out as its key driving force. As Anwar Shaikh points out, "Cheap labor is not the only source of attraction for foreign investment. Other things being equal, cheap raw materials, a good climate, and a good location . . . are also important. . . . But these factors are specific to certain branches only; cheap wage-labor, on the other hand, is a general social characteristic of underdeveloped capitalist countries, one whose implications extend to all areas of production, even those yet to be created."[17] This highlights the qualitative difference between labor and other costs of production: the cost of labor power and the value of its product are part of a social relation, a relation between people and between classes, in contrast to other factors such as climate and availability of raw materials. The cost of living labor is central not only because it forms a major share of total production costs but also, and especially, because living labor is the source of all value.

Outsourcing and International Trade Theory

A survey of outsourcing literature published by the World Trade Organization (WTO) and the Hong Kong-based Fung Global Institute (FGI) asks two highly pertinent questions: "Why did firms in advanced economies find it profitable to increasingly offshore tasks or parts of the production process to developing economies? And, does international trade theory need a new framework to study this phenomenon of global supply chains?"[18] Good questions, except that we don't need a theory of international trade, we need a theory of international *production*, one that explains how value created by super-exploited workers in low-wage nations is captured by firms, states, and consumers in imperialist nations.

Their answer to the first question: "Vast absolute differences in unskilled labour wages between developed and developing economies, driven by differences in factor endowments, made cross-border production sharing profitable," accords well with Stephen Roach's concept of global labor arbitrage, and—with the exception of driven by differences in factor endowments—shares its qualities of clarity and directness. Differences in factor endowments is a euphemistic reference to one factor in particular: the vast unemployed and underemployed reserve army of labor with which developing nations are so generously endowed, dehumanized and converted by the bourgeois mind into a factor of production with the same status as machinery and sacks of raw materials. Their answer to the second question is no, international trade theory does not need a new framework; production outsourcing to low-wage countries "stays true to the concept of comparative advantage, as defined by the Heckscher-Ohlin model of trade," in which each country "use[s] its relatively abundant factor of production relatively intensively."[19] The H-O version of Ricardo's theory of comparative advantage predicts that "a relatively unskilled, labour-abundant developing economy would complete and export the relatively unskilled labour intensive tasks. . . . Similarly, a relatively capital or skilled labour-intensive country would export intermediate products, such as capital goods and design and research and development services."[20]

In other words, each country will endeavor to maximize the utilization of its resources. The H-O model turns this banal truism into a theoretical model by making three highly dubious assumptions. The first is that products for final sale cross borders but factors of production do not. There is no place in the H-O model for foreign direct investment or indeed any international capital flows (this also rules out structural trade imbalances, since the resulting accumulation of claims by one country on the wealth of another is tantamount to foreign investment). As for the other factor of production, the immobility of labor is treated as a fact of nature that needs no explanation. The second assumption is that all factors of production are fully utilized, a necessary condition for equilibrium, that is, for supply and demand to be balanced, all commodities to find buyers, and for each factor of production to be rewarded to the full extent of its contribution to their firm's output. In other words, it accords with Say's Law, after the classical economist Jean-Baptiste Say, who more than two hundred years ago argued that supply creates its own demand. In other words, everyone receives the fruit of his or her own labor and not anyone else's.

Heterodox economists question whether the ideal state resulting from these two assumptions has ever existed or could ever exist. Marxists argue that this ideal state is itself absurd, pointing to the third and most important of the fallacious assumptions upon which modern trade theory and indeed the entire edifice of bourgeois economic theory is based—the conflation of value and price, the presumption that the price received for a commodity is identical to the value that was generated in its production. This conflation excludes the possibility that a firm's value added may differ from the value it has added, in other words that part of its value added may represent value generated in other firms; while the conflation can only be implemented by making the production process invisible, creating a world in which prices are not only discovered in the marketplace but determined there, where the value of commodities, as Marx said, "seem not just to be realised only in circulation but actually to arise from it."[21] Modern trade theory applies these microeconomic precepts directly to the global economy, substituting individual nations for individual property owners.

The WTO-FGI researchers contrast the H-O model of comparative advantage with what they call the Ricardian model: "The Heckscher-Ohlin model of trade argues that technology is freely available across countries and hence comparative advantage is determined by relative factor endowments. In contrast, the Ricardian model of trade stresses differences in technology as the basis of international trade—countries tend to specialise in activities about which their inhabitants are especially knowledgeable."[22] The Ricardian model receives its title because differences in technology imply differences in the productivity of labor—David Ricardo's original theory hinged on the difference in the productivity of weavers and wine-makers in Portugal and England. On closer inspection, however, what WTO-FGI researchers call the Ricardian model has much more in common with the H-O approach than with Ricardo's original theory.[23] Ricardo, along with Karl Marx and Adam Smith, espoused the labor theory of value, according to which only one factor of production—living labor—is value-producing; materials and machinery used up in the process of production merely impart their already-created value to the new commodities. Hecksher and Ohlin replaced Ricardo's labor theory of value with a two-factor (labor and capital) model, in which the intersection of supply and demand curves determines not just the price of commodities but also their value.[24] The so-called Ricardian model does essentially the same thing with its two-factor production function. Both are founded on a tautological conflation of value and price and are trapped in the circular reasoning that springs from it. The difference between them is where in the circle they choose to begin, but between both of them and the theories of the classical economists there is a chasm. The real roots of the H-O model are to be found not in Ricardo and the classical economists, but in Thomas Malthus, Alfred Marshall, and others who rejected the labor theory of value, arguing instead that the value of a commodity is whatever the market says it is—or would say if allowed to function free of meddling governments or militant labor unions.

With no concept of exploitation the ruling ideas of economics, and all those in thrall to them, end up denying reality rather than explaining it. We turn instead to Marx's theory of value, to test and apply its concepts to the study of global labor arbitrage.

GLOBAL LABOR ARBITRAGE AND MARXIST THEORIES OF GLOBALIZATION AND IMPERIALISM

Before we proceed, some basic definitions and concepts of Marxist value theory need to be restated, emphasizing those aspects critical to our investigation of global labor arbitrage and the global labor-capital relation.

The *wage* (or nominal wage) is the monetary expression of the value of labor-power; the *real wage* is the wage expressed in terms of purchasing power, that is, by the size of the basket of consumption goods for which it can be exchanged.

The *value of labor-power* is the quantity of socially necessary labor required to produce that basket. The value of labor-power can therefore be expressed as a sum of money or as a quantity of labor time.[25] If four hours of social labor are required to create the workers' consumption basket, then four hours of their working day is necessary labor, time spent replacing v, the values they and their families consume. The remainder of her/his working day is spent generating surplus value for the capitalist, or s.

The *rate of surplus-value*, otherwise known as *rate of exploitation*,[26] is the ratio between surplus labor time and necessary labor time, that is, s/v. There is thus an extremely close connection between the value of labor power and the rate of exploitation: assuming a working day of constant length, the higher the value of labor-power the lower the rate of exploitation, and vice versa. Since $s + v$ = the working day, s/v can be increased either by increasing s while leaving v unchanged, that is, by extending the working day; or by reducing v, the value of labor-power, and increasing s in proportion, leaving the length of the working day unchanged. Marx termed the former an increase in *absolute surplus-value*, since this way of increasing the rate of surplus-value requires an increase in the absolute length of the working day. There are two ways in which the second route to increasing *s/v* can be achieved, one of which was exhaustively studied by Marx in *Capital* and has concentrated the attention of Marxists ever since, and the other of which he put to one side—and which Marxists have neglected ever since. The first is by raising the productivity of labor *in the branches of production involved in the production of workers' consumption goods*, thereby reducing the amount of labor-time needed to produce the basket of goods consumed by the worker and her/his family. (As Marx says, "An increase in the productivity of labor in those branches of industry which supply neither the necessary means of subsistence nor the means by which they are produced leaves the value of labor-power undisturbed."[27]) Marx called this an increase in *relative surplus-value*, since this involves a change in the relative portions into which a working day of a given length is divided—specifically, by reducing necessary labor-time, that is, the value of labor-power, so that surplus labor-time can increase. The second is by reducing the size of the basket, that is, by reducing consumption, lowering the real wage. Relative surplus value, for Marx and ever since, is "that form of surplus-value which results from the *growing productivity of industry*,"[28] which, as Higginbottom has pointed out, "does *not* include paying wages below the value of labor-power."[29] Reduction of wages below the value of labor-power is therefore a third way to increase the rate of exploitation, to which we will return in the next chapter.

These preliminary concepts will be further developed as they are applied. Exploitation, surplus-value, the real wage—all of these hinge on and are deducible from the concept of the value of labor-power, for which we need much more than a pat definition. Labor-power itself is a commodity, indeed this is the defining feature of capitalism. As we have seen, *its* value is the combined value of the commodities consumed by the worker and her/his family. This basket of goods, what is in it and what workers think should be in it, is the product of a complex process of social evolution and class struggle, and can be thought of as comprising two elements: the minimum quantity of values needed to allow the subsistence of the worker and her/his family, and what Marx called the historical and moral element of the value of labor-power. The local and especially national determinants of this continues to predominate over the global dimension, yet workers' desires and needs are being transformed at an accelerating pace by heightened economic, political, social and cultural interaction across borders of all kinds. Access to health care, education, nutritious food, transport, shelter, and retirement income are part of the value of labor-power in imperialist countries—but these concessions, forced from the imperialist ruling classes by powerful trade union–led social movements, were consciously intended to pacify workers and prevent them from linking up with revolutionary struggles in oppressed nations. They are thus the fruit of revolutionary struggles abroad as much as of class struggle at home. What's more, as the analysis in chapter 1 of iconic global commodities revealed, a significant part of the revenues used by states in imperialist countries to defray the costs of the social wage derives from super-exploited workers in oppressed nations. *Access* to health, education, etc., has been achieved, to a degree, in imperialist countries, but the *fight* for a living wage sufficient to provide for these basic needs is international; where these basic rights have been won they can only be defended by generalizing them, in the first place to migrant workers.

Contemporary Marxists and the Global Labor Arbitrage

Most of the scholars and analysts cited so far in our survey of literature on the globalization of production and its driver, global labor arbitrage, have been from mainstream or heterodox schools. This is because Marxists have, by and large, neglected this subject. Global labor arbitrage foregrounds the labor-capital relation, spotlights the enormous international differences in the price of labor, encompasses both ways capitalists profit from wage differentials—outsourcing and migration—and focuses attention on the fragmented and hierarchically organized global labor market that gives rise to these arbitrage opportunities. This is why, despite being a rather opaque and technical term, global labor arbitrage is more useful and concrete than any of the core concepts so far developed by value-chain analysts and other heterodox critics of neoliberal globalization or by neo-Marxist theorists of new imperialism and transnational capitalism.

What's so special about global labor arbitrage is that it takes place entirely within the orbit of the capital-labor relation. Global labor arbitrage is capitalist imperialism par excellence. Here, capitalism has evolved ways of extracting surplus-value from the so-called emerging nations that are effected not by political-military coercion but by market forces—what Ellen Wood calls the globalization of capitalist imperatives—in contrast to the century before, when, according to Wood, "capitalist imperial power certainly did embrace much of the world but it did so less by the universality of its economic imperatives than by the same coercive force that had always determined relations between colonial masters and subject territories."[30] As she is careful to acknowledge, the exercise of military power by states continues to play an active role in constituting the imperialist world order and removing diverse obstacles in its way, whether they be traditional communities resisting expulsion from ancestral lands, radical insurgencies, or regimes that refuse to submit to imperial dictates. She makes a passing reference to the most large-scale, round-the-clock exercise of coercive violence by states in the global political economy, namely the mobilization of armies of soldiers and police against economic migrants: "Not the least important function of the nation-state in globalization is to . . . manage the movements of labor by means of strict border controls and stringent immigration policies, in the interests of capital."[31] Yet neither this nor the other dimension of global labor arbitrage, the outsourcing of production to low-wage countries, are given any further attention, despite their relevance to her stated aim, which is "to define the essence of capitalist imperialism."[32] Instead, Wood decides not "to go into the intricacies of value theory," and as a result her excellent insight can go no further.[33] By excluding the value relation from the concept of imperialism Wood empties it of both the exploitation of labor by capital and the exploitation of poor nations by rich nations, reducing imperialism to interstate rivalry between great powers before extinguishing it entirely: The "new imperialism [is] no longer . . . a relationship between imperial masters and colonial subjects but a complex interaction between more or less sovereign states."[34]

PROMINENT AMONG CONTEMPORARY MARXIST theorists, David Harvey has published a series of influential books on Marx's theory of value, on neoliberalism, and on the new imperialism. Because of the wide audience he has gained for his views, it is necessary to subject them to a severe evaluation, a task that can only be broached here.

The central argument in Harvey's theory of the new imperialism is that the overaccumulation of capital pushes capitalists and capitalism into an ever-greater recourse to non-capitalist forms of plunder, that is, forms other than the extraction of surplus-value from wage-labor, from confiscation of communal property to privatization of welfare, arising from capital's encroachment on the commons, whether this be public property or pristine nature. He argues that new imperialism is characterized by "a shift in emphasis from accumulation through expanded reproduction to accumulation through dispossession," this now being "the primary contradiction to be confronted."[35] Harvey is right to draw attention to the continuing and even increasing importance of old and new forms of accumulation by dispossession, but he does not recognize that imperialism's most significant shift in emphasis is *in an entirely different direction*—toward the transformation of its own core processes of surplus-value extraction through the global labor arbitrage-driven globalization of production, a phenomenon that is entirely internal to the labor-capital relation.[36]

Harvey's *Limits to Capital* has a deliberately ambiguous title. This book attempts to discover the limits to capital's relentless advance, and also to identify the limitations of *Capital*, of Marx's theory of capitalist development. *Limits to Capital* has far less to say about imperialism than *Capital* itself. In fact, imperialism receives just one brief, desultory mention: "Much of what passes for imperialism rests on the reality of exploitation of the peoples in one region by those in another. . . . The processes described allow the geographical production of surplus-value to diverge from its geographical distribution."[37] Instead of expanding on this important insight, it receives no further attention. Harvey returns to the subject of the geographical shift of production to low-wage countries in *The Condition of Postmodernity* (1990), where this is seen not as a sign of deepening imperialist exploitation, as is implied by his passing comment in *Limits to Capital*, but of its accelerated decline:

> From the mid-1970s onwards . . . newly industrialising countries . . . began to make serious inroads into the markets for certain products (textiles, electronics, etc) in the advanced capitalist countries, and w[ere] soon joined by a host of other NICs [Newly Industrialising Countries, such as] Hungary, India, Egypt and those countries that had earlier pursued import substitution strategies (Brazil, Mexico). . . Some of the power shifts since 1972 within the global political economy of advanced capitalism have been truly remarkable. United States dependence on foreign trade . . . doubled in the period 1973–80. Imports from developing countries increased almost tenfold.[38]

This stands reality on its head: far from signifying a power shift toward low-wage countries, the growth of foreign trade reflects an enormous expansion of the power of imperialist TNCs *over* these countries—and of the increased dependence of these corporations on surplus-value extracted from their workers. This conclusion is suggested by Harvey's recognition, in the same work, of "the enhanced capacity of multinational capital to take Fordist mass production systems abroad, and there to exploit extremely vulnerable women's labour power under conditions of extremely low pay and negligible job security."[39] Furthermore, the global shift of production processes to low-wage nations was driven by TNCs in order to buttress their competitiveness and profitability, and to great effect, yet Harvey presents this as evidence of declining imperialist competitiveness. According to Harvey, core capital attempts to resolve its overaccumulation crisis through a spatial fix, involving the production of "new spaces within which capitalist production can proceed (through infrastructural investments, for example), the growth of trade and direct investments, and the exploration of new possibilities for the exploitation of labor-power."[40] This is what Marx called a chaotic concept. Instead of the deliberate vagueness of exploration of new possibilities for the exploitation of labor-power, what about something much more straightforward like intensified exploitation of low-wage labor? In the end, Harvey's attempts to add a spatial dimension to Marxist theory of capitalism falls flat because he neglects to discuss the spatial implications of immigration controls, of the deepening wage gradient between imperialist and semicolonial nations, of global wage arbitrage.

In *The New Imperialism*, published in 2003, Harvey devotes two pages to the globalization of production processes. He begins by inserting this development into his basic overaccumulation of capital thesis: "Easily exploited low-wage workforces coupled with increasing ease of geographical mobility of production opened up new opportunities for the profitable employment of surplus capital. But in short order this exacerbated the problem of surplus capital production world-wide."[41]

Formally separating industrial capitalists and financial capitalists, he ascribes the driving source of the outsourcing wave to the unleashed power of finance capitalists asserting their domination over manufacturing capital, to the great detriment of U.S. national interests:

A battery of technological and organisational shifts . . . promoted the kind of geographical mobility of manufacturing capital that the increasingly hyper-mobile financial capital could feed upon. While the shift towards financial power brought great direct benefits to the United States, the effects upon its own industrial structure were nothing short of traumatic, if not catastrophic. . . . Wave after wave of deindustrialisation hit industry after industry and region after region. . . . The U.S. was complicit in undermining its dominance in manufacturing by unleashing the powers of finance throughout the globe. The benefit, however, was ever cheaper goods from elsewhere to fuel the endless consumerism to which the US was committed.[42]

Leaving aside its nationalist and protectionist perspective, and its failure to notice that cheaper goods from elsewhere are made possible by cheaper labor elsewhere, that is, super-exploitation, Harvey's argument contains a fatal flaw. Outsourcing was not so much driven by the awakening of finance but by stagnation and decline in the rate of manufacturing profit and the efforts of the captains of industry to counter this. Increased imports of cheap manufactured goods did much more than fuel consumerism; it also directly supported the profitability and competitive position of North Americas industrial behemoths, and was actively promoted by them. Far from ending U.S. dominance—in other words, the ability of its corporations to capture the lion's share of surplus-value—outsourcing has opened up new ways for U.S., European, and Japanese capitalists to entrench their dominance over global manufacturing production.

Harvey's fundamental error only goes so far in explaining the dreadful reformism of his conclusion to *The New Imperialism*, where he pined for "a return to a more benevolent New Deal imperialism, preferably arrived at through the sort of coalition of capitalist powers that Kautsky long ago envisaged. . . . [This] is surely enough to fight for in the present conjuncture,"[43] forgetting what he wrote two decades earlier in his conclusion to *Limits to Capital*: "The world was saved from the terrors of the Great Depression not by some glorious new deal or the magic touch of Keynesian economics in the treasuries of the world, but by the destruction and death of global war."[44]

Harvey's refusal to acknowledge that production outsourcing to low-wage countries signifies a vast expansion of direct and indirect super-exploitation of Southern labor by U.S., European, and Japanese TNCs, and his notion that this transformation marks the passing of imperialism not its apogee, has been and remains the dominant view among those in the imperialist countries who call themselves Marxists. Robert Brenner is a prominent critic of dependency theory, who, unlike Harvey, has no use at all for terms like imperialism, who offers an almost identical explanation of the outsourcing transformation. Harvey's view that "outsourcing exacerbated the problem of surplus capital production worldwide" coincides with Brenner's argument that manufacturing over-capacity emerged, was reproduced, and has been further deepened by . . . a succession of newly emerging manufacturing powers . . . combining ever increasing technological sophistication with relatively cheap labor and orienting production to exports for the world market . . . thus ma[king] huge, but often redundant, additions of manufacturing capacity to the world market, tending to squeeze global prices and profits.[45]

Like Harvey, Brenner ignores the fact that the massive expansion of what he calls "highly-competitive lower cost producers" was itself driven by capitalist firms based in the imperialist economies, impelled by their insatiable urge to cut costs by substituting relatively expensive domestic labor with cheap Southern labor. He doesn't notice the paradoxical fact that the so-called race to the bottom, that is, overcapacity in Southern labor-intensive production processes, has greatly helped the imperialist economies contain the tendency toward overproduction—by bearing down on production costs to such an extent that markets can continue to grow and high markups can persist, and by resolving the tendency to overproduction by shifting it (in particular, low value-added production activities) to low-wage countries. Global outsourcing has thus not only added to global overcapacity and overproduction, it has displaced it to the Global South. With the imperialist economies now heading into prolonged stagnation or worse, the crisis of overproduction that last reared its head in the 1970s is now set to return.

A superior definition is provided by Jack Barnes, a leader of the Socialist Workers Party (U.S.), once part of the Fourth International with Ernest Mandel:

The workings of the world capitalist market bring about an enormous, and unconscionable, transfer to the imperialist countries of the wealth produced by the workers and peasants of Africa, the Middle East, Latin America, and most of Asia and Pacific. That extortion is guaranteed not primarily by unfair terms of trade imposed from outside on world markets. It is guaranteed above all by the differential value of labor-power and the gap in productivity of labor between the imperialist countries on one hand, and those oppressed and exploited by imperialism on the other—a differential that not only underlies unequal exchange but relentlessly reproduces and increases it.[46]

There is much wisdom in these words, but they show the distance yet to be traveled. The differential value of labor-power and the gap in productivity of labor are presented as a single phenomenon, yet they are in fact two very different dimensions of the imperialist capital-labor relation. They must be strictly and rigorously separated, or else the door is opened to marginalist conceptions of productivity and associated notions that wage differentials reflect productivity differences. Nevertheless, "differential value of labor-power" acknowledges that this is much lower, and therefore the rate of exploitation much higher, than in imperialist countries.

Another important exception to the failure of the Marxist mainstream in Europe and North America is the *Monthly Review* tradition founded by Paul Baran and Paul Sweezy, which influenced and in turn championed the work of dependency theorists discussed below. We do not have the space to critically evaluate this enduring contribution, only for a brief reference to a recent addition to it. In *The Endless Crisis* by John Bellamy Foster and Robert McChesney, which is worth reading for its discussion of this topic and much else, we read this rich characterization of the imperialist reality:

> New realities dominate labor at the world level today. One is global labor arbitrage, or the system of imperial rent. The other is the existence of a massive global reserve army, which makes this world system of extreme exploitation possible. Labor arbitrage is defined quite simply by *The Economist* as taking advantage of lower wages abroad, especially in poor countries. It is thus an unequal exchange process in which one country, as Marx said, is able to cheat another due to the much higher exploitation of labor in the poor country. . . . It is such *super-exploitation* that lies behind much of the expansion of production in the Global South. The fact that this has been the basis of rapid economic growth for some emerging economies does not alter the reality that it has generated enormous imperial rents for multinational corporations and capital at the center of the system.[47]

These authors identify the centrality of global labor arbitrage; recognize that super-exploitation is central to this; and argue that this generates "enormous imperialist rents for multinational corporations and capital at the center of the system." The first two points concur with the argument being developed here. Imperial rent accords closely with the theory of imperialism developed by Samir Amin, a leading proponent of the anti-imperialist dependency school that rose to prominence in the 1960s and 1970s. The concept of rent is closely related to that of monopoly; rent signifying above-average profits resulting from some sort of monopoly, that is, any impediment to free competition and efficient markets. Rent therefore implies a violation of the law of value, and Amin's use of the term *imperialist rent* implies that imperialist domination and exploitation is based on systematic violation of this law.[48] The approach adopted here, in contrast, is to explain modern capitalist imperialism not as a *departure* from the law of value but *as a stage in its evolution*.

Samir Amin argues in the *The Law of Worldwide Value* that "labor-power has but a single value, that which is associated with the level of development of the productive forces taken globally,"[49] and from this springs a simple concept of super-exploitation: workers who are paid below this global value are by definition super-exploited. In their seminal 1979 debate with Amin, John Weeks and Elizabeth Dore founded their denial of higher rates of exploitation in oppressed nations on rejection of Amin's premise: "The concept of the value of labor-power at world level . . . we consider to be idealistic, in that it is purely a mental construction not existing in reality."[50] Weeks and Dore's argument—that the value of labor-power is determined at an exclusively national level—has since been finessed by the shift in the production of so many consumer goods to low-wage countries, with the result that the wages and productivity of workers in low-wage countries are now key determinants of the value of labor-power in imperialist countries. But their arguments were wrong when they were first enunciated: the theory of super-exploitation does not rest on the assumption of a single global value of labor-power—indeed, if we accept their argument, that there are as many labor values as there are nations, super-exploitation could then be simply defined as national rates of exploitation that are higher than the global average. Either way, TNCs move production to where the rate of exploitation is higher from where it is lower and thereby reap greater profits.

The notion of a single global value of labor-power converts the point toward which capitalism's globalizing tendency is ultimately moving into something that already exists, or to put this another way, to suppress the very real contradiction between the national and international dimensions. There are two fundamental aspects to the relation between the value of labor-power and the development of the productive forces: on the one hand, as productive forces develop so the quantity of labor required to produce a given basket of consumption goods falls, and with it, therefore, the value of labor-power. On the other hand, the development of the productive forces stimulates the expansion of human culture and with it the development of new needs that are incorporated through social evolution and class struggle into the value of labor-power, causing the value of labor-power to rise. There is a national and an international dimension to both aspects; they cannot be reduced to one or the other for many reasons, not least that the giant strides in this direction during the neoliberal era have been accompanied by ever-deepening impediments to the unification of the global labor market.[51]

Amin thus provides orthodox Marxists with an easy target—it is easy to oppose one undialectical, hypostatized concept with another.[52] This does not mean that the contending parties are equally mistaken—the purpose and effect of Amin's argument is to emphasize the centrality of imperialism, while his European Marxist critics attempt the opposite.

DEPENDENCY THEORY AND INTERNATIONAL DIFFERENCES IN THE RATE OF EXPLOITATION

Exploitation has much more terrible connotations in a Third World country than in a developed capitalist country, because it is exactly out of fear of revolution, out of fear of socialism that developed capitalism came up with some distribution schemes that, to a certain degree, do away with the great hunger that European countries were familiar with in Engels's day, in Marx's day.

—FIDEL CASTRO [53]

The debate in the 1960s and 1970s sparked by the rise of dependency theory, which sought to explain the persistence of imperialist exploitation following the dismantling of territorial empires, was the first and last sustained attempt to found the theory of imperialism on Marx's theory of value, one reason why it remains a crucial reference point for contemporary study of imperialism. We do not have the space here to do justice to this extraordinarily rich body of work, so what follows is an attempt to place dependency theory in its historical context and to identify its most important contributions and limitations. Its direct relevance to analysis of contemporary imperialism is limited by the fact that it rose and fell in the period prior to the neoliberal era, a time when developing countries exported raw materials and imported manufactured goods and when the globalization of production was still in the egg. Ironically, the hatching of this egg—the rapid exported-oriented industrial development in South Korea, Taiwan, and Singapore in the 1970s (the so-called NICS, or Newly

Industrializing Countries) partly explains why, as Gary Howe pointed out at the time, "Dependency theory itself began to flounder," since these early instances of industrial takeoff appeared to refute its insistence that imperialist domination blocked industrial development in the South.[54]

Dependency theory—really a spectrum of theories, or better still of political perspectives, since it sought to give theoretical expression to a movement for change involving hundreds of millions of people—viewed the world from a Southern perspective, as it appears to and is experienced by the peoples of poor nations, whether they be impoverished workers and farmers or domestic capitalists wishing to retain a larger share of the surplus-value extracted from them. Dependency theory's leading expo-nents were overwhelmingly Latin American, Asian, African; they were citizens of what they and all politically conscious people in those conti-nents saw as *neo-colonies*, nations that had attained formal independence but remained politically and economically subjugated to the former colonial powers. The primary difference lay between those like Arghiri Emmanuel, author of *Unequal Exchange: A Study in the Imperialism of Trade*, and Fernando Henrique Cardoso (later a neoliberal Brazilian president) who sought a path for independent capitalist development in the South, while Marxists like Samir Amin, André Gunder Frank, and Ruy Mauro Marini argued in different ways that capitalism, being intrin-sically imperialist, is itself the obstacle.

Both versions directly challenged the ruling modernization thesis, arguing that extreme disparity in development results in unequal trade relations that traps these countries in permanent underdevelopment. What this diverse array of reformists and revolutionaries had in common was a recognition that unequal exchange between developed imperialist nations and what was then known as the Third World (the Soviet Union and its allies constituting the Second World) results in a large-scale transfer of wealth from the latter to the former, spurring development in the imperialist centers and underdevelopment in the nations of the periphery.

Unequal Exchange

Raúl Prebisch, an Argentinian economist, and Hans Singer, a German Jewish economist who fled to the UK when Hitler came to power (and who, in 1940, was interned by the UK government as an enemy alien), separately devised what became known as the Prebisch-Singer hypothesis. This argued that there is a long-run tendency for primary commodity exporters to suffer deteriorating terms of trade with manufactured goods-exporting rich nations, and that this severely reduces or cancels altogether the benefits of comparative advantage for primary commodity–exporting countries, perpetuating their underdevelopment and widening the gap with developed countries. This much-disputed but now well-established fact provides an unassailable empirical basis for theories of unequal exchange, a core component of dependency theory.

The tendency for the terms of trade of raw materials to fall vis-à-vis manufactured goods contradicts one of the central arguments of Nikolai Bukharin, along with Lenin a central leader of the world's first socialist revolution. Bukharin predicted *rising* raw material prices in his influential 1915 book *Imperialism and World Economy*, reasoning that "the development of agriculture does not keep pace with the impetuous development of industry . . . [the] ever-growing disproportion between industry and agriculture" leads to "the epoch of dearth, of a general rise in the prices of agricultural products everywhere. . . . The rise in the prices of raw materials in turn reveals itself directly in [a lowering of] the rate of profit, for, other conditions being equal, the rate of profit rises and falls in inverse ratio to the fluctuations in the prices of raw materials."[55] Bukharin based his conclusions on data from 1900 to 1913, which was a period of rising raw material prices, a commodity supercycle analogous to the one that, a century later, we have just experienced. A 2012 report for the United Nations by Bilge Erten and José Antonio Ocampo identified four such supercycles over the past 150 years, finding that "for non-oil commodities, the mean of each supercycle has a tendency to be lower than that of the previous cycle, suggesting a step-wise deterioration over the entire period in support of the Prebisch-Singer hypothesis. This finding applies especially to tropical and non-tropical agricultural prices, as well as metals."[56]

Prebisch and Singer hypothesised that declining terms of trade of raw materials stemmed from the extremely asymmetric and unequal structure of the global economy—which is why their approach is commonly described as *structuralist*—and, in particular, from the different properties intrinsic to the production of raw materials vis-à-vis manufactured goods that result, inter alia, in much greater price volatility in the former. They concluded that capitalist development requires a shift away from reliance on agriculture and resource extraction and toward the development of modern industry, and that this was only possible if domestic industries are protected from foreign competition—what became known as the *import substitution industrialization* strategy, or

ISI. This strategy, in essence, introduces an amendment to the modernization thesis: for poor countries to traverse the prescribed stages and become developed capitalist nations the state must intervene to protect domestic industry from competition with firms in imperialist countries. But it accepts its premise, that the only possible development is capitalist development. This perspective expressed the interests of domestic capitalists seeking to enrich themselves while modernizing their countries, and made them the prime agents of change and progress. This blue end of the dependency spectrum also acquired strength from its considerable institutional power. In 1950 Prebisch was appointed Executive Secretary of the Economic Commission for Latin America and the Caribbean, or ECLAC (CEPAL in Spanish), a UN body founded in 1948 to promote regional economic cooperation and which, under Prebisch's direction, became an influential think-tank and source of analysis and data on Latin American economies. ECLAC promoted the ISI strategy pursued with differing intensity and effect by most nations in Latin America and many in Africa and Asia—until the U.S. Federal Reserve pulled the rug out from under it with a dramatic hike in interest rates in 1979, detonating the Third World debt crisis and a chain reaction of wrenching economic crises across the Global South.[57]

While the bourgeois-nationalist proponents of dependency theory acquired great strength from their connection with modernizing elites, UN development agencies, and academia, the Marxist-influenced wing of dependency theory acquired its great strength from anti-colonial and anti-imperialist struggles involving hundreds of millions of people, and from the socialist revolutions they spawned, in particular those in China and Cuba. The Marxist wing, however, was fragmented and deeply affected by the ideological influence of Stalinism (especially its Maoist varieties). This is reflected in its almost complete disregard for the Cuban Revolution and its leaders, cutting dependency theorists off from the most advanced debates going on anywhere at that time about the law of value, imperialism, and the transition to socialism.[58] This is all the more surprising since the leaders of the Cuban Revolution had placed denunciation of unequal exchange at the center of their struggle to unite the Global South against imperialism, as in Fidel Castro's speech to the 1979 UN General Assembly on behalf of 95 member nations of the Non-Aligned Movement:

> The first fundamental objective in our struggle consists of reducing until we eliminate the unequal exchange that . . . converts

international trade into a very useful vehicle for the plundering of our wealth. Today, one hour of labor in the developed countries is exchanged for ten hours of labor in the underdeveloped countries. . . . Unequal exchange is ruining our peoples. It must end! . . . The economic chasm between the developed countries and the countries seeking development is not narrowing but widening. It must be closed! . . .

The first fundamental objective in our struggle consists of reducing until we eliminate the unequal exchange that prevails today and converts international trade into a very useful vehicle for the plundering of our wealth. Today, one hour of labor in the developed countries is exchanged for ten hours of labor in the underdeveloped countries. The non-aligned countries demand . . . a permanent linkage between the price we receive for our products and those paid for our imports . . . such a linkage . . . constitutes an essential pivot for all future economic negotiations.[59]

Not only did Cuba's Communist leadership avail themselves of every opportunity to denounce imperialist exploitation and arouse workers, farmers, and youth to rise up in revolt against it, they also fought hard for trade with the Soviet Union and other Comecon countries to fundamentally break from the exploitative pattern of trade between rich and poor countries. Indeed, the only example of fair trade between industrialized and developing nations in the modern world is to be found in the economic relations developed between Cuba and the USSR until the latter's collapse in 1991. Carlos Tablada shows how Che and Fidel extended their campaign against unequal exchange to Cuba's struggle for trade relations with the USSR/Comecon to be based on the principle that relative prices be fixed to ensure the exchange of equal quantities of labor, thereby "reducing the brutal impact of the law of value in international trade with revolutionary underdeveloped countries."[60] This, they argued, was the minimum requirement for non-exploitative trade. Developed, industrialized socialist countries should go further, by tipping the playing field in favor of the underdeveloped country, making the overcoming of grossly uneven economic development into a conscious aim of trade policy. As Che Guevara argued in February 1964, "To prevent a widening of the differences between the developed and the more backward countries as a result of the exchange," trade between "countries of the new society" must "assume a higher form. . . . In other words it is necessary to develop terms of trade that permit the financing of industrial investments in the developing countries even if it contravenes the price systems prevailing in the capitalist world market. . . . The recent agreement between Cuba and the USSR is an example of the steps that can be taken in this direction."[61]

Che returned to this theme in his speech to a conference in Algeria in 1965, in which he made it abundantly clear that Cuba had to overcome considerable resistance to its proposals for trade of a higher form with the USSR and its allies:

> The socialist countries must help pay for the development of countries now starting out on the road to liberation. . . . There should not be any more talk about developing mutually beneficial trade based on prices forced on the backward countries by the law of value and the international relations of unequal exchange that result from the law of value. How can it be "mutually beneficial" to sell at world market prices the raw materials that cost the underdeveloped countries immeasurable sweat and suffering, and to buy at world market prices the machinery produced in todays big automated factories? . . . The socialist countries have the moral duty to put an end to their tacit complicity with the exploiting countries of the West.[62]

The 1973 agreements that led to Cuba's full integration into Comecon are now widely seen in Cuba as a source of many costly errors, not least the abandonment of the quest for self-sufficiency in food. In the decade that followed, termed by Fidel Castro "the ten despicable years," a wider use of Stalinist bureaucratic planning methods eroded the consciousness and the morale of Cuba's working people, leading Cuba, in Castro's words, toward "a system worse than capitalism, instead of leading us toward socialism and communism."[63] As we have seen, however, the trade agreements struck between Cuba and Comecon had a positive and revolutionary side: the relative prices of goods exchanged between Comecon and Cuba were to be fixed so as to equalize the quantity of labor expended by each country in the production of the exchanged goods, eliminating, in other words, the unequal exchange that typifies "free trade" between imperialist and underdeveloped countries, allowing Cuba to develop its renowned health and education systems and finance industrial development. During the 1980s the dumping of heavily subsidized U.S. and European sugar surpluses depressed the world market price to as little as five cent per pound—the "garbage dump price," according to Fidel Castro—yet Cuba received forty cents for each pound of sugar exported to the USSR. Fidel Castro explained the far-reaching significance of this:

In our economic relations with the USSR and other developed socialist countries, we have overcome the tragic law of unequal terms of
trade that has historically governed the relations between the Third
World and the developed capitalist powers. We receive fair prices .
. . that are protected by agreements against the deterioration in the
terms of trade. . . . This is of enormous importance, because, I repeat,
we have solved our problems not only through social changes but
also because. . . . Cuba has established a form of new international
economic order with the rest of the socialist community. Without
these foundations, our great economic and social successes . . . would
not have been possible.[64]

Within a decade Comecon—but not Cuba—had collapsed. In the
space of a few months, Cuba lost 85 percent of its foreign trade as former
Comecon countries submitted to U.S. pressure to break off trade relations with Cuba as a condition for promises of loans and assistance with
market reforms.

The Sino-Soviet Split

The struggle against imperialism was dealt a severe blow by the Sino-
Soviet split, which reached a head in the years between 1958 and 1960
and was formalized in 1962 with the mutual break of diplomatic relations.
That the Sino-Soviet split should coincide with the Cuban Revolution was
no coincidence—this revolution was one of many blazing at that time: a
revolutionary government was in power in Algeria following its victory
over France; a pro-British monarchy had been toppled in Iraq; national
liberation struggles in Indochina and Africa were reaching a new level
of intensity and were reinforcing each other; and Latin America was gal-
vanized by the Cuban Revolution. The Chinese and Soviet governments
vied with each other to lead the struggle against imperialism—not to
lead it to victory, but instead to subordinate it to the interests of the rival
bureaucratic castes.

In Samir Amin's words, Stalin's aim in 1945 was "to impose peaceful coexistence and hence to calm the aggressive passions of the United
States and its subaltern European and Japanese allies. In exchange, the
Soviet Union would accept a low profile, abstaining from interfering in
colonial matters that the imperialist powers considered their internal
affairs." This treacherous policy (my adjective) "was accepted without
reservation in the European Communist parties and in those of Latin

America . . . however, almost immediately it came up against resistance from the Communist parties of Asia and the Middle East. This was concealed in the language of that period, for they continued to affirm the unity of the socialist camp behind the USSR."[65] Amin summarizes the behind-the-scenes debate sparked by Stalin's policy of surrender:

> Who was to direct these anti-imperialist battles? To simplify: the bourgeoisie . . . whom the communists should then support, or a front of popular classes, directed by the communists and not the bourgeoisie? . . . The answer to this question often changed and was sometimes confused. In 1945 the Communist parties concerned were aligned, based on the conclusion that Stalin had formulated: the bourgeoisie everywhere in the world . . . has thrown the national flag into the rubbish bin. The communists were therefore the only ones who could assemble a united front of the forces that refused to submit to the imperialist, capitalist, American order.[66]

Since, as Amin explained above, following the Second World War Stalin directed the Communist parties to cease resistance to imperialism, it is little wonder that "the answer to this question often changed and was sometimes confused." Opposition to the Moscow line from within the Communist parties coalesced around Mao's thesis, and, in Amin's words:

> For the majority of the peoples of the planet, the long road to socialism could only be opened by a national, popular, democratic, anti-feudal and anti-imperialist revolution run by the communists. The underlying message was that other socialist advances were not on the agenda elsewhere, i.e., in the imperialist centers. They could not possibly take shape until after the peoples of the peripheries had inflicted substantial damage on imperialism.[67]

This "national, popular, democratic, anti-feudal and anti-imperialist revolution" was to be a bourgeois anti-feudal revolution, *not* an anti-capitalist, socialist revolution, since the Stalinist stagist theory of historical evolution said that the objective conditions for socialism did not exist in the underdeveloped periphery and that a prolonged period of capitalist development was necessary before socialism could become an option. If the national bourgeoisies in the colonies and neo-colonies were incapable of leading this revolution and open the way to independent capitalist development, the communists had to do it. Amin argues, in continuation, "The triumph of the Chinese Revolution confirmed this conclusion. . . . Later, in 1964, Che Guevara revealed similar views."[68] Both verdicts, it is argued here, are wrong.

The Chinese Communist Party had done its best to implement Stalins policy of class collaboration. In the mid-1920s, it obeyed Moscow's instruction to dissolve itself into the capitalist-led Kuomintang and to follow Chiang Kai-shek, its main leader.[69] When, in 1927, Kuomintang forces approached Shanghai, which in March had been seized by the workers in an insurrectionary general strike, the CCP told them to put down their arms and welcome the liberator—who proceeded to suppress the rebellion, smash the trade unions, and massacre 40,000 people. In the aftermath of this avoidable disaster, the CCP withdrew from the Kuomintang and from the cities and began a guerrilla war against its former allies. Following the Japanese imperialist invasion of China in 1931 the CCP assumed leadership of the national liberation struggle while the Kuomintang focused its energies on attacking the Communists. Nevertheless, in 1937 the Mao Zedong leadership accepted Moscow's diktat and proposed an alliance with Chiang Kai-shek, adopted the Kuomintang program, abandoned the fight for land reform, abolished soviets (councils of workers and peasants) that had been established in liberated areas, and dissolved the Red Army into the Kuomintang forces. In 1945, following the defeat of Japanese imperialism in the Second World War, Chiang Kai-shek resumed the civil war against the CCP. Despite this, Mao dutifully attempted to implement Stalin's line of peaceful coexistence and once again proposed a coalition government with the Kuomintang. Despite pressure from the United States, Chiang Kai-shek rejected the CCP's offer, and in 1947, with the onset of the Cold War dashing hopes of peaceful coexistence, the CCP called for the overthrow of the Kuomintang government and for the expropriation of the large landlords, while promising the industrial bourgeoisie that their property rights would be respected. Attracted by the CCP's relaunched campaign for land reform, the Kuomintang's peasant-based army refused to fight the People's Liberation Army, as it was now called. Chiang Kai-shek fled to Taiwan, and, in October 1949, the CCP took political power into its hands. The United States responded by invading Korea and moving its troops toward the Chinese border. The CCP mobilized millions of armed workers and peasants to confront the U.S. imperialist forces and, to consolidate its power, cracked down on bourgeois counterrevolutionaries in the cities. By 1952, most of heavy industry, banking, and trade were in the hands of the state. In sum, the Chinese Revolution followed the inexorable logic of the class struggle, not the false logic of Chairman Mao, and was compelled to expropriate the capitalists and landlords and embark on the socialist transition.

According to Amin, who described himself as a Leninist-Maoist in *The Law of Value and Historical Materialism*[70] but did not repeat this auto-designation in the new edition of his book, *The Law of Worldwide Value*, "The principal contradiction, that which governs all others and the vicissitudes of which largely determine the objective conditions in which the others take place" is expressed in the struggle between "the social-democratic alliance (hegemony of imperialism over the working classes at the center), . . . a constant all through the history of capitalism, except for possible moments of crisis when it can no longer function," and "the national liberation alliance of the proletariat, peasantry, and at least part of the bourgeoisie."[71] The hegemony of imperialism over the working class in the imperialist countries is indisputable, even though most who call themselves Marxists in the imperialist countries deny this—but the moments of crisis have been much more than moments, and, as we shall discuss in the concluding chapter, crisis is now a permanent condition in the imperialist centers. Much more problematic is Amin's formulation concerning the national liberation alliance, which, with the addition of the middle class, conforms to the Stalinist policy of the bloc of four classes. Defining the primary contradiction to be between this bloc and imperialism was the rationale used by Stalinist Communist parties throughout the oppressed nations to justify reining in the independent struggle of the workers and farmers against their own national bourgeoisies, as the course of the Chinese Revolution itself testifies. Amin wishes to smash the alliance between capitalists and workers in the imperialist countries, and in this is infinitely more progressive than his Euro-Marxist critics who deny the existence of this alliance, yet he wishes to preserve it, albeit under Communist leadership, in the oppressed nations.

However sharp the political differences between the Chinese and Soviet leaderships were, they had far more in common with each other than with the communists of Cuba,[72] who sought to build an alliance of the oppressed classes, a *worker-peasant alliance*, and who acted on the premise that, in Che Guevara's words, "the indigenous bourgeoisies have lost all capacity to oppose imperialism—if they ever had any. . . . There are no other alternatives. Either a socialist revolution or a caricature of a revolution."[73] This is the polar opposite of the actual course followed by

Moscow- and Beijing-oriented Communist parties, namely of renounc-
ing the struggle to bring revolutionary governments of workers and
farmers to power in favor of becoming junior partners in coalitions led
by supposedly progressive capitalists, a course that led to catastrophic
defeats in scores of countries, most notably in Iran, 1953; Iraq, 1963; and
Indonesia, 1965.[74]

AS WE HAVE SEEN ABOVE, BOURGEOIS THEORIES of dependency
ascribed agency to capitalist elites and a support role, at best, to the popular classes, and it also argued that concessions made to organized labor
in imperialist countries distorted prices of production on a world scale,
giving rise to unequal exchange. Marxists under the influence of both
Beijing and Moscow had little problem with the first of these premises,
though Maoists were apt to argue that the working classes in imperialist
nations were fully incorporated into the imperialist system, were beneficiaries of the exploitation of workers and farmers in oppressed nations,
and were willing participants in imperialism's genocidal wars against
national liberation struggles. So they felt no need to dispute the contention of Cardoso, Emmanuel, and others that concessions to these workers
is the fundamental source of unequal exchange. Indeed, this implication
could be drawn from Amin's theory of a single global value of labor-
power and the "hierarchical structure . . . of the prices of labor-power
around its value,"[75] in that he argues that these deviations are determined
by the class struggle—in particular by social-democratic concessions
made to pacify workers in the imperialist nations on the one hand, and
the brutal suppression of workers' and farmers' incomes in oppressed
nations on the other. In continuation, Amin argues that "linked to the
management practices governing access to natural resources, this globalization of value constitutes the basis for imperialist rent."

There is more than a grain of truth in Amin's argument, but both
the concept of a single global value of labor-power and the nebulous
yet tantalizing notion of imperialist rent are theoretically very problematic. The limitations of Amin's theory are brought into sharp relief by the
very different theory of dependency advanced by the Brazilian Marxist
Ruy Mauro Marini, who argued that super-exploitation of workers in
dependent economies was a "necessary condition of world capitalism,
contradicting those who, like Fernando Enrique Cardoso, understand
this to be an accidental development."[76] Marini successfully operational-
ized the law of value to explain the condition of dependency, in contrast
to Amin's argument, which—despite the title of his book—hinged on

monopoly and rent, both of which negate the law of value. Marini hinged his argument on a fundamental aspect of Marx's exposition of the law of value, namely the relation between absolute surplus-value and relative surplus-value. Marx argued that *absolute surplus-value*, that is, the exten sion of the working day to or beyond the physical limits of the worker and the restriction of her/his consumption of use-values to or below the physical minimum, was both logically and historically prior to *relative surplus-value*, that is, increasing the productivity of labor through the introduction of machinery, thereby reducing necessary labor time and increasing surplus labor, and argued that the rise of modern industry signified the growing predominance of the second of these. For Marx, the transition from the predominance of absolute surplus-value to relative surplus-value was necessitated by the limits on absolute surplus-value imposed by the finite maximum length of the working day and the minimum level of consumption required for the reproduction of labor-power, and by the rising struggle of workers for higher wages and shorter working hours. Marini argued that another factor played a crucial role in this transition: the importation of cheap foodstuffs and other consumer goods from colonies and neo-colonies, especially from Latin America. These were cheap because of the prevalence of super-exploitation in those countries, while *their* transition from absolute to relative surplus-value, that is, their capitalist development, was impeded by the appropriation of part of the surplus by industrial capitalists in the dominant nations. Marx's views on the historical progression from absolute to relative surplus-value have been misunderstood by Euro-Marxists to mean that the importance of absolute surplus-value has dwindled and all-but disappeared, but Marini argued that the opposite is true:

> The central issue in the debate is . . . should forms of exploitation distinct from those that generate relative surplus-value on the basis of increased productivity be excluded from theoretical analysis of the capitalist mode of production? The mistake of Cardoso is to respond affirmatively to this question, as if the higher forms of capitalist accumulation imply the exclusion of inferior forms and develop independently of them. . . .
>
> Capitalist production, by developing the productivity of labor-power, does not suppress but accentuates the greater exploitation of the worker, and second, forms of capitalist exploitation are combined in different ways throughout the system as a whole, generating distinct social formations according to which of these forms predominates.[77]

In other words, unequal exchange played a crucial role in the rise of modern capitalism in the nineteenth century, and continued to do so throughout the twentieth century.[78] As Amanda Latimer points out, "Marini's work undermines [the] myth that the shift to relative surplus-value in England was entirely the product of *national* class struggle."[79] Tiago Camarinha Lopes and Elizeu Serra de Araujo expand on this:

> For Marx the logical limits of capital itself, together with political campaigning by European workers to limit the length of the working day, were responsible for replacing the production of absolute surplus-value with that of relative surplus-value. Marini suggests that on the periphery the pursuit of surplus-value would focus on the production of absolute surplus-value. . . . In his view, the integration of Latin America into the capitalist world system would take place in response to changing needs at the center, specifically, the need to move from absolute toward relative production of surplus-value. According to Marini, the periphery thus has a very important role to play in the consolidation of relative surplus-value in the center. But for its own development, the production of absolute surplus-value remains the principal source of value expansion.[80]

With the increasing flow of North-South FDI yet to turn into a flood, international outsourcing yet to take off, and Third World debt yet to achieve its mountainous proportions, the dependency theorists' claims of systematic North-South exploitation crucially depended on making the theory of unequal exchange stand up; that is, to successfully operationalize the law of value, by developing the theory of unequal exchange into a theory of global capitalist production. Of all the dependency theorists, Marini went furthest down this road.

There are six aspects to his theory that underline its continuing relevance. First, Marini's theory of dependency hinges on the distinction between absolute and relative surplus-value, whereas Amin's theory of imperialist rent completely blurs these two categories. Second, the productivity of labor, and differences in it between imperialist and dependent nations, is central to Marini's analysis, yet he completely avoids falling into the Euro-Marxist trap of confusing the value of labor-power with its productivity. Amin, in contrast, argues that "there is but a single productivity, that of social labor working with adequate tools, in a given natural framework."[81] Third, Marini regards the value of labor-power to vary between nations, and to be determined by the specific way in which these different modes of surplus extraction are combined in imperialist and dependent social formations and by the interaction between them—a far more dialectical conception than Amin's timeless and static notion of a single global value of labor-power. Fourth, although Marini's research into the origins of unequal exchange necessarily analyzes the export of food and raw materials, his argument does not rest on the distinction between raw materials and manufactured goods, as in the Prebisch-Singer hypothesis. As Higginbottom points out, his theory "combines the genesis of the export-oriented capitalism at the periphery with the development of industrial capitalism at the center,"[82] and is therefore of particular relevance to understanding the outsourcing phenomenon. Fifth, Marini's concept of sub-imperialism (not discussed here), in which dependent economies like Brazil seek to compensate for the drain of wealth to the imperialist centers by developing their own exploitative relationships with even more underdeveloped and peripheral neighboring economies, such as Bolivia.[83] And finally, inspired by the Cuban Revolution, Marini argued, as Camarinha Lopes and Serra de Araujo argue, that

> the only route to overcoming the dependent condition is the revolutionary socialist one. This explains why Marini's thought is often excluded from official contexts, such as the universities. The strategy of socialist revolution is at the core of his analysis of dependency in Latin America, and the practical function of his thought in the area of political economy is to put the question of the transition to socialism on the agenda.[84]

Dependency's Euro-Marxist critics

What Marxist theories of dependency had in common, and what makes them so relevant today, was their perception that the wide and growing differences in wages and living standards between workers in imperialist nations and neo-colonial Southern nations is reflected in a higher rate of exploitation of workers in the oppressed nations and a mitigation of the rate of exploitation in the imperialist countries; the dependent nations losing and imperialist nations gaining because the former exchange more labor for less labor. What dependency theory's Euro-Marxist critics have in common, and what makes them so irrelevant today, is their denial of this reality.

Critics of dependency theory used to argue that the much higher productivity of labor in imperialist nations means that, despite their much higher levels of consumption, workers there may be subject to an even higher rate of exploitation than workers in the Third World. Thus, in their 1979 exchange with Amin, Weeks and Dore argued that "since it is in the developed capitalist countries that labor productivity is higher, it is not obvious that a high standard of living of workers in such countries implies that the exchange value of the commodities making up that standard of living is also higher."[85] Charles Bettelheim was less circumspect, arguing in his critique of Arghiri Emmanuel's *Unequal Exchange* that "the more the productive forces are developed, the more the proletarians are exploited."[86] Nigel Harris similarly argued: "Other things being equal, the higher the productivity of labor, the higher the income paid to the worker (since his or her reproduction costs are higher) and the more exploited he or she is—that is, the greater the proportion of the worker's output [that] is appropriated by the employer."[87]

Since this debate first raged, the neoliberal era and its defining transformation, the globalization of production, has fatally undermined the argument of Marxist critics of dependency theory. It cannot be seriously argued that the global shift of production to low-wage countries is of peripheral importance, so the response of the Euro-Marxists has been to largely ignore this altogether and leave the study of global value chains and production networks to bourgeois social scientists. The Euro-Marxist argument that higher productivity in the North means that higher wages are consistent with higher rates of exploitation has been negated by a simple fact: as we know from the labels, the consumption goods consumed by workers in the North are no longer produced solely or mainly in the North; to an ever-greater extent, they are produced by low-wage labor in the Global South. *Their* productivity, *their* wages substantially determine the value of the basket of consumption goods that reproduces labor-power in imperialist countries. Despite ubiquitous evidence of this, such arguments continue to be advanced to the present day; thus Alex Callinicos argues, "From the perspective of Marx's value theory, the critical error [of theorists of unequal exchange such as Arghiri Emmanuel and Samir Amin] is not to take into account the significance of high levels of labor productivity in the advanced economies."[88] And Joseph Choonara believes:

> It is a misconception that workers in countries such as India or China are more exploited than those in countries such as the U.S. or Britain. This is not necessarily the case. They probably have worse pay and conditions, and face greater repression and degradation than workers in the most developed industrial countries. But it is also possible that

workers in the U.S. or Britain generate more surplus-value for every pound that they are paid in wages.[89]

This argument rests on the higher productivity of labor that results from the higher organic composition of capital in countries such as the United States or Britain. Yet, as we shall see in the next chapter, Marxism teaches that the value and surplus-value generated by an hour of labor *is wholly independent of its productivity and of the organic composition of the capital it is employed by.*

Finally, to conclude this brief survey, let us consider the efforts of the influential Belgian Marxist Ernest Mandel to reconcile dependency theory with its Euro-Marxist critics. In his major economic work, *Late Capitalism,* Mandel acknowledges the central importance of unequal exchange to modern imperialism: "There is no doubt that the total volume of directly produced colonial surplus-profit is today less significant as a form of imperialist exploitation of the Third World than unequal exchange,"[90] and devotes a chapter to neo-colonialism and unequal exchange, in which he attempts to achieve a synthesis, a theory of unequal exchange that does not result from higher rates of exploitation in dependent, semi-colonial nations. Early on in his tome, Mandel acknowledges that "surplus-profits arise . . . when it is possible to force down the price paid for labor-power to a level below its social value . . . or what is the same thing, when it is possible to buy labor-power in countries where its value (average price) is lower than its value (average price) in the country where the commodities are sold."[91] Later on he speaks of "vast international differences in the value and the price of the commodity labor-power," giving the impression that these differences are in the same direction, implying a higher rate of surplus-value in the underdeveloped country.[92] He nevertheless adopted the strict orthodox view that there "exists in underdeveloped countries . . . a lower rate of surplus-value" than in the imperialist countries, though in his numerical models the rates of surplus-value are almost identical (100 percent in developed countries, 90 percent in underdeveloped countries), with all of his results deriving from vastly different organic compositions of capital—which is what he wanted to show, that value transfers associated with unequal exchange result only from differences in organic composition, just as between different branches of production within countries—or, as he argued in a 1964 article in *New Left Review,* value transfers from underdeveloped to imperialist countries occur "exactly in the same way as exchange between firms . . . which . . . produce at a level of productivity above the national average . . . transfers surplus profits to those firms."[93] This standard Euro-Marxist rejection of the dependency thesis of super-exploitation claims to strictly adhere to Marx's theory of value, but it is founded on an ideologically blinkered denial of the *palpable reality of super-exploitation*, and, as we shall show, on a literalist misreading of *Capital* that abandons Marx's method and ignores the really important and obvious clues to be found there that point in a radically different direction.

Mandel acknowledges and then denies the prevalence of super-exploitation; he posits this as the basis of unequal exchange, and then casts this to one side and defines unequal exchange as the consequence of differences in the composition of capital. He finally abandons efforts to conceptualize unequal exchange in terms of the law of value altogether, in favor of an explanation that rests on its antithesis, *monopoly*:

> On the world market the metropolitan countries now operate as monopolist sellers of machines and equipment goods, while the semi-colonies have lost their position as monopolist sellers of raw materials. There is thus a steady transfer of value from one zone to the other via the deterioration of the terms of trade for the semicolonies.[94]

Instead of a synthesis, Mandel serves up a confusing mess. Along with other Euro-Marxist critics of dependency, he succeeded only in confusing a generation of young people drawn to Marxism, this author included, and bears his share of responsibility for the fact that, more than a decade into the twenty-first century, Marxism still has not developed a coherent theory of imperialism.

AS WE HAVE SEEN, DEPENDENCY'S ORTHODOX Marxist critics in Europe and North America failed to notice that the center of gravity of the global proletariat and the source of the surplus-value sustaining capitalist profits in the imperialist centers was shifting toward the Global South, and paid little attention to the globalization of production and the implications of this for profits, wages, etc. The rapid growth of industrial production in Singapore, South Korea, and Taiwan heralded a broader transformation—the globalization of production and thereby of the capital-labor relation, opening the door to a new phase of capitalism's imperialist development. Yet the beginning of the outsourcing wave appeared to confound existing theories of imperialism. The response of the Euro-Marxists was, in different degrees, to maintain their distance from theories of imperialism altogether, but the dependency thesis remains an important influence among anti-imperialists today and is an important reference for renewed attempts to understand the imperialist evolution of the value relation. On crucial questions—the exploitative character of relations between core and peripheral nations, the higher rate of exploitation in the latter, and the political centrality of the struggles in the Global South—the Marxist proponents of dependency theory were right and their orthodox critics wrong.

8

Imperialism and the Law of Value

We have yet to see a systematic theory of imperialism designed for a world in which all international relations are internal to capitalism and governed by capitalist imperatives. That, at least in part, is because a world of more or less universal capitalism . . . is a very recent development.
—ELLEN MEIKSINS WOOD[1]

Critical evaluation of theoretical concepts developed in previous historical stages combines two distinct but complementary processes. First, the benefits of hindsight are brought to bear, as these concepts are tested against the subsequent course of social evolution, including both the empirical data of all that has happened since and new theoretical insights; and, second, these concepts are evaluated in relation to the data and theories that were extant at the time they were devised. These two analytical processes take place simultaneously and are often blurred, but the best results are obtained when we are conscious of these two processes going on in our heads. With this in mind, we now proceed to further enrich the concepts of value, productivity, exploitation, etc., that have so far been developed through our analysis of the empirics of neoliberal globalization and our critique of theories of dependency and new imperialism by critically evaluating the foundational ideas of Vladimir Lenin and Karl Marx, with the aim not of going back into history but of fully arriving at the present.

LENIN AND IMPERIALISM

Just as Karl Marx could not have written *Capital* before capitalism's mature, fully evolved form had come into existence with the rise of industrial capitalism in England,[2] so it is unreasonable to expect to find, in the writings of Lenin and others writing at the time of its birth, a theory of imperialism that is able to explain its fully evolved modern form. There cannot be a concrete concept of a system of interaction that is not itself fully concrete and developed, and, as Ellen Wood states in the epigraph, "A world of more or less universal capitalism . . . is a very recent development."[3]

Imperialist domination and plunder was a necessary condition of the rise of capitalism in England, but it has taken the whole course of capitalist development for the imperialist division of the world to become internalized, to become a property of the capital relation itself.

The systematic violation of equality between proletarians, a central feature of global capitalism that, as we shall see below, Marx excluded from the general theory of the capital-labor relation developed in *Capital*, derives from the systematic inequality between nations, which Marx also excluded. Both, however, were central preoccupations of Lenin, who defined this latest stage of capitalism in extremely sharp and political terms: "The division of nations into oppressor and oppressed [is] the essence of imperialism."[4] Here, Lenin was not so much stating a theory as recognizing a new fact not anticipated by theory, and in so doing, revealing himself to be the very opposite of the dogmatist his opponents accuse him of being.

Lenin's *Imperialism, the Highest Stage of Capitalism*, written in 1916, in the middle of the First World War, was written as a guide to action, a concrete analysis of a concrete situation, an attempt to lay bare the reasons why the leaderships of the mass socialist parties in the imperialist countries capitulated on the eve of world war. Lenin showed that the war itself was no aberration or accident but an expression of capitalism's nature, of the contradictions internal to it, and that the new imperialist stage of capitalism proved the objective necessity of world social revolution and the transition to a communist mode of production. Lenin's theory did what was then possible: it recognized the beginning of a new stage of capitalism's development and identified those essential characteristics of capitalism's imperialist stage evident at its birth, in particular the concentration of wealth and the rise of finance capital, its oppression of and predation on weak nations, and its militarism. Lenin could not have included a conception of how value is produced in globalized production processes because this phenomenon was only to emerge in a later phase of capitalist development.[5] These circumstances have resulted in an inevitable disconnection, persisting right to this day, between Lenin's theory of imperialism and Marxist value theory.

Despite the remarkable persistence to the present day of the key features of imperialism identified by Lenin—for example, since his time, there have been no new recruits to the select club of imperialist nations[6]—it is striking how keen currently fashionable theories of new imperialism are to take their distance from Lenin. Sam Ashman notes, in her editorial introduction to a symposium on David Harvey's *The New Imperialism,* the "general agreement that the classical theorists of imperialism, whose accounts are now nearly 100 years old, may be important reference points but they are not an adequate guide to the contemporary world." [7] Ashman is right about the consensus, but is the consensus right? A contrary view is that Lenin's nearly hundred-years-old writings are no more out of date than are Marx's writings of nearly 150 years ago. U.S. Communist leader Jack Barnes gives reasons for believing that Lenin's writings may be a more useful guide to today's imperialist reality than those of today's new imperialism theorists: "Lenin's theoretical contribution to economics is one no bourgeois economist will admit to and that petty-bourgeois radicals recoil from. Lenin's main point, more true today than when he wrote it 85 years ago, is that this monopoly stage of capitalism is one in which state-organized violence, imperialist wars, national rebellions, civil wars, and proletarian revolutions are just as much an inevitable, lawful consequence of that mode of production as business cycles, inflation, and depressions."[8]

Ellen Wood's reason for joining the consensus is her claim that Lenin believed imperialism "depends for its survival not only on the existence of . . . non-capitalist formations but on essentially precapitalist instruments of extra-economic force, military and geopolitical coercion, and on traditional interstate rivalries, colonial wars, and territorial domination."[9] This misrepresents Lenin, who emphasized that the capitalist rulers of the great powers became imperialist—that is, expansionary and predatory toward the rest of the world—as a necessary response to domestic overaccumulation of capital and rising class struggle, both of which provoked their predatory overseas expansion. The fact that imperialist finance capital emerged into a world in which pre-capitalist forms were prevalent was a circumstance, not a predicate, of Lenin's theory. David Harvey noted this in *Limits of Capital,* saying that "Luxemburg and Lenin . . . see imperialism as the external expression, dominant at a particular stage in capitalism's history and achieved under the aegis of finance capitalism, of the internal contradictions to which capitalism is systematically prone." [10] It follows that Wood's justification for a dismissal of Lenin is unsound. Wood's argument that Lenin's theory depended on the widespread existence of "non-capitalist formations" is more appropriately directed at Rosa Luxemburg, in whose opinion "Capitalism is the first mode of economy . . . which is unable to exist by itself, which needs other economic systems as a medium and soil." [11]

In *A Reply to Critics*, Wood suggests a less cavalier approach to Lenin's legacy and contemporary relevance: "Another approach I have encountered suggests that, although Lenin lived in different times, he foresaw the connections between then and now. According to that argument, he only claimed to be describing the beginning of a new development in capitalism, which would . . . never again exist without financial domination; and it was only in this sense that he described his own time as the highest stage. What we are seeing today, then, would simply be Lenin's prediction come true. As an interpretation of Lenin, this may have much to recommend it." [12]

David Harvey's study of Marx's writings led him "to conclude that the classical theorists of imperialism had not completed Marx's theoretical project." [13] Of course, it is unrealistic to expect them to have done so, since they were writing at the birth of capitalism's imperialist stage. Instead of seeking to connect with classical theorists, however, Harvey casts them aside, scolding them for bickering and for not being smart enough to complete Marx's theoretical project. The classical theorists, says Harvey,

> were desperately anxious . . . to construct a conceptual apparatus to confront the rapidly deteriorating national and international conditions. . . . The result was a body of theorising (or, in Lenin's case, pamphleteering) that was deeply marked by the conditions of the time. But I would go much further than Wood and argue that the theories they produced were not adequate to their time either, and that much of the bickering between the participants . . . reflects not only fundamentally different political positions over what was to be done, but also a theoretical failure to find a way to deal with the spatiotemporal dynamics that had long been constructing a global imperialist system. [14]

According to Harvey, "spatiotemporal dynamics," the addition of the dialectic of time and space to Marx's theory of capital, is the concept that completes Marx's theoretical project but eluded Lenin and his contemporaries. An alternative view is that this is a vacuous concept, inserted by Harvey to fill the gap left by his rejection of Lenin's thesis of the central importance of imperialist exploitation of oppressed nations. We saw in chapter 7 where Harvey has taken his theory; as for the bickering between Lenin and other classical theorists, Jack Barnes offers a much more reliable verdict:

> Kautsky and other centrist leaders did not challenge the basic facts presented by Lenin about the growing domination of monopolies, of finance capital. Rather, they denied that these tendencies increased the violence of capitalism on a world scale and created conditions for its overthrow by the toilers led by a proletarian vanguard. In fact, the centrists said, these trends fostered the conditions for the development of a stable order, based on a convergence of interests of the largest capitalist powers, that would transcend contradictions and conflicts and could lay the basis, over time, for peace on earth.[15]

Monopoly Capitalism

Most strands of Western Marxism, including many claiming adherence to Lenin's legacy, have disregarded Lenin's insistence on the economic and political centrality of the division of the world into oppressed and oppressor nations, dwelling instead on Lenin's argument that in its economic essence imperialism is monopoly capitalism.[16] Compounding the problem, neither of these antithetical definitions seems to be consistent with the concepts and categories developed by Marx in *Capital*. As Anwar Shaikh has argued:

> Ever since the publication of Lenin's *Imperialism* it has become a Marxist commonplace to assert that capitalism has entered its monopoly stage. Now, in the case of monopoly . . . the laws of price formation must be abandoned. . . . The focus shifts instead to the domestic and international rivalries of giant monopolies, to their political interaction with various capitalist states, and to the antagonisms and conflicts between these states themselves—in other words, to "imperialism" as an aspect of monopoly capitalism. The law of value, like competitive capitalism itself, fades into history.[17]

In a similar vein, Gavin Kitching contended that

The essence of Lenin's theory of imperialism as a particular stage of capitalism was precisely that it was distinguished by a growing domination of exchange and exchange relations (and of the bank capital—money—earned through exchange) over production and relations of production. . . . The major result of the shift of the theoretical focus . . . has been an almost total neglect of production and relations of production in an international context. . . . As a result, we are effectively without a theory of the world capitalist mode of production.[18]

There is an important grain of truth in this: as noted above, Lenin's theory of imperialism is more concerned with the violent struggle between dominant capitalist nations over the distribution of surplus value than with its mode of production. The problem with Shaikh and Kitching's argument is twofold: first, they dismiss facts not consistent with their theory, namely the imperialist division of the world into dominant and subject nations and the divergent rates of exploitation this makes possible; second, the tension between the rival definitions of imperialism reflects real, objectively existing, explosive contradictions in the global capitalist system itself. Andy Higginbottom has gone furthest in correctly posing the problem: "Lenin does *not* theorise imperialism with respect to the rising organic composition of capital or the tendency of the rate of profit to fall. . . . This theoretical incompleteness in the study of imperialism is atypical of Lenin, and stands in marked contrast with his own economic analyses of the development of capitalism in Russia, which are firmly based on the categories of *Capital*."[19]

How, then, can we achieve a theoretical concept of monopoly that *is* firmly based on the categories of *Capital*? This is a very large and complex question on which an extensive literature already exists. All we can do here is to outline how the phenomenon of monopoly should be analyzed and theorized.

Monopoly comes in a multiplicity of forms, and is used quite promiscuously in both bourgeois and Marxist literature to describe phenomena pertaining to production, distribution, brand loyalty, finance, concentration of capital, political and military power, and much else. In other words, it is routinely applied both to technological innovations that give capital a productive edge over its rivals as well as to any and all types of extra-economic distortion or barrier to new entrants. All of them result in above-average profits for certain capitals, but instead of a concept that explains what is common to all of these forms, resulting in a chaotic concept that includes everything and explains nothing, we must instead identify, through empirical analysis of the imperialist global economy, the specific facts that are essential to its imperialist character. Just as Marx sought the nature of surplus-value not by listing all of its forms of appearance (interest, rent, profit, etc.) but by discovering the real phenomenon that gives rise to all of these forms—the difference between the value of labor-power and the value generated by it, that is, the inherently exploitative labor-capital relation—so the *source* of imperialist profits and imperial rents is not to be found in any form of monopoly but in *super-exploitation*.

Monopoly in the marketplace and monopoly over the most advanced production process are related but distinct phenomena; a great deal of confusion results from the widespread habit of conflating the two. In the marketplace, monopoly describes the extent to which imperfections in markets result in equilibrium prices that do not equalize the rate of profit, enabling some capitalists to claim super-profits at the expense of their rivals. This form of monopoly is a secondary factor that affects the division of surplus-value between competing capitals. Monopoly over the most advanced production techniques also results in above-average profits for innovating firms; such forms of monopoly are constantly being created and destroyed by competition in each branch and sphere of production, but should only be called monopoly where insurmountable barriers stand in the way of other capitals adopting those more advanced techniques, thus locking in their higher-than-average profits. A technological innovation can become an insurmountable barrier when the innovator is given a legal monopoly over its use, as, for instance, when a pharmaceutical company brings a new drug to the market. Here, the source of monopoly power is not the technological innovation itself but the legal protection given to the innovator against potential competitors. Another form of monopoly power derives from the enormous size of the capital investments required for new firms to enter markets for many high-technology goods. In this case, it is not the size of the required capital that confers protection against new competitors, and hence monopoly power, since the centralization of finance capital through the banking system allows potential investors to easily raise whatever capital is required. What deters new entrants here is the domination of the potential market by one or a small number of incumbent producers, that is, the preexistence of monopoly or oligopoly. Once again, monopoly power derives not from the technology itself but from the size of the market and the degree of its monopolization. We could go on, but two central points emerge. First, monopoly is an extremely complex category and must be defined very concretely and precisely if it is to have explanatory power. Second, distinguishing technological innovation as such from monopoly allows rent in general and imperialist rent in particular to be seen, in essence, as a distributional phenomenon, that is, something that concerns how surplus-value is distributed between owners of capital and which is remote from the production process itself.[20]

How do these observations relate to Lenin's definition of the economic essence of imperialism to be monopoly capitalism? For Lenin, monopoly signifies the concentration of capital into giant corporations, the merging of financial and industrial capital, and of both of these with the state. The imperialist's monopoly power manifests itself in all of the ways listed above—monopolistic control of markets, of advanced technology, of the state and military power, and so on—and they all must be disentangled if monopoly is to be conceptualized in terms of the law of value. Lenin's view of a central place of monopoly in contemporary capitalist imperialism informs the *Monthly Review* tradition founded by Paul Baran and Paul Sweezy and continued today by John Bellamy Foster, Robert McChesney, among others, who, in *The Endless Crisis,* amass vast evidence to prove that

> the tendency to monopolization in the capitalist economy . . . is demonstrably stronger in the opening decade of the twenty-first century than ever before. . . . What we have been witnessing in the last quarter-century is the evolution of monopoly capital into a more generalized and globalized system of monopoly-finance capital that lies at the core of the current economic system in the advanced capitalist economies—a key source of economic instability, and the basis of the current new imperialism.[21]

At the time when Lenin was writing, monopolistic control over sources of raw materials was especially important and could be most effectively guaranteed by territorial conquest. Imperialist oil and mining corporations continue to exercise monopolistic control over raw materials and their extraction, but do so now through forming corrupt relationships with the most venal and treacherous sections of the national bourgeoisies of the subject nations, cutting them in on the proceeds. This typically involves the intervention of imperialist state power—a classic example being the U.S./UK-orchestrated military coup in Iran in 1953 that returned the Shah to the throne and returned control over Iran's oil to imperialist oil corporations—rather than through their direct subjugation through colonial possession.

The Export of Capital

In *Imperialism, the Highest Stage of Capitalism*, Lenin argued that "the export of capital, one of the most essential economic bases of imperialism . . . sets the seal of parasitism on the whole country that lives by exploiting the labor of several overseas countries and colonies."[22] Lenin's contention that the whole (imperialist) country is parasitical on the labor of workers in overseas countries and colonies resonates powerfully with the picture revealed in chapter 1's examination of the social relations objectified in the iPhone and the T-shirt, where Apple, H&M, etc., share the spoils of super-exploitation with myriad service providers and their own employees, with the biggest cut of all taken by the state.[23] There is, however, an obvious problem with applying Lenin's searing insight to contemporary imperialism. Apple, H&M, and the others *export no capital* to Bangladesh and China—their iPhones and garments are produced by arm's-length production processes. Export of capital as such comes in three forms: FDI, portfolio investment (purchases of shares and financial securities which, unlike FDI, do not give the foreign investor a controlling influence), and loan capital. All of these continue to be important, but, as we saw in chapter 3, in recent years they have been outpaced by the arm's-length relationship. The riddle can be solved by focusing on the essence of the matter, not the form–the *export* of capital being the form. Lenin's essential point is to be found in the second half of the quote above, and his argument is not that exploitation of workers in the imperialist country has ceased to take place—even if higher-paid, aristocratic layers of the working class may receive wages far in excess of the value they produce—but that the accumulated wealth of the imperialist ruling families has reached such proportions that the gigantic mass of surplus-value necessary to convert their wealth into capital, that is, self-expanding wealth, far outstrips the amount of surplus-value that can be extracted from its domestic workforce. The imperialists, Lenin argued, were compelled to export part of their capital in order to exploit the labor of workers overseas. Andy Higginbottom explains why Lenin attached such importance to this:

> With his emphasis on the export of capital as a characteristic of the new stage, Lenin has already identified a vital starting point from

which to deepen the analysis. . . . The export of capital means that there must be a new type of capital-labour relation, between Northern capital and Southern labour, it means the *export of the capital-labour relation under terms of national oppression.*[24]

What must be added is that capitalism's evolution, especially since 1980, has provided TNCs with ways to capture surplus-value extracted from workers in low-wage countries without having to export their capital to those countries, which is why arm's-length outsourcing is now a more important source of profits than FDI, portfolio investments, and debt (the three components of capital export).

To conclude this all-too-brief discussion of Lenin's contribution to the theory of imperialism, what is urgently needed is a concept that unites its economic essence—monopoly capitalism and its political essence—the division of the world into oppressed and oppressor nations; and for both of these to be explained in terms of the law of value developed by Karl Marx in his towering work, *Capital.* This would be the path to achieving what Andy Higginbottom has called a new synthesis of Marx's theory of value and Lenin's theory of imperialism. To arrive at the necessary starting point for such a synthesis, we now go back another half-century, where we will make a secure connection with Marx's great work.

MARX'S CAPITAL IN THE TWENTY-FIRST CENTURY

Dependency theory's Marxist critics were termed orthodox because they based their rejection of super-exploitation and the unequal exchange arising from it on passages from Marx's *Capital* that, on a superficial reading, appear to support their view. Marx devotes a short chapter in volume 1 of *Capital I* to "National Differences in Wages" which concludes that even though England's workers receive higher wages than in Germany or Russia they may be subject to a higher rate of exploitation: "It will frequently be found that the daily or weekly wage in the first nation is higher than in the second while the relative price of labor, that is, the price of labor as compared both with surplus-value and the value of the product stands higher in the second that in the first."[25] This is exactly the argument used by Weeks and Dore, Choonara, et al., to dismiss the possibility that the rate of exploitation is, in fact, higher in the poor nations, but there are three reasons why Marx's argument does not apply to contemporary North-South relations.

First, what these disciples of Marx forget is that each of the nations used by Marx for his comparisons—England, Germany, and Russia—were competing imperialist nations, each of them busy acquiring colonial empires of their own. The formally free nations of the Global South of today cannot be regarded merely as less-developed capitalist nations, analogous to Germany and Russia in the nineteenth century. Second, in Marx's schema not only did each worker consume domestically produced goods, each capitalist consumed domestically reared labor-power—this was an age before FDI, outsourcing, etc. Higher wages and higher rates of exploitation in more advanced England were both made possible by the higher productivity of labor in industries producing workers' consumption goods. As we have repeatedly stressed throughout this book, the defining feature of the neoliberal era is the large-scale shift of these production processes to low-wage countries. One long century later, the large-scale outsourcing of production of workers' consumption goods to low-wage countries has become a prime means of lowering the value of labor-power in the imperialist countries—or of containing its rise. The third reason why this passage in *Capital* does not apply to contemporary North-South relations is that late twentieth-century trade between imperialist and developing nations is qualitatively different to late nineteenth-century trade between England, Germany, and Russia. Marx's example assumed that English, German, and Russian capitalists competed in the production of similar goods, whereas, as we saw in chapter 3, contemporary North-South trade is in dissimilar goods. The great significance of this for the theory of value will be discussed shortly; for the moment it is sufficient to draw attention to this important contrast.

Marx fleetingly returned to the subject of international differences in the rate of profit and rate of surplus-value in a remarkable passage in volume 3 of *Capital*, in the midst of a discussion about the equalization of the rate of profit between capitals with different value compositions:

> In a European country the rate of surplus-value might be 100 percent, i.e. the worker might work half the day for himself and half the day for his employer; in an Asian country it might be 25%, i.e. the worker might work for four-fifths of the day for himself and one-fifth of the day for his employer. In the European country, however, the composition of the national capital might be $84c + 16v$, and in the Asian country, where little machinery, etc., is used and relatively little raw material productively consumed in a given period of time, the composition might be $16c + 84v$. We then have the following calculation:

In the European country, the value of the product = $84c + 16v + 16s = 116$; rate of profit = $16/100 = 16$ percent.

In the Asian country, the value of the product = $16c + 84v + 21s = 121$; rate of profit = $21/100 = 21$ percent.

The rate of profit in the Asian country would thus be some 25 per cent higher than in the European country, even though the rate of surplus-value was only a fourth as great.[26]

Marx's purpose here is to illustrate the effect of different value compositions on the rate of profit—in particular, that the rate of profit could be higher in the country A than in country B even if the rate of surplus-value was lower in that country. Unlike in the *Capital I* passage above, it says nothing about the relative wages, and contrasts two unconnected economies (there is no interaction, such as trade or investment, between them). The rate of exploitation is far lower in the less developed country, and this is because necessary labor-time, the time a worker needs to work to replace the value of her/his consumption goods, swallows up so much of the working day. There are two possible explanations for this—either the basket of consumption goods purchased by the Asian worker's wage is many times larger than in Europe, which of course is not what Marx meant, or the basket of consumption goods is *similar in size* in both continents but lower productivity in Asia means that much more labor is required to produce it.[27] Either way, it is clear that this passage does not describe contemporary interaction between imperialist and low-wage nations.

Marx's *Capital* was tasked with comprehending the capitalist form of the value relation, in order to discover the origin and nature of surplus-value, whereas the task before us is to theoretically comprehend its current, imperialist stage of development. The level of abstraction required for Marx's project is evident from his statement *in Capital I* that "In order to examine the object of our investigation in its integrity, free from all disturbing subsidiary circumstances, we must treat the whole world of trade as one nation, and assume that capitalist production is established everywhere and has taken possession of every branch of industry."[28] The corollary of this is equality between capitals, whose freedom to decide where and on what to invest their funds promotes the formation through competition of an average rate of profit across the different branches of the economy; and equality between workers, whose free mobility between trades, industries, and locations results in the equalization through competition of wages.[29] Orthodox Marxist critics of dependency theory accept that profit-equalizing value-transfers

take place *within* countries—between branches of production with differing organic compositions, and toward the most efficient producers
within each branch—and deny that there is anything qualitatively new
or different when these producers are located in countries with much
lower levels of economic and social development, different histories, and
different labor regimes. But, as we shall see, a condition of fundamental
importance assumed by Marx no longer holds: the equality of proletarians. Equalization of wages and the equality between proletarians within
a national economy is predicated on the free movement of labor, free
to sell its creative power to the highest bidder. At an international level,
this essential attribute of the proletarian condition is massively restricted
by immigration controls and by racism and segregation experienced by
Southern workers in imperialist nations.

Marx treated divergence of wages as the result of temporary or contingent factors that ceaselessly mobile capital and labor would erode
over time, and which could be safely excluded from analysis, as he made
clear in *Capital III*: "Important as the study of frictions [local obstacles
obstructing the equalization of wages] is for any specialist work on wages,
they are still accidental and inessential as far as the general investigation
of capitalist production is concerned and can therefore be ignored."[30]

This exclusion from consideration of systematic divergences of wages
from a common average, implying the exclusion of divergences in the
value of labor-power and the rate of exploitation, applies to the whole
of *Capital*. Marx's level of abstraction is clearly inappropriate for our
task. Study of workers' status in labor markets and their mobility across
borders reveals that, in today's imperialist world, the condition of equality between workers is profoundly and shockingly violated; and, as was
established in chapter 5, global competition has not produced any mea-
surable progress toward the international equalization of real wages—on
the contrary, overall wage dispersion has increased during the neoliberal era. Neoliberal globalization has greatly relaxed restrictions on the
mobility of capital across national borders, but there has been no such
relaxation of the free movement of labor—on the contrary, imperialist
governments are responding to increasing migration pressure by milita-
rizing their borders and criminalizing migrant workers.

The Third Form of Surplus-Value Increase

In *Capital I*, Marx analyzed in great depth and detail two ways in which
capitalists strive to increase the rate of exploitation. One is by lengthening

the working day, thereby increasing absolute surplus-value; and the other is to increase relative surplus-value by increasing the productivity of workers producing consumption goods, thereby reducing necessary labor time. In several places he briefly describes a third. In the chapter "The Concept of Relative Surplus Value," Marx writes: "The duration of the surplus labor . . . [could be extended] only by pushing the wage of the worker down below the value of his labor-power. . . . Despite the important part which this method plays in practice, we are excluded from considering it here by our assumption that all commodities, including labor-power, are bought and sold at their full value."[31]

Pushing the wage of the worker down below the value of his labor-power, that is, super-exploitation, is again mentioned two chapters later, during a discussion of the consequences for workers when "machinery . . . gradually seizes control of the whole of a given field of production," with the result that a "section of the working class . . . rendered superfluous by machinery . . . swamps the labor-market, and makes the price of labor-power fall below its value."[32] Here Marx is talking about the episodic, sectoral unemployment arising from the mechanization of a new branch of industry, but its relevance to the modern era hardly needs stating. A huge section of the working class in the Global South has been rendered superfluous by the inability of modern production methods to soak up enough labor to prevent rising unemployment, and this alone, even before we take into account the much harsher labor regimes and political repression prevalent in low-wage countries, exerts a powerful force that makes the price of their labor-power fall below its value. Even before we establish the precise connection between the wage, the value of labor-power, and the rate of exploitation, this already constitutes *prima facie* evidence that the value of labor-power has been forced down much more cruelly in Southern than in Northern nations, *so much so as to force a permanently lower value of labor-power upon these workers*. It is also powerful evidence that wage differentials are determined, in part at least, by factors that are quite independent of the workers' productivity when at work, such as absence of social security, structural unemployment, and repressive labor regimes.

Super-exploitation is mentioned for a third time in *Capital I*, in the midst of a discussion of how capitalists can increase the amount of surplus-value:

In the chapters on the production of surplus-value we constantly assumed that wages were at least equal to the value of labour-power. But the forcible reduction of the wage of labour beneath its value plays too important a role in the practical movement of affairs for us not to stay with this phenomenon for a moment.[33]

"A moment" is the length of Marx's digression, long enough for him to argue that "the constant tendency of capital is to force the cost of labor back towards . . . absolute zero."[34] As Higginbottom points out, this moment "has of course turned out to be somewhat longer," and persists right to this day.[35]

Not only did Marx leave to one side the reduction of wages below their value, he made a further abstraction that, though necessary for his general analysis of capital, must be relaxed if we are to analyze capitalism's current stage of development: "The distinction between rates of surplus-value in different countries and hence between different national levels of exploitation of labour are completely outside the scope of our present investigation."[36] So, the two necessary elements of a theory of contemporary imperialism—international variations in the value of labor-power and in the rate of exploitation—were explicitly excluded by Marx from his general theory as elaborated in *Capital*. Anwar Shaikh was thus wrong to contend that "the development of the law of value in *Capital* contains all the necessary elements for its extension to international exchange."[37] To connect *Capital* to the twenty-first century, necessary if we are to explain the world one and a half centuries on, we must latch on to the questions that Marx recognized were of the highest importance yet which he put to one side.

"Communism is not a doctrine but a movement; it proceeds not from principles but from facts,"[38] as Frederick Engels said. Analysis of contemporary imperialism must proceed from, and attempt to explain, a fact of transcendental importance: *the systematic international divergence in the rate of exploitation between nations*. Wage arbitrage-driven globalization of production corresponds neither to absolute surplus-value—long hours are endemic in low-wage countries, but the length of the working day is not the outsourcing firm's main attraction—nor to relative surplus-value: necessary labor is not reduced through the application of new technology. Indeed, outsourcing is *an alternative* to investment in new technology. Raising surplus-value through expanding the exploitation of Southern low-wage labor therefore cannot be reduced to the two forms of surplus-value extraction analyzed in *Capital*—absolute and relative surplus-value. Global labor arbitrage-driven outsourcing is driven by lust for cheaper labor, and corresponds most directly to the "reduction of wages below their value." In other words, global labor arbitrage, the driver of the global shift of production to low-wage nations, is the third form of surplus value recognized by Marx as a most important factor, yet excluded, as we have seen, from his theory of value.

The rediscovery of this third form of surplus-value, or rather its disinterment after being buried for so long, is a major breakthrough, providing the key to unleashing the dynamic concepts contained in *Capital*, and it was made by Andy Higginbottom in *The Third Form of Surplus Value Increase*.[39] There he comments, "Marx discusses three distinct ways that capital can increase surplus-value, but he names only two of these as absolute surplus-value and relative surplus-value. The third mechanism, reducing wages below the value of labour-power, Marx consigns to the sphere of the competition and outside his analysis." [40] Higginbottom developed this idea further in *The System of Accumulation in South Africa: Theories of Imperialism and Capital*, where, referring to the standard orthodox reading of *Capital*, he says:

> It is unclear . . . why lengthening the working day; and the indirect, unintentional and mediated effect of increasing labour productivity on decreasing the value of labour-power belong to the inner nature of capital, while capital directly decreasing wages does not. All three mechanisms increase the rate of surplus-value. Not only is direct wage decrease the mechanism that is crucial to understanding the mode of exploitation of capitalism in South Africa [the subject of Higginbottom's paper]; it is by extension crucial to the analysis of capitalism as imperialism and a world system.[41]

And he continues:

> The idea of super-exploitation needs to be conceptually generalised at the necessary level of abstraction and incorporated in the theory of imperialism. Super-exploitation is a specific condition within the capitalist mode of production . . . the hidden common essence defining imperialism. The working class of the oppressed nations/Third World/ Global South is systematically paid below the value of labour power of the working class of the oppressor nations/First World/Global North. This is not because the Southern working class produces less value, but because it is more oppressed and more exploited.[42]

This is a new fact not contained in Marx's theory of value. It is the starting point from which, and only from which, it is possible to proceed toward a value theory of imperialism. As Higginbottom concludes: "Experience of modes of oppressive exploitation is so overwhelming that not to include it in Marxism as a theoretical expression of capitalism as a world system would render Marxism itself obsolete.[43]

Why the Rate of Exploitation Is Independent of Workers' Productivity

In a much-discussed chapter in *Capital III*, Marx considers six counteracting factors that mitigate the tendency of the rate of profit to fall. One of these counteracting factors, the "Reduction of Wages below their Value," is another brief reference to this third way to increase surplus value, and is dealt with in just two short sentences: "Like many other things that might be brought in, it has nothing to do with the general analysis of capital, but has its place in an account of competition, which is not dealt with in this work. *It is nonetheless one of the most important factors in stemming the tendency for the rate of profit to fall.*"[44]

Once again, Marx mentions super-exploitation, that is, "pushing wages . . . below the value of labor-power," stressing its great importance—and then excludes it from further analysis. This and other exclusions reviewed in this chapter were overlooked by orthodox Marxists as they scoured *Capital* for ammunition to use against dependency theory, seizing instead on Marx's comment that higher real wages in England than in Germany and Russia are compatible with a higher rates of exploitation in England, his assumption of a very much lower rate of surplus-value in China than in England, and a few other scattered asides, in order to exclude the blindingly obvious fact of higher rates of exploitation from theory, and in so doing they use *Capital* itself to obscure capitalism's imperialist trajectory and shield it from criticism.

Undoubtedly the most tantalizing of the brief appearances of international differences in the rate of exploitation is contained in *Capital III*, in the midst of four dense paragraphs that make up foreign trade, the fifth of six counteracting factors restraining the fall in the rate of profit. Underlining the distance between then and now, Marx discusses a world before large-scale production outsourcing, a time when international trade took place in goods that each capitalist produced at home. In these paragraphs, Marx specifies or alludes to no less than five different ways in which "capital invested in foreign trade, and colonial trade in particular,"[45] can increase the average rate of profit in the imperialist country, thus countering its tendency to fall—and the fifth, briefest, and most allusive is to the higher rate of exploitation in the subject nations.

The first two counteracting effects are to be found in Marx's explanation that "insofar as foreign trade cheapens on the one hand the elements of constant capital and on the other the necessary means of subsistence into which variable capital is converted, it acts to raise the rate of profit by raising the rate of surplus-value and reducing the value of constant capital." The rough nature of the notes that Engels assembled into *Capital III* is evident here—the cited passage is confusing because the order of the two pairs of cause and effect are reversed: cheapening the price of raw materials ("elements of constant capital") results in the reduction in the value of constant capital, while the cheapening of workers' necessary means of subsistence results in a reduction of the value of labor power and an increase in relative surplus value.

We are already familiar with these first two counteracting effects, but the third counteracting effect of trade on the tendency of the rate of profit to fall,[46] resulting from the ability of firms in "the more advanced country [to] sell its goods above their value," needs special attention. Marx says this effect of trade is analogous to "a manufacturer who makes use of a new discovery before this has become general," thereby reaping a super-profit because his more technically advanced capital can produce a *given commodity* in less than the average socially necessary labor time required in the technically retarded country. These extra profits *only arise in competition between capitalists in the same branch*, producing similar goods in direct competition with each other, for example, cars, chemicals, or clothing, and results from capitals with differing costs of production all selling for the same price. It is important to note that, assuming labor of average intensity and complexity (we return to the subject of complex labor later in this chapter), *all* of the labor-power expended by workers employed in the less productive capitals counts *equally* toward total value, even if a disproportionate part of it is captured by the more productive capitalists. The more productive capitalists' extra profits derive not from their own more productive workers but from surplus labor extracted from workers employed by technologically deficient capitals.[47] Were these capitals to be driven out of production, the average socially necessary labor time required for the production of these commodities would decline, and with it their price and the surviving capitalists' extra profits. Thus the value generated by productive workers in a given amount of time is independent of their productivity, even if the value added captured by their employers remains highly dependent on this. This is so fundamental, it must be repeated: a steelworker operating more technologically sophisticated machinery *does not* produce more exchange value, s/he simply allows her/his capitalist employer to capture a larger share of it. It follows that the rate of exploitation—assuming equal wages, intensity of labor, etc.—is not higher in more productive capitals than in less productive capitals.

Between branches of production, when trade is in dissimilar goods, matters are very different. Producers of entirely different commodities do not confront each other directly as competitors in product markets, but indirectly, as capitals competing for new investors. *Between* branches of production, assuming a uniform value of labor-power, relative prices are determined by the different amounts of socially necessary labor time required to produce each product and by profit-equalizing transfers of value generated by differences in the organic composition of capital.[48]

Though it is certainly true that workers using advanced technology will produce more use-value, the quantity of value and of surplus-value generated by their living labor will be no different than if the same labor was performed in a less advanced firm in the same branch of production, and the same is true when we consider the value generated by a given quantity of average labor in a different branch of production. The apparently higher productivity of workers in capital-intensive branches of production is an illusion created by transfers of value from capitals with low organic composition to those where it is higher *and also* by transfers of value from capitals with higher-than-average rates of exploitation to those with lower-than-average rates of exploitation. In other words, what the capitalist thinks of as profits magically appearing out of dead labor, that is, from his machinery and other inputs, is in fact value created by living labor employed by rival capitalists with lower organic compositions and/or higher rates of exploitation. It follows that, assuming that both labors are of average intensity, and ignoring the issue of qualified or complex labor, the new value generated by a given quantity of living labor *is wholly independent of the organic composition of the capital it sets in motion.* In other words, again assuming both labors are of average intensity and assuming they are paid the same wages, the quantity of value produced in a standard working day by the hamburger-flipper standing in the car-park of a steel factory is the same as that produced during the same time by the steelworker inside that factory.[49] Not only is the relation between the productivity of labor and the exchange-value created by it not direct, as asserted by mainstream economic theory and echoed by Euro-Marxists, they are wholly independent of each other, as Marx emphasized:

> By productivity, of course, we always mean the productivity of
> concrete useful labor. . . . Useful labor becomes . . . a more or less
> abundant source of products in direct proportion as its productiv-
> ity rises or falls. As against this, however, variations in productivity
> have no impact whatever on the labor itself represented in value. As
> productivity is an attribute of labor in its concrete useful form, it nat-
> urally ceases to have any bearing on that labor as soon as we abstract
> from its concrete useful form. The same labor, therefore, performed
> for the same length of time, always yields the same amount of value,
> independently of any variations in productivity. But it provides dif-
> ferent quantities of use-values during equal periods of time.[50]

Belief in a direct relation between wages and productivity is therefore
founded on a confusion of use-value with exchange-value, a confusion
that wrecks the very foundation of Marx's theory and in fact responds to
the semblance of the relations of production in the mind of the capitalist.
Ironically, the orthodox Marxists end up promoting bourgeois economics dressed in Marxist terminology.

It follows from the foregoing that value transfers to innovating capitals
from less advanced capitals *within* a branch of production are the result
of *differences in the individual productivities of the individual capitals*
within that branch—and result in *divergence* in the rate of profit enjoyed
by individual capitals. On the other hand, value transfers *between* different branches are effected by the *different value compositions of the total
capital employed in the different branches*—and, in a unitary economy,
in which capital and commodities freely flow, this results in *convergence*
of the rate of profit between the different branches and the formation
of an average, economy-wide rate of profit. Whether trade between
countries involves competition between firms trading similar goods or
instead involves the exchange of dissimilar goods is therefore of great
importance, determining which type of value transfer is predominant. It
is therefore highly significant that, as we saw in chapter 3, trade between
imperialist nations is in similar goods, while, in contrast, trade between
imperialist and developing nations is in different goods. We thus obtain
this important result: in N-N trade differences in productivity are a
prime cause of value-transfers and a prime determinant of above- or
below-average profits, but in N-S trade *they are not*; and, for this reason,
this particular counteracting effect of foreign trade on the falling rate of
profit does not explain anything about the interaction between imperialist and low-wage economies. An alternative explanation is required, one

that rests on the central role played by the third form of surplus-value extraction, that is, super-exploitation.

Super-Exploitation in Marx's Capital

Finally, in this remarkable sentence, Marx says, "As far as capital invested in colonies, etc., is concerned, the reason why this can yield higher rates of profit is that the profit rate is generally higher there on account of the lower degree of development, and so too is the exploitation of labor, through the use of slaves and coolies, etc."[51]

Close examination of this passage reveals not one but two reasons why capital invested in colonies may return a higher than average rate of profit. Lower degree of development refers to low productivity, capital-intensity, etc., and extends to the colonies the same unequal exchange effect previously identified by Marx in trade between more and less advanced capitalist nations. It is the second part of the sentence that attracts attention. Marx says that "the profit rate is generally higher [in the colonies] . . . and so too is the exploitation of labor, through the use of slaves and coolies, etc." The few words in this single sentence are the only place in the whole of *Capital*'s three volumes and in its fourth volume, *Theories of Surplus Value*, where Marx mentions the positive effect on the rate of profit in the imperialist nations of higher exploitation in subject nations.[52]

In continuation, Marx says, "There is no reason why the higher rates of profit that capital invested in certain branches yields in this way, and brings to its country of origin, should not enter into the equalization of the general rate of profit and hence raise this in due proportion, unless monopolies stand in the way."[53] This short sentence indicates how the theory of value relates to the concept of monopoly—the latter is a second-order phenomenon that affects the distribution of surplus-value. In order to arrive at a concrete concept of monopoly, analysis must first of all abstract from it in order to analyze the value relation, as argued in the discussion of Amin's theory of imperialist rent in chapter 7.

Qualified Labor in Marx's Theory of Value

So far we have shown that, according to Marx's theory of value, and assuming throughout that all labor is of average intensity, the quantity of value objectified in commodities by one hour of living labor is entirely independent of its specific productivity. In other words, workers in firms employing more advanced technology do not themselves produce any more value in a given period of time than workers employed by more backward firms, but the higher productivity of workers in the former does allow their employer to capture part of the surplus value generated in the latter. Assuming all workers in this branch work with the same intensity, *all* of their labor is counted *equally* toward the total value generated in that branch, and if they are all paid the same wage, that is, assuming a uniform value of labor-power, they are all equally exploited, regardless of productivity differences between those working for more- and less-advanced capitals. We have also shown that the same is true of the living labor performed by workers employed in different branches of production where the organic composition of capital varies. Again, assuming labor of average intensity and a common value of labor-power, they are all equally exploited. The orthodox Marxists' rejection of the dependency thesis therefore not only fails the test of external validity, that is, it flies in the face of the reality of the extreme rates of exploitation in Bangladeshi garment factories, Chinese production lines, South African platinum mines, and Brazilian coffee farms. It also fails the test of internal validity; it contradicts the most fundamental principles of Marxist value theory. It further follows that the much lower level of wages and the value of labor-power in Bangladesh, China, and other countries in the Global South reflects the higher rate of exploitation prevalent in those countries. And finally, it is clear that this higher rate of exploitation corresponds neither to a higher rate of absolute surplus-value nor to a higher rate of relative surplus-value but to what Higginbottom has called the third form of surplus-value increase, what Marx called the reduction of wages below the value of labor-power but we call here, simply, a lower value of labor-power.

There is, however, another extremely important dimension of the problem. Though neither the specific productivity of living labor employed by a particular firm nor the average productivity of labor in a particular branch of production affects the quantity of value generated in a given period of time, this assumes that all of this labor is what Marx called average labor—labor that is equally qualified, equally skilled. This is a safe assumption when it comes to comparing the labor of Bangladeshi garment workers or Chinese iPhone assemblers to the labor of workers employed in the transportation and retail of these commodities in the countries where these commodities are sold. The huge differences in the value of labor-power between these two regions of the global economy therefore provide a reliable index of the huge differences in the rate of exploitation of those workers. But what does Marx's theory of value say about the value-generating quality of skilled labor vis-à-vis unskilled labor? In *Capital I*, Marx explains:

> All labour of a higher, or more complicated, character than aver-age labour is expenditure of labour power of a more costly kind, labour-power whose production has cost more time and labour than unskilled or simple labour-power, and which therefore has a higher value. This power being of higher value, it expresses itself in labour of a higher sort, and therefore becomes objectified, during an equal amount of time, in proportionally higher values.[54]

To the extent that the higher wages of skilled, more complex labor reflects the higher cost of its production, the ratio between necessary labor-time and surplus labor-time, i.e. the rate of exploitation, is neither higher nor lower than that endured by unskilled, simple labor. As Marx says, in continuation, "Whatever difference in skill there may be between the labour of a spinner and that of a jeweller, the portion of his labour by which the jeweller merely replaces the value of his own labour-power does not in any way differ from the additional portion of his labour by which he creates surplus-value," a point to which he returned in *Capital III*:

> Distinctions, for instance in the level of wages, depend to a large measure on the distinction between simple and complex labour that was mentioned in the first chapter of Volume 1, and although they make the lot of the workers in different spheres of production very unequal, they in no way affect the degree of exploitation of labour in these various spheres. If the work of a goldsmith is paid at a higher rate than that of a day-labourer, for example, the former's surplus labour also produces a correspondingly greater surplus-value than does the latter.[55]

It was in this context that Marx stated, as quoted earlier, that "important as the study of frictions [impeding equalization of wages] is . . . they are still accidental and inessential as far as the general investigation of capitalist production is concerned. . . . It is assumed throughout that actual conditions correspond to their concept."[56]

In *Capital I* , Marx goes on to explain why, in addition to the exclusions already discussed, he also excluded difference between qualified or complex labor and simple labor from his general theory: "In every process of creating value the reduction of the higher type of labor to average social labor is unavoidable. We therefore save ourselves a superfluous operation, and simplify our analysis, by the assumption that the labor of the workers employed by the capitalist is average simple labor." He added, in a footnote to this passage:

> The distinction between higher and simple labour, skilled labour and unskilled labour, rests in part on pure illusion or, to say the least, on distinctions that have long since ceased to be real, and survive only by virtue of a national convention; and in part on the helpless condition of some sections of the working class, a condition that prevents them from exacting equally with the rest the value of their labour-power.[57]

Here, Marx considers the distinction between skilled and unskilled labor within a single national economy, regarding it to be a transient phenomenon, destined to be eroded by competition between workers and by the deskilling of skilled labor as complex, labor-intensive production processes become mechanized and therefore simplified. Attempts to explain the huge divergences in wages and the value of labor-power between workers in imperialist and low-wage nations as the result of the distinction between skilled and unskilled labor-power, as do dependency theory's orthodox Marxist critics, rest, in very large part, on some combination of pure illusion and self-deception. To ignore, as they do, the role of "the helpless condition of some sections of the working class," namely those corralled by immigration controls and oppressed by brutal labor regimes in low-wage countries, in forcing down the value of their labor-power, in *ratcheting up their rate of exploitation,* is bad science and leads to worse politics.

Falling Rate of Profit

To conclude my attempt in this chapter to connect Marx's theory of value with today's imperialist reality, a note about a fundamental postulate of this theory, namely the tendency of the rate of profit to fall. In Marx's schema the rate of profit, $s/(c+v)$, tends to fall because s, surplus labor, is limited by the length of the working day, while c, the quantity of fixed capital that needs to be advanced, grows relative to v, living labor, and without limit. If this simple equation was applicable to a single firm, higher investment in fixed capital would mean a lower rate of profit, which would be a mighty disincentive to investment in machinery. Marx explained how capital-intensive capitals are rescued from this fate by profit-equalizing flows of value from branches of production with lower organic compositions (organic composition is the ratio of fixed capital to living labor, or c/v). The average rate of profit is thus determined by the intersection of two relations: the rate of exploitation, s/v, which Marx assumed to be constant for a given economy, and the average composition of capital, c/v, of all capitals producing all commodities. To the extent to which living labor is progressively replaced by dead labor, i.e., as c rises while v remains constant or falls, the average rate of profit will tend to fall. In the real world, this actually existing tendency is counteracted by many phenomena. We have explored one of the most important, the outsourcing of production, in this book. Outsourcing reduces both c and v, as direct responsibility for the exploitation of wage labor has been outsourced, yet part of s, the surplus value captured by the outsourcing firms, is generated by living labor in the remote locations where production now takes place. At its extreme, in the case of firms who have outsourced all production to independent suppliers, both c and v become vanishingly small, the rate of profit becomes infinite and the very concept of organic composition ceases to apply.

To account for this, to comprehend the rate of profit in the actual conditions of globalized production, we must make allow for variation in s/v (the rate of exploitation) as well as c/v (the organic composition of capital) and for interaction between the two. The very interesting debate among Marxists in the United States, Europe, and Japan on the tendency for the rate of profit to fall does not consider this; it generally ignores the fact that a substantial part of the surplus-value that is captured by firms in imperialist countries and realized as profit was extracted from workers in low-wage countries.

Relating the law of the tendential decline in the rate of profit to the real world is complicated by many other factors. The sphere of production and trade is connected at all points to the sphere of banking and finance, where surplus-value captured in production is transmuted into interest payments and dividends for the owners of financial assets. Whether or not the rate of profit is increasing or declining, what matters is whether the total mass of surplus value is sufficient to reward all those with claims on it. These claims rose faster than world GDP in the decade preceding the crisis and have grown even more strongly since then. As their wealth accumulates, so does their need for sufficient surplus-value to convert all of this wealth into capital. As the vampire grows to gargantuan proportions, so does the quantity of blood required to slake its thirst. The greatest of all "global imbalances" is what could be called the hypertrophy of capital, otherwise known as overaccumulation: a growing disproportion between the claims on surplus-value and the capacity of the productive system to meet these claims. This disproportion can only be resolved through a partial but substantial reduction in these claims, in other words a major destruction of financial assets. Everything that policy makers and central bankers have done since the crisis, and indeed in the years before it, has been designed to prevent this, yet all they have succeeded in doing is to postpone this certain eventuality. Soon, maybe the next time they kick the can, instead of being pushed further down the road it will explode.

THE PLACE OF OUTSOURCING IN THE HISTORY OF CAPITALISM

The central finding from our search of Marx's *Capital* for clues, concepts, and methodological tools useful for analyzing and theorizing super-exploitation is that global labor arbitrage is the form taken by the third form of surplus-value increase. This provides the only possible solid foundation for a renaissance of Marxism, for the achievement, at long last, of a theory of the imperialist form of the law of value, one that uses Lenin's searing insights into capitalism's imperialist trajectory to interrogate and reconnect with Marx and uses Marx's theory of value to interrogate and reconnect with Lenin, opening the way to the forging of a revolutionary Marxism-Leninism that, unlike its previous, perverse Stalinist iteration, actually deserves its name. This is a huge claim, but one I am sure will stand against the flightless arrows of sterile Marxist orthodoxy. This central finding also allows us to see the place of the neoliberal era in history. In *Grundrisse*, Marx comments:

> As long as capital is weak, it still itself relies on the crutches of past modes of production, or of those which will pass with its rise. As soon as it feels strong, it throws away the crutches, and moves in accordance with its own laws. As soon as it begins to sense itself and become conscious of itself as a barrier to development, it seeks refuge in forms which, by restricting free competition, seem to make the rule of capital more perfect, but are at the same time the heralds of its dissolution and of the dissolution of the mode of production resting on it.[58]

Thus capitalism, like any organic system, moves through stages of immaturity, maturity, and decay. This bears a startling similarity to

Lenin's argument in *Imperialism, the Highest Stage of Capitalism* that "capitalism only became capitalist imperialism at a definite and very high stage of its development, when certain of its fundamental characteristics began to change into their opposites, when the features of the epoch of transition from capitalism to a higher social and economic system had taken shape and revealed themselves in all spheres."[59]

The rise of capitalism depended on the most barbaric forms of primitive accumulation, such as the transportation of millions of African slaves, opium-trafficking, etc., and its relationship with feudalism was not only antagonistic but fed off and sucked the life out of it, spitting out only what it could not absorb. When capitalism reached its adult stage and took full control over the production process, competition flourished and the inner laws of capital became expressed most fully. Finally, in its epoch of decay, capitalism increasingly relies for its survival on forms other than free competition—monopoly, vastly increased state intervention in all aspects of economic life, accumulation by dispossession, imperialism—but at the cost of distorting the operation of its laws and erecting barriers to the expansion of the productive forces. These three phases are not strictly separated from one another; each succeeding phase contains elements of those that went before; indeed, there is a kernel of truth in David Harvey's argument that accumulation by dispossession, or the continuation of primitive accumulation in a contemporary setting, is increasingly important to capitalism's survival. Harvey's great error, as discussed in chapter 7, is to contrapose this to the super-exploitation of wage-labor in the oppressed nations.

How does this chronology relate to the three forms of surplus-value increase? In the immature phase of capitalism, absolute surplus-value was the predominant form of the capital-labor relation. As capital took control of the production process, relative surplus-value became the predominant form, though at all times this depended on the persistence of much more brutal and archaic forms of domination in the subject nations. Now, the capitalist ruling class controls a greater portion of world wealth than ever in history and that wealth is growing faster than ever before, while the fraction of it being invested productively has never been lower. Global labor arbitrage—super-exploitation—that is, forcing down the value of labor-power, the third form of surplus-value increase, is now the increasingly predominant form of the capital-labor relation. The proletarians of the semi-colonial countries are its first victims, but the broad masses of working people in the imperialist countries also face destitution. The new, youthful, and female proletarians of low-wage countries dug capitalism out of the hole in which it found itself in the 1970s. Now, together with workers in the imperialist countries, it is their mission to dig another hole—to excavate the grave in which to bury capitalism and thereby secure the future of human civilization.

9

The GDP Illusion

How is super-exploitation, and the vast S-N flows of value it generates, rendered invisible in statistics on GDP, trade, and financial flows? To answer this question of questions, in this chapter we bring together many strands of investigation pursued in preceding chapters and further develop the critique of core tenets of neo-classical economic theory, demonstrating that supposedly objective raw data on GDP, productivity, trade, and value added, universally accepted as such by mainstream and critical social science, are in fact fetishized categories that obscure at least as much as they reveal. The specific aim here is to explain the biggest conundrum posed by the investigation in chapter 1 into the social relations embodied in the "Global Commodity." How is the contribution of Bangladeshi garment workers, assembly-line workers in low-wage countries like China, and poor farmers like those who harvest our coffee beans, so undervalued in the picture of the global economy as portrayed in standard statistics on GDP and productivity? The result, if you agree with the argument developed here, will be to profoundly transform the way you perceive the world in which we live.

The two main sections, "What Is GDP?" I and II, examine GDP's claim to be an ideal measure of the amount of output *produced* by economic activity within a nation, first by critically reviewing conventional definitions and common critiques, in other words what it says on the can; we then open the can and examine its contents, exposing and critically evaluating the highly contestable core precepts of mainstream marginalist economics that are at its core, in particular the concept of value added, concluding that GDP is falsely labelled, it measures not what is *domestically produced* by the firms operating in a given national economy, but that part of the *global* product that is *captured* by them. In other words, "Gross Domestic Product" is a grossly deceptive pretension.

This argument is further developed in the third section, "The Value-Chain Concept," which examines the concepts developed by new schools of research, collectively termed "value-chain analysis," which recognize the central importance of the globalization of production processes, arguing that while they implicitly challenge the underlying premises of the GDP concept they remain trapped by them.

The fourth section, "Three Elements of the GDP Illusion," outlines three distinct ways in which GDP data obscure the exploitative and parasitic relations between imperialist nations and the Global South.

The final section, "GDP in the Era of Globalized Production," concludes the chapter.

WHAT IS GDP?—I

The standard definition of GDP offered by the United Nations provides a useful starting point: GDP "is the sum of gross value added by all resident producers in the economy plus any product taxes and minus any subsidies not included in the value of the products. It is calculated without making deductions for depreciation of fabricated assets or for depletion and degradation of natural resources."[1] The essential element of this is that GDP is the sum of the value added recorded by all firms comprising a given national economy. "Gross" value added signifies that no account is made for depreciation of capital goods; while it is true that no account is made for depletion of natural resources and other "externalities," the UN definition is confusing—capitalists don't give a damn about externalities; including depreciation in the calculation is alone sufficient to convert gross domestic product into net domestic product. GDP can be measured in three different ways: directly, by using input-output tables to calculate total value added; and indirectly, either by calculating total expenditure in an economy minus expenditure on intermediate inputs; or as the total income of firms, households, and government. In principle, these three different measures should equal one another—each expense is someone else's income, and each firm's value added becomes the income of capital, labor, and government. These three different ways of *measuring* GDP too often become three different *definitions* of GDP, leading to conceptual confusion. In *GDP: A Brief but Affectionate History*,[2] Diane Coyle, professor of economics at Manchester University, gives a fine example of such confusion, arguing at one point in her book, that "GDP is the sum of all that is spent in the national economy."[3] No, GDP aggregates the value added generated in the production of commodities; the sum spent in a national economy is a way of approximating this, but it is not the same. Even this approximation is not equivalent to GDP, since "all that is spent in the national economy" includes income generated abroad, not domestically. Coyle offers an alternative definition, that "GDP measures output,"[4] which is much closer to the mark, but GDP only measures the monetary value of commodities produced for final sale (that is, intermediate inputs are netted out) and does not include output that is not traded, such as domestic labor. This might seem a pedantic point, and Coyle's formulation to be reasonable shorthand, but she also states that "some non-marketed parts of output, such as unpaid work in the home, are not counted on the grounds that this is . . . too hard to measure,"[5] repeating this claim later in her book, when referring to "the well-known paradox . . . that a widower who marries his former housekeeper is reducing GDP since he is no longer paying her a wage."[6] No—unpaid domestic labor is not counted toward GDP for one simple reason: it doesn't produce commodities. Housework is not counted because it is outside of the money economy, outside of the capital relation; it produces use-values, but it does not produce exchange-value—a distinction that eludes neoclassical economists like Coyle. GDP, therefore, doesn't claim to measure all production, it measures *capitalist* production. It is not only "difficult" to measure the output of unpaid housework in monetary terms, it is *impossible*. Unable to find the rational solution to these and other such paradoxes, her concept of GDP entirely disintegrates: "There is no such entity as GDP out there in the real world waiting to be measured by economists. It is an abstract idea."[7] Not only abstract, according to Coyle, but arbitrary as well: she criticizes an attempt to develop a different approach to the calculation of national wealth production authored by French economics professor Jean-Paul Fitoussi and Nobel Economics Laureates Amartya Sen and Joseph Stiglitz for arguing that "'GDP mainly measures market production.' . . . This gets it backward," she says. "GDP defines market production, which is then measured by the official statisticians."[8] No, Coyle herself "gets it backward": *market production defines GDP.*[9]

In comparison to Coyle, Lorenzo Fioramonti, professor of political economy at the University of Pretoria and the author of two recent books on the use and abuse of statistics, is a beacon of clarity: "As we know, what is not exchanged through the mediation of the market is not included in the national income accounts. As a consequence, by using

GDP as a measure of economic performance, our governments pursue policies that strengthen the market at the expense of informal economic areas, such as household services, the care economy and the gift economy. Moreover, as GDP is based on market prices, what is not priced becomes valueless."[10] Fioramonti strays into the same territory as Coyle, however, with his argument that

> the invention of GDP has been instrumental in generating the most powerful narrative of all times: that is, that markets are the only producers of wealth and that endless market production is the ultimate objective of politics. . . . GDP has afforded immense power to central bankers, economic advisers, development consultants, IMF specialists, World Bankers and the like, as these technocrats know best how to propel economic growth and manage the business cycle.[11]

But GDP is not an arbitrary invention, it merely registers the economists' recognition that the only thing of interest to capitalists is the value and the surplus-value that can be extracted from living labor.[12] Thus he says, "GDP is not just a number. It is *the* number par excellence ... in the case of GDP statistics, to measure is to rule."[13] There is a grain of truth here—as we shall see in the next section, GDP data imperfectly portray a world marked by gross inequality between rich and poor countries, yet at the same time conceal the exploitative, imperialistic relation between them. This is accomplished not by arbitrarily excluding important categories of social production from the calculation of GDP, although this undoubtedly contributes to the deception, but because of what is included: the fallacious and tautological concept of *value added*. The result, as we shall see in the next section, obscures both the exploitation of labor by capital and of poor nations by rich nations, and this is indeed instrumental in maintaining the rule, not of a number, nor of the technocrats responsible for calculating it, but of the capitalist class they serve.

Dirk Philipsen, professor of economic history at Duke University and the author of yet another recent history of GDP, *The Little Big Number: How GDP Came to Rule the World and What to Do About It*, makes the same mistake as Fioramonti, but in a far more crass manner, when he argues that "the tyranny of ignorance that characterized modern economies into the 1930s and helped bring about the Great Depression has been replaced by another kind of tyranny, that of a single metric."[14] No, the tyranny is not of a number; it is not a number that rules the world, as the title of his book claims, capitalists rule the world. According to

Philipsen, "The more central GDP has become, the more wreckage it has produced: depletion of resources, climate change, erosion of communities, social decay, rapid decline of biodiversity, a stark divide between haves and have-nots—and resulting endless conflict."[15] No, *capitalism*, not "GDP," is inflicting these evils. Philipsen's anti-growth tract seeks to protect capitalism and rescue it from its malevolent consequences: "Following the GDP logic is a self-inflicted problem. It is not . . . an inevitable result of the profit motive, nor is it necessary to run modern economies. Instead, its particular logic is directly traceable to a series of responses to 1930s disaster and war."[16]

GDP and GNP

GDP differs from GNP (Gross National Product) because the former includes income generated domestically by foreign firms and individuals and excludes income generated overseas by a country's own firms and citizens. If net profit repatriation and remittance of wages abroad is positive, GNP will be smaller than GDP, and the converse is true if net transfers are negative. Clifford Cobb, Ted Halstead, and Jonathan Rowe explain the shift from GNP to GDP:

> In 1991 the GNP was turned into the GDP—a quiet change that had very large implications. Under the old measure, the gross national product, the earnings of a multinational firm were attributed to the country where the firm was owned—and where the profits would eventually return. Under the gross domestic product, however, the profits are attributed to the country where the factory or mine is located, even though they won't stay there. This accounting shift has turned many struggling nations into statistical boomtowns, while aiding the push for a global economy. Conveniently, it has hidden a basic fact: the nations of the North are walking off with the South's resources, and calling it a gain for the South.[17]

However, as I shall argue below, GDP also hides this basic fact.

GDP and Government

For two centuries before the Second World War, "the economy," the sphere in which commodities are produced and capital is accumulated, was coterminous with the private sector; government was regarded as a consumer of part of this wealth, mainly to finance foreign wars, and its activities therefore subtracted from the national product (the terms GDP and GNP had yet to be invented). As governments became more and more actively involved in diverse economic activities, reflected in their increased share of the national product, this approach became untenable. The modern concept of GNP, adopted in the midst of the Second World War, was spurred by the government's need to accurately measure national output in order to determine the size of resources available for war production. Diane Coyle argues that this involved a "switch to conceiving of government as adding to national income rather than subtracting from it."[18] She is mistaken: the shift was from seeing the services delivered by government as a subtraction from GDP to seeing its role as *neutral*. In other words, the new approach assumed that the government provides services equal in value to the taxes it raises to pay for them—thus government does *not* make a net contribution to national product, as Coyle argues, and doesn't subtract from it, either. The notion that government activities, *by definition*, produce no net addition to social wealth is a blatant absurdity and a clear indication of the ideological bias embedded in the fundamental concept used to construct GDP: the concept of value added.

"Externalities"

"Gross"—the *G* in GDP and GNP—signifies that no account is made for depreciation of capital and of inventories of unsold goods, but even if we net these out, substantial additional costs, known as "externalities," which include destruction of the environment, damage to the health of workers and consumers, and so forth, are not included in either gross or net measures of national product. This matters a lot. GDP is the ultimate measure of development, and no nation in recent years has experienced faster GDP growth and therefore faster development than China. Yet when externalities—for instance, the pollution of all its major river systems and 80% of its groundwater, heavy metal contamination of vast swathes of its farmland, its poisonous levels of air pollution—are taken into account, it is highly questionable whether China has experienced any development at all. Pan Yue, vice minister of China's State Environmental Protection Administration (SEPA), estimates that environmental damage has cost China between 8 and 15 percent of GDP per year, "which means that China has lost almost everything it has gained since the late 1970s due to pollution."[19] When we take account of the fact that capitalist development, especially over the three neoliberal decades, has brought the world to the brink of ecological catastrophe, Yue's verdict applies to the entire planet, with a considerable degree of understatement.

Cooking the GDP Books

Before moving on to look inside the box labelled "GDP," it is worth mentioning two recent significant and controversial changes to how GDP is measured: the supposed contribution of finance and the treatment of research and development (R&D) (another, "hedonic prices," in which market prices are manipulated to reflect changes in quality, affecting commodities comprising around 20 percent of the GDP of countries in North America and Europe, was discussed in chapter 5).

How to account for the financial sector in GDP accounts has long been a major headache for government statisticians. Coyle's book is a useful and accessible guide to the technical issues involved, and she underlines how the growing power of financiers influenced changes that greatly magnify the apparent contribution of banks to national output. The 1993 update of the United Nations System of National Accounts (SNA) introduced the concept of "financial intermediation services indirectly measured," or FISIM, which treats the risks taken on by banks as a service on behalf of their depositors and shareholders, confects a value for it, and counts this as an addition to GDP, with the result that increased risk-taking is recorded as increased real growth in financial services. This change accounts for a substantial part of reported growth in GDP over the past two decades, particularly in the United States and United Kingdom. Coyle points out that "ironically, the United Kingdom's Office for National Statistics implemented the treatment of FISIM fully for the first time in the 2008 figures. . . . The absurdity of recording big increases in the contribution made by financial services to GDP as the biggest financial crisis in a generation or two got underway indicates that the statistical approach is mistaken."[20]

Another major revision to GDP accounts is a radical change in the treatment of R&D. Until the 2008 update of the UN's SNA, R&D was regarded as a business cost, similar to its purchase of intermediate inputs, and made no separate addition to measures of GDP. With SNA 2008, Coyle informs us, "henceforth, R&D is supposed to be counted as investment . . . leading to upward revisions of 1–4 percent in the level of GDP, depending on the country."[21] She adds that "a second change made in the US statistics at the same time had the same kind of effect. That was to switch from counting purchases of software by companies as a form of investment rather than a purchase of an intermediate good."[22] Alan Greenspan, former head of the U.S. Federal Reserve, has justified these changes with the argument that "the market capitalization in the stock market—not its levels, but its difference from company to company . . . is telling us that the markets are saying that certain outlays are indeed capital expenditures irrespective of what the accountants call them."[23]

Each of these "adjustments" blatantly contradicts the UN's definition of GDP given at the beginning of this section. Hedonic prices convert a change in the usefulness of a commodity into an entirely notional, non-existent increase in the value-added of the firm that has produced it. FISIM goes a step further—it converts reckless risk-taking into something that is socially useful, concocts a monetary value for this, and records this as an addition to national output. The change to the treatment of R&D and software expenses is an even more radical violation of the standard definition of GDP as the sum of gross value added. In this case, an increase in the capital value of a firm, as measured by its share price, is arbitrarily ascribed to an increase in the firm's intangible assets; this is transformed into a purely imaginary addition to this firm's value-added, yet depreciation of this firm's tangible assets remains, as before, excluded from the calculation of its gross value added. Each of these highly dubious procedures raises many complex issues that require a much more detailed examination than is possible here. It is sufficient to note, for present purposes, that if it wasn't for these changes, the long-term and accelerating decline in GDP growth in imperialist economies discussed in the next chapter, would look even more dramatic.

WHAT IS GDP?—II

GDP is frequently criticized for what is omitted from its measure of domestic product—so-called externalities such as pollution, the depletion of non-renewable resources, destruction of traditional societies, as well as for where it draws the "production boundary," excluding all those productive activities that take place outside of the commodity economy, especially household labor.[24] Yet GDP has never been criticized for what it claims to measure, not even by Marxist and other heterodox critics of the mainstream. Part of the explanation for this reticence lies in the fact that marginalist and Marxist value theory coincide at one point: though Marxist value theory reveals that individual prices of commodities systematically diverge from the values created in their production, at the aggregate level all these individual divergences cancel out. In the aggregate, total value is equal to total price,[25] or as Marx put it, "The distinction between value and prices of production . . . disappears whenever we are concerned with the value of labor's total annual product, i.e. the value of the product of the total social capital."[26] The problem facing anyone seeking to use GDP data to analyze the international political economy is that in the era of globalized production the nation and the national economy can less than ever serve as the aggregate level.

GDP's claim to measure the value of domestically produced commodities is accepted without question. The contrary argument here is that GDP and trade data are artifices conjured from the fundamental premises and precepts of mainstream marginalist economic theory. These walk through the door every time we uncritically report GDP and trade data, each time implicitly accepting that Gross Domestic Product does indeed measure the wealth generated within a nation's borders and that statistics on world trade—including the superior, new measures of "trade in value added"—do serve as a more-or-less accurate measure of that which is traded between nations. But if GDP is a true measure of a nation's product then the residents of Bermuda, a "British overseas territory," which in 2006 boasted the world's highest per capita GDP, are among the most productive members of humanity.[27] This tax haven leapt above Luxemburg to take the top spot after becoming a favorite destination for hedge funds left homeless by the destruction of the World Trade Center in 2001, and was given a further boost by the devastation of New Orleans by Hurricane Katrina in 2005. The *Financial Times* reported that "Bermuda's reinsurance business has exploded in scale. The rapid growth started after the September 11 attacks in 2001 and gathered pace following . . . Hurricane Katrina. These disasters . . . pushed up the cost of insurance premiums . . . prompt[ing] hedge funds and private equity groups to dash into the sector, hoping to reap fat profits if premiums stay high. Bermuda became their favoured location."[28] Yet, apart from cocktails in beach bars and other luxury tourist services, and the output of some 1,500 Bermudians employed in agriculture and fishing, nothing is produced in Bermuda; its official status as the "world's most productive nation" rests on the allegedly extraordinary productivity of its expatriate community of hedge-fund traders and offshore bankers.

Sixteen hundred kilometers south-southwest of Bermuda lies another nation, the Dominican Republic (DR), which shares the island of Hispaniola with Haiti,[29] where 154,000 workers toil for a pittance in fifty-seven export processing zones, producing footwear and clothing mainly for the North American market.[30] Its per capita GDP in 2006 stood at PPP$5,549, 8 percent of Bermuda's, or just 3 percent at market exchange rates. According to Raphael Kaplinsky, workers in its footwear factories make shoes out of imported components, thereby adding 30¢ to the value of each pair of shoes—just 2 percent of the final selling price—and to the DR's GDP, to be shared between the state, the capitalist owners of the shoe factory, and the workers.[31] "Yet, in international trade statistics, the unit value of shoe exports was not the added value of 30¢ but the gross value of the final product, which was more like $15,"[32] while trade in value-added (TiVA) statistics (were they available) would count $0.30 toward DR's exports—and if the shoe factory is a foreign-owned subsidiary, part of this $0.30 would be repatriated to the parent company. The argument here is that neither gross nor net value-added measures even begin to approximate to the value actually generated by the living labor of Dominican shoe workers.

We can get closer still to seeing through the GDP illusion by considering the paradox that arises when the DR's employers reduce wages in response to intensifying competition with footwear and hosiery producers in China and other low-wage countries for access to the shelves of Walmart, Top Shop, and other large retailers. Assuming that this increased competition results from China's lower wages rather than from more advanced production techniques (in other words, assuming that the socially necessary labor-time required to produce these commodities is unaltered), lower real wages signify an increased rate of exploitation, a higher rate of surplus-value. The fall in the price of shoes signifies that only a portion of the surplus-value resulting from this increased exploitation of shoe workers appears in the profits of their immediate employers, the remainder being a contribution to total surplus-value, and is shared between Northern firms, supporting profit of all kinds; Northern governments, through tariffs, VAT, and taxes on profits and wages; and Northern consumers, raising consumption levels without raising nominal wages. A reduction in the real wage in DR therefore means that its living labor becomes *more* important as a source of surplus-value and profits, that is, it is *more productive of capital*. Surface appearances, however, as recorded in GDP and trade data, lead us to the very opposite conclusion: falling real wages in DR allow the prices of its export products to also fall, and with them the apparent contribution of DR to global wealth and profits. And the same goes for measures of our Dominican sisters' productivity, too: falling output prices directly translate into falling "value added per worker," the standard measure of productivity. These sisters make the same amount of shoes as before, and they are subject to an even higher rate of exploitation than before. Yet economic statistics record a *decline* in their productivity and in DR's GDP per capita. This hypothetical example illustrates what has actually occurred on a grand scale during the past three neoliberal decades, as summed up in the term "race to the bottom," and indicates that the GDP illusion is very far from being a minor distortion. As soon as it is recognized that the "financial services" that Bermuda "exports" are nonproduction activities that consist of filling treasure chests with wealth produced in countries like the DR, a very different perception is formed of which of these two island nations contributes more to global wealth—and of where their relative position in the league table would be if "GDP per capita" was a true measure of the respective contribution of hedge-fund traders and workers in Caribbean shoe factories to global wealth.

GDP, Value Added, and the Theory of the Firm

Despite its claim to be a measure of *product*, GDP measures the *results* of transactions in the marketplace. Yet nothing is produced in marketplaces, the world of the exchange of money and titles of ownership. Production takes place elsewhere—behind high walls, on private property, in production processes.

To assess the validity of GDP's claim to be an objective measure of a nation's domestic wealth production we must examine the premises on which it stakes this claim. The essential concept within GDP is "value added"—GDP being the aggregate of the value added produced by all firms within a national economy. Value added itself is the net addition to value that is thought to result from the productive activity of that firm, obtained by subtracting the cost of all inputs from the proceeds of the sale of the outputs.[33] But all that this price data tells us, all that is needed for value added to be computed, is the price of what goes in and the price of what comes out, with the production process remaining safely concealed inside its black box. Before moving on to evaluate the false premises and invalid assumptions contained in the value-added concept, we should note its one entirely valid implication: Value is created (or "added") in production processes, prior to the realization of this value in marketplace transactions. However, cognition of this elementary fact is confounded by the neoclassical economists' dogmatic insistence that value has no independent, transitory, existence separate from price prior to the realization of this value in the marketplace. As Marx said of this highly fetishized notion, "Both the restoration of the values advanced in production, and particularly the surplus-value contained in the commodities, seem not just to be realized only in circulation but actually to arise from it."[34]

Apart from profit repatriation from foreign direct investment (FDI) by TNCs, the only S-N flow of value recognized by bourgeois economists to arise from firms' international activities is that which results from transfer pricing—as occurs when a TNC over- or under-invoices for imports and exports or overcharges for business expenses, etc., in order to shift profits to low-tax locations, often offshore tax havens. In 2008 Christian Aid estimated that TNCs defrauded developing countries of $160bn a year in unpaid taxes through these activities.[35] UNCTAD comments, "To the extent that domestic value added is created by foreign affiliates of TNCs—a high share, in the case of many developing countries—the profit component of value added (about 40 percent in developing countries on average) may be affected by transfer price manipulation, potentially 'leaking' value added."[36] But this pertains exclusively to FDI; as we saw in the case of Bangladeshi garment workers and global clothing retailers analyzed in chapter 1, value flows generated by arm's-length outsourcing remain completely hidden from view.

According to the bourgeois economists' metaphysical concept of value, the marginal product of any one factor of production is derived by extrapolating the firm's total value added backwards in time onto the production process. The contribution made by each factor, including labor, is conceptualized by retrospectively apportioning slices of the residual value added to the various factors of production—to labor, capital, R&D, etc.—and is calculated by estimating the difference a unit increase in any one of them makes to the value of the firm's final output.[37] This is a pure tautology—a complex relationship between value and price is replaced by a simple equals sign. What is more, the arrow of time is reversed: unable to deny the elementary fact that values are created in production processes, the marginalist doctrine nevertheless insists that the magnitudes of these values are determined retrospectively by what Michael Prowse (see below) calls "the subjective evaluations of consumers." As Shaikh and Tonak comment, "The orthodox argument turns on the notion that marketability is equivalent to production. But ... marketability is only a measure of the ability to attract money."[38]

The value-price identity does not stop at mere tautology, that is, a forced equation of two separately existing phenomena; the two are conflated, the very existence of value as something distinct from price is excluded out of hand. Yet, and the marginalists cannot get around this stubborn fact, *value is added in production processes*. The conflation of value with price collapses the time between them, allowing the marginalist concept to evade the contradiction, but creating a looking-glass world where relationships are inverted and processes reversed. Evasion of this contradiction is only made possible by an arbitrary and far-fetched assumption. Even though the various firms and their production functions proceed simultaneously, as part of an organic whole, the marginalist "theory of the firm" does not permit them to influence one another. No value added is allowed to leak between them. Instead, the quantity of value added that remains after subtracting the price of inputs from the price of the outputs *is assumed to be entirely and solely the result of the production process taking place within that firm*. No leak or transfer is allowed between boxes, or else it would violate the forced identity of price with value. The famous "black boxes," it turns out, are not only black, in that all that's visible is what goes in and what comes out, but *they are also hermetically sealed from one another*.

Financial Times columnist Michael Prowse provides a classic example of the economists' fetishized view of value creation:

> What determines the value of goods and services? The correct answer is our subjective valuations as consumers. A good is valuable only to the extent that people demonstrate a desire to purchase it rather than something else. If our tastes change even a good that is scarce will cease to command a high price. Such a theory of value ought to be intuitively obvious; after all what could confer value on inanimate objects but the decisions of valuing individuals?[39]

In this schema, the production process is completely offstage, the only actors are buyers and sellers, and the only activity is buying and selling. The marginalist counterrevolution of the nineteenth century, succinctly articulated by Prowse, replaced a complexity (the transformation of values into prices) with an absurdity (that no such transformation takes place because value and price are the same thing), a counterrevolution made permanent by the post–Second World War "neoclassical synthesis."[40] The economists' "production function," in its many variants, mathematically expresses this unconditional identity: inputs multiplied by their factoral productivity are placed on one side of an equals sign, output on the other. Anything still unexplained can be lumped together and called "total factor productivity" (TFP) and inserted into the equation in order to ensure identity. As Lance Taylor sardonically comments, "Despite the fact that TFP and similar constructs basically boil down to manipulation of accounting identities, they are viewed as engines of great analytical power by the mainstream."[41]

The Marxist concept of value is diametrically opposed to this. Values are not disaggregated prices; according to Marx, *prices are transformed values*. In this approach, time is not forced to go backwards and value is not seen as a mere number or quantity of money, but as the expression of a complex, living social relation between each individual capital and all other capitals, what Marx called "the total social capital." However difficult it may be to conceptualize or solve what has come to be called the "transformation problem,"[42] values, which are prior to prices, *must be transformed into prices in a really existing process*. The consequences of this are profound. Once we open our eyes to the fact that, as part of the process of price formation, value generated in one firm may be transferred or reassigned to competing capitals, we are obliged to radically redefine value added to signify not the value it has added but *the share of the total value created by all firms* competing within the economy as a whole that this firm succeeds in capturing. And the economy as a whole is the *global* capitalist economy, not the national economy. This overturns universally held notions of what is meant by GDP. As we have seen, standard WB/IMF data on GDP, trade, etc., are compiled by adding up the value added contributed by each firm in a nation's economy. They are therefore projections of the tautological fallacy that forms the keystone of marginalist economics: the value-price identity, and its corollary, that what a firm actually adds to total value in the whole economy is the same thing as its value added.

The globalization of production processes signifies that the process of value-production itself, and the transformation of these values into prices, now takes place at an international level to a qualitatively greater extent than before the neoliberal era. If value can be produced by one firm in one production process and condense in the prices paid for commodities produced in other firms within a national economy, then it is irrefutable that, in the era of globalized production processes, this also occurs between firms in the global economy. In other words, as David Harvey once surmised, "The geographical production of surplus-value [may] diverge from its geographical distribution."[43] To the extent that it does, GDP departs ever further from being an objective, more-or-less accurate measure of a nation's product and instead becomes a veil concealing not just the extent but the very existence of North-South exploitation. It was therefore with unintended irony that J. Steven Landefeld, Director of the U.S. Bureau of Economic Analysis, described GDP as "one of the great inventions of the twentieth century."[44]

THE VALUE-CHAIN CONCEPT

Distinguishing between *value creation* and *value capture*, and even counterposing them, has recently become commonplace in business literature, but this is invariably done to provide practical advice to capitalists about how they may maximize their value added, not to inform a critique of it. A good example of this was provided by a study of the Nokia value chain by a team of Finnish economists, in which the two terms are interchangeable: "Value capture is increasingly detached from cross-border flows of physical goods. It is, rather, in-house and market services as well as various forms of intangible assets that command the lion's share of value added (and thus income and profits earned)."[45] The value creation vs. value capture terminology has also recently found its way into UNCTAD's annual reports, as in 2011's *World Investment Report*: "The externalization of any part of the value chain through the use of an NEM will cause a firm to capture less of the total value created in the chain. . . . This is balanced by . . . potential cost advantages that can be obtained through the externalization of activities (e.g. to low-cost providers and locations)."[46] UNCTAD does not explore the radical implication of this—that value created in "low-cost locations" is captured by lead firms based in imperialist countries—but it nevertheless represents an important step forward, and reflects the growing influence of value-chain analysis, to which we now turn.

Value Chains and Value Theory

The critique of value added developed in the preceding section can be used to inform a critical evaluation of new and highly active areas of multidisciplinary research into what its exponents variously call "global value chains" (GVC), "value-added chains," "global commodity chains" or "global production networks" (GPN)—collectively referred to here as *GVC theory*. These related heterodox schools have emerged in response to the same transformative phenomenon that is the focus of this book, namely the globalization of production processes, and have generated many insights and ideas as the many references to this literature in earlier chapters of this book indicate. Furthermore, the focus on globally extended production processes includes both the in-house and arm's-length forms of outsourcing in its field of vision, making GVC theory particularly suited to study of multiform arm's-length relationships. In this respect GVC theory is a big improvement on increasingly anachronistic approaches that peer exclusively through the foreign direct investment lens (discussed in chapter 3), whose starting point is formal titles of ownership of production facilities rather than the production process itself.

Gary Gereffi, John Humphrey, and Timothy Sturgeon, three prominent GVC theorists, state that "for us, the starting point for understanding the changing nature of international trade and industrial organisation is contained in the notion of a value-added chain."[47] Raphael Kaplinsky, another scholar who has made a major contribution to this field of research, explains the basic concept like this: "The value chain describes the full range of activities that are required to bring a product or service from conception, through the different phases of production (involving a combination of physical transformation and the input of various producer services), delivery to final consumers, and disposal after use."[48] A compatible definition was published in a 2007 report under the imprimatur of the World Bank, titled *Moving Toward Competitiveness: A Value-Chain Approach*. This publication gave the stamp of official approval of the value-chain approach, stating:

> Value-chain analysis is a method for accounting and presenting the value that is created in a product or service as it is transformed from raw inputs to a final product consumed by end users. Value-chain analysis typically involves identifying and mapping the relationships of four types of features: (i) the activities performed during each stage of processing; (ii) the value of inputs, processing time, outputs and value added; (iii) the spatial relationships, such as distance and logistics . . . and; (iv) the structure of economic agents, such as suppliers, the producer, and the wholesaler.[49]

Also feeding into the modern value-chain concept is the closely related global production network school. Its leading proponents have sought to differentiate this from the value-chain approach, thus Jeffrey Henderson, Peter Dicken, Martin Hess, Neil Coe, and Henry Wai-Chung Yeung argue:

A major weakness of the "chain" approach is its conceptualization of production and distribution processes as being essentially vertical and linear. In fact, such processes are better conceptualized as being highly complex network structures in which there are intricate links—horizontal, diagonal, as well as vertical—forming multidimensional, multi-layered lattices of economic activity.[50]

As GVC research has refined its concepts and developed typologies to examine simple and complex value chains, diverse contractual relationships, and so forth, these objections have become redundant. The difference in emphasis between the GVC and GPN approaches partly owes to their respective origins in sociology and geography, and—to no small degree—to the rivalry between academic schools anxious to exalt their approach above the others. Henderson et al., for instance, argued that "the value chain or value-adding chain is an old-established concept in industrial economics and in the business studies literature . . . [with] little relevance for the study of economic development."[51] However, far more unites the GVC and GPN paradigms than divides them—indeed there is a great deal of creative collaboration and cross-fertilization between these schools—and the critique of GVC theory developed in the next pages applies equally to both.

A fundamental distinction is made in GVC literature between "producer-led" chains, whose lead firms are industrial producers outsourcing labor-intensive production tasks, and "buyer-led" chains, whose lead firms are commercial capitalists, like Walmart and Tesco, who outsource production of mass consumer goods and low-tech intermediate inputs to independent Southern producers. Research has since discovered a multiplicity of hybrid forms between these polar ideal types. We should note one feature they have in common that is rarely mentioned, or when it is, is seen as the natural order of things: whether the value chains are buyer-driven or producer-driven, the lead firms are overwhelmingly headquartered in the developed nations, though more and more of the production takes place in the South. As Gary Gereffi argues, "It is important to recognise the fundamental asymmetry in the organisation of the global economy. . . . To a great extent, the concentrated higher value-added portion of the value chain is located in developed countries, while the lower value-added portion of the value chain is in developing economies."[52]

To all variants of GVC analysis, the desire to gain access to low-wage labor is just one determinant on a long list including such diverse factors as the communication revolution, reduced transport costs, infrastructure, skills, and other qualities of the local workforce. GVC analysis attempts to explicate the different factors determining the relation *between* capitals participating in the chain; the relations *internal to each capital* are beyond its field of vision. Not only is GPN/GVC's central concept not founded on the labor-capital relation, it sidelines this altogether. The result is a chaotic concept, founded on what Marcus Taylor has called the "fetish of labour as simply a factor of production."[53]

Jennifer Bair, in a lucid review of the different strands of GVC research, argues that the "principal task" of GVC analysts must be "to understand where, how, and by whom value is created and distributed" in "global industries."[54] The strong implication is that value is "created" in some of the links in the chain (say, the South's fields and factories), and "distributed" to others (say, retail giants), TNC parent companies headquartered in imperialist countries. In other words, values created in one link condense as prices received elsewhere, by other links in the chain, even though these separate links are different firms operating in different continents. Value-chain theorists have hesitated (perhaps explained by their reluctance to engage with Marxism or of being accused of it) to consider the far-reaching implications of this, preferring to talk of "rents" rather than "value transfers," or instead they ignore the problem altogether, worshipfully accepting the sanctity of the market's determination of value. Raphael Kaplinsky, who regards all income received by a firm above break-even as rent, is an exemplar of the former approach, and all of them lapse into the latter.

Bair followed up her call with a general plea for fellow GVC researchers to pay "closer attention to the role of workers as chain participants . . . [and for] more serious attention to labour than it has been given to date," and, even more promisingly, that "beyond looking at the extent to which workers benefit from processes of upgrading . . . discussions of upgrading also need to examine how workers contribute to the creation of value in terms of the labour process."[55] Unfortunately, her call for GVC theory to examine how workers contribute to the creation of value is not included in the "research agenda for the second generation of GVC research" that concludes her paper, and she avoids asking an obvious question: why has GVC theory had so little to say about this?

For all of its insights and empirical research into the forms and functions of value chains, GVC theory fails Bair's test; it is unable to explain "where, how, and by whom value is created and distributed along a commodity chain."[56] The root of this is a refusal to break with the neoclassical identification of value with value added. This failure is compounded by another of similar proportions: it has nothing to say about how value, once captured by a firm, is then divided between capital and labor. As Carr et al. comment, "Few of the global value-chain studies focus on who is employed, under what types of employment relations, and for what returns."[57]

That the prices received by a link in a value chain (or, if you prefer, a node in a production network) typically diverge from its contribution to the value generated in the chain as a whole is anathema to orthodox economics, but a fundamental postulate of Marxist value theory. And if such price-value divergences and corresponding value-transfers can occur *within* value chains, they must also occur *between* value chains. Value chain theory makes the same error that neoclassical economics makes with its hermetically sealed production functions, but now the error is transferred from the level of the individual firm to the level of the individual value chain. Just as neoclassical economic theory assumes that a firm's value added was generated entirely by its own productive activities and none of it was captured from other firms, so the value-chain concept assumes that the total value added captured by all participants in a value chain equals the total value generated in that value chain. In other words, economic orthodoxy says "no value leaks between firms," value-chain heterodoxy says "no value leaks between chains."[58] Though orthodox economics rules out regular, large-scale transfers of value between firms, the value-chain concept implies that this does happen, yet it excludes *a priori* that such transfers might take place between chains. The value-chain approach effectively regards the total value added created in the entire value chain as a pie to be sliced up and retrospectively assigned to each link—exactly the same tautological procedure we identified in our examination of the neoclassical production function. Here we see the limited scope of its heterodoxy. The radical implication of value chain-theory is that individual firms within the chain may leak value to other links or absorb value from them, destroying the value/value-added identity. Now the firms are porous, but the chains themselves are hermetically sealed from one another. Recognizing that value is enclosed neither by firms nor by value chains, that *all* of what bourgeois economists call value added is actually *value captured*, is the logical next step, but one that would signify a decisive and explicit break with the premises of neoclassical economics and necessitate a reengagement with Marxist value theory.

The consequence of GVC theory's failure to carry through the logic of their hesitant critique of the ruling marginalist doctrine of value and value added is that it has become conceptually bound by this doctrine. This is only natural, since its most influential authors (Gereffi, Kaplinsky, and others) explicitly approach global-commodity chains from the standpoint of capitalist entrepreneurs in developing nations and with their interests in mind, as they seek to discover how they may "upgrade," that is, improve on their meager ration of the profits' cake. It is therefore not so surprising that GVC theory's focus on the distribution of value between the links of the chain says nothing about how these proceeds are distributed within these links, in particular between capital and labor. There is no sense in the GVC literature that, in studying global-commodity chains, we are studying relations of exploitation, that this is a terrain not just of competition between capitals but of struggle between classes. GVC theorists claim to "explicitly recognize that . . . input-output structures [that is, firms] within the networks are centrally important, not least because it is these that constitute the sites where value is generated and where . . . enormous variations in working conditions . . . exist around the world."[59] GPN theorists arrived at exactly the same juncture as GVC theory, its leading proponents uneasily and hesitantly admitting the "possibilities that exist for value to be captured. It is one thing for value to be created and enhanced in given locations, but it may be quite another for it to be captured for the benefit of those locations."[60] But without a theory of value, no further progress can be made, and about this they just cannot make up their minds: "By 'value' we mean both Marxian notions of surplus-value and more orthodox ones associated with economic rent."[61]

The recent move by some of the leading researchers in the field to favor the term "value chain" over "commodity chain" indicates their progress toward adopting an explicit theory of value. Unfortunately, it is the mainstream, neoclassical concept of value with which they are more openly aligning themselves, as leading value-chain researcher Timothy Sturgeon explains:

We . . . chose to replace the term "commodity" with "value" because of popular connotations of the word commodity . . . and because the term value captured both the concept of "value added," which fits well with the chain metaphor we were using, and focused attention on the main source of economic development: the application of human effort, often amplified by machines, to generate returns on invested capital.[62]

Aligning value-chain analysis with the bourgeois economists' concept of value added aids efforts to get value-chain analysis into the mainstream. But is this where it belongs? Acceptance of the mainstream concept of value added deprives Sturgeon and others moving in his direction of the conceptual tools they need to understand this phenomenon, with the result that the most important discovery unearthed by value-chain analysis—the existence of value flows between different "black boxes," that is, different firms or links in the chain—is left lying in the ground for others to disinter.

THE THREE DIMENSIONS OF THE GDP ILLUSION

Bermuda and other tax havens are spectacular examples of how data on GDP, whether at market exchange rates or in PPP$, can depart very far from being a measure of a nation's contribution to global wealth.[63] But this highlight just one of three distinct ways in which GDP departs from being what it claims to be: a measure of how much value is added by economic activity within a nation's borders.

The first dimension, incarnated in an extreme and pure form by Bermuda (and other offshore financial centers including the largest of them all, the City of London), results from the non-productive and parasitic nature of financial services and the distance separating them from the sphere of production, while, in contrast, the second and third dimensions—differences in the organic composition of capital and differences in the rate of exploitation—are intrinsic to the globalized production process. As discussed in chapter 2, nonproduction activities also include security, administration, advertising, all activities that, from the standpoint of capital, may be no less necessary than production activities but in themselves add nothing to social wealth and should instead be regarded as forms of social consumption. Nonproduction activities have increased their share of GDP in all imperialist countries, and to a much greater extent than in the nations of the South, to which increasingly falls the task of production. This growing asymmetry therefore implies that a significant and growing proportion of value consumed in nonproductive activities in imperialist countries was generated in low-wage countries, and that Northern capitals operating in nonproduction sectors are valorized in part by the living labor expended in Southern production activities.

The second distortion comprising the GDP illusion results from the higher capital intensity of capitals in imperialist nations than in the Southern nations, that is, investment in fixed capital forms a higher proportion of total investment, with proportionally less invested in wages (in Marxist terms, the organic composition of capital is higher in the imperialist nations). Capital-intensive capitals can only harvest a small amount of fresh surplus-value from their own relatively small workforce, and the rest they capture in circulation. The capital invested in their more expensive means of production is therefore valorized by value transfers from capitals of lower intensity. This process was summarized by Marx in an oft-cited passage in *Capital III*:

> If the commodities are sold at their values . . . very different rates of profit arise in the various spheres of production. . . . But capital withdraws from a sphere with a low rate of profit and invades others which yield a higher profit. Through this incessant outflow and influx . . . it creates a ratio of supply and demand that the average profit in the various spheres of production becomes the same, and values are, therefore, converted into prices of production. It follows . . . that in each particular sphere of production the individual capitalist . . . takes direct part in the exploitation of the total working class by the totality of capital.[64]

This effect takes place whether or not the competing capitals are operating within the borders of a single economy, and occurs even if we assume perfect competition among capitals and a uniform rate of exploitation. To the considerable extent that capital-intensive capitals are concentrated in imperialist nations and labor-intensive capitals in low-wage nations, the N-S difference in organic composition directly implies a S-N transfer or redistribution of value that, once again, is not captured in GDP data. This, the only basis for unequal exchange accepted by dependency theory's Euro-Marxist critics, therefore points to a second way that Northern capitals may be valorized by Southern labor.

The third, least acknowledged but most important of all, and the specific focus of this book, are the distortions to GDP produced by *international differences in the rate of exploitation,* the subject of chapters 7 and 8. The evidence collected in chapters 2 to 5 on the condition of the emergent Southern working class and the strenuous efforts of Northern firms to "extract value" from them strongly suggests that these differences exist, and that the notion that international wage differentials reflect international differences in labor productivity is fallacious, tautological, and conflicts with reality.

A Note on Technological Advances in ICT and Transportation

Chapter 7 explained that the desire to exploit low-wage labor is the motive force of the globalization of production processes, while technological advances in information and communications technology (ICT) and transportation are facilitators, their role being to open up more and more production tasks to cost-cutting via outsourcing. This study has emphasized the impact of technological advances in ICT and transportation on production outsourcing. A value theory of imperialism requires a much richer concept of the many-sided impact of these technologies. Here we can do no more than briefly outline some of the issues that need to be addressed.

The impact of innovations in ICT and transportation on outsourcing, important as it is, is only one of the ways technological advances affect the rate of profit. They have, of course, had the most profound impact on finance, that is, on the circulation of titles to financial assets, which provides the nervous and circulatory systems for globally integrated currency and capital markets. ICT, in particular, has eliminated much of the nonproduction labor previously employed in this sector. The same goes for the wholesale and retail sector, collectively known as commercial capital, which straddles the boundary between production and exchange. A major part of the living labor expended in this sector is transportation, which Marx considered to be part of the sphere of production. Thus much of the living labor expended by workers employed by Amazon and Walmart is productive.[65] Aside from reducing necessary labor time, perhaps the greatest effect of ICT and containerization on the rate of profit is to be found in the acceleration of the turnover time of capital, providing a crucial prop to the sagging rate of profit that defined the systemic crisis in the 1970s.[66] To illustrate this, a $10 million investment yielding a profit of $1 million translates to a 5 percent rate of return if two years are required to accomplish this, but if this can be squeezed down to one year, the rate of return is 10 percent.

Most of the literature reviewed in this book regards labor costs as one factor among many, and often gives priority to technological changes in general and revolutions in ICT and transportation in particular. On one thing, however, perhaps all could agree: there are no technological innovations on the horizon that are capable of repeating the impact of the ICT-transport revolution on turnover times and profit rates. Efforts to squeeze more drops from these qualitative leaps in technology will continue: cost pressures driving outsourcing are becoming even more intense and are spreading to new branches of production, and there still is considerable unrealized potential for outsourcing services. But most of their benefits have already been realized, and there are no new technologies in waiting that could have a similar transformative effect.

Here we will briefly consider transportation and ICT technology separately, and look at the distinct role of each in the individual phases of the overall circuit of capital. This, following Marx in volume 2 of *Capital,* can be schematically represented as M–C–C′–M′, where each pair of letters separated by a dash represents a distinct phase in this circuit. Thus M represents the capitalist's initial capital, a sum of money used to purchase C, a set of commodities comprising means of production, raw materials, and labor-power. The ensuing process of production, C–C′, transforms this set of commodities into a new set of commodities, C′, which are subsequently sold and turned into a new, larger sum of money, M′. The difference between M and M′ (ΔM) is gross profit, and corresponds to the firm's "value added." In this schema, M–C and C′–M′ describe the circulation of commodities while C–C′ encompasses the production process.[67]

Transportation of commodities from field or factory to markets is a production activity and the labor of transport workers is productive labor. This is so because the change in their location is a physical change, one that is no less necessary to their social existence as use-values than any other transformation performed during their production,[68] as Anwar Shaikh and Ahmet Tonak explain:

> By shipping oranges from their point of production to their point of consumption, a trucker transforms a useful objective property of these oranges (their location in space) which is crucial to them as objects of consumption. To be consumed, an orange must not merely be an orange somewhere, it must be an orange where the consumer is. Transportation from the orange grove to the consumption region is therefore productive transformation [and] is internal to the process of production.[69]

That transportation is also a part of the production process is perhaps clearest of all in the movement of intermediate inputs; the disintegration and dispersal of production processes across different countries and continents implies a major expansion of this role. But, as with all other categories associated with commodity value, what is essential is not the physical transformation per se but the social relation to which this physical transformation pertains.[70] In the case of transportation, what is crucial is not the physical movement of the useful good, but the social relation that governs this change of location. Shaikh and Tonak, in the continuation of the above quote, lucidly explain this subtle yet funda-mental distinction:

> It is important to understand that not all transportation consti-tutes production activity. . . . Suppose our oranges are produced in California to be sold in New York, but are stored in New Jersey because of cheaper warehouse facilities. . . . The loop through New Jersey has no (positive) effect on the useful properties of the orange as an object of consumption. . . . This loop is internal to the distribu-tion system . . . a nonproduction activity.[71]

Shaikh and Tonak's example is hypothetical; for a real-world example, consider the decision by Scottish firm Young's Seafood to send shrimp caught in Scottish waters on a 12,000-mile round-trip to Thailand, where they are hand-peeled by cheap labor, repacked, and then shipped back to Scotland, in which the deciding factor was the "prohibitive wage costs" of Young's minimum-wage, mainly female employees who were thereby made redundant.[72]

With this very important qualification, transportation is part of the production process and is therefore an element in the C–C′ stage of the circuit of capital. Technological advances in transportation also speed up the circulation-time of inputs and outputs; in other words they impact on both M–C and C′–M′, exerting their beneficial effect on the rate of profit by compressing the time required to circulate commodities, rather than through cutting the costs of transport in absolute terms.[73] Advances in ICT also reduce circulation time and increase profit rates, by speeding up the time needed to match buyer with seller and complete a sale, enabling just-in-time inventory management and in other ways. As with advances in transportation technologies, ICT has also had a transformative effect on each stage of the process of production, that is, on C–C′, to a greater or lesser extent depending on the characteristics of each process. The application of ICT to production processes has, in a word, accelerated advances in the social productivity of living labor.

According to Marx's theory of value, it is precisely the increased social productivity of living labor that finds its ultimate expression in the tendency for the rate of profit to fall. As Marx emphasized: "The rate of profit does not fall because labor becomes less productive, but because it becomes more productive. Both the rise in the rate of surplus-value and the fall in the rate of profit are but specific forms through which growing productivity of labor is expressed under capitalism."[74] According to Marx this is because growing productivity of labor is the result of a higher organic composition of capital; in other words, the application of technology replaces living labor, the sole source of new value, with dead labor (means of production). ICT has a specific characteristic that counters this effect. "Organic composition," in Marx's theory, combines capital's technical composition (the ratio of workers to means of production) and its value composition (in which these two factors are expressed in value terms). Normally—as, for instance, in the case of transport— technological advances increase both the technical composition and the value composition, for example, by doubling the size of a cargo ship while keeping its crew the same. But continuous advances in the production of ICT goods, as well as outsourcing of labor-intensive production tasks, have resulted in continuous falls in their prices, reducing the cost of these means of production in both relative and absolute terms. Thus the increased technical composition is not fully reflected in an increased value composition, slowing the feedback between productivity advances and downward pressure on average profits.

"Rate of profit" in this discussion refers to the rate of profit of productive capital and ignores the claims made on the mass of surplus-value by non-productive sectors, owners of debt, etc. This is not the rate of profit that matters to the industrial capitalist, who is concerned only with his share of it. As we have seen in the case of Dhaka's garment sweatshops and Shenzhen's production lines, the surplus-value extracted by productive enterprises in low-wage countries supports and feeds many ancillary industries in imperialist countries, where it also funds governments and is transmuted by the financial system into higher asset values across the board.

CONCLUSION: GDP IN THE ERA OF GLOBALIZED PRODUCTION

Our analysis of global outsourcing, of the asymmetries between Southern sweatshops and the lead firms headquartered in the imperialist nations, and of the forces driving and shaping the rapid growth of the Southern proletariat that dictate the terms on which it can sell its labor-power, has provided many reasons to question the universal acceptance of GDP as a measure of the output of a national economy.[75] The case for a radical reinterpretation of GDP is further supported by examination of some paradoxes and anomalies thrown up by these data, such as the relative GDP of Bermuda and the Dominican Republic, and the intriguing mystery of why an arm's-length relationship might be more profitable to a TNC than an in-house relationship even though in the arm's-length relationship there are no visible flows of profits. This chapter's investigation into what GDP actually measures as opposed to what it claims to measure has exposed the highly contestable neoclassical premises on which it stakes its claim. Closer examination of these ruling neoclassical ideas, of their explanation of how value is created in production processes, and of heterodox theories that remain in thrall to orthodox conceptions of value, leads us to reject these explanations and the core assumptions that underlie them, and to redefine GDP as a measure of the part of the global product that is captured or appropriated by a nation, not a measure of what it has produced domestically. The D in GDP, in other words, *is a lie*.

To the extent that that GDP exaggerates or diminishes the real contribution of individual nations to global wealth, each nation is either a net consumer of wealth produced by the living labor of other nations, or it is a net contributor, producing more wealth than it consumes. I argue that just this happens, routinely, systematically, and on a grand scale, and so GDP in the neoliberal era has departed further than ever from being a measure of domestic production, magnifying the "GDP illusion." This illusion occurs not so much in the data themselves, but in their interpretation, which, in line with the fallacious premises of the ruling economic doctrine, assumes that economic actors (individual citizens, or individual countries in the global community) consume only what they produce and produce only what they consume—as in the *Financial Times* editorial stating that "the richest fifth of the world's population generates—and enjoys—85 percent of world output. The poorest fifth produces—and struggles to survive on—just 1.4 percent."[76] Correcting for the GDP illusion gives us a more accurate and more objective picture of the global economy, in which capitalists and citizens in Triad nations are now seen as appropriators and consumers of wealth produced by workers and small producers in the nations of the Global South. A picture, in other words, of the emergent, fully evolved form of capitalism's imperialist stage of development.

——10——

All Roads Lead into the Crisis

Apart from their original purposes [trade unions] must now learn to act deliberately as organising centres of the working class in the broad interest of its *complete emancipation*. They must aid every social and political movement tending in that direction. . . . They must look carefully after the interests of the worst-paid trades. . . . They must convince the world at large that their efforts, far from being narrow and selfish, aim at the emancipation of the downtrodden millions.[1]
— KARL MARX, 1866, *Trade Unions: Their Past, Present, and Future*

This chapter shows why the global transformation and shift of production examined in earlier chapters is essential to understanding the unfolding global crisis. This crisis is still in its early stages, will endure for decades, is inescapable, and inevitably leads to wars and revolutions. What is not inevitable is the outcome of coming battles that will determine not merely the future of humanity, but whether humanity has a future. The remedies being offered by different economic commentators and practitioners—from austerity for all, advocated by adherents of laissez-faire economics, prominent on the right wing of the U.S. Republican Party, which opposes government intervention to prevent bankruptcies and asset destruction, to the current policy being pursued by governments in Europe and North America of succor for the rich and austerity for the rest, to the anti-austerity policies espoused by Keynesian economists and left social democrats such as Jeremy Corbyn, leader of the British Labour Party, who call for governments to print money to finance government expenditure and personal consumption—are all different routes toward the same destination: a systemic crisis that poses the question of questions: Who rules the world—the toilers or the exploiters?

While bankers and financiers have crowded the stage, the hugely powerful commercial and industrial capitalists who command non-financial TNCs appear in this drama only as victims. Since they have featured so prominently in this book's investigation of the transformation of production, it is only natural that our investigation of the crisis should put these powerful actors in the spotlight and reveal their true roles. The deepest roots of the financial whirlwind currently on world tour are to be found not in finance but in capitalist production. The series of financial heart attacks that began on August 9, 2007, were provoked by the side effects of the two principal measures that allowed the imperialist economies to escape, for a while, the crises of the 1970s—the enormous expansion of debt and the epochal global shift of production to low-wage countries. The first propped up demand, alleviating overproduction (the production of more goods than can be sold for a profit); the second helped restore sagging profits by substituting relatively expensive domestic labor with cheap labor in low-wage countries. Together, these two therapies helped put global capitalism back on the rails for another thirty years. But piling up debt has destabilized the global financial system, and the shift of production to low-wage countries, as we shall see, is deeply implicated in other factors commonly pointed to by commentators as the causes of the global crisis, from increased debt to structural trade imbalances. In a word, these *therapies* have turned into *pathologies*, and the underlying disease that they have helped to suppress for so long, the tendency toward overproduction of commodities and overaccumulation of capital, can now only be contained by even more concentrated doses of the same toxic medicine that brought on the crisis in the first place.

In this chapter we will form a timeline of the crisis, but it is important to be aware that the sequence of events is highly deceptive. The standard interpretation of the 2007 crisis was neatly expressed by the OECD in its April 2009 *Interim Report*, which began by stating that "the world economy is in the midst of its deepest and most synchronised recession in our lifetimes, caused by a global financial crisis and deepened by a collapse in world trade."[2] The operative word here is *caused*. The story goes, repeated a thousand times, that a global financial crisis *caused* a crisis in the system of production and trade. This understanding is strongly suggested by the chronology of the crisis: what began in August 2007 when the freezing of financial markets was quickly followed by a credit crunch and a slump in consumer confidence. The resulting sudden contraction of demand for goods and services led to a sharp reduction in orders to factories, so production fell, factories closed, and unemployment more than doubled in many countries. Thus a financial crisis led to a commercial crisis that in turn led to a production crisis. This is fine as a description but not as an explanation, because it is characteristic of capitalist crises that *the true direction of cause and effect is the very opposite of what is suggested by the sequence of events.* This was explained more than half a century before by Evald Ilyenkov, a dissident communist living in Moscow. Despite his very different times and extremely different circumstances, these three sentences provide a finer description and superior definition of the events of 2007 and 2008 than any written since:

> Very often . . . the genuine objective cause of a phenomenon appears on the surface of the historical process later than its own consequence. For instance, the general crisis of overproduction in the capitalist world is empirically manifested first of all in the form of disturbances in the sphere of bank credits, as a financial crisis, later it involves commerce and only at the very end does it reveal itself in the sphere of direct production as a real general crisis of overproduction. The superficial observer, who takes succession in time for the only historical principle, concludes from this that misunderstandings and conflicts in bank clearances are the cause, the basis, and the source of the general crisis.[3]

THE ROOTS OF THE FINANCIAL CRISIS

Unsure who was holding U.S. subprime mortgage securities, on August 9, 2007, European banks suddenly stopped lending to one another, compelling the European Central Bank to make an emergency transfusion of €94.8 billion ($131 billion) into the Eurozone's banking system. When U.S. markets opened a few hours later, the U.S. Federal Reserve followed with an injection of $24 billion into the U.S. banking system. Writing in the *Financial Times* soon afterward, Martin Wolf called this "the moment when credit dried up even to sound borrowers. Panic had arrived."[4] This momentous moment marked the completion of the transition from a postwar world order to a prewar world order. "Bubble" is an oft-used metaphor to describe the approach of a financial crisis, but bubbles are weightless and burst with an imperceptible pop, so a more apt image is of a bursting dam or an exploding bomb. August 9, 2007, was the day the debt bomb exploded, by coincidence the sixty-second anniversary of another detonation—of the nuclear bomb that killed 80,000 human beings in the Japanese city of Nagasaki. The symbolism is powerful—the first detonation marked the end of the Second World War, the second detonation marked the definitive end of the postwar world order.[5]

A broad consensus among policymakers, economists, and many critics of capitalism sees an otherwise healthy "real economy" damaged by a financial crisis that itself resulted from a fatal mix of lax regulation, excessive indebtedness, and reckless risk-taking. Some go further, and point to the rapid growth in the decade leading up to the crisis of "global imbalances"—huge structural trade deficits and surpluses that generated destabilizing financial flows. Another important school of thought emphasizes the major increase in finance's share of profits and its weight in the GDP of developed countries. Yet, as we shall see, each of these supposed causes can be seen as symptoms and side effects of transformations in the sphere of production, in particular its global shift to low-wage countries.

In the years preceding the global crisis a period of calm had descended on global markets, characterized by low interest rates, low inflation, and low volatility. This magical alignment was dubbed the "Great Moderation" by Ben Bernanke, later to become chair of the U.S. Federal Reserve, and was also known as the "'Goldilocks economy'," after the fairy-tale heroine who liked porridge that was "not too hot, not too cold," and led Nobel Laureate Robert Lucas, then president of the American Economic Association, to conclude that "the central problem of depression prevention has been solved, for all practical purposes, and has in fact been solved for many decades."[6] Low interest rates, low inflation, and low volatility were regarded at the time as the perfect recipe for sustainable growth, but in retrospect have come to be seen as a toxic cocktail that encouraged the inflation of an enormous credit bubble. Directly or indirectly, these proximate causes of the financial crisis were effects of the global shift of production.

Low interest rates encouraged households and corporations to take on more debt and at the same time pushed banks and other private investors to make riskier bets in their hunt for yield. Interest rates were kept low in large measure because China and other manufactures-exporting countries, compelled by what Lawrence Summers called the "financial balance of terror,"[7] recycled their export earnings to the U.S. government as loans at zero or negative real rate of interest—a Marshall Plan in reverse, in which poor countries lend the richest the money they needed to purchase the product of their factories.

Inflation, too, was kept low by falling prices of intermediate inputs and consumer goods whose production was shifting to low-wage countries. How times change—as *Financial Times* columnist Gabriel Wildau commented, "cheap made-in-China goods contained price rises around the world when that was a force for good. Now, as Europe, Japan, and the United States struggle with stagnant or falling prices, the spectre of exported deflation is a far from benevolent force,"[8] one that has helped push inflation below zero in Japan, the UK, and the Eurozone and is threatening to do so in the United States. This is greatly feared: negative inflation, that is, deflation, gives consumers an incentive to postpone purchases, makes the burden of debt heavier, and if falling prices were to become entrenched, would deal a final blow to hopes for a revival of capital investment. No one wants to invest in producing things whose prices are falling.

Volatility is the amount by which asset prices gyrate about their supposed equilibrium, and is related to *correlation*, the degree to which the prices of different types of assets move as a herd. Both measure the mood of serenity or panic among investors and both fell to extremely benign levels in the run-up to the crisis. Along with low interest rates, they also encouraged risk-taking behavior and more borrowing, and their quiescence was a key condition for the creation of the complex derivatives and highly leveraged speculative bets that characterized the pre-2007 financial feeding frenzy. Volatility and correlation were attenuated by the constant wall of dollars being recycled into the United States by China and other surplus countries—more than a billion dollars a day, day-in, day-out, for more than a decade. As Andrew Gamble has pointed out, "It was the cheapness of Chinese goods and its willingness to fund U.S. deficits which kept the bubble inflating as long as it did."[9]

We have not had to look very far or very hard to discover that the global financial crisis is connected with transformations in capitalist production, and when we come to discuss global trade imbalances and financialization, this connection will become clearer still.

Repeatedly throughout the two decades leading up to the crisis, G7 governments countered threats of recession by increasing spending, slashing interest rates, and relaxing credit controls, only to cautiously retrace their steps as recessionary forces abated and inflation started to raise its ugly head. Governments acted this way out of fear that if a recession was allowed to take hold it would quickly develop a momentum of its own, causing unsold goods to pile up, falling prices, and rising bankruptcies. Governments were terrified they might join Japan in a deflationary spiral from which there is no escape.

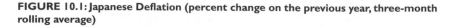

FIGURE 10.1: Japanese Deflation (percent change on the previous year, three-month rolling average)

Source: Thomson Reuters Datastream.

Why did Japan's predicament evoke such dread? By the 1980s Japanese car and electronics industries were winning the competitive battle against their European and North American rivals, but they were denied the fruits of their victory by quotas on exports and other protectionist measures. Threats by the Reagan administration to intensify its aggressive protectionism helped persuade Japan and other members of what was then the G5 to engineer a devaluation of the dollar in return for reining in the U.S. budget deficit—the Plaza Accord of September 1985.[10] Within two years the dollar-yen exchange rate fell by 50 percent, dealing a crippling blow to Japan's export competitiveness, discouraging Japanese investors from investing their profits in expanded production, and inducing them to indulge in an orgy of property speculation. The resulting real estate bubble burst in 1990, plunging the Japanese banking system into the same sort of crisis that has now become familiar to us all—another financial crisis with roots in overproduction.

In Figure 10.2 "deflation" means falling prices; since GDP is merely the sum of the prices of all final goods, it can fall even if the volume of

FIGURE 10.2: The Descent into Deflation

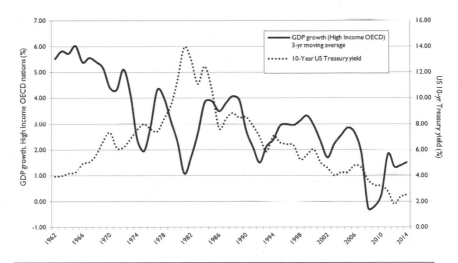

Source: World Economic Outlook Database; U.S. Federal Reserve.

In Figure 10.2 "deflation" means falling prices; since GDP is merely the sum of the prices of all final goods, it can fall even if the volume of production stays the same or even increases GDP. The graph shows that GDP turned negative in 2009–2010, but this was primarily the effect of sharp cuts in the volume of production. "10-year U.S. Treasury yield" is the interest rate paid on ten-year bonds issued by the U.S. government. Rates on ten-year bonds issued by other imperialist governments are even lower—in mid-September 2015, yields were 0.3 percent on ten-year Japanese government bonds; 0.7 percent on the German bonds; 1 percent on French bonds; and 1.8 percent on Italian and UK bonds. The interest rate is the cost of money capital, and according to mainstream theory the equilibrium interest rate ensures that all savings are invested. It is related to the broadest definition of the rate of profit: the ratio between the total mass of surplus-value and the total quantity of capital. Its descent to historically low levels is therefore a sign of a deepening crisis of profitability, which is a different way of saying a crisis of capitalism.

production stays the same or even increases GDP. The graph shows that GDP turned negative in 2009–2010, but this was primarily the effect of sharp cuts in the volume of production. "10-year U.S. Treasury yield" is the interest rate paid on ten-year bonds issued by the U.S. government. Rates on ten-year bonds issued by other imperialist governments are even lower—in mid-September 2015, yields were 0.3 percent on ten-year Japanese government bonds; 0.7 percent on the German bonds; 1 percent on French bonds; and 1.8 percent on Italian and UK bonds.[11] The interest rate is the cost of money capital, and according to mainstream theory the equilibrium interest rate ensures that all savings are invested. It is related to the broadest definition of the rate of profit: the ratio between the total mass of surplus-value and the total quantity of capital. Its descent to historically low levels is therefore a sign of a deepening crisis of profitability, which is a different way of saying a crisis of capitalism.

Despite a massive injection of public funds into the crippled banking system that raised Japanese government debt from 10 percent of GDP to over 180 percent, despite the relocation of labor-intensive production processes on a colossal scale to low-wage Asian neighbors, and despite booming growth in the rest of the world, Japan barely succeeded in keeping its head above the mire. Fear of what *Financial Times* journalist John Plender and others have called "Japanification" has now become rampant, as in a report of that title published by PIMCO, the world's largest investors in global bond markets:

> Ballooning fiscal deficits, record low interest rates, depressing economic growth, private sector deleveraging, uncoordinated and ineffective governmental responses and monetary authorities increasingly exhausted and reluctant to act. Over the past two decades, people would have associated this characterization with Japan. However, more recently, they are accurate descriptions of the status quo in many other developed countries, raising the question: is the developed world becoming "Japanified"?[12]

Japan's experience is ominous. As Plender comments, "Japan had an advantage that today's deficit countries may not have. The rest of the world was growing, while it confronted the threat of stagnation and deflation, permitting Japanese exports to keep the economy afloat."[13] "Japanification" is another word for what Lawrence Summers and others call "secular stagnation," defined by the *Financial Times* as "a condition of negligible or no economic growth."[14] Now that mutually reinforcing Japanese-style deflation is tightening its grip on all the imperialist economies, and because the spread to China and other so-called emerging markets means there are no external sources of growth to counteract this, prolonged anemic growth is actually a best-case scenario. More likely, the onset of global crisis signifies that the world capitalist economy has passed an event horizon and now cannot escape from being sucked into a deflationary black hole.[15]

Global Imbalances

Blaming the symptoms—excessive debt, reckless risk-taking, and lax regulation—typifies most of the public discourse relating to the financial crisis. Some analysts seek to go further than these superficial explanations, and give a central place in the gestation of the global financial

crisis to "global imbalances," that is, the accumulation of large and growing trade surpluses in some countries and large and growing deficits in
others. These current account imbalances generate equal and opposite
capital account imbalances, in which China and other countries lend
their trade surpluses to deficit countries, in particular the United States.
But these global imbalances are themselves symptoms of the deeper
transformation of capitalist production that is the subject of this book.
Martin Wolf, chief economics commentator at the *Financial Times*, is
prominent among those who emphasize the role of global imbalances.
In his *The Shifts and the Shocks: What We've Learned—And Have Still To
Learn—From the Financial Crisis*, he explains:

> Between 1996, just before the Asian financial crisis, and 2006, [cur-
> rent account] imbalances increased roughly five times relative to
> world output. Three categories of large net capital exporters emerged:
> China and emerging Asia; aging high-income, export-oriented econ-
> omies (Germany and Japan); and the oil exporters. . . . There also
> emerged just two groups of large net capital importers—the U.S. and
> "peripheral Europe"—Western, Southern and Eastern Europe.[16]

Wolf highlights the singular role of the U.S. trade deficit, which by
itself absorbed 60 percent of the fast-growing surpluses of the rest of
the world, and which more than tripled in relation to U.S. GDP from
1.6 percent of GDP in 1997 to a colossal 5.8 percent in 2006.[17] This huge
deficit exemplifies the global imbalances that Wolf is talking about, and
yet, perhaps because he is fixated on the resulting financial imbalances,
he doesn't pause to examine the trade deficit more closely.

In 2006, when, as Wolf reports, the U.S. trade deficit equalled 5.8 percent of its GDP, the deficit in its *merchandise* trade with the rest of the
world was higher still—6.4 percent of GDP, the surplus on trade in services
making up the difference. In that year, the United States imported nearly
twice as much stuff in value terms as it exported—total U.S. merchandise
exports were just 53.5 percent of its merchandise imports. Zooming in a
bit closer, most of the deficit in merchandise trade reflects the deficit in
manufactured goods trade, which alone equalled 3.7 percent of U.S. GDP
in 2006. After a wobble in 2009, the manufactured goods deficit resumed
its upward path and reached 4 percent of GDP in 2014, or $695 billion, of
which $496 billion represents the deficit in U.S. manufactured trade with
developing economies. Its recent surge to these astronomical heights is
not fully reflected in the overall trade deficit, where it is partly offset by

the rising surplus in services trade, which grew from $86 billion in 2006 to $227 billion in 2013.

The impressive size of the deficit in manufactured trade, and the fact that since 2007 more than 70 percent of it arose from trade with developing economies, all points to the global shift of production to low-wage economies as the prime contributor to global imbalances. Notable, too, is the surge of this deficit to new highs since 2009, another pre-crisis trend that has continued with full force during the supposed recovery. Yet this epoch-defining shift is not among the "shifts and the shocks" explored by Martin Wolf in his book of that name.

In Wolf's account, a ballooning trade deficit was inflicted on the United States by "massive intervention in currency markets by governments, mainly of emerging countries . . . pursu[ing] export-led economic growth—the most successful of all development strategies."[18] To prevent their currencies appreciating against the dollar Chinese and other central banks purchased trillions of dollars of supposedly safe U.S. assets. Wolf charges that "the governments of emerging countries organized these flows. . . . The consequent accumulations of foreign-currency reserves . . . reached $11.4tn at the end of September 2013, quite apart from over $6tn in sovereign wealth funds."[19]

However, Wolf omits to mention another very powerful group of actors who were arguably far more important than governments in emerging countries in driving this process: transnational corporations headquartered in high-income, high-wage economies. UNCTAD reported in 2013 that "about 80 percent of global trade (in terms of gross exports) is linked to the international production networks of TNCs,"[20] three-quarters of which "consists of trade in intermediate goods and services that are incorporated at various stages in the production process of goods and services for final consumption."[21] China, "the supplier of choice in virtually all labour-intensive global value chains,"[22] as Gary Gereffi described it in 2005, rose so fast in large part because U.S., European, and Japanese TNCs used it as a giant export-processing zone. If, as Wolf emphasizes, governments of emerging countries organized the financial flows, the global shift of production that obligated this was organized by Western firms seeking to cut production costs by, as the IMF delicately put it, increasing their "access" to the "global pool of labor."[23] Morgan Stanley's Stephen Roach gave a more forthright explanation of what this involves: the substitution of "high-wage workers here with like-quality, low-wage workers abroad,"[24] and why this became a compulsion: "In an era of excess supply, companies lack pricing leverage as never before

[and] must be unrelenting in their search for new efficiencies . . . offshore outsourcing that extracts product from relatively low-wage workers in the developing world has become an increasingly urgent survival tactic for companies in the developed economies."[25]

Wolf's book does contain one significant discussion of the global shift of production in which he acknowledges the central part it played in the gestation of the crisis:

> Without the explosive rise in global commerce and particularly the growth of exports and production in emerging countries, especially China, the scale of the imbalances . . . could not have emerged. This rapid growth in trade . . . was also associated with a rapid shift in production from high-income economies to cheaper low-cost producers. China emerged over a remarkably short time as the world's largest manufacturing country and largest exporter of goods. This was . . . made possible by the ease with which know-how could be transferred across frontiers. That in turn followed in part from the rise of integrated global companies, which were themselves the product of liberalization and improved information and communications technology.[26]

Apart from its superbly succinct summary of the transformation of production, what's most striking about this passage is the shadowy role Wolf accords to "integrated global companies." TNCs are not even referred to by name. No account is made of their agency, what motivated them, of the enormous power they have come to wield; no recognition that their desire to cut costs by cutting labor costs has driven the global shift of production, and is therefore the *source* of the global imbalances that, he argues, were so central to the drama that began in 2007.

The world of production and trade connects at every point with the world of finance. Each is relatively autonomous and powerfully influences the other, yet a theoretical concept of the global crisis must give primacy to the production of the wealth that courses through the tubes and vesicles of the global financial system. If Martin Wolf had extended his search for the causes of the global imbalances beyond the sphere of finance to the transformations and shifts in production, he would have discovered their ultimate source and completed his quest. But he would then have to acknowledge that this global financial crisis is a financial crisis *in form only*, that its ultimate roots lie in the imperatives and contradictions that govern the behavior of powerful capitalist firms, overwhelmingly concentrated in rich countries, and why they responded to them by cutting production costs through shifting as much of it as possible to low-wage countries.

The Investment Strike

In a letter sent in April 2015 to chief executives of the 500 biggest firms listed on the U.S. stock market, Larry Fink, the head of Blackstone, the largest asset manager in the world, with a $4.65 trillion portfolio, roundly accused U.S. corporate bosses of attempting to "deliver immediate returns to shareholders . . . while underinvesting in innovation, skilled workforces or essential capital expenditures necessary to sustain long-term growth." In 2014, Fink reminded the CEOs, U.S. corporations returned more than $900 billion to shareholders in dividends and buybacks, and concluded by politely pointing out that "with interest rates approaching zero, returning excessive amounts of capital to investors . . . sends a discouraging message about a company's ability to use its resources wisely and develop a coherent plan to create value over the long term."[27]

Buybacks are popular because those who sell their shares receive a handsome price, and those who don't sell can expect their shares to rise because buybacks concentrate ownership and magnify dividends. And, most important of all, corporate bosses can't think of anything better to do with the money—investing in means of production is the last thing on their minds. Luce remarks, "In theory companies are meant to raise money from the stock market to invest in their future growth. Exactly the reverse is taking place."[28] David Bowers, another astute observer of the corporate scene, adds, "It is very unusual for the corporate sectors to run sustained financial surpluses. Look back at the UK and the US for more than half a century and the corporate sector has tended to be a net borrower, not a net saver."[29]

Companies are not only spending their profits on share buybacks, they are borrowing to finance them, boosting shareholder value by loading their firm with debt! Yet it all makes sense, at least for the participants: buybacks concentrate share ownership, and the surge of bond issuance seeks to take advantage of historically low interest rates before the Federal Reserve presses the button and begins to raise the rate at which banks can borrow money from the rock-bottom 0.25 percent where it has been since December 2008. (At the time of writing, November 2015, the first interest hike was thought to be imminent.) Between 2009 and 2015, the top 500 U.S. companies returned $2.7 trillion to investors through share buybacks, a period, according to *Bloomberg News*, that "coincides with the second-longest U.S. bull market since the 1950s."[30] Most of the buyback binge has occurred since 2013, and buybacks have since spiked higher still, averaging more than $100 billion per month in mid-2015.[31] Bloomberg reported that in 2014 the top 500 U.S. companies had returned the equivalent of 95 percent of their profits to shareholders in dividends and buybacks.[32] These vast oceans of cash have passed through investors' hands and on to stock and multiple other markets, keeping asset prices aloft, some of it fueling bubbles in distant parts of the world and reinforcing the effects of the Federal Reserve's extreme monetary policies, which are also aimed at pumping cash into markets to support asset prices, in the forlorn hope that confidence will return and investors will start investing in production and growth.

According to Robin Harding, "Experts are struggling to explain a great puzzle of the U.S. economy . . . one that dates back to the late 1980s, but has become ever more pressing as a fifth year of sluggish recovery begins. Profits in the United States are at an all-time high but, perversely, investment is stagnant."[33] Citing data from GMO, a global asset management company, Harding reports that "profits and overall net investment in the US tracked each other closely until the late 1980s, with both about 9 percent of gross domestic product. Then the relationship began to break down. After the recession, from 2009, it went haywire. Pre-tax corporate profits are now at record highs—more than 12 percent of GDP—while net investment is barely 4 percent of output."[34] "Net investment" is the sum of investment in "tangible" fixed capital in the form of buildings, machinery, etc., plus expenditure on so-called intangibles, including R&D but also branding and other forms of intangible capital that, since changes to the UN System of National Accounts (discussed in chapter 9), are now counted as investment rather than as business expenses, minus depreciation of tangible assets. GMO data show that tangible investments in plant and machinery by U.S. private industry have steadily declined from 14 percent of output in 1980 to around 7 percent by 2011, whereas intangible investments have gone in the opposite direction and now make up more than two-thirds of total investments by U.S. industrial firms. Harding adds, "This change is profoundly odd. Economic theory says investment is driven by profitable opportunities on one side and the cost of capital on the other. High profits suggest there are decent opportunities to make money; historic lows in interest rates and highs in the stock market mean that capital is dirt cheap. Yet investment does not follow." In November 2013, Credit

Suisse published research confirming this, showing "U.S. net business investment has rebounded—but, at around 1.5 percent of GDP, still only stands at the trough levels seen during the past two recessions."[35] Credit Suisse showed that since the early 1980s the peaks reached by net business investment as a share of GDP have been declining in each economic recovery, an unmistakable downward trend that closely follows the decline in GDP growth depicted in Figure 10.2. A notable effect of the investment strike is that the age of the capital stock in the United States has been on a long-term rising trend since 1980 and started climbing rapidly after the turn of the millennium, reaching record levels several years before the crisis.

The capitalists' investment strike is not restricted to the United States. In 2011, the UK government's fiscal deficit (the excess of spending over income, also know as the budget deficit) was 8.8 percent of GDP. The biggest counterpart to this was a corporate surplus of 5.5 percent of GDP, unspent cash that sucked huge demand out of the UK economy.[36] David Bowers commented:

> Much has been written about how the developed world must tackle its structural budget deficits. But the link that remains to be properly recognised is that the counterparts to those "unsustainable" public-sector budget deficits are equally "unsustainable" corporate-sector surpluses. . . . It is not that governments have been spending "too much" that is the problem; it is that corporates have been spending "too little." Moreover, because this corporate saving is the main counterpart to the government's borrowing, until companies start to spend again, the burden of fiscal adjustment will have to fall on cutbacks in public services and higher personal taxation.[37]

In Japan, where huge corporate surpluses and low rates of investment have characterized the economy since it entered deflation in the early 1990s, the situation is even more extreme. Martin Wolf argues that in Japan "the underlying obstacle is structural: it lies in what is now a dysfunctional corporate sector. . . . The sum of depreciation and retained earnings of corporate Japan was a staggering 29.5 percent of GDP in 2011, against just 16 percent in the U.S., which is itself struggling with a corporate financial surplus."[38] The phenomenon is indeed global in scale. UNCTAD noted in 2012 that "despite the gradual advance of international production by TNCs, their record levels of cash have so far not translated into sustained growth in investment levels. UNCTAD estimates that these cash levels have reached more than $5 trillion, including earnings retained overseas."[39] In 2008, the 963 non-financial companies in the S&P Global 1200 index sat on cash piles totalling $1.95 trillion. By 2012, total reserves had grown by 62 percent to $3.16 trillion.[40] As Bowers explained, "Prompt[ing] the recent move into financial surplus has been the decision by companies to step away from investment. Investment-to-gross domestic product ratios in the developed world are now close to the lowest levels seen in 60 years. Corporates appear to have decided to run themselves for cash, and not for growth."[41]

It is clear that the owners and CEOs of non-financial corporations, the commercial and industrial TNCs, are far from being passive victims of bankers' excesses. The capitalists' investment strike is real, it is massive, it predates the crisis, and it has widened since the crisis. It is exerting enormous, unabated strain on the weakened financial system, yet this startling truth gets surprisingly little attention in the financial press and almost none beyond it. Still less have capitalism's supporters and apologists acknowledged the connection between this investment strike and the shift of production to low-wage countries, which, as our study of global labor arbitrage in this book has revealed, has been enthusiastically pursued as an alternative to investment in new plant and machinery. Very occasionally, some commentators have made a glancing reference to this; for example, Edward Luce, who has argued, "It is no accident that the rise of buybacks has coincided with the boom in downsizing,"[42] and Citigroup researcher Tobias Levkovich, who has pointed out that "a reluctance to hire more employees as well as outsourcing to lower-cost alternatives have left management teams with lean and mean companies."[43]

How can we understand the astonishing lack of attention to the capitalists' investment strike? Two possible reasons spring to mind. One is what psychologists call cognitive dissonance—when a mental conviction is contradicted by reality, the thinker remains blind to what should be blindingly obvious. In this case, possible explanations are so awful (from the standpoint of believers in capitalism) they simply cannot be true. Another is more cynical—to protect capitalists from public criticism, by blaming instead their servants, the bankers, or governments for spending too much or too little, or indeed anyone except the real villains. There is undoubtedly a large element of truth in this. The enormous fuss that has been generated over bankers' bonuses has deflected attention from the vastly greater profits that they have made for their billionaire clients, profits that have been turbo-charged by "quantitative easing" (QE)

294   IMPERIALISM IN THE TWENTY-FIRST CENTURY

and zero interest rates,[44] and it is these billionaires, rather than the CEOs hired to run their corporations, who make the investment decisions.

Euro-Marxist Theories of the Crisis

The outbreak of the global crisis in 2007 also led to a flurry of analyses and theories from Marxists based in Europe and North America. As we saw in chapter 7, with few exceptions Marxists have failed to identify the significance or even existence of the vastly increased flows of surplus value from low-wage nations to imperialist nations during the neoliberal era, and it is therefore no surprise that this forms no part of their analyses of the crisis. What follows is a brief postscript to the chapter 7 discussion of their views.

David McNally is one of the few Marxists based in imperialist countries to attempt to integrate transformations in the spheres of production and finance into analysis of the global economic crisis. We will consider how far he gets in this endeavor, but first it is useful to report his typology of radical analyses of the crisis. McNally observes:

> On the Left, most analyses of the crisis have tended to fall into one of two camps. On the one hand, we find a series of commentators who view the financial meltdown as just the latest manifestation of a crisis of profitability that began in the early 1970s. . . . In another camp is a large number of commentators who see the crisis as essentially caused by an explosion of financial transactions and speculation that followed from de-regulation of financial markets over the past quarter-century.[45]

He assails the second camp's commentators for their

> failure to grasp the deep tendencies at the level of capital accumulation and profitability that drove deregulation and that underpin this crisis. . . . As a result, they are prone to describe the problem in terms of neoliberal policy-changes, rather than capitalism; they advocate a return to some sort of Keynesian re-regulation of financial markets.[46]

The defects of the second camp are on full display in Robin Blackburn's *The Subprime Crisis*, which provides a well-informed account of the subprime loans crisis and other financial excesses, one that is completely divorced from analysis of contradictions and transformations in the sphere of production, and arrives at a hopelessly reformist and fantastic conclusion: "The solution [to the crisis] . . . is not to abandon money or finance but to embed them in a properly regulated system . . . a global system of financial regulation."[47] Leo Panitch and Sam Gindin, in *The Current Crisis: A Socialist Perspective*, provide an insightful account of the evolution of "financialized capitalism," in particular demonstrating the glaring discrepancy between the neoliberal doctrine of minimal state intervention and the reality of the highly activist role of the U.S. state. On the relationship between the evolution of finance and the transformation of production, they have nothing to say save for one passing comment: "New York and London's access to global savings simultaneously came to depend on the surplus extracted through the high rates of exploitation of the new working classes in emerging markets."[48] Despite its non-trivial nature, Panitch and Gindin have nothing more to say about this. And though they note the dependence of New York and London's financial institutions on super-exploited Southern labor, they ignore the increasing dependence of *non*-financial TNCs headquartered in those same cities.

Robert Brenner also suffers from this blind spot, failing to perceive the importance of the relationship between workers in low-wage countries and firms based in imperialist countries. He attributes continued if unimpressive growth in the "advanced capitalist economies," despite continued overcapacity, exclusively to the inflation of credit bubbles: "All else equal, the build-up of overcapacity . . . could have been expected to lead, sooner rather than later, to serious crisis. But the governments of the advanced capitalist economies were long able to forestall this outcome by making sure that titanic volumes of credit were made available to firms and households."[49] McNally points to the weakness of this answer: "It will not do to say that for 25 years crisis was 'postponed' because credit was pumped into the system. . . . If this was the whole answer, if everything had simply been credit-driven, then all the evidence suggests that an enormous global financial crisis of the sort we are witnessing today would have had to occur much earlier."[50]

According to McNally, the postponement of the crisis is the outcome of many factors acting in combination:

> The partial but real successes of capital in restoring profit rates throughout the 1980s; the generation of new centers of global accumulation, such as China; the creation of huge new labour reserves (by means of ongoing "primitive accumulation"); the re-subordination of

the South under neoliberalism; and the associated metamorphoses in financial markets, all of which enabled neoliberal capitalism to avoid a generalized economic and financial slump for a quarter of a century, only to lay the grounds for new crises of overaccumulation and financial dislocation.[51]

This is a comprehensive list—yet it omits mention of global labor arbitrage, that is, of super-exploitation, in the temporary stabilization of capitalism in the neoliberal era. This heightened exploitative, imperialist tendency is obscured by his dubious notion of "new centers of global accumulation." The old "centers of global accumulation" are the imperialist economies that capture the lion's share of the surplus-value generated by the proletarians of the world, the wealth generated by its small farmers, and the proceeds of brutal accumulation by dispossession. What exactly does it mean to refer to China and other low-wage Southern nations as "new centers of global accumulation"? Is China or any other of the so-called emerging economies about to gate-crash into the elite club of imperialist "developed economies," unchanged since the accession of Japan at the end of the nineteenth century? It is unclear whether McNally actually believes they are, since he also emphasizes the "re-subordination of the South under neoliberalism." There are many capitalists in China, and their number and wealth is rapidly increasing, and there is indeed a great deal of capitalist accumulation taking place in China today, but a large portion of this capital is being accumulated by the TNCs of Japan, the United States, and other rich nations—whose foreign subsidiaries today produce around half of Chinese exports, and also by lead firms like Walmart and Apple whose relationship to Chinese workers is mediated through independent suppliers like Foxconn and Huawei. Despite its strenuous attempts to attain development, China is still characterized by dependence on exports of low-value-added goods to the imperialist economies, or, in the case of its high-tech exports, low-value-added assembly of imported inputs. This particular "new center of global accumulation" continues to be a major source of surplus-value for U.S., European, and Japanese firms, as we have seen in earlier chapters. It is therefore essential to identify this and other new centers of accumulation as new sources of imperialist super-profits.

According to McNally, the rise of the new centers of accumulation underpinned a "dynamic period of growth, centered on industrial expansion in East Asia [that] enabled capitalism to avoid a world crisis for twenty-five years."[52] The central question, however, is how did the growth of manufacturing production in the Global South allow not just capitalism in general, but U.S., European, and Japanese capitalism in particular, to avoid systemic crisis? How have capitalist firms *in these imperialist nations* benefited from the enormous expansion of manufacturing industry in the low-wage emerging economies? For McNally, the restoration of profits in the imperialist nations is explained not even in part by the proceeds of greatly expanded super-exploitation in the Global South, but at home through "neoliberal wage compression," which "underwrote the significant partial recovery of the rate of profit between 1982 and 1997 . . . [and was] a key component of the increase in the rate of surplus-value in the neoliberal period."[53] Wages have indeed been repressed, production lines have been speeded up, but his account ignores the international dimension, the mighty but invisible flows of surplus-value that travel from Southern workers into Northern coffers.

OUTSOURCING AND FINANCIALIZATION

Another candidate for the cause of the crisis that has attracted the attention of many researchers is the rising weight of finance in the imperialist economies, also known as financialization. This certainly is a real and highly significant phenomenon, a defining feature of the neoliberal era. Martin Wolf has pointed out that "between its low in the first quarter of 1982 and its high in the second quarter of 2007, the share of the financial sector's profits in U.S. gross domestic product rose more than six-fold. Behind this boom was an economy-wide rise in leverage [debt]. Leverage was the philosopher's stone that turned economic lead into financial gold. Attempts to reduce it now risk turning the gold back into lead again."[54] As John Bellamy Foster and Robert McChesney observe, "something fundamental has changed in the nature of capitalism in the closing decades of the 20th century. . . . Accumulation—real capital formation in the realm of goods and services—has become increasingly subordinate to finance. Keynes's well-known fear that speculation would come to dominate over production seems to have finally materialized."[55]

Financialization requires a detailed and careful empirical and theoretical analysis. All I seek to do here is to establish an intimate connection between outsourcing and financialization, neoliberal globalization's two defining transformations, to show that both are aspects of a single complex system of interaction, and to give some reasons why making this connection is the key to understanding why the global crisis heralded by the 1987 stock market crash did not erupt for another two decades, why this crisis is ultimately rooted not in finance but in capitalist production, and why we can only begin to comprehend the form, dynamics, and possible trajectories of this crisis if developments in the sphere of finance are seen within this broader context.

Both outsourcing and financialization have generated huge literatures. We have reviewed the outsourcing literature in previous chapters and we shall now briefly look at some important contributions to the financialization literature. As William Milberg has pointed out, they display two symmetrical gaps: "The value chain literature has not considered in any detail the implications of globalized production for the flow of funds or what has become widely known as financialization,"[56] while "studies of financialization tend to leave as implicit the link to production and investment," adding that "many analysts . . . fail to consider the changes in the structure of production, and specifically the rise of global value chains that have provided the continued capacity of the major industrialized countries to sustain profit growth."[57] Seven years later this verdict remains true, and also applies to the burgeoning literature on the global economic crisis, which is overwhelmingly regarded as a financial crisis, in essence as well as in form, and consequently pays little attention to the accompanying transformation of production.

Financialization and outsourcing have been inextricably interconnected from the beginning of the neoliberal era, when TNCs pioneered the use of offshore financial centers and international money markets to handle their increasingly global operations, thereby forcing open the doors to international financial integration. As Gérard Duménil and Dominique Lévy have explained, "In the 1960s, a new international finance developed . . . the most crucial element was probably the convergence between the rise of the new international finance and the internationalization of production (the development of multinational corporations). International firms needed financial institutions allowing for the circulation of funds internationally."[58] Conversely, financial engineering aimed at boosting "shareholder value," combined with the pressures of fierce competition, compelled Northern firms to cut production costs by outsourcing production to low-wage countries. Outsourcing supported the rate of profit in the imperialist countries, and has become an increasingly favored alternative to investments in new productivity-enhancing and capacity-expanding technology, enabling operating profits to be diverted from investment in plant, machinery, and living labor into financial speculation of different kinds. Non-financial corporations don't just sit on the piles of uninvested cash discussed earlier in this chapter. They use it to become more like financial corporations, often earning more through the operations of their treasury departments than through whatever they are making and selling.

William Milberg is alone in making the crucial connection between financialization and outsourcing and exploring its implications. His holistic approach and excellent research questions have allowed him to partially escape the limitations of the value-added framework he shares with the rest of mainstream and heterodox economists. Yet without a theory of value capable of explaining this connection he can do no more than state the problem. In 2004 he wrote: "The enormous expansion of global value chains has . . . coincided with a decline in manufacturing in most countries [he means most *rich* countries], and thus has permitted companies to return a greater share of net revenues to shareholders rather than reinvesting these revenues in new productive capacity."[59] Writing four years later, on the eve of the crisis, Milberg drew an even clearer connection between outsourcing and financialization: the "impetus to the process of financialization," he argued, is a result of the "rapid expansion of manufacturing productive capacity in low-wage countries," which generates "capital flows from the low-wage to the industrialized countries . . . supporting asset values in the industrialized countries and especially the U.S."[60] This connection was observed in empirical data reviewed by Elisa Parisi-Capone, an analyst working for Roubini Global Economics, who concluded that "at the TNC level, the cost savings from offshoring are considerable and coincide with historic highs in profit shares."[61] But their coincidence, as Milberg explains, is no coincidence.

The critique of value added and the revelation of the GDP illusion presented in the last chapter, along with the mass of data reviewed in earlier chapters, leads us to conclude that the rising weight of financial assets and their associated revenue streams in GDP, a key characteristic of financialization, is not all fizz, froth, and fictitious capital but is to a significant extent a materialization of surplus-value extracted from super-exploited workers in low-wage countries. There is a very real connection, therefore, between the vertiginous growth of the financial wealth of the world's "high net-worth individuals" (or HNWIs, those with more than $1 million in financial assets), which has grown from $32.8 trillion in 2008 to $56.4 trillion in 2014, a 72 percent increase in just six years, and the inhuman work and living conditions of the Bangladeshi and Chinese workers we met in chapter 1.[62]

Finance capital has indeed indulged in alchemy, using debt to amplify profit streams and inflate asset values, with the perversity that the more readily an asset can be stripped and turned into an income flow the more valuable that asset becomes; the more it is cannibalized the more flesh it seems to have on it.[63] However, as well as conjuring value out of thin air, the financial sector also captures value created in productive sectors of the economy, including those it has helped to relocate to low-wage nations. Fleeting references to outsourcing in the financialization literature treat these two processes as if they are completely unconnected. *The Financialization of the American Economy*, a founding document of the financialization literature, provides a classic example of this error. There, Greta Krippner defines financialization as "a pattern of accumulation in which profits accrue primarily through financial channels rather than through trade and commodity production."[64] "Accrue" is ambiguous. It could be understood to mean the accrual of profits whose source is elsewhere, but she evades any such suggestion, talking instead of "the growing importance of the financial sector as a *source* of profits for the economy"[65] (my emphasis) and again, where she justifies her focus on finance by stating: "This paper. . . examines *where profits are generated in the U.S. economy*"[66] (her emphasis). Criticizing this, Till van Treeck makes the essential point: "It is undoubtedly true that many profits are nowadays linked to financial activities. Yet . . . aggregate profits ultimately rely on the production and trade of real goods and services. . . . It is in our view at least semantically, if not conceptually, problematic to consider "the financial sector as a source of profits for the economy."[67] The fundamental problem with this dominant, almost consensus view was identified in *What the 1987 Stock Market Crash Foretold*, a resolution adopted by U.S. Communists in 1988:

> Capitalists are not refraining from major new capacity-expanding investment because they are choosing to divert too much capital into securities markets, real estate speculation, loan sharking, and speeding up production in outmoded factories. The cause and effect are the other way around. The exploiters are sinking their capital into "labor-saving" retooling and speculative paper claims on values because they can get a better rate of return there than from investments in building new factories, installing major new technologies, and hiring on large amounts of additional labor-power.[68]

This critique of financialization does not deny the relative autonomy of finance or the agency of financiers, nor does it imply that financialization can be reduced in some deterministic fashion to the contradictions in the sphere of production. Detailed study of the autonomous role of finance in the global economy is beyond the scope of this investigation. All we can do here is to insist on its inseparable connection with the transformation of production, and use the conceptual tools of value theory to take steps beyond the reach of analysts blinkered by the bourgeois concept of value added.

THE GLOBAL SOUTH IN THE GLOBAL CRISIS

Between 2003 and 2007, the years immediately before the global economic crisis, so-called emerging markets (EMs) in Africa, Asia, and Latin America grew at a faster rate than at any time since the Second World War, and more than twice as fast as imperialist countries. Their average rate of growth during these years exceeded 7 percent (5.9 percent if China is included), compared to 2.6 percent in rich countries. Even in the most crisis-affected year, 2009, they grew by 2.9 percent (0.9 percent excluding China), compared to a 3.7 percent decline in imperialist countries, and in 2010 growth rates in emerging nations shot back up to 7.7 percent (6.9 percent excluding China). Even though EM growth rates declined in each of the next four years, in 2014 they still grew on average by 4.3 percent (3.1 percent excluding China), compared to 1.7 percent GDP growth in the imperialist countries. This raises an obvious question: Why should a crisis be termed global when it affects the richest 20 percent of the world's population, but only a Third World crisis when it is devastating the other 80 percent? Indeed, the 2007–2009 crisis is known as the "North Atlantic Crisis" in China and elsewhere. The short answer is that systemic crisis affecting all imperialist nations is by definition a world crisis. In autumn 2015, at the time of this writing, events are delivering a more complete answer: the global economic crisis is far from over, and *is now set to engulf the entire developing world,* posing a mortal danger to the anemic economic recovery struggling to take hold in the imperialist heartlands. As Andrew Haldane, chief economist at the Bank of England, explained, "Recent events form the latest leg of what might be called a three-part crisis trilogy. Part one of that trilogy was the 'Anglo-Saxon' crisis of 2008/09. Part Two was the 'Euro-Area' crisis of 2011/12. And we may now be entering the early stages of Part Three of the trilogy, the 'Emerging Market' crisis of 2015 onwards."[69]

Before we analyze this historic moment in more detail, it is important to understand why the high rates of growth experienced by emerging nations in the half-decade before 2008 were in large measure a direct consequence of deepening contradictions in the imperialist countries. Figure 10.2 (page 285) above shows that even before the outbreak of the crisis, interest rates in the imperialist centers were already unusually low, forcing investors to look abroad for higher rates of return. "Hot money" flows into emerging markets soared as investors hunted for yield, amplifying the stimulating effects of the big pre-crisis surge of production outsourcing. The first years of the new millennium also saw the beginning of the "commodities super-cycle," a period of rising world prices of the metals, oil, and other primary commodities upon which many emerging nations, particularly in Africa and Latin America, depend for the bulk of their export earnings. This super-cycle was driven by China's insatiable demand for raw materials, in part a function of the outsourcing surge, and by speculation by yield-hungry investors. As *The Economist* observed, "The credit boom in emerging markets was in large part a response to the credit bust in the rich world. Fearing a depression in its richest export markets, the authorities in China brought about a massive increase in credit in 2009. Meanwhile a flood of capital escaping the paltry yields on offer in developed economies pushed interest rates lower in developing ones. This search for yield by rich-world investors took them to ever more exotic places."[70] High rates of growth in emerging markets were therefore more a reflection of deteriorating economic conditions in the imperialist centers than of their own economic vitality. As Ousmène Mandeng of the Reinventing Bretton Woods Committee points out, of all the acronyms that have been coined to define different groups of emerging nations, one stands out: "WIMP: without international monetary power. Most emerging markets are too heterogeneous to be reduced to a simple acronym. . . . However, one common trait does exist unambiguously. Those countries suffer from the fact that they are without international monetary power: they are WIMPs."[71] Expanding on this, Mandeng explains:

> In economic policy gatherings, it is striking how many policy makers attest that one of the most pressing concerns today is the effect of an increase in the Federal Reserve's policy rate. It is this aspect, that a single central bank possesses this extraordinary influence on the rest of the world, that represents one of the greatest defects of the international economy. On the one hand there is a core country with economic policy autonomy, and on the other hand, a periphery dependent on its ability to adjust to the core.[72]

Before the outbreak of the crisis, it was possible to pretend that buoyant economic growth in emerging nations was a sure sign of their progress toward convergence with the imperialist nations; since then it has become abundantly clear that their fate is hostage to the actions of imperialist investors and of central banks beholden to them. As the *Financial Times* pointed out in April 2015, "One big and insidious trend is working to forge a common destiny for almost all emerging markets. The gush of global capital that flowed into their economies in the six years since the 2008–09 financial crisis is in most countries now either slowing to a trickle or reversing course to find a safer home back in developed economies."[73]

Stagnant or declining demand in the imperialist countries poses an obvious threat to the export-oriented industrialization development strategies pursued by low-wage nations. To this must be added another potent transmission mechanism that is sucking the entire Global South into the maelstrom: the reversal of the flows of "hot money" into developing countries, also known as emerging markets, which we will now examine in more detail.

Emerging Market Corporate Debt

According to the IMF, the total corporate debt of indigenous non-financial firms in major emerging markets, which in 2004 stood at $4 trillion, by 2014 had skyrocketed to more than $18 trillion, or 73 percent of GDP, and almost all of this growth was recorded since the financial crisis broke in 2008.[74] By autumn 2015, according to the Institute of International Finance (IIF), total EM corporate debt had reached $23.7 trillion, or 90 percent of total emerging market GDP. "The speed in the buildup of debt has been staggering," said Hung Tran, IIF executive managing director.[75] Chinese non-financial companies alone account for more than half of total EM corporate debt; their $12.5 trillion debt to banks and bond-holders costs them an estimated $812 billion in annual interest payments. According to an editorial in the *Financial Times*, this is "significantly more than China's projected total industrial profits this year," and amounts in real terms to $1.35 trillion once account is made of factory gate prices, which had fallen in 42 consecutive months to September 2015 and were by then declining by around 6 percent a year. Deflation in producer prices means that real interest rates in China are rising sharply, reaching 10.8 percent in March 2015.[76] Chinese firms are far from alone in suffering from falling prices for their products:

Morgan Stanley reports that, by 2015, nine of the top ten EMs were experiencing falling producer prices, with only Indonesia bucking the trend.[77] Rising debts and falling product prices are a fatal combination that threaten a wave of corporate bankruptcies, with the potential to torpedo the banking systems in the affected countries. The IMF warns that "shocks to the corporate sector could quickly spill over to the financial sector and generate a vicious cycle,"[78] especially in those EMs where loans to corporations form a high proportion of bank assets. Indicating the global extent of the phenomenon, the most-exposed banking systems, excluding China, are to be found in Turkey, the Philippines, Chile, and Bulgaria.

Exacerbating the plunge into deflation is the decline in Asian EM exports, which fell by 7.7 percent in July 2015 compared to the year before, the ninth consecutive month of year-on-year declines. As *Financial Times* columnist John Plender points out, "The reason for the evaporation in Asian trade growth, however, is of more concern than the trend itself. Weakening currency values against the dollar are failing to boost export performance—as would normally be expected—but they are nevertheless driving down demand for imports, thus worsening the deflationary trend."[79] The slump in Asian exports, which has "turned emerging markets from contributors to global trade growth to detractors,"[80] is part of a broader trend—throughout the neoliberal era, global trade grew twice as fast as global GDP, but since the crisis it has barely kept pace. *The Economist* warns that emerging market corporations are in poor shape to withstand falling exports, falling factory gate prices, and rising real interest rates: "Over the last five years companies have . . . become less profitable, and so less able to pay [the debt] back. Despite enjoying low yields and the chance to refinance on better terms, 40 percent still have to pay interest amounting to nearly half their pre-tax earnings." *Financial Times* editors add that "the nightmare deflationary scenario is that falling prices in Asia continue to cut corporate profits, prompting mass redundancies and reducing consumer demand. The drag that this imposes on global demand may then intensify, depressing feeble economic growth in Europe and Japan and damping dynamism in the U.S. Aspects of this scenario are already in place."[81]

Loans and Bonds

Debt comes in two forms: bank loans and debt in the form of bonds. When a company or a government issues a bond, say for a million dollars, it agrees to return the million dollars in full to the lender at a definite point in the future and to pay a "coupon" of, say, 5 percent each year until then. Banks intermediate between the owners of capital and those wishing to borrow it; in bond markets they meet each other face-to-face. Unlike bank loans, bonds are sold directly to individual investors as well as to financial institutions, and are actively traded on secondary markets, so the borrower never knows until the bond reaches its term to whom repayment must be made. It is the secondary markets that create "more volatile financial market conditions," as Jonathan Wheatley explains: "If a bond falls sharply in price, any investor who has borrowed money to buy it—as hedge funds habitually do—will have to sell others to make up the loss. Such waves of selling can spread quickly, not only to other bonds but also to other asset classes." [82] Wheatley cites research by UBS to the effect that the total global stock of debt held by banks fell by a half in the period between 2010 and 2015, reflecting the restrictions placed by financial authorities on the amount of money banks can lend, while the volume of assets held by investors in the form of bonds has quadrupled. He goes on to explain why, even before we consider the increase in corporate debt, the change in its composition is itself a source of increased instability:

> The likelihood of [instability] is greater because of changed conditions on secondary markets, where bonds are traded, as opposed to on primary markets, where they are issued. Quantitative easing has pumped up the primary markets but, since the financial crisis, regulatory and other changes have caused a drought of liquidity on secondary markets. Investment banks that used to hold large inventories of bonds on their books can no longer do so. . . . "When there are bouts of buying there are no sellers and when there are bouts of selling there are no buyers," says David Spegel [global head of EM sovereign and corporate bond strategy at BNP Paribas]. "It creates the perfect environment for distressed markets to get worse. This is the year of negative feedback loops."[83]

The IMF estimates that bond finance, "which exposes firms more to volatile financial market conditions," has increased its share from 9 percent of total EM corporate debt in 2004 to 17 percent in 2014.[84] Since total EM corporate debt has quintupled in this period, the near doubling of the share of it in the form of bonds means that EM corporate bond debt increased around tenfold over this decade; what's more, this stellar increase has been concentrated in some particularly vulnerable EMs, such as Brazil, where corporate bond debt has increased twelve-fold since 2007.[85]

Hard Currency Debt

Emerging market corporate debt, as with household debt and sovereign debt, can also be divided into domestic debt, that is, debt issued in domestic currencies, and "hard currency" external debt, mostly in dollars. The loudest alarm bells of all are sounding over a steep rise in that part of EM corporate debt that is denominated in hard currencies. Borrowing in hard currency is attractive to firms in emerging markets because the rate of interest is generally much lower than on debt issued in domestic currencies. On the other hand, to the extent that debt-issuing firms receive their income in domestic currencies, they are exposed to "currency risk" should their domestic currency fall in value vis-à-vis the dollar. Bankruptcies caused by such "currency mismatches" were a prominent feature of all Third World debt crises. In the first three quarters of 2015, the currency of every emerging market has fallen sharply against the dollar. Four of them have declined by at least a fifth: Malaysia, Colombia, Turkey, and Brazil, the last by a third.

Although only around 8 percent of corporate debt is foreign currency denominated,[86] this has grown tenfold since 2004 and nearly doubled between 2012 and 2014, and now exceeds $2 trillion.[87] In addition, there are many EM firms with most of their debt in hard currencies. This is particularly true of oil and mineral companies, whose products are priced in dollars, thereby evading currency risk and making it much easier for them to borrow hard currency, but these companies are exposed to risk of a different sort: plunging commodity prices. For example, 80 percent of Gazprom's debts are in hard currency; Vale, the Brazilian mining company, has more than 60 percent of its debt in hard currency; and Petrobras, the partly state-owned Brazilian oil company currently embroiled in a huge corruption scandal, owes around half of its debt in hard currency.[88] On the other hand, the most prolific Chinese issuers of hard-currency debt are property firms, which have little if any foreign income and which are in the midst of a real estate bubble of biblical proportions. Their appetite for hard-currency loans is a sign of their extreme distress.[89]

Furthermore, corporate exposure to hard-currency debt is concentrated in particular countries, especially in Latin America, where it

equals around 9 percent of Latin America's GDP.[90] Reporting the findings of Fitch, the international credit-rating agency, Jonathan Wheatley
notes that by 2015 Latin American firms had accumulated around $802
billion in debt, of which $501 billion, more than 60 percent, is in U.S.
dollars.[91] Eleven big oil and mineral exporters account for around 40
percent of this total. They receive their earnings in dollars, so are not
exposed to currency risk, although this is little compensation in a time of
plunging world market prices for their exports. Wheatley explains why
other indebted Latin American firms, who owe $471 billion, of which
$232 billion is in dollars, are especially vulnerable to declines in their
national currencies:

> Unless they buy currency hedges on financial markets—fixing their
> dollar liabilities with forward currency contracts—they risk danger-
> ous currency mismatches. But to do so, they must borrow on local
> markets. In Brazil, the cost of doing this—at least 14.25 percent a year
> (the overnight rate) plus a spread of two or three points—is prohibi-
> tively expensive. Many issuers prefer just to take the currency risk.[92]

Foreign currency denominated corporate debt plus household debt
is thought to constitute 47 percent of total private debt in Mexico, 43
percent in Hungary, 40 percent in Singapore, 27 percent in Turkey, and
23 percent in Brazil.[93]

Another indication of the dangerous dynamics of hard currency debt
is the increasing use by EM firms of offshore tax havens to issue this debt.
In this case, a firm sets up a subsidiary in, say, the Cayman Islands, often
amounting to nothing more than a postal address, and uses it to borrow
dollars from investors. Counted by the standard method, such debt is
invisible because the debt has been issued by a Caribbean entity, not a
Chinese or Brazilian one. This practice allows firms to skirt capital controls, creates a conduit for flight capital, and helps firms to conceal their
level of indebtedness from shareholders and regulators and thus preserve
their credit rating. It also makes calculation of total debt outstanding
much more difficult.

Total Debt

One of the most important lessons of the financial crash is that when
crisis breaks it does not matter a whole lot whether the mountains of
debt were accumulated by private firms, households, or governments.

Defaulting private debt brings down banks, which in turn forces government bailouts; hence the warning by Christine Lagarde, the IMF's Managing Director, that "rising U.S. interest rates and a stronger dollar could reveal currency mismatches, leading to corporate defaults—and a vicious cycle between corporates, banks and sovereigns."[94] What matters most of all, therefore, is aggregate debt. According to a study by McKinsey, total emerging market debt rose to $49 trillion at the end of 2013, accounting for 47 percent of the growth in global debt since 2007.[95] China's total debt as a proportion of GDP has gone from 156 percent in 2008 to 244 percent in 2014, and South Korea's debt is even higher at 254 percent, though it is not growing as fast. Malaysia, Taiwan, and Thailand are also weighed down by aggregate debt twice or more as high as their GDP. In contrast, India's ratio is lower, at 135 percent, and has barely moved since the crash,[96] and Brazil's debt-GDP ratio is similar to India's, but grew by 27 percent between 2007 and 2013.

All three categories of debt—corporate, household, and sovereign—have been rising rapidly in developing countries since the global crisis. Household debt in Thailand, for example, rose from 60 percent of GDP in 2007 to 85 percent of GDP by spring of 2015,[97] and very high levels of household debt are also flashing danger signals in a host of other countries in Asia and Latin America, notably South Korea, Malaysia, and Brazil. Analysis by JPMorgan indicates that emerging market private debt (companies plus households) has jumped from 73 percent of GDP in 2007 to 106 percent at the end of 2014. The problem is most acute in Asia. Leaving aside Hong Kong and Singapore, whose extremely high private debt-GDP ratios are skewed by their status as regional financial centers, the highest ratios are found in Asian countries such as Malaysia (170.7 percent), South Korea (167.2 percent), mainland China (147.1 percent), and Thailand (134.4 percent).[98]

The Flight from the South

A net total of $2.2 trillion in capital flooded into the fifteen largest emerging markets between July 2009 and June 2014, when the flow abruptly reversed and began gushing out, reflecting a dramatic loss of confidence by imperialist investors in the prospects for developing countries. Total net outflows from the fifteen largest emerging markets rose to $600.1 billion over three quarters to the end of March 2015, higher than the $545.2 billion in outflows seen during the crisis-ridden three quarters to April 2009. More dramatic still is the unprecedented plunge in EM foreign exchange reserves since December 2014. In March 2015 alone, total reserves held by the fifteen EM countries fell by $374.4 billion, their first decline since records began in 1995, and reflects efforts by central banks to defend their currencies against waves of depreciation and stagnant exports.[99] Driving this reversal is the end of the commodity super-cycle and the big fall in commodity prices (in which China's deceleration weighs heavily) and, even more important, the impending move by the U.S. Federal Reserve away from its zero-interest policy rate. The latter is important because the prospect of higher interest rates in the United States and continued appreciation of the dollar is sucking hot money back home while investors' fear of the consequences of a rise in interest rates for debt-burdened emerging markets is spurring its departure.

As the old saying goes, "What's sauce for the goose is sauce for the gander," so the same pressures acting on imperialist investors in emerging markets are also acting on their native capitalists, who are also moving to shift their fortunes out of depreciating soft currencies into dollars and euros. Capital flight is undoubtedly one of the factors explaining the big increase in FDI outflows from emerging markets since 2009, which have jumped from 21.3 percent of total FDI flows in 2009 to 35.7 percent in 2014,[100] although there are many other factors involved in this—for instance, the growth of corporate debt has been used, in part, to finance a spate of mergers and acquisitions among EM corporations. Henny Sender comments:

> It is hard to know what represents prudent diversification and what constitutes capital flight on the part of Chinese groups and wealthy travellers. But for those who track capital outflows from China, the distinction does not much matter. . . . China's mountain of foreign reserves, once around $4tn, are now down to less than $3.7tn and are expected to drop further to $3.3tn by the end of the year.[101]

A *Financial Times* editorial adds that "even the current pace cannot be assumed to be a maximum. The biggest reserves will drain rapidly if markets completely lose faith in a country."[102] The gathering storm in the Global South is therefore not only generating tremendous deflationary pressures as declining prices set in for both raw materials and manufactured goods, but the deepening crisis is also pressuring the governments of China and other developing nations to slow or halt the recycling of hard currency reserves into U.S. Treasury bonds, making it much more difficult for the U.S. government to finance its trade deficit and threatens to force a tightening of monetary policy. The effect of this is to withdraw liquidity from international financial markets, nullifying the effects of quantitative easing by imperialist central banks. George Saravelos, a Deutsche Bank currency strategist, comments "It is neither the sell-off in Chinese stocks nor weakness in the currency that matters most. It is what is happening to China's FX reserves and what this means for global liquidity. The People's Bank of China's actions are equivalent to an unwinding of QE or, in other words, Quantitative Tightening."[103] James Kynge and Jonathan Wheatley point out the significance of this:

> Deflation was blamed for turning the 1929 US stock market crash into the Great Depression. Fears that a downward price spiral might follow the 2008/09 financial crisis was a key impetus behind the decision of Ben Bernanke, then chairman of the US Federal Reserve, to unleash quantitative easing—the monetary policy that has dominated the world's economic cycle ever since. For these reasons, evidence of a deepening deflationary spiral in Asia—sparked by manufacturing overcapacity, an evaporation of trade demand and anaemic productivity—is a major cause for concern. That anxiety is amplified because . . . it is taking place just as the EU and Japan are slipping back into deflation while the US is struggling with weak corporate earnings, [and this] makes Asia's falling prices a pivotal issue.[104]

ALL ROADS LEAD INTO CRISIS

The greatest surprise about the eruption in 2007 of the deepest and most profound crisis in capitalism's history was not that it happened. On the contrary, it was long expected by Marxists, myself included, who became accustomed to being derided for crying wolf. Nor was it a surprise that the crisis first appeared as a fit of panic in financial markets—this is invariably the case. Instead, the surprise was that it took so long. The outbreak of sovereign debt crises in the spring of 2010, initially centered on Greece, Ireland, Iceland, and Portugal, marked the beginning of a new and qualitatively more dangerous phase of the global crisis. Two factors, above all, determined that these developments marked the beginning of a new stage in what was then a three-year-old global economic crisis. First, the insipid response of the imperialist economies, and the United States in particular, to a succession of colossal stimulus packages—involving unprecedented near-zero interest rates, and massive bailouts not of workers unable to meet mortgage repayments

or of the peoples of Greece, Ireland, and Portugal but of their private
creditors. Second, in reaction to the Greek crisis, governments raced to
replace stimulus packages with their opposite, sharp pro-cyclical cuts in
public spending.[105] Despite the very obvious risk that radical and simultaneous cuts in government spending would reinforce recessionary
trends, imperialist governments were frightened into taking this course
by the even greater peril of not doing so: the fear that, as in Greece and
other so-called peripheral Eurozone countries, investors would begin to
demand sharply higher rates of interest on new loans, making their debt
burden even more unsustainable, creating a vicious circle that could
quickly turn into a death spiral. The Gadarene rush toward austerity is
not limited to imperialist countries, far from it. Reporting on a survey of
128 developing countries, UNICEF has warned of a "new age of austerity sweeping across the developing world."[106]

While governments across the world turn toward austerity, citizens
and corporations are reducing consumption and paying down debt, and
if aggregate debt is nevertheless continuing to increase, this is a sign
of economic distress, not of confidence in the future. In this situation,
export-led growth is the only way individual countries can attempt to
avert contraction. However, the absence of growth turns export-oriented
growth strategies into a zero-sum game, in which each competing nation
struggles to export unemployment and asset destruction onto its neighbors, near and far. The high level of global economic integration means
that a return to economic warfare between the major imperialist powers
will be even more damaging and destructive than last time around. This
does not mean it will not happen, because the source of irrationality is
not to be found in the brains of the capitalists, but in the capitalist system
itself, as Michael Pettis explains:

> Nearly everyone agrees that a world that retreats into direct and indi-
> rect forms of trade protection is a world that is worse off and likely
> to recover more slowly from the global crisis. But the fact that every-
> one seems to agree on this point should not allay our worries. In the
> 1930s, it was also well understood that the crisis would be exacerbated
> by plunging international trade. This did not stop a descent into pro-
> tectionism which put the "Great" into the Great Depression.[107]

At the time of this writing, the eye of the financial storm and the
eyes of the world had moved from the crisis in the Eurozone, which has
been temporarily stabilized by money printing and ultra-low interest

rates, to China and the entire so-called developing world. With interest rates "zero bound"—in other words, they've been cut to zero and can't be reduced further—central banks are deprived of their chief monetary weapon against new shocks. The huge growth of public debt makes further additions to it very risky, despite currently low interest rates, and so fear of adverse market reaction deprives governments of fiscal tools, that is, large budget deficits to support sagging demand. All that remains are "unorthodox" solutions, involving the same conjuring tricks used by private banks to inflate financial bubbles in the first place. Thus Mervyn King, Governor of the Bank of England, refers to "the paradox of policy . . . almost any policy measure that is desirable now appears diametrically opposite to the direction in which we need to go in the long term,"[108] a view echoed by Lawrence Summers, who was beaten by Janet Yellen in the contest for the equivalent post at the U.S. Federal Reserve: "It is the central irony of the financial crisis—caused by too much confidence, borrowing and lending and spending—that it cannot be resolved without more confidence, more borrowing and lending and more spending."[109] Others go further. In 2011 Martin Wolf called on governments to turn on the printing presses and keep them running around the clock—"The time has come to employ this nuclear option on a grand scale"—and to use this freshly minted money not only to support the prices of financial assets (the main beneficiaries so far of government largesse) but also to finance the government's wage bill and investment in infrastructure.[110] Wolf dismissed criticisms that his proposal courted the danger of hyperinflation on the grounds that the detectable pressures on interest rates were pushing in the opposite direction, toward deflation, threatening "financial collapses and sovereign debt crises that ricochet across the globe."[111]

It is now widely recognized that the emergency measures taken by governments to alleviate the financial crisis have prevented wholesale asset destruction but at the cost of inflating new and even bigger bubbles. Martin Wolf has concluded that "without an unsustainable credit boom somewhere, the world economy seems incapable of generating growth in demand sufficient to absorb potential supply. . . . A great deal more trouble surely lies ahead."[112] Nouriel Roubini, one of the few economists to sound the alarm about the pre-2007 bubble, argued that "the combined effect of the Fed policy of a zero Fed funds rate, quantitative easing and massive purchase of long-term debt instruments is seemingly making the world safe—for now—for the mother of all carry trades and mother of all highly leveraged global asset bubbles."[113] As fellow *Financial Times* columnist Tony Jackson explained, wealthy investors merrily move from one credit bubble to the next: "Not only are investors aware they are in yet another bubble, they seem not to care. . . . In recent years, world markets have become so unstable that spotting and exploiting the next bubble has become the name of the game. So if doomsters warn that a bubble is forming, that is taken not as a threat but as a promise."[114]

The next time that panic grips financial markets, which may well be soon, central banks will have neither the resources nor the credibility to mount a second rescue. They can only postpone the inevitable bursting of what Roubini has dubbed "the mother of all asset bubbles," but there is nothing they can do to prevent a protracted, calamitous global depression, competitive currency devaluations, and therefore of vicious trade wars and sharpening inter-imperialist rivalry.

CONCLUSION

The vast wave of outsourcing of production processes to low-wage countries, enabled by the fortuitous arrival of ICT and rapid advances in transportation technology, was a strategic response to the twin crises of declining profitability and overproduction that resurfaced in the 1970s in the form of stagflation and synchronized global recession. This course that was conditioned by the imperialists' reluctance to reverse the expensive concessions that helped convert the workers of the Global North into passive bystanders, or even accomplices, to their subjugation of the rest of the world. Along with a huge expansion of domestic, corporate, and sovereign debt, the global shift of production gave the outmoded and destructive capitalist system a respite that lasted for barely twenty-five years. The "financial crisis" that brought this to an end is a secondary infection, a sickness caused by the medicine imbibed to relieve a deeper malaise, one for which capitalism has no alternative remedies. Exponentially increasing indebtedness succeeded in containing the overproduction crisis, but it has brought the global financial system to the point of collapse. Outsourcing has boosted profits of firms across the imperialist world and helped to sustain the living standards of its inhabitants, but this has led to deindustrialization, has intensified capitalism's imperialist and parasitic tendencies, and has piled up global imbalances that threaten to plunge the world into destructive trade wars. All of the factors that produced this crisis—increasing debt, asset bubbles, global imbalances—are being amplified by the effects of the emergency measures designed to contain it. The irony of zero-interest rate policy and quantitative easing is that their greatest success—preserving the value of financial assets and thus the wealth of those who own these financial assets—blocks the only possible capitalist solution to the crisis, namely a massive cancellation and reassignment of claims on social wealth. QE and ZIRP—Zero Interest Rate Policy, or "crack cocaine for the financial markets," in a memorable phrase uttered by a Goldman Sachs banker[115]—are therefore means of postponing the inevitable, of kicking the can down the road while waiting and hoping for the growth engine to restart.

Although the global crisis first manifested in the sphere of finance and banking, what's now engulfing the world is far more than a financial crisis. It is the inevitable and now unpostponable outcome of the contradictions of capitalist production itself. In just three decades, capitalist production and its inherent contradictions have been utterly transformed by the vast global shift of production to low-wage countries, with the result that profits, prosperity, and social peace in imperialist countries have become qualitatively more dependent upon the proceeds of super-exploitation of living labor in countries like Vietnam, Mexico, Bangladesh, and China. It follows that this is not just a financial crisis, and it is not just another crisis of capitalism. It is a crisis of imperialism.

The rise of neoliberalism after a decade of wars, crises, and revolutions was not inevitable. The 1970s was, after all, the decade of the expulsion of the United States from Vietnam, the Nicaraguan and Iranian revolutions, Cuba's defeat of South Africa's invasion of Angola, and the Soweto uprising that followed. It was the result of battles whose outcome was not determined in advance. Neither, four decades later, is the future predetermined, but this does not mean that there are an infinite number of possible futures. In fact, there are just two: socialism or barbarism. Which of these futures will come to pass will depend on the struggle of millions, and on the capacity of revolutionaries to forge a leadership of the caliber of Russia's Bolsheviks or Cuba's July 26 movement.

The enormous growth of the working class, and in particular the industrial working class, in China and in nations oppressed by imperialism is the most significant transformation of the neoliberal era and ranks among the most important developments in the history of capitalism. The southward shift of the working class, the reinforcement of the working class in imperialist countries through migration from oppressed nations, and the influx of women into wage labor in all countries means that the working class now much more closely resembles the face of humanity, greatly strengthening its chances of prevailing in coming battles. Surplus-value extracted from these new legions of poorly paid workers helped to dig the capitalism system out of its hole in the 1970s, when the imperialist order was challenged by overproduction, falling profits, and rising class struggle in its heartlands and by rebellions and revolutions in Asia, Africa, and Latin America. Together with their sisters and brothers in the imperialist countries, workers have the capacity, the mission, and the destiny to dig a new hole, a grave in which to bury capitalism and bring an end to what Marx called "the pre-history of human society."[116]

The interaction between living labor and nature is the source of all wealth. Capitalism's frenzied exploitation of both has resulted not only in a grave social and economic crisis, but also in a spreading ecological catastrophe. Rising concentrations of CO_2 in the atmosphere, along with the rest of the filth generated by capitalist production and dumped on land and into rivers and oceans, are already causing extreme weather conditions across the Global South. Capitalism's tendency to exhaust labor and nature is as old as capitalism itself, but like its voracious appetite for cheap labor and its dream of circumventing production altogether through financial alchemy, all of its destructive tendencies are reaching their most extreme expression at the same time. The *capitalist destruction of nature* means that this is not just capitalism's greatest-ever crisis, it is capitalism's final crisis, an existential crisis for humanity.

From here, then, *all roads lead into the crisis.* This, in the words of Cuban revolutionary leader Raúl Valdés Vivó, is *un crisis sin salida del capitalismo,* a crisis with no capitalist way out. The only way forward for humanity is to "begin the transition to a communist mode of production. . . . Either the peoples will destroy the imperialist power and establish their own or the end of history. It is not 'socialism or barbarism,' as Rosa Luxemburg said in 1918, but socialism or nothing."[117]

Notes

1. The Global Commodity

1. Karl Marx, [1865] 1987 "Value, Price and Profit," in Marx and Engels, *Collected Works*, volume 20 (Moscow: Progress Publishers) 149.

2. A report by British Parliamentarians noted that "the building, which hosted a total of three garment factories, was built for purely retail purposes. The thousands of workers and electrical generators exerted a weight estimated to be almost six times greater than the building was intended to bear. Load bearing support columns were found to have been erected haphazardly and experts have reason to suspect that the building materials and methods were below par." Bangladesh All-Party Parliamentary Group, 2013, *After Rana Plaza: A Report Into he Ready-Made Garment Industry in Bangladesh*, 18, available at http://www.annemain.com/pdf/APPG_Bangladesh_Garment_Industry_Report.pdf.

3. In December 2013, thirteen months after the blaze that killed 112 workers, Tazreen Fashion owners Mahmuda Akter, her husband, Delwar Hossain, and eleven of their managers were charged with "culpable homicide"—the first time in its history that the Bangladeshi state has attempted to prosecute factory bosses for violations of health and safety legislation. If found guilty, they face imprisonment for between seven years and life. On 3 September 2015 it was announced that their trial could begin in October of that year. On 1 June 2015 Sohel Rana, the owner of Rana Plaza, and 41 managers were charged with murder, whose maximum penalty in Bangladesh is execution. At the time of writing no date has been set for their trial.

4. K. Fernandez-Stark, S. Frederick, and G. Gereffi, 2011, *The Apparel Global Value Chain: Economic Upgrading and Workforce Development* (Durham, NC: Center on Globalization, Governance, and Competitiveness, Duke University), 7.

5. "Bangladesh factory collapse the result of appalling working conditions, says TUC [Britain's Trades Union Congress]." Press release, 25 April 2013.

6. Hasan Kamrul reports that the Bangladeshi government currently spends fully half of its annual budget repairing roads, culverts, and bridges damaged by seasonal floods in "A threat to us all," *Dhaka Tribune*, 9 November 2009, http://www.dhaka-tribune.com/op-ed/2013/nov/09/threat-us-all#sthash.DGHBxoAn.dpuf.

7. Rana Plaza itself was built on a reclaimed swamp.

8. Amy Kazmin, "Bangladesh factory collapse a catalyst for workers' rights," *Financial Times*, May 3, 2013.

9. Peter Custers, 2012 [1997], *Capital Accumulation and Women's Labor in Asian Economies* (New York: Monthly Review Press), 162.

10. Peter Custers quotes an interview with Michael Chossudovsky, who noted that "for each shirt which is produced in Bangladesh and sold in the world market for three dollars, the GNP of the importing OECD countries is going up by about $32." Ibid., 141n.

11. Tony Norfield, 2011, *The China Price*, available at http://economicsofimperialism.blogspot.com/2011/06/what-china-price-really-means.html. His source: "Das Welthemd" (The World Shirt), *Die Zeit*, 17 December 2010, http://www.zeit.de/2010/51/Billige-T-Shirts.

12. Ibid.

13. ILO, 2013, *Decent Work Country Profile—Bangladesh* (Geneva: ILO).

14. Bangladesh All-Party Parliamentary Group, 2013, *After Rana Plaza: A report into*

the ready-made garment industry in Bangladesh, http://www.annemain.com/pdf/APPG_Bangladesh_Garment_Industry_Report.pdf, 26.

15. McKinsey & Co., 2011, *Bangladesh's Ready-Made Garments Landscape: The Challenge of Growth,* http://www.mckinsey.de/sites/mck_files/files/2011_McKinsey_Bangladesh.pdf, 7.

16. See http://www.thedailystar.net/beta2/news/factory-watch-just-farcical/.

17. See https://www.cleanclothes.org/livingwage/calculating-a-living-wage and http://www.cleanclothes.org/livingwage/living-wage-versus-minimum-wage.

18. Rhian Nicholson, 2011, *The 5 biggest retail markups,* Yahoo! Finance UK, http://uk.finance.yahoo.com/news/The-5-biggest-retail-mark-ups-yahoofinanceuk-2638718762.html.

19. See *Practical Stock Investing,* a blog by Dan Duane, at http://practicalstockinvesting.com/2013/05/21/pricing-out-a-low-end-shirt-investment-implications/.

20. Rubana Huq, "The Economics of a $6.75 Shirt," *Wall Street Journal,* May 16, 2013, http://online.wsj.com/article/SB10001424127887323582904578485300080843278.html.

21. Bangladesh All-Party Parliamentary Group, *After Rana Plaza,* 15.

22. Dara Brown, "'We were trapped inside': Pakistan factory fires kill at least 261," NBCNews.com, September 12, 2012. http://worldnews.nbcnews.com/_news/2012/09/12/13819640-we-were-trapped-inside-pakistan-factory-fires-kill-at-least-261?lite

23. John Pickles, 2013, *Economic and Social Upgrading in Apparel Global Value Chains: Public Governance and Trade Policy,* http://papers.ssrn.com/sol3/papers.cfm?abstract_id=2209720, 104–5. 2004 was the final year of the Multi-Fibre Arrangement, which since 1974 had restricted apparel imports into imperialist countries in order to protect domestic clothing industries.

24. UNCTAD, *World Investment Report 2013,* 158–62.

25. Sarah Labowitz and Dorothée Baumann-Pauly, 2014, *Business as Usual Is Not an Option: Supply Chains and Sourcing after Rana Plaza* (New York: NYU Leonard N. Stern School of Business), 25, http://www.stern.nyu.edu/cons/groups/content/documents/webasset/con_047408.pdf.

26. Ibid., 6.

27. Ibid., 9.

28. "Rankle is too strong a word. . . . There's nothing on international trade on which I've not written with some success. I shouldn't be saying it myself but a lot of other people say it." David Pilling, "Lunch with the FT: Jagdish Bhagwati," *Financial Times,* April 17, 2014.

29. Jagdish Bhagwati, "Responsibility Is Local, Not Global," *New York Times,* May 2, 2013, http://www.nytimes.com/roomfordebate/2013/05/02/when-does-corporate-responsibility-mean-abandoning-ship/responsibility-for-sweatshops-is-local-not-global.

30. Available from http://www.cleanclothes.org/img/pdf/accord-on-fire-and-building-safety-in-bangladesh/at_download/file.

31. See "Detailed list of 2012–2014 garment factory fire incidents," compiled by the AFL-CIO's Solidarity Centre in Dhaka, at http://www.aflcio.org/Blog/Global-Action/1-Year-After-Rana-Plaza-Survivors-Families-Struggle-to-Survive.

32. See http://www.industriall-union.org/we-made-it-global-breakthrough-as-retail-brands-sign-up-to-bangladesh-factory-safety-deal; http://www.industriall-union.org/industriall-uni-and-ituc-visit-bangladesh.

33. See http://www.unitetheunion.org/news/workersunitingstatementonbangladesh/.

34.   See http://www.aflcio.org/Press-Room/Press-Releases/Statement-by-AFL-CIO-Presi-dent-Richard-Trumka-on-News-that-U.S.-Government-Plans-to-Suspend-Bang-ladesh-s-Trade-Benefits.

35.   "U.S. suspends GSP for Bangladesh," *Daily Star,* 28 June 2013, http://archive.the-dailystar.net/beta2/news/us-set-to-suspend-bangladeshs-gsp/.

36.   ILO, 2013, *Decent Work Country Profile: Bangladesh* (Geneva: ILO).

37.   Ravi Kanth Devarakonda, *New Labor Norms Could Hurt Bangladesh,* July 13, 2013, Inter Press Service, http://www.source.ly/10SWJ#.VizZbH7hBQI

38.   Palash Baral, n.d. UBINIG, Policy Research for Development Alternative, *Struc-tural Adjustment and the Global Terms of Trade: Perspectives from the Workers' Movement of Bangladesh,* paper presented to seminar organized by War on Want.

39.   Charles Duhigg and Keith Bradsher, "How U.S. Lost Out on iPhone Work," *New York Times,* January 21, 2012, http://www.nytimes.com/2012/01/22/business/apple-america-and-a-squeezed-middle-class.html.

40.   This huge migrant workforce, the result of the largest population movement in his-tory in terms of sheer numbers, is 40 percent of China's total workforce and more numerous than all of Europe's workers,

41.   Marty Hart-Landsberg, 2012, *Apple and the Labor Process,* http://blogs.lclark.edu/hart-landsberg/. Under China's labor law the legal limit on overtime is 36 hours a month.

42.   Pun Ngai and Jenny Chan, 2012, "Global Capital, the State, and Chinese Work-ers: The Foxconn Experience," *Modern China* 38/4: 383–410, available at http://burawoy.berkeley.edu/Public percent20Sociology, percent20Live/Pun percent-20Ngai/ModernChinaPun percent20and percent20Chan2012.pdf.

43.   Duhigg and Bradsher, "How U.S. Lost Out on iPhone Work."

44.   "Foxconn Chairman Likens His Workforce to Animals," *Want China Times,* January 21, 2012, http://www.wantchinatimes.com/news-subclass-cnt.aspx-?id=20120119000111&cid=1102.

45.   Jagdish Bhagwati, *In Defence of Globalization* (Oxford: OUP), 172.

46.   Ibid., 173.

47.   Ibid.

48.   UNCTAD, *World Investment Report 2013,* 162. It adds, with unintended irony, "While there is strong consensus on the normative dimension of what should be done, the practical implementation of CSR standards is the key challenge."

49.   Ibid., 85.

50.   Naila Kabeer, 2000, *The Power to Choose—Bangladeshi Women and Labor Market Decisions in London and Dhaka* (London: Verso).

51.   "The example of Bangladeshi garments illustrates well how the patriarchal divi-sion of labor is enforced through definitions of skill. . . . By defining their work as 'semi-skilled,' the owners make sure that the workforce is disciplined, and that their wages remain far below those of the average male employee." Custers, *Capital Accumulation and Women's Labor in Asian Economies,* 153–54.

52.   Greg Linden, Kenneth L. Kraemer, and Jason Dedrick, 2007, *Who Captures Value in a Global Innovation System? The Case of Apple's iPod* (Irvine: University of Cali-fornia Irvine), http://www.signallake.com/innovation/AppleiPod.pdf, 7.

53.   Greg Linden, Jason Dedrick, Kenneth L. Kraemer, 2009, *Innovation and Job Crea-tion in a Global Economy: The Case of Apple's iPod* (Irvine: University of California Irvine), http://pcic.merage.uci.edu/papers/2008/InnovationAndJobCreation.pdf, 2.

54.   The distribution of the resulting profits brings to mind words written by Lenin more than a century ago: "The British bourgeoisie . . . derives more profit from the

many millions of the population of India and other colonies than from the British
workers. In certain countries this provides the material and economic basis for
infecting the proletariat with colonial chauvinism." V. I. Lenin, 1907, "The International Socialist Congress in Stuttgart," in *Lenin's Fight for a Revolutionary International,* ed. John Riddell (New York: Pathfinder), 76–77.

55. Yuqing Xing and Neal Detert, 2010, *How the iPhone Widens the United States
     Trade Deficit with the People's Republic of China,* ADBI Working Paper Series No.
     257, May 2011, 4–5. http://www.adbi.org/files/2010.12.14.wp257.iphone.widens.
     us.trade.deficit.prc.pdf.

56. The gross value of a nation's exports is the sum of domestically generated value
     added plus the cost of imported inputs. GDP sums the former and does not count
     imports, which of course were produced in other countries and count toward their
     GDPs.

57. Xing and Detert, *How the iPhone Widens the United States Trade Deficit,* 8.

58. Ibid.

59. Ibid., 9.

60. The trend of ever-higher markups of imperialist countries' imports from low-wage
     countries is an outstanding feature of the neoliberal era. William Milberg and Deb-
     orah Winkler report: "Import price declines [relative to final sale price, i.e. the
     markup] were greatest in those sectors which have both the technological and the
     value-chain characteristics identified with profitable offshore outsourcing—com-
     puters and electrical and telecommunications products. But many of the non-elec-
     tronics manufacturing sectors showed large and persistent import price declines,
     especially those with well-developed GVCs [Global Value Chains]. . . . Clothing,
     footwear, textiles, furniture, miscellaneous manufactures (which includes toys) and
     chemicals all experienced import price declines (relative to U.S. consumer prices)
     over two decades of more than 1 percent per year on average, or 40 percent over the
     period 1986–2006." Milberg and Winkler, 2010, *Economic and Social Upgrading in
     Global Production Networks: Problems of Theory and Measurement, Capturing the
     Gains,* Working Paper 10, 13, available at: http://ssrn.com/abstract=1987682.

61. Neil Mawston, executive director at Strategy Analytics, quoted in Steven Musil,
     2014, "Apple, Samsung see drop in global smartphone market share," http://www.
     cnet.com/uk/news/apple-samsung-see-declining-shares-in-global-smartphone-
     market/.

62. Ben Rooney, 2013, "What Does It Cost to Make an iPhone?," http://blogs.wsj.com/
     tech-europe/2013/09/30/how-much-does-it-cost-to-make-an-iphone/.

63. Lex, "China: An Apple a Day Helps Profits Decay," *Financial Times,* April 24, 2014.

64. Source for Hon Hai, Apple's profits, market capitalization and workforce: Forbes'
     list of "2000 World's Biggest Companies," http://www.forbes.com/global2000/list.

65. John Authers, "Apple Core to Earnings Growth," *Financial Times,* April 20, 2012.

66. Anousha Sakoui, "Huge Cash Pile Puts Recovery in Hands of the Few," *Financial
     Times,* January 21, 2014.

67. Julie Froud, Sukhdev Johal, Adam Leaver, and Karel Williams, 2012, *Apple Busi-
     ness Model—Financialization Across the Pacific,* CRESC [Centre for Research in
     Socio-Cultural Change, University of Manchester] Working Paper No. 111, 20.

68. Lex, "Hon Hai / Foxconn: Wage Slaves," *Financial Times,* August 30, 2011.

69. Robin Kwong, "Hon Hai Bracing for Recession," *Financial Times,* January 10, 2012.

70. Lorraine Luk, "iPhone 5S Wait Time Drops as Foxconn Boosts Production," *Wall
     Street Journal* blog, November 27, 2013, http://blogs.wsj.com/digits/2013/11/27/
     iphone-5s-wait-time-drops-as-foxconn-boosts-production/.

71. Kwong, "Hon Hai Bracing for Recession."
72. The sharp decline in farmers' share of final value is evident in other "soft commodities." According to Edward George, head of soft commodities research at Ecobank, in 2012 cocoa farmers received 6 percent of the value of a standard €0.79 chocolate bar, down from 16 percent in 1980. Edward George, 2013, "Overview of Global Cocoa, Coffee and Sugar Markets," http://www.globalgrainevents.com/pdfs/Geneva percent202013/EdwardGeorgeEcobankOverview.pdf.
73. The "fair trade" price of Arabica coffee is 20¢ above the world market price, with a floor of $1.40. However much "fair trade" coffee mitigates the effects on coffee farmers of imperialist domination of the global coffee economy, this is not expressed in lower markups by Northern retailers and coffee chains, who often use the small "fair trade" cost premium as a pretext for much larger increases in retail prices.
74. Oxfam, 2003, *Europe and the Coffee Crisis*, Oxfam Briefing Paper, 9, http://www.oxfam.org/en/policy/pp030226-EUcoffee10.
75. "IMF and World Bank adjustment lending was not designed to reduce poverty directly, and so it is not surprising that they were not unusually effective at doing so." William Easterly, 2003, *IMF and World Bank Structural Adjustment Programs and Poverty*, http://www.nber.org/chapters/c9656.
76. Isaac Kamola, 2007, "The Global Coffee Economy and the Production of Genocide in Rwanda," *Third World Quarterly* 28/3: 571–92, quote at 584.
77. Michel Chossudovsky, 1997, *The Globalization of Poverty: Impacts of IMF and World Bank Reforms* (Goa: Other India Press), 120.
78. Karen St Jean-Kufuor, 2002, *Coffee Value Chain*, http://www.maketradefair.com/en/assets/english/CoffeeValueChain.pdf.
79. Galina Hale and Bart Hobijn calculate that "on average, of every dollar spent on an item labeled 'Made in China,' 55 cents go for services produced in the United States." Galina Hale and Bart Hobijn, 2011, *The U.S. Content of "Made in China,"* Federal Reserve Bank of San Francisco Economic Letter, http://www.frbsf.org/publications/economics/letter/2011/el2011-25.html.
80. William Milberg and Deborah Winkler, 2010, *Economic and Social Upgrading in Global Production Networks: Problems of Theory and Measurement, Capturing the Gains*, Working Paper 10, 13, available at http://ssrn.com/abstract=1987682.

2. OUTSOURCING, OR THE GLOBALIZATION OF PRODUCTION
1. Karl Marx, 1867, *On the Lausanne Congress*, http://www.marxists.org/archive/marx/iwma/documents/1867/lausanne-call.htm.
2. Kate Bronfenbrenner and Stephanie Luce, 2004, *The Changing Nature of Corporate Global Restructuring: The Impact of Production Shifts on Jobs in the U.S., China and Around the Globe* (Washington, DC: U.S.-China Economic and Security Review Commission), 37–38, http://digitalcommons.ilr.cornell.edu/cgi/viewcontent.cgi?article=1017&context=cbpubs.
3. Chhabilendra Roul, 2009, *The International Jute Commodity System* (Delhi: New Book Centre).
4. Anthony Cox, 2013, *Empire, Industry and Class: The Imperial Nexus of Jute, 1840–1940*. After independence and partition in 1948, Bangladeshi capitalists established their own jute mills to process it raw jute. Today Bangladesh is the top exporter of jute and jute products, earning $1bn between July 2012 and June 2013, compared to $21.5bn from garment exports over the same period. "Bangladesh Jute Exports Grow 6.54 Percent in FY13," http://www.fibre2fashion.com/news/jute-news/news-details.aspx?news_id=148556.

5. Aviva Chomsky, 2008, *Linked Labor Histories* (Durham, NC: Duke University Press), 294.

6. Gary Gereffi, 2005, *The New Offshoring of Jobs and Global Development*, ILO Social Policy Lectures (Geneva: ILO Publications), 4.

7. Nelson Lichtenstein, 2007, "Supply-Chains, Workers' Chains and the New World of Retail Supremacy," *Labor* 4/1:17–31. http://www.law.yale.edu/documents/pdf)/Lichtenstein_SupplyChains_WorkersChains.pdf, pp 3–4.

8. UNCTAD, *World Investment Report 2013*, xxi.

9. Ari Van Assche, Chang Hong, and and Veerle Slootmaekers, 2008, *China's International Competitiveness: Reassessing the Evidence*, http://www.econ.kuleuven.ac.be/licos/DP/DP2008/DP205.pdf, 13.

10. It was no coincidence that these two first-movers are frontline states in U.S. imperialism's efforts to contain and encircle China. U.S. electronics companies had very close relations with U.S. generals and politicians and obtained special licenses to transfer what were considered strategic technologies to these two client dictatorships. See Jeffrey Henderson, 1989, *The Globalization of High-Technology Production: Society, Space and Semi-Conductors in the Restructuring of the Modern World* (London: Routledge).

11. Jörg Mayer, Arunas Butkevicius, and Ali Kadri, 2002. *Dynamic Products In World Exports*. UNCTAD Discussion Paper No. 159, 20, http://ideas.repec.org/p/unc/dispap/159.html.

12. UNCTAD, *World Investment Report* 2013, 122.

13. Bronfenbrenner and Luce, *The Changing Nature of Corporate Global Restructuring*, 80. In 2000 Mexico and China were the first- and second-most important destinations for U.S. outsourcers.

14. Ibid., 56.

15. Ibid., 35.

16. Chomsky, *Linked Labor Histories*, 294.

17. Aviva Chomsky draws attention to another specific quality that immigration and outsourcing have in common: "immigration and capital flight ... relieve employers of paying for the reproduction of their workforce" (ibid., 3) by giving employers access to a ready-made workforce in Southern nations. These workers are sustained in part by remittances from migrant workers in the imperialist economies, by foreign aid and public debt, and not least by unpaid labor performed in the family or informal economy. William Robinson makes the same point: "The use of immigrant labor allows employers in receiving countries to separate reproduction and maintenance of labor, and therefore to 'externalise' the cost of social reproduction." Robinson, 2008, *Latin America and Global Capitalism: A Critical Globalization Perspective* (Baltimore: Johns Hopkins University Press), 204.

18. Jeffrey Henderson and Robin Cohen, 1982, "On the Reproduction of the Relations of Production," in *Urban Political Economy and Social Theory*, ed. Ray Forrest, Jeff Henderson, and Peter Williams (Aldershot: Gower).

19. Tasneem Siddiqui, 2003, *Migration as a Livelihood Strategy of the Poor: The Bangladesh Case*, Refugee and Migratory Movements Research Unit, Dhaka University, Bangladesh, http://r4d.dfid.gov.uk/PDF/Outputs/MigrationGlobPov/WP-C1.pdf, 2.

20. IMF, *World Economic Outlook 2007*, 179. This confirmed UNCTAD's earlier verdict that, in industrial countries "cheaper manufactured imports ... greatly helped to maintain income levels and reduce inflation" (*Trade and Development Report 1999*, 11), a conclusion stated more bluntly by Gene M. Grossman and Esteban

Rossi-Hansberg: "Increased offshoring has been a countervailing force that has supported American wages." See *The Rise of Offshoring: It's Not Wine for Cloth Anymore* (Princeton: Princeton University Press, 2006), http://www.kc.frb.org/publicat/sympos/2006/pdf/grossman-rossi-hansberg.paper.0728.pdf, 28.

    In his study of Walmart, Nelson Lichtenstein reports: "Wal-Mart argues that the company's downward squeeze on prices raises the standard of living of the entire U.S. population, saving consumers upwards of $100bn each year, perhaps as much as $600 a year at the checkout counter for the average family.... 'These savings are a lifeline for millions of middle- and lower-income families who live from payday to payday,' argues Wal-Mart CEO H. Lee Scott. 'In effect, it gives them a raise every time they shop with us.'" Lichtenstein, 2005, *Wal-Mart: The Face of Twenty-First-Century Capitalism* (New York: New Press).

21.   Christian Broda and John Romalis, 2008, *Inequality and Prices: Does China Benefit the Poor in America?*, http://faculty.chicagogsb.edu/christian.broda/website/research/unrestricted/Broda_TradeInequality.pdf, 3.

22.   William Milberg, 2004, *The Changing Structure of International Trade Linked to Global Production Systems: What Are the Policy Implications?* Working Paper No. 33 (Geneva: Policy Integration Department, World Commission on the Social Dimension of Globalization, International Labor Office), 38.

23.   IMF 2007, *World Economic Outlook,* 165.

24.   Consumer goods are inputs in the domestic production of a very special commodity: labor-power. Outsourcing the production of consumer goods implies the globalization of the production of labor-power, a fact of immense importance to a value theory of imperialism. Different aspects of this phenomenon are discussed in various chapters in this book.

25.   Richard Baldwin, 2006, *Globalization: The Great Unbundling(s)*, Economic Council of Finland, http://appli8.hec.fr/map/files/globalizationthegreatunbundling(s).pdf, 23.

26.   The Plaza Accord involved the United States' competitors agreeing to help engineer a decline in the relative value of the dollar, thereby stimulating U.S. exports and U.S. economic recovery, in return for U.S. government promises to promote growth and increase access to the U.S. market. In the two years following the Plaza Accord, the Japanese yen almost doubled in value, destroying Japanese competitiveness and creating the conditions for Japan's economic meltdown in 1990. The Plaza Accord thereby helped lay the basis both for the resurgence of the U.S. economy and for the deflationary crisis that has held Japan in its grip ever since.

27.   Margit Molnar, Nigel Pain, and Daria Taglioni, 2007, *The Internationalization of Production, International Outsourcing and Employment in the OECD,* Economics Department Working Paper No. 561, 11.

28.   Milberg and Winkler, *Economic and Social Upgrading in Global Production Networks,* 41.

29.   Data from the WTO-OECD "Trade in Value Added" database, which reports the value of exports net of imported inputs, thereby providing a more accurate picture of trade between nations.

30.   Johannes Van Biesebroeck and Timothy J. Sturgeon, 2010, "Effects of the 2008-09 Crisis on the Automotive Industry in Developing Countries," in *Global Value Chains in a Post-Crisis World, A Development Perspective* (Washington, DC: World Bank), 214.

31.   For a useful review of the literature on ways to estimate the extent of outsourcing, see João Amador and Sónia Cabral, 2014, *Global Value Chains: Surveying Driv-*

ers, *Measures and Impacts,* Working Paper 3/214, Banco de Portugal, http://www.bportugal.pt/pt-PT/BdP percent20Publicaes percent20de percent20Investigao/wp20143.pdf.

32. Peter Dicken, 2007, *Global shift—mapping the changing contours of the world economy (fifth edition)* (London: Sage Publications Ltd.), 38.

33. "Related party imports . . . accounted for more than 60 percent of total U.S. imports from Mexico in 1992." Grossman and Rossi-Hansberg, *The Rise of Offshoring: It's Not Wine for Cloth Anymore,* 8–9. Related party imports include those to subsidiaries in the United States of non-U.S. firms, e.g. the U.S. subsidiaries of Japanese car companies. Latin America has remained characterized by resource extraction rather than outsourcing, with the important exception of the U.S.-Mexican *maquiladora* program.

34. William Milberg, 2008, "Shifting Sources and Uses of Profits: Sustaining U.S. Financialization with Global Value Chains," *Economy and Society* 37/3: 420–51. "Vertical disintegration" or "deverticalization" are sometimes used to denote the outsourcing of previously in-house production tasks, the idea being that vertical links within a firm are replaced by horizontal links between formally equal independent firms.

35. William Milberg and Deborah Winkler, 2012, "Trade, Crisis, and Recovery: Restructuring Global Value Chains," in *Global Value Chains in a Post-Crisis World, A Development Perspective* (Washington, DC: World Bank), 29; my emphasis. Milberg first proposed this in 2008 ("Shifting Sources and Uses of Profits"): "Many 'manufacturing' firms now do no manufacturing at all, providing only brand design, marketing and supply chain and financial management services. Thus a better measure of offshore outsourcing may simply be imports from low-wage countries" (425).

36. Milberg and Winkler, "Trade, Crisis, and Recovery," 30. European nations' relatively low share is due, in part, to the fact that trade between European nations is counted as foreign trade, but not so the trade between firms in different states of the United States.

37. Rashmi Banga, 2013, *Measuring Value in Global Value Chains*, UNCTAD Background Paper No. Rvc-8, 14.

38. In continuation, UNCTAD lists three forms: "either as intra-firm trade, through NEMs [Non-Equity Modes] (which include, among others, contract manufacturing, licensing, and franchising), or through arm's-length transactions involving at least one TNC." *World Investment Report 2013*, 135.

39. Ibid., 122.

40. Paul Krugman, 1995, *Growing World Trade: Causes and Consequences,* Brookings Papers on Economic Activity, http://www.brookings.edu/~/media/Projects/BPE-A/1995-1/1995a_bpea_krugman_cooper_srinivasan.PDF, 327–77.

41. Baldwin, *Globalization: The Great Unbundling(s),* 5.

42. The existence of a socialist option is proved by Cuba, whose revolution has survived more than half a century of economic warfare, terrorism, and subversion orchestrated by successive U.S. governments. Cubans have paid a high price for their defiance, yet they enjoy a higher life expectancy, lower infant mortality, and greater access to education and culture than their powerful neighbor to the north. For an excellent account of the Cuban revolution's staying power, see Emily Morris, 2014, "Unexpected Cuba," *New Left Review* 88: 5–45, available at http://newleftreview.org/II/88/emily-morris-unexpected-cuba.

43. Gary Gereffi, 2005, *The New Offshoring of Jobs and Global Development,* ILO Social

Policy Lectures. (Geneva: ILO Publications), available at http://library.fes.de/pdf-files/gurn/00062.pdf, 18. The situation changed somewhat in the decade following the publication of this book—TNCs have increasingly sought lower-wage hosts such as Vietnam, Cambodia, and Bangladesh, and China has had some limited successes in its efforts to move into higher value-added activities.

44. Ajit K. Ghose, 2005, *Jobs and Incomes in a Globalizing World* (New Delhi: Bookwell), 12.

45. Ibid., 14.

46. After Nigeria, the next three most populous developing nations whose manufactured exports are below half of total exports are Ethiopia, Iran, and Myanmar.

47. The trace for Europe was obtained by subtracting intra-Eurozone manufactured imports from the Eurozone total.

48. Remember, as you study Figure 2.4, that it shows the changing composition of Southern nations' exports and doesn't reveal anything about their absolute size, which, apart from a dip in 2008, grew strongly throughout the entire period.

49. Dostani Madani, 1999, *A Review of the Role and Impact of Export Processing Zones,* Policy Research Working Paper 2238 (Washington, DC: World Bank), 44.

50. World Bank, 1992, *Export Processing Zones,* PRS 20, Industry Development Division (Washington, DC: World Bank), 7.

51. World Bank, 1998, *Export Processing Zones,* PremNotes 11, http://www1.worldbank.org/prem/PREMNotes/premnote11.pdf, 1.

52. William Milberg, 2007, *Export Processing Zones, Industrial Upgrading and Economic Development* (Geneva: International Labor Organization), 7.

53. ILO, 2003, *Employment and social policy in respect of export processing zones (EPZs),* Committee on Employment and Social Policy, http://www.ilo.org/public/english/standards/relm/gb/docs/gb286/pdf/esp-3.pdf, 2; number of countries with EPZs in 2005–6, http://www.wepza.org/.

54. F. Fröbel, J. Heinrichs, and O. Kreye, 1980, *The New International Division of Labor: Structural Unemployment Industrialized Countries and Industrialization in Developing Countries* (Cambridge: Cambridge University Press), 313.

55. Milberg, *Export Processing Zones,* 6.

56. UNCTAD, 2004, *The Least Developed Countries Report 2004—Linking International Trade with Poverty Reduction* (Geneva: UNCTAD), 119.

57. Milberg, *Export Processing Zones,* 6.

58. Richard B. Freeman, 2005, "What Really Ails Europe (and America): The Doubling of the Global Workforce," *The Globalist,* June 3, 2005, http://www.theglobalist.com/StoryId.aspx?StoryId=4542.

59. Alan S. Blinder, 2006, "Offshoring: The Next Industrial Revolution?" *Foreign Affairs* 85/2: 114.

60. Gereffi, *The New Offshoring of Jobs,* 15.

61. Blinder, "Offshoring," 117–18. Other professors criticized Blinder for hyperbole and headline-grabbing, citing an array of bottlenecks, obstacles, and hidden costs that will slow the pace of services outsourcing. Columbia University's Arvind Panagariya, in a direct reply to Blinder, who, he claimed, represents a "minority view" among "informed analysts," even argued that global wage differentials are a temporary phenomenon. During the next half-century, he believes, "The chances are excellent that India and China themselves will turn into rich countries. . . . [Thus Blinder's] fear of having to compete against low-skilled-wage workers in these countries is perhaps exaggerated." Arvind Panagariya, 2007, *Outsourcing: Is the Third Industrial Revolution Really Around the Corner?* http://www.colum-

bia.edu/~ap2231/Policy%20Papers/Tokyo%20club%20Outsourcing%20November%2013-14%202007.pdf, 33.

62. Source: Word Development Indicators.

63. UNCTAD, *World Investment Report 2013,* 135.

64. See http://www.economist.com/economics-a-to-z/.

65. Construction shares one important characteristic with services: the absence of portability. A building must be consumed where it has been built—and for this reason is often given a category of its own, as, for example the UK's Office of National Statistics.

66. Heterodox economic theories question whether, in the real world, market forces do efficiently result in the discovery of equilibrium, market-clearing prices. They challenge neoclassical theory on the grounds that it lacks external validity. In contrast, the Marxist critique focuses on the theoretical incoherence of bourgeois economists' theory of value, and this critique stands even if, as Marx did in *Capital,* we assume that markets function as bourgeois theory says they should, i.e. that all factors of production are used up, and that all commodities are sold at their value.

67. John Maynard Keynes, 1978, *Collected Writings,* vol. 29 (Cambridge: Cambridge University Press), 81–82.

68. Karl Marx, [1883] 1978, *Capital,* vol. 2 (London: Penguin), 137. In the second edition, Frederick Engels inserted a comment that rings true of the decade or so leading up to the global crisis: "All nations characterized by the capitalist mode of production are periodically seized by fits of giddiness in which they try to accomplish the money-making without the mediation of the production process."

69. Anwar M. Shaikh and E. Ahmet Tonak, 1994, *Measuring the Wealth of Nations* (Cambridge: Cambridge University Press), 21–24.

70. As Anwar Shaikh and E. Ahmet Tonak point out, "This physicalist notion [was] embodied in the Soviet-type measure of 'national material product' [which] only serves to strengthen the grip of the official Western concepts" (ibid., 229). Marx explicitly criticized Adam Smith for his physicalist concept of value: "The materialization, etc., of labor is however not to be taken in such a Scottish sense as Adam Smith conceives it. When we speak of the commodity as a materialization of labor—in the sense of its exchange value—this itself is . . . a purely social mode of existence of the commodity which has nothing to do with its corporeal reality. . . . Therefore the materialization of labor in the commodity must not be understood in that way. (The mystification here arises from the fact that a social relation appears in the form of a thing)." Karl Marx, [1862] 1963, *Theories of Surplus Value,* Part 1 (Moscow: Progress Publishers), 171–72.

71. Marx, *Capital,* vol. 3, 406–7.But commerce also includes the transportation of commodities and the preservation of their value. Whether these activities fall within the circuit of production or of circulation depends on their specific social relation; thus maintaining chickens in a frozen state prior to their consumption is a production task, but keeping them frozen so they can be driven from poultry sheds in northeast England to Hungary for filleting by cheap Hungarian labor is not.

72. Ibid., 171.

73. Shaikh and Tonak, *Measuring the Wealth of Nations,* 23–24.

74. For a groundbreaking discussion of this, see Andy Higginbottom, 2011, "The System of Accumulation in South Africa: Theories of Imperialism and Capital," *Économies et Sociétés* 45/2: 261–88.

75. "Reporting of service transactions with unaffiliated foreigners is only required if the transaction exceeds $1 million or with affiliated services if the affiliate's assets, sales, or net income exceed $30 million." Susan Houseman, 2006, *Outsourcing,*

Offshoring, and Productivity Measurement in U.S. Manufacturing, Upjohn Institute Staff Working Paper No. 06-130, 11.

76.   Shaikh and Tonak, *Measuring the Wealth of Nations,* 33.

77.   Ibid., 25.

78.   Since the distinction between productive and nonproductive labor exists in all modes of production, we do not need to begin with the assumption of a capitalist economy. This agrees with Shaikh and Tonak in *Measuring the Wealth of Nations*: "All economic theory contains an elementary distinction between production and nonproduction activities. What distinguishes the classical/ Marxian tradition from the neoclassical/ Keynesian one is the location of the dividing line. The former places distribution and social maintenance activities in the sphere of nonproduction activities, whereas the latter places them in production" (25). It disagrees with Ben Fine and Alfredo Saad-Filho's assertion that "the productive-unproductive distinction is specific to capitalist labor." Fine and Saad-Filho, 2004, *Marx's Capital* (London: Pluto Press), 47. The difference could be overcome if the words "form taken by" were inserted after "the."

79.   Katharine G. Abraham, 2005, "What We Don't Know Could Hurt Us: Some Reflections on the Measurement of Economic Activity," *Journal of Economic Perspectives* 19/3: 3–18, quote at 7.

80.   Ibid., 1.

81.   The decline in manufacturing employment must be "even faster" than the decline in manufacturing's share of GDP because investment in capital goods and raw materials makes up an ever-growing fraction of industrial value added, that is, of industry's share of GDP .

82.   Houseman, *Outsourcing, Offshoring,* 4.

83.   Ibid., 27. "Improvements in the feasibility of offshoring are economically equivalent to labor-augmenting technological progress." Gene M.Grossman and Esteban Rossi-Hansberg, 2006, *The Rise of Offshoring: It's Not Wine for Cloth Anymore* (Princeton: Princeton University Press), 15.

84.   Houseman, *Outsourcing, Offshoring,* 27.

85.   Stephen S. Roach, 2003, *Outsourcing, Protectionism, and the Global Labor Arbitrage,* Morgan Stanley Special Economic Study, http://www.neogroup.com/PDFs/casestudies/Special-Economic-Study-Outsourcing.pdf, 6.

3. The Two Forms of the Outsourcing Relationship

1.   UNCTAD, *World Investment Report 2004—The Shift Toward Services* (Geneva, UNCTAD), 345.

2.   Lex, "Walmart Nation," *Financial Times,* June 5, 2009.

3.   William Milberg, 2004, *The changing structure of international trade linked to global production systems: what are the policy implications?* Working Paper No. 33, Policy Integration Department, World Commission on the Social Dimension of Globalization, International Labour Office: Geneva., 9.

4.   Peter Dicken, 2007, *Global Shift: Mapping the Changing Contours of the World Economy* (London: Sage Publications), 6. *Global Shift*, now in its 6th edition, is a trove of information about many aspects of the outsourcing and the globalization of production.

5.   UNCTAD, *World Investment Report 2011,* 127. This definition of TNC is no more than a thin description of its external form, useful because it underlines the fact that formal ownership of a production facility is not a prerequisite for effectively controlling it and subordinating it to a TNC's profit-maximizing imperative. In a

rich definition that captures the essence of the TNC as well as its form, Fidel Castro described "transnationals [as] the most perfect synthesis, the most developed expression of monopoly capitalism in this phase of its general crisis. . . . Transnational corporations are the international vector of all the laws that govern the capitalist mode of production in its present imperialist stage, all its contradictions, and they are the most efficient instrument available to imperialism for developing and intensifying the subordination of labor to capital throughout the world." Fidel Castro, 1983, *The World Economic and Social Crisis: Its Impact on the Underdeveloped Countries, Its Somber Prospects, and the Need to Struggle If We Are to Survive* (Havana: Publishing Office of the Council of State), 146.

6.   United Nations, n.d., *Underlying Definitions and Concepts,* available from http://www.un.org/esa/sustdev/natlinfo/indicators/methodology_sheets/global_econ_partnership/fdi.pdf. The UN briefing adds: "In practice, many countries set a higher threshold. Also, many countries fail to report reinvested earnings, and the definition of long-term loans differs among countries."

7.   Ricardo Hausmann and Eduardo Fernández-Arias, 2000, *Foreign Direct Investment: Good Cholesterol?,* paper prepared for the seminar on "The New Wave of Capital Inflows: Sea Change or Just Another Tide?," Annual Meeting of the Board of Governors, Inter-American Development Bank and Inter-American Investment Corporation, New Orleans, March 26, 2000, 14.

8.   Jörg Mayer, Arunas Butkevicius, and Ali Kadri, 2002, "Dynamic Products in World Exports," UNCTAD Discussion Paper No. 159, http://ideas.repec.org/p/unc/dispap/159.html.

9.   David Held, A. McGrew, D. Goldblatt, and D. Perraton, 1999, *Global Transformations: Politics Economics and Culture* (Cambridge: Polity Press), 248.

10. Kavaljit Singh, 2007, *Why Investment Matters: The Political Economy of International Investments* (Delhi: Madhyam Books), 26–27.

11. Sam Ashman and Alex Callinicos, 2006, "Capital Accumulation and the State System," *Historical Materialism* 14/4: 107–31.

12. Chris Harman, 2003, "Analyzing Imperialism," *International Socialism* 99: 39–40. For an exchange between myself and another adherent of the International Socialist Tradition, see Jane Hardy, "New Divisions of Labor in the Global Economy," 2013, *International Socialism Journal* 137, isj.org.uk/new-divisions-of-labor-in-the-global-economy: and John Smith, 2013, "Southern Labor: Peripheral No Longer: A Reply to Jane Hardy," *International Socialism Journal* 140: 185–200, http://isj.org.uk/southern-labor-peripheral-no-longer/.

13. lex Callinicos, 2009, *Imperialism and Global Political Economy* (Cambridge: Polity Press), 199–201.

14. UNCTAD, 2008, *World Investment Report 2008,* "Transnational Corporations and the Infrastructure Challenge" (Geneva: UNCTAD), 4.

15. "Developing economies absorbed an unprecedented $142 billion more FDI than developed countries. They accounted for a record share of 52 percent of FDI inflows in 2012. . . . Four developing economies now rank among the five largest recipients in the world; and among the top 20 recipients, nine are developing economies." UNCTAD, *World Investment Report 2013,* 2.

16. Source: Annex table "Estimated World Inward FDI Flows, by Sector and Industry," UNCTAD *World Investment Reports* 2005, 2008, 2011 and 2014.

17. Source: Table 19 "Value of Announced Greenfield FDI Projects, by Destination," 2003–2014, http://unctad.org/en/Pages/DIAE/World%20Investment%20Report/Annex-Tables.aspx.

18.   Alexander Lehmann, 2002, *Foreign Direct Investment in Emerging Markets: Income, Repatriations and Financial Vulnerabilities,* IMF Working Paper WP/02/47, http://www.imf.org/external/pubs/ft/wp/2002/wp0247.pdf, 4.

19.   UNCTAD, *World Investment Report 2007,* 28.

20.   Or more, depending on how it counts agency and temporary contract labor.

21.   "Endesa Announces Full Year 2007 Results," *Business Wire,* February 21, 2008.

22.   UNCTAD, *World Investment Report 2015,* 8.

23.   Ibid., Annex Table 4.

24.   Milberg, *The Changing Structure of International Trade Linked to Global Production Systems: What Are the Policy Implications?,* 9.

25.   Gary Gereffi, 2005, *The New Offshoring of Jobs and Global Development,* ILO Social Policy Lectures (Geneva: ILO Publications), 40.

26.   Data for 2003. UNCTAD, *World Investment Report 2007,* Table 1.6.

27.   This conclusion is supported by an interesting argument advanced by David Harvie and Massimo de Angelis, who proposed an alternative way to interpret data on N-S FDI flows: "In the United States, $20 will . . . command just a single hour of labor time. But in China or Thailand, $20 can put four people to work for 10 hours, while in India, that $20 is sufficient to put 10 people to work, each for 10 hours. When the difference that $20 makes is between commanding one hour of labor time, on the one hand, and commanding 40 hours or 100 hours, on the other, it matters much less that FDI goes to the South." They calculate that between 1997 and 2002 flows of around $3.4 trillion of N-N FDI commanded 190 billion hours of labor time, while the $0.8 trillion that flowed into low-wage countries commanded 330 billion hours, and that, during this period, N-S flows accounted for 19 percent of global FDI, yet resulted in 63 percent of total "labor commanded." David Harvie and Massimo de Angelis, 2008, "Globalization? No Question! Foreign Direct Investment and Labor Commanded," *Review of Radical Political Economics* 14/4: 429–44, quote at 433.

28.   UNCTAD, 2008, *Development and Globalization: Facts and Figures* (Geneva, UNCTAD), 30.

29.   Source for data on the global distribution of subsidiaries: UNCTAD, *World Investment Report 2007,* "Transnational Corporations, Extractive Industries and Development" Geneva: UNCTAD), 217.

30.   UN, n.d., *Underlying Definitions and Concepts,* available from http://www.un.org/esa/sustdev/natlinfo/indicators/methodology_sheets/global_econ_partnership/fdi.pdf.

31.   In continuation, he reports: "A survey jointly sponsored by the IMF and OECD in 1997 showed that of the 14 largest emerging markets only six correctly recorded all three components of FDI income. . . . None of these countries reported a continuous series in published balance of payments statistics." Lehmann, *Foreign Direct Investment in Emerging Markets,* 6.

32.   Ibid., 24.

33.   UNCTAD, *World Investment Report 2013,* 33. Elsewhere the report contradicts itself: Figure I.31, "FDI Income By Region," provides data that implies an average rate of return on FDI in developing nations during this period of 6.7 percent.

34.   UNCTAD, *World Investment Report 2013,* xvi.

35.   Raymond W. Baker, 2005, *Capitalism's Achilles' Heel* (Hoboken, NJ: John Wiley and Sons), 162.

36.   Raymond Baker and Jennifer Nordin, "How Dirty Money Thwarts Capitalism's True Course," *Financial Times,* 10 October 2005.

37. Gene M. Grossman and Esteban Rossi-Hansberg, 2006, *The Rise of Offshoring: It's Not Wine for Cloth Anymore* (Princeton: Princeton University Press) http://www.kc.frb.org/publicat/sympos/2006/pdf/grossman-rossi-hansberg.paper.0728.pdf, p13. The effects on production, wages, and prices, according to the authors, are that U.S. production will become more concentrated in capital-intensive activities; the wages of workers engaged in labor-intensive tasks will come under pressure while skilled workers' wages will rise; and the prices in the United States of goods whose production has been outsourced will fall relative to those produced domestically.

38. Gereffi, *The New Offshoring of Jobs and Global Development,* 4.

39. Timothy J. Sturgeon, 2008, *From Commodity Chains to Value Chains: Interdisciplinary Theory Building in an Age of Globalization,* http://web.mit.edu.eresources.shef.ac.uk/ipc/publications/pdf)/08-001.pdf, 8.

40. Milberg, *The Changing Structure of International Trade Linked to Global Production Systems: What Are the Policy Implications?,* 15.

41. Grossman and Rossi-Hansberg, *The Rise of Offshoring: It's Not Wine for Cloth Anymore,* 8–9.

42. Foreign trade statistics from http://www.census.gov/foreign-trade/balance/c5700.html#2005.

43. William Milberg, 2004, "Globalized Production: Structural Challenges for Developing Country Workers," in *Labor and the Globalization of production: Causes and Consequences of Industrial Upgrading,* ed.William Milberg (New York: Palgrave Macmillan), 7–8.

44. Milberg, *The Changing Structure of International Trade Linked to Global Production Systems: What Are the Policy Implications?,*34.

45. Martin Wolf, 2005, *Why Globalization Works* (New Haven and London: Yale University Press), 235. More investigation is needed to see how casualization affects these calculations, since TNC affiliates' wages may only reflect direct labor.

46. Ibid., 236.

47. Jagdish Bhagwati, 2004, *In Defense of Globalization* (Oxford: Oxford University Press),172.

48. Clive Crook, 2001, "Globalization and Its Critics: A Survey of Globalization," *The Economist,* September 29, 2001.

49. Lesley Gill, 2004, *Labor and Human Rights: "The Real Thing" in Colombia: Report to the Human Rights Committee of the American Anthropological Association,* http://killercoke.org/downloads/reports/gill.pdf.

50. Coca-Cola spokesman Rafael Fernandez, quoted in Julian Borger, "Coca-Cola sued over bottling plant 'terror campaign,'" *Guardian,* 21 July 2001.

51. Mark Thomas, 2008, *Belching Out the Devil: Global Adventures with Coca-Cola* (London: Ebury Press).

52. UNCTAD, *World Investment Report 2011,* 151.

53. B. J. Silver and Giovanni Arrighi, 2000, "Workers North and South," in *The Socialist Register 2001,* ed. L. Panitch and C. Leys (London: Merlin Press), http://www.wildcat-www.de/dossiers/forcesoflabor/workers_north_and_south.pdf, 10.

54. UNCTAD also offers a list of four key advantages of arm's-length outsourcing over FDI: "(1) the relatively lower upfront capital expenditure and working capital needed for operation; (2) related to this, the reduced risk exposure; (3) greater flexibility in adapting to changes in the business cycle and in demand; and (4) the externalization of non-core activities that can be carried out at lower cost or more effectively by other operators." UNCTAD, *World Investment Report 2011,* 142. UNCTAD's list does not mention the FDI wage premium; (2) and (3) are different

330 Notes to pages 81–88

aspects of risk, both are covered by my third reason why outsourcing firms might favor arm's-length relationships.

55. Anwar M. Shaikh and E. Ahmet Tonak, 1994, *Measuring the Wealth of Nations* (Cambridge: Cambridge University Press), 229.

56. *Positive Economics* is the title of a widely used economics textbook by Paul Samuelson. Positivism is a pseudo-scientific approach to natural and social phenomena that privileges the induction of theoretical concepts from empirical data to their deduction from scientific principles. Since value generated in production cannot be empirically measured—it only appears in the form of price, which measures the deposition of value, not its generation—bourgeois economics ignores it.

57. If profit is the return on invested capital, rent can be defined as extra profits arising from some form of monopoly.

58. Quoted in Michiyo Nakamoto, "Asia: Displacement Activity," *Financial Times*, August 22, 2010.

59. Ari Van Assche, Chang Hong, and Veerle Slootmaekers, 2008, *China's International Competitiveness: Reassessing the Evidence*, http://www.econ.kuleuven.ac.be/licos/DP/DP2008/DP205.pdf, 15–16.

60. Ibid., 16.

61. Ibid., 2, 16.

62. Ricardo Hausmann, César Hidalgo et al., 2011, *The Atlas of Economic Complexity*, http://atlas.cid.harvard.edu/media/atlas/pdf/HarvardMIT_AtlasOfEconomicComplexity.pdf, 18.

63. Arnelyn Abdon, Marife Bacate, Jesus Felipe, and Utsav Kumar, 2010, *Product Complexity and Economic Development*, Levy Economics Institute Working Paper No. 616, http://www.levyinstitute.org/pubs/wp_616.pdf,, 3.

64. Hausmann, *The Atlas of Economic Complexity*, 22.

65. Timothy J. Sturgeon, Peter Bøegh Nielsen, Greg Linden, Gary Gereffi and Clair Brown, 2013, "Direct Measurement of Global Value Chains: Collecting Product- and Firm-Level Statistics on Value Added and Business Function Outsourcing and Offshoring," in *The Fragmentation of Global Production and Trade in Value-Added: Developing New Measures of Cross Border Trade*, ed. Aaditya Mattoo, Zhi Wang, and Shang-Jin Wei (Washington, DC: World Bank), 289–319. Available from https://openknowledge.worldbank.org/handle/10986/15809.

66. Hausmann, *The Atlas of Economic Complexity*, 23.

67. Over 40 percent of Greek export earnings derive from its large merchant shipping fleet. Unlike the ships themselves, this service does not figure in complexity calculations.

68. Samuel Brittan, "The Futile Attempt to Save the Eurozone," *Financial Times*, November 4, 2010.

69. Jesus Felipe and Utsav Kumar, 2011, *Unit Labor Costs in the Eurozone: The Competitiveness Debate Again*, Levy Economics Institute Working Paper No. 651, Asian Development Bank, Manila, 11. Hausmann et al. comment: "The least complex countries in Western Europe are Portugal (35) and Greece (53), two countries whose high income cannot be explained by either their complexity or their natural resource wealth. We do not think that this is unrelated to their present difficulties." *The Atlas of Economic Complexity*, 63.

70. Fred Halliday adds that yet there is "a continued failure of social scientists or anyone else to provide a convincing explanation of why it is so." Halliday, 2001, "'For an International Sociology,'" in *Historical Sociology of International Relations*, ed. Stephen Hobden and John M, Hobson (Cambridge: Cambridge University Press), 244–64.

71. Hausmann, *The Atlas of Economic Complexity*, 83.
72. Arnelyn Abdon, Marife Bacate, Jesus Felipe, and Utsav Kumar, 2010, *Product Complexity and Economic Development*, Levy Economics Institute Working Paper No. 616, http://www.levyinstitute.org/pubs/wp_616.pdf, 13–14.
73. Mayer, "Dynamic Products in World Exports," 20.
74. William R. Cline, "Can the East Asian Model of Development Be Generalized?," *World Development* 10/2 (1982): 89.
75. Raphael Kaplinsky, 2005, *Globalization, Poverty and Inequality* (Cambridge: Polity), 230.
76. Ibid., 108.
77. Ibid., 177. *Oligopsony* is when demand for a product is dominated by a small number of buyers.
78. Gereffi, *The New Offshoring of Jobs and Global Development*, 46–47.
79. Robert Feenstra and Gordon Hanson, 2001, *Global Production Sharing and Rising Inequality: A Survey of Trade and Wages*, NBER Working Paper No. 8372, 17.
80. Ibid., 10.
81. UNCTAD, *Trade and Investment Report 1999*, vi.
82. UNCTAD, *Trade and Development Report 2002*, 80.
83. William Milberg and Deborah Winkler, 2010, *Economic and Social Upgrading in Global Production Networks: Problems of Theory and Measurement*, Capturing the Gains Working Paper 10, *Capturing the Gains* (CtG), Convenor: Stephanie Barrientos, University of Manchester http://www.capturingthegains.org/pdf/ctg-wp-2010-4.pdf 1.
84. Ibid., 18.
85. The nine weak upgraders: Cameroon, China, Ethiopia, India, Indonesia, Malaysia, Thailand, Tunisia, Vietnam. Those achieving no detectable upgrading: Argentina, Angola, Bangladesh, Bolivia, Brazil, Cambodia, Chile, Colombia, Gabon, Ghana, Kenya, Malaysia, Mexico, Morocco, Peru, Senegal, South Africa, Uruguay, Venezuela, Zimbabwe
86. Raúl Prebisch and Hans Singer argued that the terms of trade were constantly moving against primary commodity-exporting poor countries and in favor of the rich nations exporting manufactured goods. This became a key element of the theory of "unequal exchange," a core concept of dependency theory (see chapter 7 in this book).
87. Milberg and Winkler, *Economic and Social Upgrading in Global Production Networks*, 13.
88. Ibid.
89. Ibid., 18.
90. Manufacturing value-added shares all of the defects of value added: it presumes that the value added is entirely the result of activities taking place within that firm, and not the result of the ability of that firm to capture a share of the total value created by all competing firms. I argue here that part of the value captured by Northern firms, appearing as part of their manufacturing and services value-added, represents value created by living labor in Southern production processes. Thus Apple's enormous markups boost U.S. manufacturing value-added (MVA), even though Apple itself does little or no manufacturing. Once this is appreciated it becomes clear why the large-scale relocation of production processes to low-wage nations does not in the slightest signify that manufacturing production has ceased to be a prime source of use-values and surplus-value sustaining the supposedly post-industrial capitalisms of the North.

91.   High-income nations: Australia, Austria, Canada, Denmark, Finland, Germany, Ireland, Italy, Japan, Netherlands, New Zealand, Norway, Portugal, Switzerland, United Kingdom, United States.

      Low- and middle-income nations: Algeria, Argentina, Bangladesh, Benin, Bolivia, Brazil, Cameroon, Central African Republic, Chile, Colombia, Costa Rica, Croatia, Ecuador, Egypt, El Salvador, Ghana, Guatemala, Honduras, Hong Kong, Hungary, India, Indonesia, Jamaica, Jordan, Kenya, South Korea, Madagascar, Malawi, Malaysia, Mauritius, Mexico, Morocco, Nepal, Nicaragua, Nigeria, Oman, Pakistan, Panama, Papua New Guinea, Paraguay, Peru, Philippines, Romania, Saudi Arabia, Senegal, Slovenia, Sri Lanka, Thailand, Togo, Trinidad and Tobago, Tunisia, Turkey, Uruguay, Venezuela, Yemen, Zimbabwe.

92.   The World Development Indicators do not provide a value for Chinese MVA in 2002. Including China, total trade of low- and middle-income nations increased by 434.3 percent. In 2001, these 55 nations produced 61.2 percent of the combined GDP of all 156 low- and middle-income nations listed in the WDI tables; this rises to 79.4 percent if China is included.

93.   The World Bank's World Development Indicators provide data on total manufacturing value-added (MVA) for nearly all nations since 1980, but do not distinguish between MVA that is domestically consumed and that which is exported.

94.   UNCTAD, *Trade and Development Report 2002,* 80.

95.   The chart shows the two lines crossing in the late 1990s, but the precise date when the two lines crossed is of no significance, since MVA does not distinguish between value added in the production of export goods and goods for domestic consumption, while "manufactured exports" do not distinguish between export of imported value and domestically produced value. More significant is the kink in the trace for manufactured exports—the brief plateau in 1997 coincided with the outbreak of economic crisis in Thailand, South Korea, Indonesia. and other Asian countries; the ensuing spurt resulted from the hugely increased competitiveness that flowed from large currency devaluations.

96.   Milberg, "Globalized Production," 10.

97.   NIPA, Table 1.2.5, http://www.bea.doc.gov; Bureau of Labor Statistics, http://www. bls.gov/ces/home.htm#data.[National Income and Product Accounts]

4. Southern Labor Peripheral No Longer

1.   Epigraph: Gary Gereffi, 2005, *The New Offshoring of Jobs and Global Development,* ILO Social Policy Lectures (Geneva: ILO Publications), 5.

2.   According to the World Bank, this level had already been reached in 1995: "Low- and middle-income countries already account for almost 80 percent of the world's industrial workforce." (World Bank, 1995, *World Development Report 1995—Workers in an Integrating World,* 4). KILM [Key Indicators of the Labor Movement] 5th edition data used to generate Figure 3.3 indicate that the figure in 1995 was 69 percent.

3.   John Bellamy Foster, Robert W. McChesney, and R. Jamil Jonna, 2011, "The Global Reserve Army of Labor and the New Imperialism," *Monthly Review* 63/6, http://monthlyreview.org/2011/11/01/the-global-reserve-army-of-labor-and-the-new-imperialism.

4.   See Figure 5.1 in IMF, *World Economic Outlook, April 2007,* 162.

5.   ILO, *Global Employment Trends,* various editions. "Population and Economically Active Population, 2004," cited in Figurte 4.1, is no longer available from ILO's website. After 2004, data on world employment by sector is contained in annex

tables in annual editions of the ILO's Global Employment Trends, http://laborsta.
ilo.org/.

6. World Bank, World Development Indicators, last updated: 09/09/2015.
7. Federal Reserve Economic Data, https://research.stlouisfed.org/fred2.
8. ILO, 2006, *Report of the Director General: Changing Patterns in the World of Work*, http://www.ilo.org/public/english/standards/relm/ilc/ilc95/pdf/rep-i-c.pdf,, 27.
9. Ibid., 28.
10. Nomaan Majid, 2005, *On the Evolution of Employment Structure in Developing Countries*, Employment Strategy Papers 2005/18, (Geneva: ILO), 3–4.
11. M. Ismail Hossain, Syed A. Hye, and Amin Muhammad Au, 1998, *Structural Adjustment Policies and Labor Market in Bangladesh* (Dhaka: CIRDAP (Centre on Integrated Rural Development for Asia and the Pacific), 223.
12. ILO, *Report of the Director General: Changing Patterns in the World of Work*, viii.
13. Fidel Castro, Speech to the 12th Summit of the Non-Aligned Movement, Durban, 2 September 1998, translated by author, http://www.cuba.cu/gobierno/discursos/1998/esp/f020998e.htm.
14. Eugene Rostow, 1960, *The Stages of Economic Growth: A Non-Communist Manifesto* (Cambridge: Cambridge University Press), 5–6.
15. Karl Marx, [1867] 1976, *Capital*, vol. 1 (London: Penguin), 915–25.
16. Eugene Rostow, *The Stages of Economic Growth: A Non-Communist Manifesto* (Cambridge: Cambridge University Press, 1960), 163.
17. [Eli] Hecksher and [Bertil] Ohlin are sometimes joined by Wolfgang Stolper and Paul Samuelson to give the "H-O-S-S model of international trade." Despite its claims, the H-O version of comparative advantage has very little to do with Ricardo's theory. Instead, it is better understood as the application of marginalist value theory to international trade. Marginalist value theory claims that, at equilibrium, each factor is rewarded in accordance with its contribution to the value created. This seems logical: if a worker produced more value than he/she receives in the form of wages, it would be in the interest of the employer to hire more workers until the "marginal product," the extra production resulting from the hiring of an extra worker, becomes equal to the wage. This is what is supposed to happen within a national economy; the HOS model assumes that it happens internationally as well. The fallacy at the heart of this approach is the assumption that a firm's value-added is identical to the value that its workers have created. I examine this assumption elsewhere in this work, especially in chapter 9, "The GDP Illusion."
18. Mike Davis, 2006, *Planet of Slums* (London: Verso), 174.
19. Deepak Nayyar, 2003, "Globalization and Development," in *Rethinking Development Economics*, ed. Ha-Joon Chang (London: Anthem Press), 70. The Balfour government's 1905 Aliens Act, which closed Britain's door to Central European Jews fleeing tsarist pogroms, is widely considered to be the first piece of modern immigration legislation in the UK; in the United States the imposition of a literacy test in 1917 and the introduction of quotas in 1921 marked the end of unrestricted (European) immigration. For a useful comparison of immigration in the late nineteenth and late twentieth centuries, see Timothy J. Hatton and Jeffrey G. Williamson, 2008, "The Impact of Immigration: Comparing Two Global Eras," *World Development* 36/3: 345–61. Cited data is from Teresa Hayter, 2000, *Open Borders* (London: Pluto Press), 9.
20. Ajit K. Ghose, 2005, *Jobs and Incomes in a Globalizing World* (New Delhi: Bookwell), 17.

21. 800 million is approximately 1/6 of the 4.9 billion people living in what Laborsta calls the "less developed countries" in 2000.

22. Ghose, *Jobs and Incomes in a Globalizing World,* 83.

23. Ibid., 89. There are important exceptions, mostly in Latin America and the Caribbean. Perhaps the most significant exception is Mexico, around 10 percent of whose workforce has emigrated to the United States. Alejandro Portes and Kelly Hoffman, 2003, "Latin American Class Structures: Their Composition and Change during the Neoliberal Era," in *Latin American Research Review,* 38:1: 42–82 , 70) report that 8 percent of the Ecuadorean population migrated to the United States during the 1990s.

24. Davis, *Planet of Slums,* 183.

25. International Organization for Migration (IOM), 2008, *World Migration 2008: Managing Labor Mobility in the Evolving Global Economy* (Geneva: International Organization for Migration), 32.

26. Nayyar, "Globalization and Development," 70. He continues, "The present phase of globalization has found substitutes for labor mobility in the form of trade flows and investment flows."

27. United Nations, *Trends in International Migrant Stock: Migrants by Destination and Origin,* POP/DB/MIG/Stock/Rev.2013. The IOM adds" "Given the amount of political attention it attracts, the total knowledge about the nature and magnitude of the international labor force, which represents around three per cent of the global workforce, is remarkably limited. This is particularly the case in relation to irregular migration, which by its very nature is difficult to measure" (31).

28. Ibid., 80. To begin to put this in context, the ILO reports that 63 million industrial workers are employed in the South's export processing zones, around one-eighth of the South's industrial workforce.

29. The remaining 50 percent of migrant workers and 72 percent of native-born workers are employed in "services." Ibid., 81, Table 3.2.

30. Ghose claimed, in *Jobs and Incomes in a Globalizing World,* that in 1998 the United States was home to "75 percent of all immigrant workers from developing countries working in the industrialized world. Only 13 percent of these workers were in Western Europe" (83).

31. UN, *Trends in International Migrant Stock.*

32. 710,000 migrant workers with permits, 192,000 without. IOM, *World Migration 2003: Managing Migration—Challenges and Responses for People on the Move* (Geneva: International Organization for Migration), Table 11.2, 199.

33. Ibid.,200.

34. Robin Harding and Jonathan Soble, "Not Made in Japan," *Financial Times,* July 20 2009.

35. OECD, 2013, *World Migration in Figures,* OECD-UNDESA,http://www.oecd.org/els/mig/World-Migration-in-Figures.pdf, 4.

36. Ghose, *Jobs and Incomes in a Globalizing World,* 89.

37. Royal Africa Society, 2005, *A Message to World Leaders: What About the Damage We Do to Africa,* http://www.royalafricansociety.org/index.php?option=com_content&task=view&id=212&Itemid=208.

38. Akhenaten Benjamin Siankam Tankwanchi, Çaglar Özden, and Sten H. Vermund, 2013, "Physician Emigration from Sub-Saharan Africa to the United States: Analysis of the 2011 AMA Physician Masterfile," *PLOS Medicine* 10/12, http://journals.plos.org/plosmedicine/article?id=10.1371/journal.pmed.1001513, 16.

39. Ibid., 3.

40. Davis, *Planet of Slums,* 14.
41. IOM, 2012, *Global Estimates and Trends,* http://www.iom.int/cms/en/sites/iom/home/about-migration/facts--figures-1.html.
42. Nearly one billion of the world population live on less than 1.25 PPP$ per day, or around 50¢ at Forex exchange rates. Their total annual income is less than half the size of migrant workers' remittances to their families in developing countries.
43. Dani Rodrik, 2002, *Feasible Globalizations,* NBER Working Paper No. 9129 http://www.nber.org/papers/w9129.pdf ,19–20. He adds , "What is equally important, the economic benefits would accrue directly to workers from developing nations. We would not need to wait for trickle-down to do its job" (21).
44. EAP data from Laborsta.
45. The ILO reports that in 2004 218 million children were "trapped in child labor, of which 126 million were in hazardous work." ILO, *Report of the Director General: Changing Patterns in the World of Work,* 22.
46. Richard B. Freeman, 2005. "What Really Ails Europe (and America): The Doubling of the Global Workforce," in *The Globalist,* June 03, 2005, http://www.theglobalist.com/StoryId.aspx?StoryId=4542
47. Calculated by applying the simple idea that if X percent of a nation's production is internationally traded, then X percent of its workers participate in global trade. Since exports, for most nations, are growing faster than GDP, the "effective global workforce" is growing much faster than the world's total economically active population. See Figure 5.1 in the IMF's *World Economic Outlook, April 2007,* 162.
48. ILO, *Global Wage Report 2008–9* (Geneva: ILO), 9.
49. Hernando de Soto, 2000, *The Mystery of Capital: Why Capitalism Triumphs in the West and Fails Everywhere Else* (New York: Basic Books), 4. Jan Breman comments, "Bitter experiences of the recession-struck informal economy ... can be repeated for region after region across India, Africa and much of Latin America. Confronted with such misery it is impossible to concur with the World Bank's and *Wall Street Journal's* optimism about the sector's absorptive powers. As for their praise for the 'self-reliance' of those struggling to get by in these conditions: living in a state of constant emergency saps the energy to cope and erodes the strength to endure. To suggest that these workers constitute a 'vibrant' new class of self-employed entre- preneurs, ready to fight their way upward, is as misleading as portraying children from the chawls of Mumbai as slumdog millionaires." Jan Breman, 2009, "Myth of the Global Safety Net," *New Left Review* 59: 32.
50. ILO, 2002, *Decent Work and the Informal Economy,* Report 6, International Labor Conference, 90th Session, Geneva, 1.
51. Kristina Flodman Becker, 2004, *The Informal Economy,* Sida Fact-Finding Study (Stockholm: Edita Sverige AB), 8, 18–19. Flodman Becker reports that Southern governments deploy a variety of techniques to determine the size of their informal economy. For instance, authorities in India, Indonesia, Thailand, Bangladesh, and the Philippines count all firms with less than ten employees as part of the informal economy (16).
52. ILO, *Decent Work and the Informal Economy,* 38.
53. Ibid., 3.
54. Alessandra Mezzadri, 2010, "Globalisation,informalisation and the state in the Indian garment industry." *International Review of Sociology,* 20/3: 491-511, 26.
55. ILO, 2002, *Women and Men in the Informal Economy, a Statistical Picture,* Employ- ment Sector (Geneva: ILO), http://www.wiego.org/publications/women and men in the informal economy.pdf, 19.

56. ILO, *Decent Work and the Informal Economy,* 21.

57. Davis, *Planet of Slums,* 178. Yes, but the "global informal working class" is not a class in and of itself, it is *part of* the global working class, of the global proletariat. Whether formal or informal, all are defined by owning nothing except their labor-power and survive only by selling it for a wage or by rendering direct labor services in the informal economy.

58. ILO, *Decent Work and the Informal Economy,* 19n.

59. Swarna Jayaweera, 2002, "Women Subcontracted Workers in Sri Lanka," in *The Hidden Assembly Line—Gender Dynamics of Subcontracted Work in the Global Economy*, ed. Radhika Balakrishnan (West Hartford, CT: Kumarian Press), 63–86.

60. Martha Chen, Jennifer Sebstad, and Lesley O'Connell, 1999, "Counting the Invisible Workforce: The Case of Home-Based Workers," *World Development* 27/3: 603–10.

61. Stephanie Barrientos , Naila Kabeer, and Naomi Hossain, 2004, *The Gender Dimension of the Globalization of Production,* Policy Integration Department, Working Paper No. 17 (Geneva: ILO), 1.

62. Henry Bernstein, *"Capital and Labor from Centre to Margins,"* keynote address for conference on "Living on the Margins, Vulnerability, Exclusion and the State in the Informal Economy," Cape Town, 26–28 March 2007, http://www.povertyfrontiers. org/ev_en.php?ID=1953_201&ID2=DO_TOPIC, 4.

63. Flodman Becker, *The Informal Economy,* 9.

64. Ibid., 5.

65. Marilyn Carr, Martha Chen, and Jane Tate, 2000, "Globalization and Home-Based Workers," *Feminist Economics,* 6/3: 123-42Carr et al., 2000, 126.

66. W. Arthur Lewis, 1954, *Economic Development with Unlimited Supplies of Labor,* http://www.unc.edu/~wwolford/Geography160/368lewistable.pdf.

67. Alejandro Portes and Kelly Hoffman, 2003, "Latin American Class Structures: Their Composition and Change during the Neoliberal Era," *Latin American Research Review* 38/1, 42–82.

68. William Robinson , 2008, *Latin America and Global Capitalism—A Critical Globalisation Perspective* (Baltimore: Johns Hopkins University Press), 242.

69. Ibid., 242–3.

70. Chen, "Counting the Invisible Workforce, " 604.

71. Davis, *Planet of Slums,* 178.

72. Ibid., 178–79.

73. Ibid., 30. In continuation, the ILO says: "The main authors of these policies, the international financial institutions, are therefore now emphasizing poverty eradication and sustainable development, although they still fail to give adequate attention to the employment implications of their policies." In other words, they now kindly provide Band-Aids as they inflict more wounds.

74. ILO, *Decent Work and the Informal Economy,* 35.

75. Ibid., 33–34.

76. Ibid., 2.

77. Stephanie Barrientos, Naila Kabeer, and Naomi Hossain, 2004, "The Gender Dimension of the Globalization of Production." Policy Integration Department, Working Paper No. 17. Geneva: ILO,10.

78. Ibid., 10.

79. Ibid., 4.

80. Socialist Workers Party, [1988] 1994, "What the 1987 Stock Market Crash Foretold," 1988 resolution adopted by the Socialist Workers Party (U.S.) in *New International #10* (New York: 408 Printing and Publishing Corp.), 144.

81. Marx, [1867] 1976, *Capital, Volume 1* (London: Penguin), 796.
82. Ibid., 782–74.
83. ILO, 2013, *Decent Work Country Profile: Bangladesh* (Geneva: ILO), 8.
84. ILO, *Decent Work and the Informal Economy,* 68.
85. ILO, 2003, *Employment and Social Policy in Respect of Export Processing Zones (EPZs)* (ILO: Geneva), 6.
86. United Nations, 1999, *World Survey on the Role of Women in Development: Globalization, Gender and Work,* Department of Economic and Social Affairs (New York: United Nations Publications), http://www.ucl.ac.uk/dpu-projects/drivers_urb_change/urb_society/pdf)_gender/UN_1999_World_Survey_Women_in_Development.pdf, 29.
87. Guy Standing, 1999, "Global Feminization through Flexible Labor: A Theme Revisited," *World Development* 27/3: 585.
88. Barrientos et al., *The Gender Dimension of the Globalization of Production,* 3.
89. Ibid., 3–4.
90. ILO, *Employment and Social Policy,* 6.
91. See Frederick Engels, 1845, *The Condition of the Working Class in England* (New York: Oxford University Press); Katrina Honeyman, 2000, *Women, Gender and Industrialisation in England, 1700–1870* (Basingstoke: Macmillan); Lyn Reese, 2005, *Women's Work in Industrial Revolutions: Primary Source Lessons from Europe and East Asia* (Berkeley: Women in World History Curriculum).
92. UNCTAD, *The Least Developed Countries Report 2004—Linking International Trade with Poverty Reduction* (Geneva, UNCTAD), 126–27.
93. Merete Lie and Ragnhild Lund, 2005, "From NIDL to Globalization: Studying Women Workers in an Increasingly Globalized Economy," *Gender, Technology and Development* 9/1: 730.
94. Shahra Razavi and Jessica Vivian, 2002, "Introduction," in *Women's Employment in the Textile Manufacturing Sectors of Bangladesh and Morocco,* ed. Carol Miller and Jessica Vivian (Geneva, UNRISD), 3.
95. Merete and Lund, "From NIDL to Globalization," 23.
96. M. Laetitia Cairoli, 1999, "Garment Factory Workers in the City of Fez," *Middle East Journal* 53:1. She adds that "hiring young, unmarried girls rather than mature married women helps ameliorate the contradictions inherent in allowing females to labor in what is a public, and more traditionally male, role."
97. Saba Gul Khattak, 2002, "Subcontracted Work and Gender Relations: The Case of Pakistan," in Balakrishnan, *The Hidden Assembly Line,* 35–62.
98. Razavi and Vivian, "Introduction," 6–8.
99. Barbara Ehrenreich and Annette Fuentes, 1981, "Life on the Global Assembly Line," in *Ms.,* January 1981, 58. Maria Mies made the same connection: "Governments, like pimps, offer their young women to foreign capital," in *Patriarchy and Accumulation on a World Scale* (London: Zed Press, 1986), 117.
100. Ibid., "Governments, like pimps," 117.
101. Barrientos et al., *The Gender Dimension of the Globalization of Production* 7.
102. ILO, *Decent Work and the Informal Economy,* 10–32.
103. Stephanie Seguino, 2000, "Accounting for Gender in Asian Economic Growth," *Feminist Economics* 6/3: 27–58, quote at 55.
104. Elizabeth Monk-Turner and Charlie G. Turner, 2001, "Sex Differentials in Earnings in the South Korean Labor Market," *Feminist Economics* 7/1: 63–78, quote at 63. South Korea continues to have one of the widest gender pay gaps in the world, with female earnings just 52 percent of male earnings for similar work. See World

Economic Forum, *Global Gender Gap Report 2013* (Geneva: World Economic Forum).

105. Kim Mikyoung, 2003, "South Korean Women Workers' Labor Resistance in the Era of Export-Oriented Industrialization, 1970–1980," *Development and Society* 32/1: 77–101, quote at 78.
106. Mies, "Patriarchy and Accumulation on a World Scale," 118–20.
107. Guy Standing, "Global Feminization through Flexible Labor," 599–600.
108. William Rau and Robert Wazienski, 1999, "Industrialization, Female Labor Force Participation, and the Modern Division of Labor by Sex," *Industrial Relations* 38/4: 504–21, quote at 509.
109. UNCTAD, *World Investment Report 2013*, 157.
110. Barrientos et al., *The Gender Dimension of the Globalization of Production*, 5
111. Richard Baldwin, 2006, *Globalisation: The Great Unbundling(s)*, Economic Council of Finland http://www2.dse.unibo.it/naghavi/baldwin.pdf, 22.
112. Barrientos et al., *The Gender Dimension of the Globalization of Production*, 5.
113. Mayumi Murayama and Nobuko Yokota, 2008, *Revisiting Labor and Gender Issues in Export Processing Zones: The Cases of South Korea, Bangladesh and India*, IDE Discussion Paper No. 174. Institute of Developing Economies, http://ir.ide.go.jp/dspace/bitstream/2344/793/3/ARRIDE_Discussion_No.174_murayama_yokota.pdf, 29.
114. Ibid.
115. ILO, 2006, *Decent Work and the Informal Economy*, 32.
116. See Remco H. Oostendorp, 2004, *Globalization and the Gender Wage Gap*, World Bank Policy Research Working Paper No. 3256 (Washington, DC: World Bank). Often jobs are counted as higher skilled not because they are higher skilled but because they are carried out by men.
117. Marva Corley, Yves Perardel, and Kalina Popova, 2005, *Wage Inequality by Gender and Occupation: A Cross-Country Analysis*, Employment Strategy Papers 2005/20, Employment Trends Unit, Employment Strategy Department (Geneva: ILO), 1.
    Corley et al. discover an interesting exception to Oostendorp's finding that the gender pay gap in low-skilled occupations is narrowing: between 1996 and 2003; all of the so-called transitional economies, with the exception of Hungary, showed a sharp rise in the gender pay gap, which they ascribe to "the worsening labor market conditions resulting from the adjustments to a market economy, which have disproportionately impacted on women" (19).
118. ILO, 2008, 2008, *Global Wage Report 2008-9* (Geneva: ILO), 29.
119. Barrientos et al., *The Gender Dimension of the Globalization of Production*, 7.
120. Stephen Roach, 2003, *Outsourcing, Protectionism, and the Global Labor Arbitrage*, Morgan Stanley Special Economic Study, 6.
121. Lie and Lund, "From NIDL to Globalization," 22. This paper contains many insights, e.g.: "The most peculiar of the local change processes we have observed, is that a formerly most protected group, namely young women, have been the spearheads in the process of transformation of the local community" (23).
122. Ibid., 19.
123. Richard Anker, 1997, 'Theories of Occupational Segregation by Sex: An Overview," *International Labor Review*, ILO, Geneva, 136/3: 315–39.
124. Zafiris Tzannatos, 1999, "Women and Labor Market Changes in the Global Economy: Growth Helps, Inequalities Hurt and Public Policy Matters," *World Development* 27/3: 551–69.
125. Mary-Alice Waters, 1992, "The Capitalist Ideological Offensive against Women

Today," in *Cosmetics, Fashions, and the Exploitation of Women*, ed. Joseph Hansen, Evelyn Reed, and Mary-Alice Waters (New York: Pathfinder Press), 11.

126. Ibid.

127. Rakhi Sehgal, 2005, "Social Reproduction of Third World Labor in the Era of Globalization," *Economic and Political Weekly*, May 28–June 4, 2005, 2286–94.

5. Global Wage Trends in the Neoliberal Era

1. BLS, n.d., *Technical Notes,* http://www.bls.gov/fls/archived_FTP/ichcctn.txt

2. ILO, *October Inquiry,* 2008, 9.

3. Remco H. Oostendorp, *The Occupational Wages around the World (OWW) Database: Update for 1983–2008*, Background Paper for *World Development Report 2013*, 3.

4. Timothy J. Sturgeon, Peter Bøegh Nielsen, Greg Linden, Gary Gereffi and Clair Brown, 2013, "Direct Measurement of Global Value Chains: Collecting Product- and Firm-Level Statistics on Value Added and Business Function Outsourcing and Offshoring," 289–319, in *The Fragmentation of Global Production and Trade in Value-Added—Developing New Measures of Cross Border Trade*, Aaditya Mattoo, Zhi Wang, and Shang-Jin Wei (eds.) (Washington: World Bank), https://openknowledge.worldbank.org/handle/10986/15809, 291.

5. ILO, *Global Wage Report* 2012–13, 36.

6. Nomaan Majid, 2004, *What Is the Effect of Trade Openness on Wages?*, Employment Strategy Papers 2004/18. Employment Analysis Unit, Employment Strategy Department (Geneva: ILO), 9–10.

7. ILO, *Global Wage Report* 2008, 11.

8. The Occupational Wages around the World database is downloadable at http://www.nber.org/oww/.

9. ILO, *Global Wage Report 2012–13*, 69.

10. The ICP (International Comparison Program) was founded in 1968, and built on the earlier work of Simon Kuznets and Irving Kravis at the University of Pennsylvania and by Cambridge University's Richard Stone. The ICP's vast database of prices, covering nearly every country on earth and every year since 1950, are known as the Penn World Tables. For more on the history of the ICP, and access to the Penn World Tables, see https://pwt.sas.upenn.edu/icp.html.

11. OECD, 2006, *Eurostat-OECD Methodological Manual on Purchasing Power Parities* (Luxembourg: Publications Office of the European Union), 431.

12. Asian Development Bank, 2007, *Purchasing Power Parities and Real Expenditures* (Manila: Asian Development Bank), 63.

13. For the corrections in detail see ICP, 2008, *Global Purchasing Power Parities and Real Expenditures: 2005 International Comparison Program*, App. G (rev.) (Washington, DC: World Bank), http://siteresources.worldbank.org/ICPINT/Resources/AppendixGrevized.pdf.

14. Quoted in Shawn Donnan, "World Bank Eyes Biggest Global Poverty Line Increase in Decades," *Financial Times*, May 9, 2014.

15. ICP. *Global Purchasing Power Parities*, 3.

16. Robert Ackland, Steve Dowrick and Benoit Freyens, 2007, http://adsri.anu.edu.au/pubs/Ackland/GlobalPoverty_14Aug2007.pdf, 14.

17. Tables A2 and A4 in Nicholas Oulton, 2012, *The Wealth and Poverty of Nations: True PPPs for 141 Countries*, rev. ed., Centre for Economic Performance, CEP Discussion Paper 1080, http://cep.lse.ac.uk/pubs/download/dp1080.pdf.

18. ICP, n.d., *Poverty PPPs,* http://web.worldbank.org/WBSITE/EXTERNAL/

DATASTATISTICS/T/0,,contentMDK:22412218~pagePK:60002244~piP-
K:62002388~theSitePK:270065,00.html.

19. ICP, 2014, *Purchasing Power Parities and Real Expenditures of World Economies—
     Summary of Results and Findings of the 2011 International Comparison Program*
     (Washington: International Bank for Reconstruction and Development/The World
     Bank), 24.

20. *ICP News* 3/1, February 2006, http://siteresources.worldbank.org/ICPINT/
     Resources/ICPe-Newsletter_Feb2006.pdf.

21. ICP, *Purchasing Power Parities and Real Expenditures of World Economies*, 24.

22. The *Financial Times* reported in 2014 that "to reflect the changing realities in the
     cost of living for the world's poor" the World Bank is considering raising its inter-
     national poverty line from $1.25 to $1.75 per day. Such a change would not, in
     principle, result in any change to the real poverty level or to the numbers trapped
     below it, it would simply register the fact that one dollar in 1990 is equal in value
     to $1.75 in 2014. Shawn Donnan, 2014, "World Bank Eyes Biggest Global Poverty
     Line Increase in Decades," in *Financial Times*, May 9, 2014.

23. See Mukul Devichand, 2007, *When a dollar a day means 25 cents*, BBC Radio 4,
     Sunday, 2 December 2007, http://news.bbc.co.uk/1/hi/business/7122356.stm.

24. Martin Ravallion, 2010, *World Bank's $1.25/day poverty measure—countering the
     latest criticisms*, http://econ.worldbank.org/WBSICTE/EXTERNAL/EXTDEC/
     EXTRESEARCH/0,,contentMDK:22510787~pagePK:641. A BBC journalist asked
     Ravallion "whether he thought this poverty level target was too low. He explained
     that … according to his data, even at the frugal 25 cents a dollar is worth in India,
     the very poor could just about afford to eat 2,100 calories for this amount, with a
     couple of rupees to spare for non-food items. But he accepted the line was very
     frugal. 'You've just got to realise that a lot of people are very poor in the world.'"
     Mukul Devichand, 2007, *When a dollar a day means 25 cents*, BBC Radio 4, Sun-
     day, 2 December 2007, http://news.bbc.co.uk/1/hi/business/7122356.stm.

     Replying to criticism, in 2008 Ravallion reported that "an effort is underway
     at the Bank to estimate 'PPPs for the poor,'" by reweighting the 2005 ICP prices
     to accord more closely with consumption patterns of poor people." Martin Rav-
     allion, 2008, *How Not to Count the Poor? A Reply to Reddy and Pogge*, http://
     siteresources.worldbank.org/INTPOVRES/Resources/477227-1208265125344/
     HowNot_toCount_thePoor_Reply_toReddy_Pogge.pdf. This is a fascinating and
     revealing debate—for Reddy and Pogge's original critique, see Sanjay Reddy and
     Thomas Pogge, 2005, *How Not To Count the Poor (version 6.2)*, http://www.colum-
     bia.edu/~sr793/count.pdf; for Pogge's rejoinder to Ravallion's reply see Thomas
     Pogge, 2008, *How Many Poor People Should There Be? A Rejoinder to Ravallion*,
     http://www.columbia.edu/~sr793/RejoinderToRavallion7.pdf

25. Another highly dubious procedure used by the World Bank to massage poverty fig-
     ures is its practice of attaching a notional cash value of the housing "consumed" by,
     for instance, slum dwellers living in shacks on squatted land, which is then counted
     toward their income, lifting some of them above the extreme poverty threshold of
     $1.25 per day.

26. ILO, *October Inquiry*, 17.

27. One distortion not discussed here arises from the standard practice of comparing
     wages in low-wage countries with those in the United States rather than imperialist
     nations as a whole. Capitalists in the United States have been much more successful
     than their European counterparts in holding down real wages, whose median has
     barely moved in the last three decades.

28. "Our valuation of a foreign currency in terms of our own ... mainly depends on the relative purchasing power of the two currencies in their respective countries," Gustav Cassel, 1922, *Money and Foreign Exchange after 1914* (New York: Macmillan), 139.

29. Alan Freeman, 2009, "The Poverty of Statistics and the Statistics of Poverty," *Third World Quarterly* 30/8, 1427–48.

30. Ibid., 1441.

31. Ibid. Intermediate inputs are by definition used up in production and therefore do not count toward private sector fixed-capital formation.

32. PPP conversion indices for most developing nations are only available from 1980. Alan Taylor and Mark Taylor report on the basis of an extensive literature review that the purchasing power anomaly "has been intensifying since 1950." Alan M. Taylor and Mark P. Taylor, 2004, "The Purchasing Power Parity Debate," *Journal of Economic Perspectives* 18/4, 135–58.

33. What became known as the "Volcker shock" (after Paul Volcker, then head of the U.S. Federal Reserve) was a huge hike in U.S. and therefore global interest rates that touched off the Third World debt crisis and waves of economic convulsions across Asia, Africa, and Latin America. It was likened by Naomi Klein to "a giant Taser gun fired from Washington, sending the developing world into convulsions," whose immediate consequence was "soaring interest rates [that] meant higher interest payments on foreign debts, and often the higher payments could only be met by taking on more loans. The debt spiral was born." Naomi Klein, 2007, *The Shock Doctrine* (London: Penguin), 198.

34. Goldman Sachs, quoted in Richard Tomkins, "Profits of doom," *Financial Times*, October 13, 2006.

35. According to classical economic theory, a nation's income can be resolved into not two but three parts; thus Adam Smith argued that "the exchangeable value ... of all the commodities which compose the whole annual produce of the labor of every country, taken complexly, must . . . be parcelled out among different inhabitants of the country, either as the wages of their labor, the profits of their stock, or the rent of their land." Adam Smith, 1986 [1776], *The Wealth of Nations*, Book 1 (Harmondsworth: Penguin Books), 155. "Land" stands for the feudal aristocracy, which since Adam Smith's day has been absorbed into the capitalist class.

36. This is sometimes rendered as labor's share of GDP. The income definition and the output definition are equivalent because the net output of firms (i.e., their value added, whose aggregate is GDP) is, according to the ruling economic theories, nothing else than their net income. Why this is profoundly false will be discussed in chapter 9, "The GDP Illusion."

37. Ann Harrison, 2005, *Has globalization eroded labor's share? Some cross-country evidence.* http://www.iadb.org/res/publications/pubfiles/pubS-FDI-9.pdf , 26.

38. Ibid., 25.

39. Not all government spending on welfare, health, education, etc., is part of workers' social wage. A substantial part of these "transfer payments," e.g. housing rent that is paid straight to landlords, should be counted as income to capital rather than income to labor. Furthermore, middle-class and elite layers benefit disproportionately from some categories of social expenditure, e.g. higher education, while their greater longevity extends their pensionable age.

40. Harrison, *Has globalization eroded labor's share?*, 11. Stock options are only counted toward labor's share when they are realized, that is, when the discounted shares distributed to managers and highly paid employees are sold. Elsby et al.

report that "extensive use of stock options in the compensation of employees in the tech and investment banking industries substantially affected compensation and profits measures in the national accounts between 1998 and 2003.... Many tech and investment banking employees decided to exercise their options at the height of the tech bubble, propping up the payroll shares in tech and investment banking." Michael Elsby, Bart Hobijn, and Ayşegül Şahın, *The Decline of the U.S. Labor Share*, Brookings Papers on Economic Activity, Fall 2013, 23.

41. Anne O. Krueger, 2002, *A New Approach to Sovereign Debt Restructuring*, International Monetary Fund, 46. Krueger was chief economist at the World Bank from 1982 to 1987, the period when neoliberal dogma consolidated its grip on this institution, and served as First Deputy Director of the IMF between 2001 and 2004 and as Acting Managing Director from 2004 to 2007. She was appointed Assistant Treasury Secretary for Economic Policy by President Obama in March 2009.

42. IMF, 2007, *World Economic Outlook, April 2007,* 182.

43. Paul Gomme and Peter Rupert, 2004, *Measuring Labor's Share of Income*, Federal Reserve Bank of Cleveland Policy Discussion Paper No. 7, 4. Another common approach is to attribute two-thirds of the income of the self-employed to labor and one-third to capital—see Malte Lübker, 2007, *Labor Shares*, ILO Technical Brief No. 1, http://www.ilo.org/wcmsp5/groups/public/—dgreports/—integration/documents/publication/wcms_086237.pdf, 1. For a useful summary of different approaches to this problem, at least with respect to calculations of labor's share in imperialist countries, see Marta Guerriero, 2012, *The Labor Share of Income around the World: Evidence from a Panel Dataset*, Development Economics and Public Policy Working Paper No. 32.

44. Elsby, *The Decline of the U.S. Labor Share*, 15.

45. ILO, *Key Indicators of the Labour Market* (KILM), 8th ed.

46. The 14 percent decline from 42 percent to 28 percent is a 33.3 percent decline from its initial starting figure, 42 percent. Confusion often arises from a failure to recognize that a "decline of x percent" means something very different from an "x percent decline"—for example, if the rate of unemployment declines from 20 percent to 10 percent the number of unemployed has actually declined by 50 percent.

47. The blip in 2008–9 reflects the fall in income to capital at the height of the global crisis, but capitalists quickly resumed their outsized income gains and wealth accumulation, and so after just two years labor's descent resumed at full speed.

48. ILO, 2011, *World of Work Report 2011: Making Markets Work for Jobs*, 58.

49. Ibid., 58.

50. Ibid.

51. Ibid., 56–57.

52. A line from "Solidarity Forever," lyrics by Ralph Chaplin, ca. 1915, http://unionsong.com/u025.html.

53. Harrison, *Has globalization eroded labor's share?*, 2.

54. Ibid., 18.

55. Paul Ormerod noted that, in mainland Europe, "the late 1960s and early 1970s saw a sharp rise in the share of national income going to the labor force, and a corresponding erosion of profitability. The rise was made up of a combination of rapid increases in real wages in excess of productivity growth, and of rises in the costs of employing labor." Paul Ormerod, "Don't Follow the European Model: It's Collapsing," *Independent*, 27 August 1996.

56. ILO, *October Inquiry,* 22. A sign of the limitations caused by extensive gaps in the data is that the furthest the ILO could go toward generating a time series was

to estimate an average for the 1995–2000 period and another for the 2001–2007 period and compare the two.

57. Harrison, *Has Globalization Eroded Labor's Share?*, 3. The IMF's calculations yield an almost identical result: "The decline in the labor share since 1980 has been much more pronounced in Europe and Japan (about 10 percent) than in Anglo-Saxon countries, including the United States (about 3–4 percent)." IMF, 2007, *World Economic Outlook—Spillovers and Cycles in the Global Economy*, 168.

58. IMF, *World Economic Outlook—Spillovers and Cycles in the Global Economy*, 167.

59. Ibid., 183.

60. Majid, *What Is the Effect of Trade Openness on Wages?*, 6. His actual periods were 1983–89 and 1990–98, and his source was the ILO *October Inquiry*.

61. Nicholas Kaldor, 1957, "A Model of Economic Growth," *Economic Journal* 67/268: 591–624. Two decades earlier, John Maynard Keynes noted the "stability of the proportion of the national dividend accruing to labor, irrespective apparently of the level of output as a whole and of the phase of the trade cycle. . . . [This is] one of the most surprising, yet best-established facts in the whole range of economic statistics, both for Great Britain and for the United States." Keynes, 1939, "Relative Movements of Real Wages and Output," *Economic Journal*, 49/193: 34–51.

62. Jesus Felipe, 2005, *A Note on Competitiveness, Unit Labor Costs and Growth: Is "Kaldor's Paradox" a Figment of Interpretation?* Macroeconomics and Finance Research Division, Asian Development Bank, http://cbe.anu.edu.au/research/papers/camawpapers/Papers/2005/Felipe_62005.pdf, 7–9.

63. Jesus Felipe and Utsav Kumar, 2011, *Unit Labor Costs in the Eurozone: The Competitiveness Debate Again*, Levy Economics Institute Working Paper No. 651, Asian Development Bank, Manila, 5. This accords with the OECD definition of what it calls a "key statistical concept": "The annual labor income share is . . . total labor costs divided by nominal output.... The division of total labor costs by nominal output is sometimes also referred to as a real unit labor cost." See http://stats.oecd.org/mei/default.asp?lang=e&subject=1.

64. ILO, *October Inquiry*, 22.

65. IMF, *World Economic Outlook—Spillovers and Cycles in the Global Economy*, 172.

66. Loukas Karabarbounis and Brent Neiman, 2013, *The Global Decline of the Labor Share*, NBER Working Paper 19136, http://faculty.chicagobooth.edu/brent.neiman/research/KN.pdf, 1.

67. Ibid., 27.

68. Ibid., 19.

69. The Boskin Commission (mentioned above) reckoned that failure to quantify qualitative changes in electronic goods concealed sharp falls in their "real" price and caused overall U.S. inflation to be overestimated by 1.3 percent per year. Karabarbounis and Neiman, in another example of their bad science, provide no information on the weight of hedonic adjustments in their calculations—but if we assume that these electronic goods make up the same proportion of capital investment goods as they do in the basket of commodities used to calculate the rate of inflation, it would take twenty-two years for the price of investment goods to be hedonically adjusted downward by 25 percent, and over the period of their survey (1975–2012), the cumulative hedonic price falls would be 40 percent. In other words, the empirical data on which they construct their thesis is not empirical at all.

70. Dave Wasshausen and Brent R. Moulton, 2006, "The Role of Hedonic Methods in Measuring Real GDP in the United States," in 31st CEIES Seminar, "Are we meas-

uring productivity correctly?," Bureau of Economic Analysis, http://www.bea.gov/papers/pdf/hedonicGDP.pdf, 97–112 (102).

71. The Boskin Commission concluded that "by failing to take account of the quality changes in goods such as computers, cameras, and phones, the U.S. consumer price index had been overstating the rate of inflation by 1.3 percentage points a year, and correspondingly understating real GDP growth . . . [giving] Alan Greenspan and the Federal Reserve more confidence about the economy's potential growth than they might otherwise have had." Diane Coyle, 2014, *GDP: A Brief but Affectionate History* (Princeton: Princeton University Press), 88.

Hedonic adjustments are being increasingly adopted by other governments and international bodies, but even before they become widespread, their impact on U.S. inflation and on the domestic purchasing power of the dollar also distorts calculation of PPP exchange rates.

72. Ibid., 10.
73. Elsby, *The Decline of the U.S. Labor Share,* 31.
74. Ibid., 37.
75. Ibid., 35–36.
76. Ibid., 23.
77. UNCTAD, 2013, *Trade and Development Report 2013: Adjusting to the Changing Dynamics of the World Economy,* 14–15.
78. ILO, *October Inquiry,* 60.
79. Majid, *What Is the Effect of Trade Openness on Wages?,* 19.
80. ILO, *October Inquiry,* 29.
81. Corley et al., 2005, 1.
82. ILO, 2008, 29.
83. Richard B. Freeman and Remco Oostendorp, 2001, 'The Occupational Wages Around the World Data File," *International Labor Review,* Vol. 140, No. 4, 380–401, 2001, 392.
84. Alan Freeman. 2004, p83.
85. ILO, 2008, 25.
86. Ibid., 26.
87. Marva Corley, Yves Perardel, and Kalina Popova, 2005, *Wage Inequality by Gender and Occupation: A Cross-Country Analysis.* Employment Strategy Papers 2005/20. Employment Trends Unit, Employment Strategy Department. Geneva: ILO, 26.
88. Robert Hunter Wade, 2004, "On the Causes of Increasing Poverty and Inequality, or Matthew Effect Prevails," *New Political Economy* 9/2: 166.
89. Richard B. Freeman and Remco Oostendorp, 2001, "The Occupational Wages Around the World Data File," *International Labor Review* 140/4: 380–401.
90. Werner International's data from 2008 is shown here (market exchange rates converted to PPP$ by the author) in preference to their more recent 2011 report, because the latter omits information on three of the seven lowest-wage entries—Bangladesh, Egypt, and Inland China, but otherwise presents an almost identical picture. For a different set of national wage comparisons for textile production workers, given in PPP$, see *KILM*, 5th ed., Figure 16a, "Wages and earnings in textile occupations relative to the United States (2004 U.S.$ PPP basis)." The discrepancies between the ILO/KILM and those derived from Werner International reflect the general lack of precision surrounding wage data.
91. Werner International, 2012, *International Comparison of the Hourly Labor Cost in the Primary Textile Industry,* Winter 2011, 3.
92. Worker Rights Consortium, 2013, *Global Wage Trends for Apparel Workers, 2001–*

2011, http://www.americanprogress.org/wp-content/uploads/2013/07/RealWag-eStudy-3.pdf, 2.

93. Ibid., 12.
94. Ibid., 16.
95. ILO, *October Inquiry*, 15. This confirms Onaran's 2005 observation that "although labor's share does not respond to growth in good years, it decreases as the economy contracts" (Özlem Onaran, 2005), *The Effect of Neoliberal Globalization on Labor's Share in Developing Countries*. Association for Heterodox Economics 7th Annual Conference City University, London, 15–17 July 2005 (25). Falling per capita GDP in the Global South means growth of anything less than 1.3 percent per annum, the rate at which its population is growing. Population growth in the imperialist nations is 0.6 percent per annum.
96. Harrison, *Has globalization eroded labor's share?*, 29.
97. Onaran, *The Effect of Neoliberal Globalization on Labor's Share in Developing Countries,* 14.
98. Thus the ILO reports that "countries which recorded the largest increases in wage inequality are those that were hit by severe economic crises." ILO, *October Inquiry*, 24–25.
99. Ibid., 15.
100. Diwan defined a crisis to be when a national currency declines by more than 25 percent against the dollar. Ishac Diwan, 2001, *Debt as Sweat: Labor, Financial Crises, and the Globalization of Capital*. World Bank Working Paper, http://info.world-bank.org/etools/docs/voddocs/150/332/diwan.pdf.
101. Ibid., 27.
102. Ibid., 24.
103. Ibid., 10.
104. Unsigned editorial, *Financial Times*, 28 April 1995.
105. Özlem Onaran, 2007, *Wage Share, Globalization, and Crisis: The Case of the Manufacturing Industry in Korea, Mexico, and Turkey*. Political Economy Research Institute PERI Working Paper Series #132. (http://www.peri.umass.edu/fileadmin/pdf/working_papers/working_papers_101-150/WP132.pdf, 14–15.
106. Ibid.
107. World Bank, 2009, *Swimming Against the Tide: How Developing Countries Are Coping with the Global Crisis,* paper presented at the G20 Finance Ministers and Central Bank Governors meeting, Horsham, UK, March 13–14, 2009, 10.
108. Diwan, *Debt as Sweat*, 26.
109. Arvind Panagariya, 2007, *Outsourcing: Is the Third Industrial Revolution Really Around the Corner?*, http://www.columbia.edu/~ap2231/Policy percent20Papers/Tokyo percent20club percent20Outsourcing percent20November percent2013-14 percent202007.pdf, 3.
110. PricewaterhouseCoopers, 2013, *The BRICs and Beyond: Prospects, Challenges and Opportunities,* http://www.pwc.com/en_GX/gx/world-2050/assets/pwc-world-in-2050-report-january-2013.pdf, 4.
111. ILO, 2014, *World of Work 2014: Developing with Jobs*, xix.
112. Bhanu Baweja, global head of emerging markets strategy at UBS, quoted in Jonathan Wheatley and James Kynge, "Emerging Markets: Trading Blow," *Financial Times*, June 10, 2015.

6. The Purchasing Power Anomaly and the Productivity Paradox

1.   Kenneth Rogoff, 1996, "The Purchasing Power Parity Puzzle," *Journal of Economic*

Literature 34/2: 647–68. For reviews of the extensive literature on PPP, see Alan M. Taylor and Mark P. Taylor, 2004, "The Purchasing Power Parity Debate," in *Journal of Economic Perspectives*, 18.4: 135–158; Mohsen Bahmani-Oskooee and A. B. M. Nasir, 2005, "Productivity Bias Hypothesis and the Purchasing Power Parity: A Review Article," *Journal of Economic Surveys* 19/4: 671–95; Imed Drine and Christophe Rault, 2008, "Purchasing Power Parity for Developing and Developed Countries: What Can We Learn from Non-Stationary Panel Data Models?," *Journal of Economic Surveys* 22/4: 752–73.

2.   Rogoff, "The Purchasing Power Parity Puzzle," 655.

3.   Ibid., 647.

4.   Robert A. Blecker, 2005. "Financial Globalization, Exchange Rates and International Trade," in *Financialization and the World Economy*, ed. Gerald A. Epstein (Cheltenham: Edward Elgar), 183–209.

5.   Rogoff, "The Purchasing Power Parity Puzzle," 647.

6.   Ibid., 665.

7.   Ibid., 653.

8.   Drine and Rault, "Purchasing Power Parity for Developing and Developed Countries," 761.

9.   Named after Béla Balassa and Paul Samuelson, who independently and simultaneously advanced the hypothesis in 1964. It is sometimes called the Harrod-Balassa-Samuelson hypothesis, recognizing the contribution of Roy Harrod in 1933; and sometimes the Ricardo-Harrod-Balassa-Samuelson hypothesis, because of the Ricardian comparative advantage model of international trade that the hypothesis deploys.

10. To simplify this narrative, we ignore the fact that not all those working in the service sector are capitalistically employed waged workers. Except where specified, wages include the incomes of self-employed producers of goods and services.

11. "Not So Absolutely Fabulous," *The Economist*, November 4, 1995.

12. See Irving B. Kravis and Richard E. Lipsey, 1983, *Toward an Explanation of National Price Levels*. Princeton Studies international Finance. Princeton: Princeton University, International Finance Section; Jagdish Bhagwati , 1984, "Why are services cheaper in poor countries?" *Economic Journal* 94:279–286; Bhagwati, 1984.

13. Bhagwati, "Why are services cheaper in poor countries," 281.

14. Susan Houseman, 2006, *Outsourcing, Offshoring, and Productivity Measurement in U.S. Manufacturing*, Upjohn Institute Staff Working Paper No. 06-130, 2.

15. Ibid., 1.

16. Ibid., 2. "Improvements in the feasibility of offshoring are economically equivalent to labor-augmenting technological progress." Gene M.Grossman and Esteban Rossi-Hansberg, 2006, *The Rise of Offshoring: It's Not Wine for Cloth Anymore* (Princeton: Princeton University Press), 15.

17. Houseman, *Outsourcing, Offshoring, and Productivity*, 27.

18. Katharine Abraham, one of the foremost authorities in the field of national accounts, reports that, in the United States, "labor productivity in the services industries . . . actually declined over the two decades from 1977 through 1997. . . . Among the individual service industries showing declines in labor productivity were educational services and health services, as well as auto repair, legal services and personal services. Construction was another problem industry, with the implied labor productivity falling by 1 percent per year over the entire 20-year period." Abraham, 2005, "What We Don't Know Could Hurt Us: Some Reflections on the Measurement of Economic Activity," *Journal of Economic Perspectives* 19/3: 3–18.

19. William J. Baumol, 1967, "Macroeconomics of Unbalanced Growth: The Anatomy of Urban Crisis," *American Economic Review* 57: 415–26.

20. Also known as the "Baumol disease." See ibid.

21. "The best points in my book are: 1) the twofold character of labor, according to whether it is expressed in use value or exchange value (all understanding of the facts depends upon this) . . . 2) the treatment of surplus-value, independently of its particular forms as profit, interest, ground rent, etc." Marx to Engels, 24 August 1867, Karl Marx and Frederick Engels, 1987 [1867] *Collected Works*, volume 42 (Moscow: Progress Publishers), 407.

22. "The desire to get rid of contradictions in definitions . . . results in disintegration of theory rather than in its development. Since life compels a development of theory all the same, in the end it always turns out that an attempt to construct a theory without contradictions leads to the piling up of new contradictions that are still more absurd and insoluble than those that were apparently got rid of. . . . Dialectics proceeds from a diametrically opposite view. Its solution of the problem is based first of all on the assumption that the objective world itself, the objective reality, is a living system unfolding through emergence and resolutions of its internal contradictions. The dialectical method, dialectical logic demands that, far from fearing contradictions in the theoretical definition of the object, one must search for these contradictions in a goal-directed manner and record them precisely—to find their rational resolution, of course, not to pile up mountains of antinomies and paradoxes." Evald Ilyenkov, 1960, *The Dialectic of the Abstract and the Concrete in Marx's Capital* (Moscow: Progress Publishers), 243–44.

23. Marx, [1867] 1976, *Capital*, vol. 1 (London: Penguin), 137. In continuation, he says, "The same labor, therefore, performed for the same length of time, always yields the same amount of value, independently of any variations in productivity. But it provides different quantities of use-values during equal periods of time. . . . On the one hand, all labor is an expenditure of human labor-power, in the physiological sense, and it is in this quality of being equal, or abstract, human labor that it forms the value of commodities. On the other hand, all labor is an expenditure of human labor-power in a particular form and with a definite aim, and it is in this quality of being concrete useful labor that it produces use-value."

24. Or, as Samir Amin has pointed out, "The orthodox argument linking wages to sectorial productivity is necessarily a marginalist argument, and one that is tautological, since it is not possible to compare the productivity of different branches." Amin, 1979, "Reply to Weeks and Dore," *Latin American Perspectives* 6/2: 88–90.

25. Marx, *Capital*, vol. 1, 1038–39.

26. Ibid., 644.

27. The *OECD* provides a classic definition of ULCs: "Unit labor costs (ULC) measure the average cost of labor per unit of output. They are calculated as the ratio of total labor costs to real output, or equivalently, as the ratio of mean labor costs per hour to labor productivity (output per hour). As such, a ULC represents a link between productivity and the cost of labor in producing output." R. McKenzie and D. Brackfield (2008), *The OECD System of Unit Labor Cost and Related Indicators*, OECD Statistics Working Papers 2008/04, http://dx.doi.org/10.1787/243142116028, 14.

28. Blecker, "Financial Globalization, Exchange Rates and International Trade," 186.

29. Martin Wolf, 2005, *Why Globalization Works* (New Haven and London: Yale University Press), 175.

30. In the first of a series of papers on this subject, Golub stated that he is "unaware of any previous studies that have attempted to carry out such comparisons [of

unit labor costs] for a wide range of countries. Perhaps this is because economists accept as an article of faith that real wages reflect productivity." Stephen Golub, 1995, *Comparative and Absolute Advantage in the Asia-Pacific Region*, Federal Reserve Bank of San Francisco, Centre for Pacific Basin Monetary and Economic Studies, Working Paper No. PB95-09, 11.

31.   Mehrene Larudee and Timothy Koechlin, 2008, "Low-Wage Labor and the Geography of Production: A Qualified Defense of the 'Pauper Labor Argument,'" *Review of Radical Political Economics* 40: 228–36.

32.   Ibid., 230.

33.   Stephen Golub, 1995, "Productivity and Labor Costs in Newly Industrializing Countries," *Pacific Basin Notes* 95/27: 1–3.

34.   Anthony G. Turner and Stephen Golub, 1997, "Multilateral Unit-Labor-Cost-Based Competitiveness Indicators for Advanced, Developing, and Transition Countries," in *Staff Studies for the World Economic Outlook*, by the Research Department of the International Monetary Fund, 47–60.

35.   Stephen Golub, 1999, *Labor Costs and International Trade* (Washington, DC: American Enterprise Institute), 21.

36.   Larudee and Koechlin, "Low-Wage Labor and the Geography of Production," 231.

37.   Ibid., 232.

38.   Wolf, *Why Globalization Works*, 183.

39.   Janet Ceglowski and Stephen Golub, 2005, *Just How Low Are China's Labor Costs?*, http://www.swarthmore.edu/SocSci/sgolub1/chinaslaborcosts11_7_2005.pdf, 2–3.

40.   Ibid., 16.

41.   Wolf, *Why Globalization Works*, 183.

42.   Ibid., 230.

43.   International Committee of Free Trade Unions (ICFTU), 2005, *Whose Miracle? How China's Workers Are Paying the Price for Its Economic Boom*, http://www.dossiertibet.it/sites/default/files/documenti/WhoseMiracleChinaReport.pdf,11.

44.   I have excluded one country from the dataset: Iran, which the WDI reports to have a value added per worker that is second only to Japan. This was the most egregious single example of the poor data quality that is part of the reason for the dispersion of the markers.

45.   Jesus Felipe and Utsav Kumar, 2011, *Unit Labor Costs in the Eurozone: The Competitiveness Debate Again*, Levy Economics Institute Working Paper No. 651 Asian Development Bank, Manila, 5.

46.   Jesus Felipe, 2005, *A Note on Competitiveness, Unit Labor Costs and Growth: Is "Kaldor's Paradox" a Figment of Interpretation?* Macroeconomics and Finance Research Division, Asian Development Bank, http://cbe.anu.edu.au/research/papers/camawpapers/Papers/2005/Felipe_62005.pdf, 7–9.

47.   Ibid., 7.

48.   The economic concept and statistic of competitiveness that most closely conforms to ruling economic theory is not unit labor cost but "total factor productivity," where the different productivities of each factor of production are combined into a single value. However, calculation of economy-wide TFP is an immensely complex and fraught task and is only carried out for a small number of countries.

          "A basic measure of TFP requires data on deflated output, labor input, capital services, intermediate inputs, and the distribution of income to factors of production. . . . If they are assembled from different sources, they may not be comparable for a variety of reasons, even if the descriptions of the activities covered are the same . . . the underlying micro data may have been collected in an inconsistent manner.

Data sets may be organized using disparate classification systems. Even if the data come from one source, the classification system can vary over time. Sometimes different classification schemes reflect more fundamental differences." Eric J. Bartelsman and J. Joseph Beaulieu, *A Consistent Accounting of U.S. Productivity Growth, Finance and Economics Discussion Series*, Federal Reserve Board, Washington, DC, 1.

49.   Richard Lewney (Team Leader), 2011, *Study on the Cost Competitiveness of European Industry in the Globalization Era: Empirical Evidence on the Basis of Relative Unit Labor Costs (ULC) at Sectoral Level, Final Report*, http://ec.europa.eu/enterprise/newsroom/cf/_getdocument.cfm?doc_id=7060, 16.

50.   Ibid., 102. Emphasis in original.

51.   Ibid., 5.

52.   "There have been several proposals to deal with [exchange-rate distortions]. The two most common are the use of unit value ratios (UVR) and the use of purchasing power parities (PPP). The first one consists in estimating local-currency price levels with unit values, computed by dividing the value of manufacturing output at the industry level by measures of the quantities of those outputs. . . . A PPP exchange rate is the ratio of the local currency price of a particular basket of goods in two different countries." Felipe, *A Note on Competitiveness, Unit Labor Costs and Growth*, 4. UVRs and PPPs tend to be closely aligned in imperialist countries, but UVRs are much higher than PPPs in most developing countries (and closer to those in imperialist countries) since international differences in the price of the highly traded industrial commodities used to compute UVRs are much lower than in the non-internationally traded services that form part of the basket of goods used to calculate PPP.

53.   Just as the University of Pennsylvania has a long association with the collection and analysis of consumption data and helped to develop and implement PPP etc., so has the University of Groningen in the Netherlands long played a key role in the collection and analysis of production data, including the devising of *unit labor costs*. The opinions expressed in this quote are much more than opinions—they express how unit labor costs are conceptualized by the IMF, ILO, etc.

54.   Bart van Ark, Edwin Stuivenwold, and Gerald Ypma, 2005, *Unit Labor Costs, Productivity and International Competitiveness*, Research Memorandum GD-80, Groningen Growth and Development Centre, http://ggdc.eldoc.ub.rug.nl/FILES/root/WorkPap/2005/200580/gd80.pdf, 3–4.

7. GLOBAL LABOR ARBITRAGE

1.   ILO, 2006, *Report of the Director General: Changing Patterns in the World of Work*, http://www.ilo.org/public/english/standards/relm/ilc/ilc95/pdf/rep-i-c.pdf, 8.

2.   Arbitrage, as used by economists, is the reaping of profits from market imperfections that result in different prices for the same product or asset. By communicating prices across segmented or partially connected markets, arbitrage causes existing price differences to narrow—unless some artificial factor (in this case, immigration controls) intervenes to prevent price differences from being arbitraged away. Arbitrage is very different from speculation: speculators bet on the future movement of prices, typically amplifying price swings. In general, the bigger the market imperfections, the bigger the price differences and the bigger the potential profits—and there is no market more imperfect than the global labor market.

3.   World Bank researchers reported that "lower migration barriers (due to decreased transportation costs) led directly to mass movements of people and an erosion of

international wage gaps prior to 1914. A similar, massive convergence in wages has been observed following more recent reductions in migration barriers, such as German reunification in 1990 and many others. But there has been much less discussion of the fact that international wage price gaps exceed any other form of border-induced price gap by an order of magnitude or more." Michael A. Clemens, Claudio Montenegro, and Lant Pritchett, 2008, *The Place Premium: Wage Differences for Identical Workers Across the US Border,* background Paper to the *2009 World Development Report,* Policy Research Working Paper 4671 (New York: World Bank), 33.

4.   IMF, 2007, *World Economic Outlook, April 2007,* 180. But not precisely enough: by the global pool of labor they mean the global pool of labor in low-wage countries.

5.   Stephen S. Roach, "More Jobs, Worse Work," *New York Times,* July 22, 2004.

6.   Stephen S. Roach, 2003, *Outsourcing, Protectionism, and the Global Labor Arbitrage,* Morgan Stanley Special Economic Study, http://www.neogroup.com/PDFs/casestudies/Special-Economic-Study-Outsourcing.pdf, 6.

7.   Ibid., my emphasis.

8.   Charles J. Whalen, 2005, "Sending Jobs Offshore from the United States: What Are the Consequences?," *European Journal of Economics and Economic Policies: Intervention* 2/2: 33-40, 35.

9.   David L. Levy, 2005, "Offshoring in the New Global Political Economy," *Journal of Management Studies* 42/3: 685–93. According to Levy, two things have unleashed this new wave: "low-cost and instantaneous transmission of data that embed engineering, medical, legal, and accounting services" combined with "the increasing organizational and technological capacity of companies, particularly multinational corporations, to separate and coordinate a network of contractors performing an intricate set of activities." However, Levy considers "the increasing organizational and technological capacity" of TNCs to be the "core driver of the latest form of offshore sourcing," confusing the driving force with the means of harnessing it.

10. Samuel J. Palmisano, 2006, "The Globally Integrated Enterprise," *Foreign Affairs* 85/3:127–36.

11. UNCTAD, 2007, *World Investment Report 2007,* 31n.

12. UNCTAD, *World Investment Report 2013,* 145.

13. In continuation, the report says: "In addition to downward pressure on wages, the drive for reduced costs often results in significant occupational safety and health violations. . . . Downward pricing pressure has created economic incentives for violating environmental regulations and industry best practices, leading to the increased release of disease-causing pollutants and climate-change-related emissions. Cutting costs by engaging in negative social and environmental practices is a particularly acute trend in developing countries." UNCTAD, *World Investment Report 2013,* 162.

14. Ibid., 158.

15. William Milberg, 2004, "Globalised Production: Structural Challenges for Developing Country Workers," in *Labour and the Globalisation of Production—Causes and Consequences of Industrial Upgrading,* William Milberg (ed.), 1–19 (New York: Palgrave Macmillan), 10.

16. Or to shareholders so they can do the same: "At a time of soaring profitability, US companies have piled up huge amounts of cash, much of it parked offshore. Yet investing it in long-term growth is the last thing on their mind. According to Barclays, US companies have lavished more than $500bn in the past year on stock buybacks—a multiple of what most are spending on research and development and other capital investments. In the first six months of the year, buybacks surged

to $338.3bn, the largest half-yearly volume since 2007." Edward Luce, "The Short-Sighted US Buyback Boom," *Financial Times,* September 21, 2014.

17. Anwar Shaikh, 1980, "The Laws of International Exchange," in *Growth, Profits and Property: Essays in the Revival of Political Economy,* ed. Edward J. Nell (Cambridge: Cambridge University Press), 104–35, quote at 228.

18. Albert Park, Gaurav Nayyar, and Patrick Low, 2013, *Supply Chain Perspectives and Issues: A Literature Review,* World Trade Organization and Fung Global Institute, WTO Publications, Geneva, http://www.wto.org/english/res_e/booksp_e/aid4tradesupplychain13_e.pdf, 29. Fung Global Institute takes its name from its chairman, Victor Fung, who is also the Group Chairman of Li and Fung Ltd., a major mid-tier corporation based in Hong Kong, two-thirds of whose business is supplying Western brands with garments made in 12,000 factories in forty low-wage economies.

19. Ibid., 30. [Eli] Hecksher and [Bertil] Ohlin are sometimes joined by Wolfgang Stolper and Paul Samuelson to give the H-O-S-S model of international trade.

20. Ibid., 29–30.

21. Marx, [1894] 1991, *Capital,* vol. 3 (London: Penguin), 966.

22. Park et al., *Supply Chain Perspectives and Issues,* 30.

23. For an excellent discussion of Marx's critique of Ricardo's theory, see Shaikh, "The Laws of International Exchange."

24. This changes Ricardo's theory beyond all recognition. That trade promotes specialization that benefits all participating countries to a greater or lesser degree irrespective of their levels of development is a *theorem* that unites all schools of economic thought (even, with some qualifications, by Marxists). But the *theory* advanced by HOS to explain why this is true is radically different from the one advanced by David Ricardo.

25. According to Marx's value theory, money is abstract labor, that is, labor that has been stripped of its concrete differences and equalized with all other labors. This abstraction is a real event, effected by competition and exchange.

26. The *rate of surplus-value* and the *rate of exploitation* are interchangeable, except for one sense in which they differ. The labor of workers in non-productive sectors such as finance, advertising, etc., produces no value or surplus-value, so it is not appropriate in their case to talk of a rate of surplus-value. But if four hours are required to produce a worker's consumption goods and her/his working day is eight hours, this worker endures a 100 percent rate of exploitation, regardless of how the capitalist employs her/his labor.

27. Marx, [1867] 1976, *Capital,* vol. 1 (London: Penguin), 432.

28. Karl Marx, 1972, *Theories of Surplus Value,* Part 3 (London: Lawrence and Wishart), 350.

29. Andy Higginbottom, 2011, "Gold Mining in South Africa Reconsidered: New Mode of Exploitation, Theories of Imperialism and 'Capital,'" Économies et Sociétés, 45:/2: 261–88, https://www.academia.edu/11419055/Gold_Mining_in_South_Africa_Reconsidered_New_Mode_of_Exploitation_Theories_of_Imperialism_and_Capital.

It might be objected that if the value of labor-power differs from one country to another, outsourcing production to where this value is lower does not involve paying wages below its value, whereas keeping production at home by slashing wages does. From the point of view of its effect on the firm's profits the objection is semantic, since slashing a worker's wage or replacing her/him with another worker on lower wages, at home or abroad, has an identical effect on the firm's profits.

30.   Ellen Meiksins Wood, [2003] 2005, *Empire of Capital* (London: Verso), 125. Wood's capitalist imperatives are synonymous with what Marx called "the silent compulsion of economic relations [that] sets the seal on the domination of the capitalist over the worker. Direct extra-economic force is still of course used, but only in exceptional cases." Karl Marx, *Capital*, vol. 1, 899. William Robinson also recognizes that "globalization [is] the near culmination of a centuries long process of the spread of capitalist production around the world and its displacement of all precapitalist relations." Robinson, 2004, *A Theory of Global Capitalism* (Baltimore: Johns Hopkins University Press), 6.

31.   Only once does *Empire of Capital* stray into the terrain of value theory, vaguely noting that "one overriding indication that the global market is still far from integrated: the fact that wages, prices and conditions of labor are still so widely diverse throughout the world. . . . The global movements of capital require . . . a kind of economic and social fragmentation that enhances profitability by differentiating the costs and conditions of production." Wood, *Empire of Capital*, 137.

32.   Ibid,. 7.

33.   Ibid.

34.   Wood, *Empire of Capital,* 12. Alex Callinicos has the same idea: "The global hierarchy of economic and political power that is a fundamental consequence of the uneven and combined development inherent in capitalist imperialism was not dissolved, but was rather complicated by the emergence of new centres of capital accumulation," producing what he calls sub-imperialisms, a broad category that includes Vietnam, Greece, Turkey, India, Pakistan, Iran, Iraq, and South Africa. Alex Callinicos, 2009, *Imperialism and Global Political Economy* (Cambridge: Polity Press), 186.

35.   David Harvey, 2003, *The New Imperialism* (Oxford: Oxford University Press), 176–77.

36.   Shaikh and Tonak explain the crucial difference between surplus-value extracted in capitalist production process and capitalist profits deriving from interaction between capital and, for example, petty-commodity producers: "At the most abstract level of Marxist theory, aggregate profit is simply the monetary expression of aggregate surplus value. But it is often forgotten that profit can also arise from transfers between the circuit of capital and other spheres of social life. Marx calls this latter form of profit alienation, which—unlike a profit on surplus value—is fundamentally dependent on some sort of unequal exchange. Its existence enables us to solve the famous puzzle of the difference between the sum of profits and sum of surplus values brought about by the transformation from values to prices of production." Anwar M. Shaikh and E. Ahmet Tonak, 1994, *Measuring the Wealth of Nations* (Cambridge University Press), 35.

37.   David Harvey, [1982] 2006, *The Limits to Capital* (London: Verso), 441–2.

38.   David Harvey, 1990, *The Condition of Postmodernity* (Oxford: Blackwell Publishing), 165.

39.   Ibid., 153.

40.   Ibid., 183.

41.   Harvey, *The New Imperialism*, 63–64.

42.   Ibid., 64–65.

43.   Ibid., 209–11.

44.   Harvey, *The Limits to Capital,* 444.

45.   Robert Brenner, 2009, "What Is Good for Goldman Sachs Is Good for America: The Origins of the Current Crisis," prologue to the Spanish translation of *Econom-*

ics of Global Turbulence, http://www.sscnet.ucla.edu/issr/cstch/papers/Brenner-CrisisTodayOctober2009.pdf (9).

46. Jack Barnes, 2005, "Our Politics Start with the World," in *New International*,13: 9–80, 35.

47. John Bellamy Foster and Robert McChesney, 2012, *The Endless Crisis: How Monopoly Finance Capital Produces Stagnation and Upheaval from the USA to China* (New York: Monthly Review Press), 138–39.

48. The antithesis of Amin's approach is to be found in Anwar Shaikh's theory of imperialism, which abstracts from monopoly factors in order to derive imperialism from the laws of competition. Imperialism, he argues, results from "the automatic tendencies of free and unhampered trade among capitalist nations at different levels of development . . . not monopoly . . . free trade is as much a mechanism for the concentration and centralization of international capital as free exchange within a capitalist nation is for the concentration and centralization of domestic capital" (Shaikh, *The Laws of International Exchange*, 227). Shaikh reduces imperialism to unequal development not by excluding monopoly but by ignoring a fact about the global system not found in competition between capitals within a single country: widely divergent rates of exploitation. Shaikh recognizes inequality between capitals but ignores inequality between workers and forgets that the world is not merely divided into rich countries and poor countries but into oppressor and oppressed nations: "What Emmanuel sees as an inequality between nations is in fact the international manifestation of the inequality between capitals which is inherent in the necessarily uneven development of capitalist relations of production" (210).

49. Samir Amin, 2010, *The Law of Worldwide Value* (New York: Monthly Review Press), 84. This is a revised and expanded edition of Samir Amin, 1978, *The Law of Value and Historical Materialism* (New York: Monthly Review Press).

50. John Weeks and Elizabeth Dore, 1979, "Reply to Samir Amin," *Latin American Perspectives* 6/3: 114–16.

51. John Bellamy Foster and Robert McChesney comment in *The Endless Crisis*: "It should be noted that the term 'superexploited' appears to have two closely related, overlapping meanings in Marxist theory: (1) workers who receive less than the historically determined value of labor power, as it is defined here; and (2) workers who are subjected to unequal exchange and overexploited, primarily in the Global South. In Amin's framework, however, the two meanings are united. This is because the value of labor power is determined globally, while actual wage rates are determined nationally, and are hierarchically ordered due to imperialism. In the global South therefore workers normally receive wages that are less than the value of labor power. This is the basis of imperial rent. John Smith and Andy Higginbottom have developed a similar approach to superexploitation based on Marx" (212). Similar, but different: the concept of exploitation and super-exploitation developed here does not rest on the notion of a global value of labor-power.

52. Hypostatization is the representation of one pole in a dialectical unity of opposites as reality.

53. Fidel Castro, 28 January 1994 speech to an international solidarity conference in Havana, reprinted in *The Militant*, 7 March 1994.

54. Gary Howe 1981, "Dependency Theory, Imperialism, and the Production of Surplus Value on a World Scale," *Latin American Perspectives* 8/3–4: 82–102. Anthony Brewer also argued that "in less developed countries . . . a widespread process of (capitalist) industrialisation is under way . . . dependency theory gives no use-

ful guidance to the analysis of [this]." Anthony Brewer, 1990, *Marxist Theories of Imperialism—A Critical Survey*, 2nd ed. (London: Routledge), 197.

55. Nikolai Bukharin, 1915, *Imperialism and World Economy* (London: Merlin Press), 91–93. According to Bukharin, "The faster the tempo of capitalist development… the more disturbed is the equilibrium between industry and agriculture, the stronger is the competition between industrially developed countries for the possession of backward countries, [and] the more unavoidable becomes an open conflict between them" (95).

56. Bilge Erten and José Antonio Ocampo, 2012, *Super-Cycles of Commodity Prices since the Mid-Nineteenth Century,* UN-DESA [United Nations Department of Social Affairs] Working Paper No. 110 ST/ESA/2012/DWP/110, 23.

57. Prebisch led ECLAC until 1963 before becoming the founding secretary-general of the United Nations Conference on Trade and Development (UNCTAD) in 1964.

58. See the chapter on unequal exchange in the outstanding book by Carlos Tablada, 1989, *Che Guevara: Economics and Politics in the Transition to Socialism* (Sydney: Pathfinder). This book, an English translation of *El Pensamiento Economico de Ernesto Che Guevara,* was highly influential in Cuba, and played an important role in the return to Che's ideas during the "rectification campaign" launched by the Third Congress of the Communist Party of Cuba in December 1986.

59. Fidel Castro, [1979] 1993, Address to UN General Assembly, in *To Speak the Truth* (New York: Pathfinder), 184–86. Cuba was voted into the leadership of the Non-Aligned Movement because of its extraordinary and unprecedented solidarity with the struggle against apartheid. Tens of thousands of Cuban soldiers had turned back the South African invasion of Angola in 1975/76, inspiring the June 1976 Soweto uprising that opened a new stage in the struggle against apartheid. China, to the disgust of millions who had looked to China as an ally of the oppressed, gave political and military support to the USA/South African forces, on the grounds that Soviet social imperialism was a bigger enemy than U.S. imperialism and South Africa's white supremacy. SA and the United States retaliated to the stinging defeat of 1975–76 by escalating their intervention; Cuba responded by escalating its solidarity, even to the point of dismantling antiaircraft defenses around its own cities and shipping them across the Atlantic in order to win the air war. A total of 425,000 Cuban soldiers, all volunteers, served in Angola from 1975 until 1988, when Cuban and Angolan forces defeated South African troops at the historic battle of Cuito Cuanavale. As Nelson Mandela told a rally of tens of thousands in Matanzas, Cuba, in 1991, "The crushing defeat of the racist army at Cuito Cuanavale was a victory for the whole of Africa . . . [and] broke the myth of the invincibility of the white oppressors!" For the full text of his speech, see Nelson Mandela and Fidel Castro, *How Far We Slaves Have Come!* (New York: Pathfinder Press, 1991).

60. Tablada, *Che Guevara,* 157–58.

61. Che Guevara, 1964, "Planning and Consciousness in the Transition to Socialism (On the Budgetary Finance System)," in *Che Guevara and the Cuban Revolution* (Sydney: Pathfinder/Pacific and Asia).

62. Che Guevara, 1965, *Speech at the Second Economic Seminar of Afro- Asian Solidarity, February 24, 1965,* https://www.marxists.org/archive/guevara/1965/02/24.htm.

63. Fidel Castro, 1987, "Important problems for the whole of international revolutionary thought," in *New International #6* (New York: 408 Printing and Publishing), 209–30.

64. Fidel Castro, 1982, interview with the Mexican newspaper *Excelsior* in *Fidel Castro Speeches,* vol. 3: *War and Crisis in the Americas* (New York: Pathfinder Press), 222–23.

65. Amin, *The Law of Worldwide Value*, 121–22.

66. Ibid., 123.

67. Ibid., 124.

68. Ibid.

69. For an excellent introduction to the Chinese Revolution, see Cindy Jaquith, "The Origins and Defeat of 1925–27 Chinese Revolution," *The Militant*, December 10, 2007, http://www.themilitant.com/2007/7146/714656.html; and Cindy Jaquith, "How Chinese Working People Overthrew Capitalism," *The Militant*, December 24, 2007, http://www.themilitant.com/2007/7148/714854.html.

70. Amin, *The Law of Value and Historical Materialism*, 108.

71. Amin, *The Law of Worldwide Value*, 93.

72. The Cuban Revolution was led by the July 26 Movement. M-26-7, as it was known, arose independently of the pro-Moscow Cuban Communist Party (then known as the Popular Socialist Party, or PSP), whose adherence to the Stalinist popular front policy, which proposed an anti-fascist alliance with a supposedly progressive, democratic wing of the bourgeoisie in both imperialist and oppressed nations, and was therefore the pre-WW2 precursor of peaceful coexistence, had led the PSP into a wartime alliance with the dictatorship of Fulgencio Batista (in which they accepted a ministerial post), and to later denounce M-26-7 and its leader, Fidel Castro, as ultra-left adventurists.

73. Ernesto Che Guevara, [1967] 1987, "Vietnam and the World Struggle for Freedom (Message to the Tricontinental)," in *Che Guevara and the Cuban Revolution: Writings and Speeches of Ernesto Che Guevara* (Sydney, Pathfinder), 351–52.

74. The Communist Party of Iran, known as the Tudeh party, was the largest party in Iran and one of the largest communist parties in the world. Tudeh supported the liberal-reformist Mossadeq regime from the left. When the US-UK military coup came in 1953 Tudeh offered no resistance. Iraq (1963) and Indonesia (1965) followed the same script.

75. Amin, *The Law of Worldwide Value*, 11.

76. Ruy Mauro Marini, 1973, *Dialéctica de Dependencia* (Mexico DF: Ediciones Era), 91. My translation.

77. Ibid., 93. Marini quotes Marx in support: "The prolongation of the working day beyond the point at which the worker would have produced an exact equivalent for the value of his labor-power, and the appropriation of surplus labor by capital—this is the process which constitutes the production of absolute surplus-value. It forms the general foundation of capitalist system, and the starting point for the production of relative surplus-value." Marx, *Capital*, vol. 1, 645.

78. "Marini places the necessity of super-exploitation of labor in the mid-nineteenth century, that is, before the appearance of modern imperialism as a world system as portrayed by Lenin. The transition in England from production dominated by methods of absolute surplus to relative surplus-value depended on cheap imports as well as greater productivity. . . . Marini's work shows that Marx was not correct on every point, even in his own time." Andy Higginbottom, 2014, "Imperialist Rent in Practice and Theory," *Globalizations* 11/1: 23–33.

79. Amanda Latimer, "Superexploitation, the Race to the Bottom and the Missing International," in *The Palgrave Encyclopedia of Imperialism and Anti-Imperialism*, ed. S. M. Bâ and I. Ness (New York: Palgrave Macmillan, forthcoming).

80. Tiago Camarinha Lopes and Elizeu Serra de Araujo, 2013, "Marx and Marini on Absolute and Relative Surplus Value," *International Critical Thought* 3/2: 165–82.

81. Amin, *The Law of Worldwide Value*, 52.

82. Higginbottom, "Imperialist Rent in Practice and Theory," 30.

83. See Ruy Mauro Marini, 1972, "Brazilian Subimperialism," *Monthly Review* 23/9: 14–24, http://archive.monthlyreview.org/index.php/mr/article/view/MR-023-09-1972-02_2.

84. Lopes and Araujo, "Marx and Marini on Absolute and Relative Surplus Value," 171.

85. John Weeks and Elizabeth Dore, 1979, "International Exchange and the Causes of Backwardness," *Latin American Perspectives* 6/2: 62–87.

86. Charles Bettelheim, 1972, "Some Theoretical Comments by Charles Bettelheim," in *Unequal Exchange, A Study in the Imperialism of Trade*, by Arghiri Emmanuel (London: NLB), 271–322.

87. Nigel Harris, 1986, "Theories of Unequal Exchange," *International Socialism* 2/33: 119–20.

88. Callinicos, *Imperialism and Global Political Economy,* 179–80.

89. Joseph Choonara, 2009, *Unravelling Capitalism* (London: Bookmarks Publications), 34.

90. Ernest Mandel, [1972] 1975, *Late Capitalism,* trans. Joris de Bres (London: NLB), 350. "Colonial surplus-profit" refers to the profits reaped by FDI in agriculture and resource extraction in subject nations. "Surplus" signifies a rate of profit that is higher than the domestic average.

91. Ibid., 77. In this quote, Mandel equates the value of the commodity labor-power with its (average) price. This is true only for this particular commodity, which alone of all commodities is not brought to market by capitalists. Competition for profits between capitalists causes the value of all other commodities to systematically diverge from their price. Workers do not sell their labor-power in order to make a profit, but to subsist, and so the identity between the value of labor-power and its price remains intact.

92. Ibid., 353. These vast international differences in the value and the price of labor-power were not considered important enough to be included in the 10 features defining the structure of the world market that concludes his tome.

93. Ernest Mandel 1964, "Contemporary Imperialism," *New Left Review* 25: 17–25.

94. Mandel, *Late Capitalism,* 371. The semi-colonies have "lost their position as monopolist sellers of raw materials" because, says Mandel, of the development of synthetic substitutes.

8. IMPERIALISM AND THE LAW OF VALUE

1. Epigraph: Ellen Meiksins Wood, 2005, *Empire of Capital* (London: Verso), 127.

2. "No period of modern society is so favourable for the study of capitalist accumulation as the period of the last 20 years . . . but of all countries England again provides the classical example, because it holds the foremost place in the world market, because capitalist production is fully developed only in England, and finally because the introduction of the free-trade millennium since 1846 has cut off the last retreat of vulgar economics." Karl Marx, [1867] 1976, *Capital,* vol. 1 (London: Penguin), 802.

3. Wood, *Empire of Capital,* 127. William Robinson also recognizes that "globalization [is] the near culmination of a centuries-long process of the spread of capitalist production around the world and its displacement of all precapitalist relations." Robinson, 2004, *A Theory of Global Capitalism* (Baltimore: Johns Hopkins University Press), 6.

4. V. I. Lenin, [1915] 1964, "The Revolutionary Proletariat and the Right of Nations

to Self–Determination," in *Collected Works,* vol. 21 (Moscow: Progress Publishers), 407–11.

5.   "The core of the problem is to be found in the nature of peripheral industrializa-tion, a historical phenomenon that could not be studied by thinkers in the rel-atively remote past." Tiago Camarinha Lopes and Elizeu Serra de Araujo, 2013, "Marx and Marini on Absolute and Relative Surplus Value," *International Critical Thought* 3/2: 165–82.

6.   South Korea is one of the few relatively small countries (in the past century) to show signs of having graduated from the ranks of emerging nations. Taiwan is the other notable candidate for developed status. There is no space here for a detailed examination of these exceptions to the general rule. The global systemic crisis, now in its early stages, will severely test the durability of their elevated status.

7.   Sam Ashman, 2006, "Symposium on David Harvey's *The New Imperialism,* Intro-duction," in *Historical Materialism* 14/4: 3–7.

8.   Jack Barnes, 2005, "Capitalism's Long Hot Winter Has Begun," *New International* 12:99–204.

9.   Wood, *Empire of Capital,* 127.

10.   David Harvey, [1982] 2006, *The Limits to Capital* (London: Verso), 440.

11.   Rosa Luxemburg, [1913] 1971, *The Accumulation of Capital,* trans. Agnes Schwartz-child (London: Routledge and Kegan Paul), 467.

12.   Ellen Meiksins Wood, 2007, "A Reply to Critics," *Historical Materialism* 15/3: 143–70.

13.   David Harvey, 2007, "In What Ways Is the New Imperialism Really New?," *Histor-ical Materialism,* 15/3: 57–70.

14.   Ibid, 58–59.

15.   Barnes, "Capitalism's Long Hot Winter Has Begun," 123–24. Centrism means vac-illation between revolution and reform.

16.   V. I. Lenin, [1916] 1964, *Imperialism, the Highest Stage of Capitalism,* in *Collected Works,* vol. 22 (Moscow: Progress Publishers), 185–305, quote at 266.

17.   Anwar Shaikh, 1980, "The Laws of International Exchange," in *Growth, Profits and Property: Essays in the Revival of Political Economy,* ed. Edward J. Nell (Cambridge: Cambridge University Press), 204–35.

18.   Gary Kitching, 1981, "The Theory of Imperialism and Its Consequences," *MERIP Reports* 100/101: 36–42.

19.   Andy Higginbottom, 2011, "The System of Accumulation in South Africa: Theo-ries of Imperialism and Capital," in *Économies et Sociétés,* 45/2: 261–288, 268.

20.   The degree of concentration of capital and of the power wielded by its owners can be glimpsed in the striking results of research by Stefania Vitali, James Glattfelder, and Stefano Battiston, three researchers at the Swiss Federal Institute of Technol-ogy in Zurich at 2011. Their attempt to measure the degree of TNC dominance "is not a trivial task because firms may exert control over other firms via a web of direct and indirect ownership relations which extends over many countries." See *The Network of Global Corporate Control* at http://arxiv.org/PS_cache/arxiv/pdf/1107/1107.5728v2.pdf, 1.

       Using "complex network analysis" to uncover the "structure of control," they find that "only 737 top holders accumulate 80% of the control over the value of all TNCs. . . . Network control is much more unequally distributed than wealth. In particular, the top ranked actors hold a control 10 times bigger than what could be expected based on their wealth" (6). These top-ranked actors are a group of 147 TNCs who control nearly 40 percent of the economic value of the world's TNCs, via a complicated web of ownership relations, and three-quarters of these core firms are financial institutions. "The core is . . . very densely connected. . . . As a result, about 3/4 of the ownership of firms in the core remains in the hands of firms of the core itself. In other words, this is a tightly knit group of corporations that cumulatively hold the majority share of each other" (ibid.).

21.   John Bellamy Foster and Robert McChesney, 2012, *The Endless Crisis: How Monopoly Finance Capital Produces Stagnation and Upheaval from the USA to China* (New York: Monthly Review Press), 67.

22.   Lenin, *Imperialism, the Highest Stage of Capitalism,* 277.

23.   In their 2012 work *The Making of Global Capitalism: The Political Economy of American Empire* (London: Verso), Leo Panitch and Sam Gindin present yet another variant of the standard Euro-Marxist theory of imperialism as a system of inter-state relations, in which neither the division of the world into oppressor and oppressed nations nor the super-exploitation of workers and farmers which this division makes possible gets a mention, let alone the central place it deserves. Thus they castigate the "theorists of imperialism writing at the beginning of the twentieth century" for "treat[ing] the export of capital itself as imperialist," arguing instead that Lenin et al.'s "insight that the export of capital was transforming the role of the state in both the capital exporting and importing countries, was the[ir] most important contribution" (Panitch and Gindin, *The Making of Global Capitalism,* 5).

24.   Higginbottom, *The System of Accumulation in South Africa,* 268.

25.   Marx, *Capital,* vol. 1, 702.

26.   Karl Marx, [1894] 1991, *Capital,* vol. 3 (London: Penguin), 249–50.

27.   There is a third possibility: the productivity of consumer goods–producing labor in the European country may be so much higher than in China that it more than outweighs the higher consumption levels of European workers. In this case, the labor-time required to produce their larger basket (and therefore the value of their labor-power) may be lower than in China. However, there is nothing in this passage to suggest that Marx intended such an interpretation.

28.   Marx, *Capital,* vol. 1, 727n.

29.   "Even though the equalisation of wages and working hours between one sphere of production and another, or between different capitals invested in the same sphere of production, comes up against all kinds of local obstacles, the advance of capitalist production and the progressive subordination of all economic relations to this mode of production tends nevertheless to bring this process to fruition." Marx, *Capital,* vol. 3, 241–42. This either fails to anticipate or tries to see beyond capitalism's imperialist stage.

30.   Ibid.

31.   Marx, *Capital,* vol. 1, 430–31.

32.   Ibid., 557.

33.   Ibid., 747–48.

34.   Ibid., 748.

35.   Andy Higginbottom, 2012, "Structure and Essence in *Capital I*: Extra Surplus-Value and the Stages of Capitalism," *Journal of Australian Political Economy* 70:251–70, https://www.academia.edu/11419215/structure_and_essence_in_capital_i_extra_surplus–value_and_the_stages_of_capitalism.

36.   Marx *Capital,* vol. 3, 242.

37.   Shaikh, "The Laws of International Exchange," 208.

38.   Frederick Engels, [1847] 1987, *The Communists and Karl Heinzen,* in *Marx and Engels, Collected Works,* vol. 6 (Moscow: Progress Publishers), 291.

39. Ruy Mauro Marini was the inspiration for Higginbottom's insight. In *Dialéctica de Dependencia,* Marini argues: "The concept of super-exploitation is not identical to that of absolute surplus-value since it also includes a type of production of relative surplus-value—that which corresponds to an increase in the intensity of labour. On the other hand, the conversion of part of the wages fund into a source of capital accumulation does not strictly represent a form of absolute surplus-value production, since it simultaneously affects both parts of the working day, not only of surplus labour-time as is the case with absolute surplus-value. Above all, super-exploitation is defined most of all by greater exploitation of the worker's physical capacity, in contrast to the exploitation resulting from an increase in her/his productivity, and tends normally to express itself in the fact that labour power is remunerated below its actual value." Ruy Mauro Marini, 1973, *Dialéctica de Dependencia* (Mexico DF: Ediciones Era), 93. My translation.

40. Andy Higginbottom, 2009, *The Third Form of Surplus Value Increase,* paper presented at Historical Materialism Conference, London https://www.academia.edu/1141897/9/Third_form_of_extraction_surplus_value.

41. Higginbottom, *Structure and Essence in Capital I,* 282–83.

42. Ibid., 284.

43. Ibid., 284–85.

44. Marx, *Capital,* vol. 3, 342, my emphasis. This was also a premise of Marx's analysis of capitalist exploitation in *Capital 1*: "I assume that commodities are sold at their value, [and] that the price of labour-power occasionally rises above its value, but never sinks below it. On these assumptions . . . the relative magnitudes of surplus-value and price of labour-power are determined by three circumstances: (1) the length of the working day, or the extensive magnitude of labour, (2) the normal intensity of labour, or its intensive magnitude, whereby a given quantity of labour is expended in a given time; and (3) the productivity of labour, whereby the same quantity of labour yields, in a given time, a greater or smaller quantity of the product, depending on the degree of development attained by the conditions of production." Marx, *Capital,* vol. 1, 655.

45. He continues, "unless monopolies stand in the way," i.e., when the surplus profit is captured by individual firms and not shared, through competition, with other capitals. Marx, *Capital,* vol. 3, 345.

46. "The rate of profit does not fall because labour becomes less productive, but because it becomes more productive. Both the rise in the rate of surplus–value and the fall in the rate of profit are but specific forms through which growing productivity of labour is expressed under capitalism." Marx, *Capital,* vol. 3, 240.

47. "When Marx states that enterprises operating with below-average productivity obtain less than the average profit . . . all this . . . means is that the value or surplus-value actually produced by their workers is appropriated on the market by firms that function better. It does not at all mean that they have created less value or surplus-value than is indicated by the number of hours worked in them." Ernest Mandel, 1975, *Late Capitalism* (London: NLB), 101.

48. Organic composition of capital is, simply, the relative proportions of dead labor and living labor in the different branches. If we assume the organic composition of capital to be the same in all branches and supply and demand to be in balance, the relative prices of two dissimilar commodities would coincide with the relative amounts of average socially necessary labor-time required to produce them, and price would be synonymous with value. In reality, of course, huge differences in organic composition exist, and so the competition between capitals for a share of

total profits results in the redistribution of value from labor-intensive capitals to capital-intensive capitals, thereby giving rise to an average, economy-wide rate of profit.

Price formation, or the process of social equalization of different concrete private labors, is also a process of abstraction from everything that makes these private labors different and concrete—a real abstraction, one that is actually performed by the marketing of the products of these diverse concrete labors, through which they are measured against all others. It is clear from this that the value of each commodity is, and therefore must be conceived as, a social relation, in other words a specific magnitude of abstract, socially necessary labor that contains within it the entire universe of social relations.

49. This assumes that both labors are of average intensity, and ignores the issue of qualified or complex labor, which may amplify the value-producing properties of labor. But this difference does not correlate with organic composition. The important point here is that the value-creating power of a worker *is wholly independent of the organic composition of the capital s/he sets in motion.*

50. Marx, *Capital,* vol. 1, 137.

51. Marx, *Capital,* vol. 3, 345.

52. It is noteworthy that Marx talks about the exploitation of labor, not the rate of exploitation, and labor, not labor-power. That this might be due to the provisional, draft form of the original can be discounted—even in rough drafts, Marx is meticulous in his choice of words. It is more likely that he deliberately chose not to use the developed capitalist form of these categories, because in the colonies, at that time, the commodification of labor-power and the univerzalisation of the capital/wage labor relation had a way to go. This again underlines the evolutionary distance separating the past three decades from the stage of capitalist development observed and analyzed by Marx.

53. Marx, *Capital,* vol. 3, 345.

54. Marx, *Capital,* vol. 1, 305.

55. Marx, *Capital,* vol. 3, 241–42.

56. Ibid., 241–42.

57. Ibid.

58. Karl Marx, 1973, *Grundrisse* (London: Penguin), 651. I am grateful to Walter Daum for pointing out the relevance of this passage.

59. Lenin, *Imperialism, the Highest Stage of Capitalism,* 265.

9. The GDP Illusion

1. United Nations, n.d., *Foreign Direct Investment (FDI): Net Inflows and Net Outflows as Share of GDP, Department of Economic and Social Affairs,* http://www.un.org/esa/sustdev/natlinfo/indicators/methodology_sheets/global_econ_partnership/fdi.pdf.

GDI, or Gross Domestic Income, also exists in the economists' lexicon: "Gross Domestic Income (GDI) is analytically equivalent to gross domestic product: both measure the level of economic activity. . . . GDP measures the product side of the economy (the value of final sales) while GDI measures the income side (labor compensation, profits, rent, and proprietors' incomes). In theory GDP always exactly equals GDI, but, due to measurement error there are slight differences between the two. When assessing profits' share, GDI is the more appropriate metric because they are measured directly through the GDI accounts." L. Josh Bivens, 2006, *Gross Domestic Income: Profit Growth Swamps Labor Income,* Economic Policy Institute,

Washington, DC, http://www.epi.org/economic_snapshots/entry/webfeatures_snapshots_20060330/.

2. The propagandist nature of this book is evident in Coyle's statement, while discussing the global financial crisis, that this was caused "above all, [by] the loss of perspective about the *purpose* of business, which is not at all the maximisation of short-term profit or even shareholder value, but rather delivering goods and services to customers (in ways they might not even know they want), in a mutually beneficial transaction. Profit and share price increases are a side effect, not a goal." Diane Coyle, 2014, *GDP: A Brief but Affectionate History* (Princeton: Princeton University Press), 95.

3 Ibid., 27.

4. Ibid., 40.

5. Ibid., 38.

6. Ibid., 106–8.

7. Ibid., 27, 24.

8. Ibid., 139.

9. Dirk Philipsen makes the same conceptual error: "Success and well-being is largely defined by growth. Growth, in turn, is defined by GDP…. The logic of GDP foresees no end to growth." Philipsen, 2015, *The Little Big Number: How GDP Came to Rule the World and What to Do About It* (Princeton: Princeton University Press), 3–4.

10. Lorenzo Fioramonti, 2014, *How Numbers Rule the World: The Use and Abuse of Statistics in Global Politics* (London: Zed Books), 200.

11. Ibid., 207.

12. Fioramonti's lack of a theory of value is evident in his statement that "mankind does not produce anything. It simply turns natural wealth into money." Fioramonti, 2013, *Gross Domestic Problem* (London: Zed Books), 137.

13. Ibid., 3.

14. Philipsen, *The Little Big Number*, 12.

15. Ibid., 6.

16. Ibid., 14

17. Clifford Cobb, Ted Halstead, and Jonathan Rowe, "If the GDP Is Up, Why Is America Down?," *The Atlantic Monthly*, October 1995, http://www.theatlantic.com/past/politics/ecbig/gdp.htm.

18. Coyle, *GDP: A Brief but Affectionate History*, 16–17.

19. Sholto Byrnes, "Person of the Year: The Man Making China Green," *New Statesman*, December 18, 2006.

20. Coyle, *GDP: A Brief but Affectionate History*, 103–4.

21. Ibid., 39.

22. Ibid., 89.

23. Alan Greenspan, in J. Steven Landefeld, *GDP: One of the Great Inventions of the 20th Century*, http://www.bea.gov/scb/pdf/BEAWIDE/2000/0100od.pdf, 12.

24. The UK's Office for National Statistics reports that "domestic and personal services produced and consumed by members of the same household are omitted [from the UK's national accounting system]. Subject to this one major exception, GDP is intended to be a comprehensive measure of the total gross value added in production by all resident institutional units." Office for National Statistics (ONS), 1998, *United Kingdom National Accounts—Concepts, Sources and Methods* (London: The Stationery Office), 11.

    See chapter 1 of Anwar M. Shaikh and E. Ahmet Tonak, 1994, *Measuring the*

Wealth of Nations (Cambridge University Press) for a lucid discussion of attempts to extend the coverage of national production accounts to include domestic labor and other activities.

In September 2009 two Nobel Economics Laureates, Joseph Stiglitz and Amartya Sen, proposed a "broader, more encompassing measure of well-being" that would augment traditional measures of domestic product with measures of popular access to "health, education, security and social connectedness." Joseph Stiglitz, "Towards a Better Measure of Well-Being," *Financial Times*, September 13, 2009.

25. This considers only the relations internal to capitalism, and abstracts from profits arising from "accumulation by dispossession," that is, the interaction between capitalism and procapitalist or noncapitalist forms. Shaikh and Tonak (*Measuring the Wealth of Nations*, 35) point out that "it is often forgotten that profit can . . . arise from transfers between the circuit of capital and other spheres of social life. Marx calls this latter form of profit on alienation, which—unlike a profit on surplus-value—is fundamentally dependent on some sort of unequal exchange. Its existence enables us to solve the famous puzzle of the difference between the sum of profits and sum of surplus-values brought about by the transformation from values to prices of production."

26. Karl Marx, [1894] 1991, *Capital,* vol. 3 (London: Penguin), 971.

27. Bermuda is one of six British overseas territories in the Caribbean–North Atlantic region; the other five are Anguilla, Cayman Islands, British Virgin Islands, and the Turks and Caicos Islands. Gibraltar and the Falklands/Malvinas are among eight other territories elsewhere in the world over which the UK exercises sovereignty. Bermuda's per capita GDP (in PPP$) in 2013 stood at $86,000 (more than 90 percent of it contributed by financial services), 63 percent greater than that of the United States, according to the *CIA Factbook* (http://www.indexmundi.com/g/r.aspx?c=bd&v=67). By 2013 Bermuda had slipped to fourth place, overtaken by Qatar, Liechtenstein (another tax haven), and Macau (a gambling den). Qatar's top spot is dubious, because the migrant workers who do most of the work are not counted as citizens,

28. Andrea Felsted and Gillian Tett, "Hedge Funds Find Bermuda a Favourable Climate, *Financial Times*, July 4, 2007.

29. The pre-Columbian name for Hispaniola is unknown because European colonists exterminated the original inhabitants.

30. In 2001, "95% of these were exported to the United States." Robert C. Shelburne, 2004, "Trade and Inequality: The Role of Vertical Specialization and Outsourcing," *Global Economy Journal* 4/2: 23. Data on the DR's EPZ workforce in Jean-Pierre Singa Boyenge, 2007, *ILO Database on Export Processing Zones*, Sectoral Activities Programme Working Paper WP.251, http://www.ilo.org/public/english/dialogue/sector/themes/epz/epz–db.pdf.

31. Some of the state's share, received as taxes or royalties, is used to service the Dominican Republic's external debts. The OECD reports that, in 2004, debt servicing consumed around 5 percent of GDP, "a percentage that altogether surpasses the resources assigned by the government to the sectors of health and education, which represented only 3.6%" while a large portion of the capitalists' profits will likewise be expatriated through capital flight. OECD, 2008, *Reviews of National Policies for Education—Dominican Republic*, 90.

32. Raphael Kaplinsky, 2005, *Globalization, Poverty and Inequality* (Cambridge: Polity),164.

33. According to the *Oxford English Dictionary*, "value added" is "the amount by which

the value of an article is increased at each stage of its production by the firm or firms producing it, exclusive of the cost of materials and bought-in parts and services." Apart from earlier usage in connection with taxation, the term first appeared in Paul Samuelson, 1951, *Economics: An Introductory Analysis* (New York: McGraw Hill), e.g. his reference to "the value-added approach which cancels out at every stage all purchases of intermediate goods by one firm from another" (247).

34.   Marx, *Capital*, vol. 3, 966.
35.   Christian Aid, 2008, *Death and Taxes: The True Toll of Tax Dodging.* http://www. christianaid.org.uk/images/deathandtaxes.pdf.
36.   UNCTAD, *World Investment Report 2013*, 156.
37.   The seeds of this modern pseudo-science were planted more than two centuries ago by Adam Smith, whom Marx castigated for his "stupid blunder": "After he has begun by correctly defining the value components of the commodity and the total value product embodied in them, and then by showing how these components form an equal number of different sources of revenue, thus after he has derived revenues from value, he proceeds in the reverse direction—and this remains the predominant idea in his work—and makes these revenues, instead of just 'component parts,' into 'original sources' of all exchangeable value, thereby throwing the doors wide open to vulgar economics." Karl Marx, [1883] 1978, *Capital*, vol. 2 (London: Penguin), 449.
38.   Shaikh and Tonak, *Measuring the Wealth of Nations*, 33.
39.   Michael Prowse, *Financial Times*, September 8, 1996.
40.   Mark Blaug comments, "The publication of the Arrow-Debreu paper of 1954, proving the existence of general equilibrium, and Samuelson's announcement of 'the neoclassical synthesis' in the third edition of his *Economics: An Introduction* (1955) marks the true birth of what has ever since been called 'neoclassical economics.'" Blaug, 2001, "No History of Ideas, Please, We're Economists," *Journal of Economic Perspectives* 15/1: 145–64.
41.   Lance Taylor, 2004, *Reconstructing Macroeconomics: Structuralist Proposals and Critiques of the Mainstream* (Cambridge, MA: Harvard University Press), 351.
42.   "That which needs to be clear, and which also contains a moment of real difficulty, is that the labor objectified in the exchange-value of a commodity does not correspond to the quantity of labor immediately spent in its production. Instead, it is the fruit of a mediation with socially allocated labor." Massimiliano Tomba, 2007, "Differentials of Surplus-Value in the Contemporary Forms of Exploitation," *The Commoner* 12: 23–37.
43.   David Harvey, [1982] 2006, *The Limits to Capital* (London: Verso), 441–42.
44.   J. Steven Landefeld, *GDP: One of the Great Inventions of the 20th Century*, http:// www.bea.gov/scb/pdf/BEAWIDE/2000/0100od.pdf.
45.   Jyrki Ali-Yrkkö, Petri Rouvinen, Timo Seppälä, and Pekka Ylä-Anttila, 2011, *Who Captures Value in Global Supply Chains? Case Nokia N95 Smartphone*, ETLA Keskusteluaiheita Discussion Paper No. 1240, 3.
        An interesting exception to the conflation of value added and value captured is *How Value Is Created, Captured and Destroyed*, by Cliff Bowman and Véronique Ambrosini, who make "a distinction in particular between use-value (UV) and exchange-value (EV), and between value creation and value capture," yet who do not acknowledge that Marx founded his theory of value on the distinction, possibly to smooth its acceptance by the journal's peer reviewers, who should, of course, have insisted on such an acknowledgment. Bowman and Ambrosini, 2010, "How Value Is Created, Captured and Destroyed," *European Business Review* 22/5: 479–95.

The authors distinguish between labor and labor-power—the use-value supplied by "suppliers of human inputs is their capacity to work" (484)—and even develop a notion of exploitation, without, however, using that term or acknowledging that these insights form the basis of Marxist value theory: "As a location of silver-bearing ore . . . [a] mine creates no value. It has UV, but it creates no more UV than it has. Moreover, 'it' cannot receive any payments; 'it' is a piece of land. What makes it a valuable piece of land are the past efforts of prospectors and miners.... I could ask someone to use it to build a mining company around it, and I would become its sole shareholder. . . . What was my contribution to the value-creating process?... I get a payment for owning the mine, not for creating any new value. The people that do create new value, the miners and other workers, must ergo get less EV than they create, otherwise how else could I be paid my 'share'?" (489–90).

46. UNCTAD, *World Investment Report 2011,* 142–43.
47. Gary Gereffi, John Humphrey, and Timothy Sturgeon, 2004, "The Governance of Global Value Chains," *Review of International Political Economy*12/1: 78–104.
48. Raphael Kaplinsky, *Globalization, Poverty and Inequality,* 101. Not included in this concept is the fact that these value chains are only being studied because they cross borders, in particular the borders between the North and South.
49. Uma Subramanian, 2007, *Moving toward Competitiveness: A Value Chain Approach,* Foreign Investment Advisory Service (FIAS) occasional paper (Washington, DC: World Bank), ix–x, http://documents.worldbank.org/curated/en/2007/08/10137616/moving-toward-competitiveness-value-chain-approach.
50. Jeffrey Henderson, Peter Dicken, Martin Hess, Neil Coe, and Henry Wai-Chung Yeung, 2002, "Global Production Networks and the Analysis of Economic Development," *Review of International Political Economy* 9/3: 436–64.
51. Ibid., 439.
52. Gary Gereffi, 2005, *The New Offshoring of Jobs and Global Development,* ILO Social Policy Lectures (Geneva: ILO Publications), 46–47. Gereffi adds, "A similar pattern is apparent in agricultural production. Although it is true that there has long been a global production system in agriculture, today production is much more controlled by a limited number of TNCs located in the developed world."
53. Taylor, "Rethinking the Global Production of Uneven Development," in *Globalizations,* 4/4: 529–542, 538.
54. Jennifer Bair, 2004, *From Commodity Chains to Value Chains and Back Again?,* http://www.irows.ucr.edu/conferences/globgis/papers/Bair.htm, 5.
55. Jennifer Bair, 2005, "Global Capitalism and Commodity Chains: Looking Back, Going Forward," *Competition & Change* 9/2: 153–80.
56. Ibid., 157.
57. Marilyn Carr, Martha Chen, and Jane Tate, 2000, "Globalization and home-based workers," in *Feminist Economics,* 6/3: 123-42, 129–130.
58. "Within a supply chain, each producer purchases inputs and then adds value, which then becomes part of the cost of the next stage of production. The sum of the value added by everyone in the chain equals the final product price." Greg Linden, Kenneth L. Kraemer, and Jason Dedrick, 2007, *Who Captures Value in a Global Innovation System? The Case of Apple's iPod* (Irvine, CA: Personal Computing Industry Center, University of California), 2.
59. Ibid., 446.
60. Henderson et al., *Global Production Networks and the Analysis of Economic Development,* 449.
61. Ibid., 448.

62. Timothy Sturgeon, 2008, *From Commodity Chains to Value Chains: Interdisciplinary Theory Building in an Age of Globalization*, Massachusetts Institute of Technology Working Paper Series, MIT-IPC-08-001,10. https://ipc.mit.edu/sites/default/files/documents/08-001.pdf.

63. Three other offshore financial centers—Jersey, Cayman Islands, and the British Virgin Islands—made it into the top ten nations in the world for per capita GDP in 2006.

64. Karl Marx, *Capital,* vol. 3, 193–94.

65. I am grateful to Joseph Choonara for pointing this out to me.

66. If an initial investment reaps the same return in half the time, its rate of profit is effectively doubled.

67. A crucial difference between the marginalist and Marxist theory of value is to be found in the final part of the circuit, C′–M′. According to the ruling marginalist doctrine, ∆M (i.e., M′–M, a firm's gross profits) is merely the monetary expression of ∆C (C–C′ i.e., new value created in this firm's production process). From the perspective of Marx's theory of value, this is a false tautology upon which is constructed the entire tottering edifice of bourgeois economic theory. For an individual firm, ∆M bears no relationship to ∆C, instead it represents instead the share of total economy-wide commodity value that the owners of this firm succeed in *capturing* through the sale of its commodities. M–C–C′–M′, therefore, corresponds to the capitalist economy as a whole, rather than to an individual firm within that economy—or, to put it differently, it schematically describes the circuit of an individual capital abstracted from value-redistributing, profit-equalizing competition with other capitals.

68. Marx explains that, in the transportation of commodities, "there certainly takes place, in the labor process, a change in the object of labor, the commodity. Its spatial existence is altered, and along with this goes a change in its use-value. . . . Its exchange-value increases in the same measure as this change in use-value requires labor." Karl Marx, [1863] 1969, *Theories of Surplus-Value,* Part 1 (London: Lawrence and Wishart), 412.

69. Shaikh and Tonak, *Measuring the Wealth of Nations,* 23.

70. Thus the extraction of juice from this orange is only productive from the point of view of capital if that process is performed not in one's own kitchen but by wage labor in the production of a commodity that is sold to a customer for a profit.

71. Ibid., 24.

72. BBC News, November 15, 2006, http://news.bbc.co.uk/2/hi/uk_news/scotland/south_of_scotland/6150240.stm.

73. "Ocean shipping, which constitutes 99 percent of world trade by weight and a majority of world trade by value . . . experienced a technological revolution in the form of container shipping, but dramatic price declines are not in evidence." David Hummels, 2007, 'Transportation Costs and International Trade in the Second Era of Globalization," *Journal of Economic Perspectives* 21/3: 131–54. What has become both faster and much cheaper is air transport: "Even after these improvements, ocean shipping is still a slow process. Shipping containers from Europe to the U.S. Midwest requires 2–3 weeks; from Europe to Asia requires five weeks. In contrast, air shipping requires a day or less to most destinations. Consequently, the ten-fold decline in air shipping prices since the late 1950s means that the cost of speed has fallen dramatically" (152).

74. Marx, *Capital,* vol. 3, 240. Productivity and the rate of profit received further development in chapter 6, in the discussion of the contrasting marginalist and Marxist concepts of productivity.

75.   Here, "wealth" is used in preference to "value" to emphasize that the social product consists of a mass of use-values. Of course, the social product necessarily takes the form of prices, that is, transformed exchange-values, and it is only in this form that value makes its appearance and different values can be measured and compared.

76.   Editorial, *Financial Times*, June 2, 1994. This makes no correction for the purchasing power anomaly, discussed in some detail in chapter 6, wherein a low-wage nation's GDP measured in dollars at market exchange rates appears to be smaller than it is. Expressing such comparisons in PPP dollars became the norm after the mid-1990s.

10. All Roads Lead into the Crisis

1.   Karl Marx, 1866, *Trade Unions: Their Past, Present, and Future*, http://www.marx-ists.org/history/international/iwma/documents/1866/instructions.htm#06.

2.   Quoted in Martin Wolf, "Why the 'Green Shoots' of Recovery Could Yet Wither," *Financial Times*, April 21, 2009.

3.   Evald Ilyenkov, 1960, *The Dialectic of the Abstract and the Concrete in Marx's Capital* (Moscow: Progress Publishers), 217.

4.   Martin Wolf, "Fear Makes a Welcome Return," *Financial Times*, August 14, 2007.

5.   This term was coined by the authors of *A Green New Deal*, who blame the crisis on deregulation of the banking system: "Financial deregulation has facilitated the creation of almost limitless credit. With this credit boom have come irresponsible and often fraudulent patterns of lending, creating inflated bubbles in assets such as property, and powering environmentally unsustainable consumption. This approach hit the buffers of insolvency and unrepayable debts on what we think of as 'debtonation day,' 9 August 2007." Green New Deal Group, 2008, *A Green New Deal*, http://www.neweconomics.org/publications/entry/a-green-new-deal.

6.   Robert E. Lucas, *Macroeconomic Priorities*, address to the 115th meeting of the American Economic Association, January 4, 2003, Washington, DC, http://pages.stern.nyu.edu/~dbackus/Taxes/Lucas%20priorities%20AER%2003.pdf, 1.

7.   To keep their export boom going, both to finance U.S. imports and to prevent their currencies appreciating against the dollar, China and other low-wage exporters were compelled to recycle their export earnings into low-risk, low-yielding U.S. Treasury bonds. "It is hard not to imagine that there are geopolitical risks associated with reliance on what might be called a financial balance of terror to assure continued financial flows to the United States," Summers said, conjuring the image of Uncle Sam pointing a gun to his own head, declaring "hand over your money or I'll shoot!" Lawrence H. Summers, 2006, *Reflections on Global Account Imbalances and Emerging Markets Reserve Accumulation*, L. K. Jha Memorial Lecture, Reserve Bank of India, Mumbai, March 24, 2006, http://www.harvard.edu/president/speeches/summers_2006/0324_rbi.php.

8.   Gabriel Wildau, "China Central Bank Admits Defeat in War on Deflation," *Financial Times*, June 11, 2015.

9.   Andrew Gamble, 2009, *The Spectre at the Feast—Capitalist Crisis and the Politics of Recession* (Basingstoke: Palgrave Macmillan), 131.

10.   G5: United States, Japan, West Germany, France and the UK, superseded in 1986 by the G7: these five countries plus Italy and Canada.

11.   Sebastian Lyon, "Safety Margin Is Becoming Perilously Thin," *Financial Times*, March 1, 2013.

12.   Scott Mather and Dirk Jeschke, 2012, "Japanification," in *Viewpoint* (Newport Beach, CA: PIMCO), https://media.pimco.com/Documents/PIMCO_Viewpoint_Japanification_Mather_Jeschke_August2012.pdf.

13. John Plender, "Return to Risk Differences and Imbalances," *Financial Times*, January 3, 2010.

14. Financial Times Lexicon, http://lexicon.ft.com/Term?term=secular-stagnation. The term, originally coined by Alvin Hansen in 1938, was reintroduced by Lawrence Summers in his *Address to Fourteenth Annual Research Conference in Honor of Stanley Fischer*, Washington, DC, November 8, 2013, http://larrysummers.com/imf-fourteenth-annual-research-conference-in-honor-of-stanley-fischer/.

15. "Event horizon" is a term used by cosmologists to describe the point of no return when an object becomes too close to a black hole and cannot escape its gravitational pull.

16. Martin Wolf, 2014, *The Shifts and the Shocks—What We've Learned, and Have still to Learn, from the Financial Crisis* (London: Penguin), 159.

17. Ibid., 164–65.

18. Ibid., 162.

19. Ibid., 10.

20. In continuation, UNCTAD lists three forms "either as intra-firm trade, through NEMs [Non-Equity Modes] (which include, among others, contract manufacturing, licensing, and franchising), or through arm's-length transactions involving at least one TNC." UNCTAD, *World Investment Report 2013*, 135.

21. Ibid., 122.

22. Gary Gereffi, 2005, *The New Offshoring of Jobs and Global Development*, ILO Social Policy Lectures (Geneva: ILO Publications), 18. The situation changed somewhat in the decade following the publication of this book—TNCs have increasingly sought lower-wage hosts such as Vietnam, Cambodia, and Bangladesh, while China has had some limited successes in its efforts to move into higher value-added activities.

23. IMF, *World Economic Outlook—Spillovers and Cycles in the Global Economy*, 180.

24. Stephen S. Roach, "More Jobs, Worse Work," *New York Times*, July 22, 2004.

25. Wolf, *The Shifts and the Shocks*, 6.

26. Ibid., 184–85.

27. Larry Fink, 2015, *Letter to S&P 500 CEOs in the United States*, http://www.businessinsider.com/larry-fink-letter-to-ceos-2015-4?IR=T. Edward Luce commented, "Among efficient market theorists, maximising shareholder value remains the watchword. In practice MSV should stand for minimising social value." Luce, "US Share Buybacks Loot the Future," *Financial Times*, April 26, 2015.

28. Ibid.

29. David Bowers, "Watch Out as Sovereigns Eye Company Cash Piles," *Financial Times*, February 8, 2012.

30. Oliver Renick, 2015, "Bonds for Buybacks Never Bigger in U.S. as $58 Billion Sold," Bloomberg Politics, http://www.bloomberg.com/politics/articles/2015-06-19/record-cash-wrung-from-bond-market-to-cover-u-s-stock-buybacks.

31. Rick Rieder, 2015, "Why to Pay Attention to Today," Blackrock blog, June 1, 2015, http://www.blackrockblog.com/2015/06/01/pay-attention-todays-buyback-boom/.

32. Lu Wang and Callie Bos, 2014, "S&P 500 Companies Spend Almost All Profits on Buybacks," Bloomberg Business, http://www.bloomberg.com/news/articles/2014-10-06/s-p-500-companies-spend-almost-all-profits-on-buybacks-payouts.

33. Robin Harding, "Corporate Investment: A Mysterious Divergence," *Financial Times*, July 24, 2013.

34. Ibid.

35. Cardiff Garcia, "The U.S. Capital Stock: Old and Busted, But Why?," *FT Alphav-*

ille, November 1, 2013, http://ftalphaville.ft.com/2013/11/01/1683962/the-us-cap-ital-stock-old-and-busted-but-why/.

36. Households' surplus was 0.9 percent of GDP; the external balance made up the difference. Martin Wolf, "Britain Needs to Whittle Down Corporate Cash Piles," *Financial Times*, February 16, 2012.

37. Bowers, "Watch Out as Sovereigns Eye Company Cash Piles."

38. Martin Wolf, "Japan's Unfinished Policy Revolution," *Financial Times*, April 9, 2013. Depreciation is a charge on income, so the sum of the two is less than gross retained earnings.

39. UNCTAD, *World Investment Report 2012*, xv.

40. John Burn-Murdoch and Magnus Bennetzen, 2014, "Where Are the World's Corporate Cash Reserves?," *Financial Times*, January 21, 2014.

41. Bowers, "Watch Out as Sovereigns Eye Company Cash Piles."

42. Luce, "US Share Buybacks Loot the Future."

43. Tobias Levkovich, *January 2012 Chart of the Month: Predicting Profitability Plunges*, Citi Blog, January 13, 2012, http://blog.citigroup.com/2012/01/janu-ary-2012-chart-of-the-month-predicting-profitability-plunges.

44. "Quantitative easing" (QE) is a way of pumping vast quantities of cash into the financial system, in which the government creates money and uses it to buy back its own debt, thereby converting privately owned government bonds held by banks, pension funds, and rich investors into a huge pool of cash which then surges through the rest of the economy as its owners use it to buy other financial assets, thereby supporting the value of these assets. By entering the market as purchasers of its own debt, governments exert downward pressure on interest rates, useful when nominal interest rates have already been cut close to zero.

45. David McNally, "From Financial Crisis to World-Slump: Accumulation, Financial-isation, and the Global Slowdown," *Historical Materialism* 17 (2009): 35–83.

46. Ibid., 42.

47. Robin Blackburn, 2008, "The Subprime Crisis," *New Left Review* 50: 63-106, quote at 106.

48. Leo Panitch and Sam Gindin, *The Current Crisis: A Socialist Perspective*, Socialist Project E-Bulletin No. 142, September 30, 2008, http://www.socialistproject.ca/bullet/bullet142.html.

49. Robert Brenner, 2009, "What Is Good for Goldman Sachs Is Good for America: The Origins of the Current Crisis," prologue to the Spanish translation of *Econom-ics of Global Turbulence*, http://www.sscnet.ucla.edu/issr/cstch/papers/Brenner-CrisisTodayOctober2009.pdf, 12.

50. McNally, "From Financial Crisis to World-Slump," 54.

51. Ibid., 53–55.

52. Ibid., 53.

53. Ibid., 60.

54. Martin Wolf, "The Prudent Will Have to Pay for the Profligate," *Financial Times*, April 1, 2008.

55. John Bellamy Foster and Robert McChesney, 2012, *The Endless Crisis: How Monop-oly Finance Capital Produces Stagnation and Upheaval from the USA to China* (New York: Monthly Review Press), 49.

56. William Milberg, 2008, "Shifting Sources and Uses of Profits: Sustaining U.S. Financialization with Global Value Chains," *Economy and Society* 37/3: 420–51, quote at 421.

57. Ibid., 445.

58. Gérard Duménil and Dominique Lévy, 2004, "The Economics of US Imperialism at the Turn of the 21st Century," *Review of International Political Economy* 11/4: 657–76.

59. William Milberg, "Globalised Production: Structural Challenges for Developing Country Workers," in *Labour and the Globalisation of Production: Causes and Consequences of Industrial Upgrading*, ed. William Milberg (New York: Palgrave Macmillan, 2004), 3.

60. Milberg, "Shifting Sources and Uses of Profits," 421.

61. Elisa Parisi-Capone, 2006, *Offshore Outsourcing: What Is the Impact on Domestic Productivity?*, RGE Analysis, http://www.roubini.com/analysis/38534.php.

62. Data from CapGemini, *World Wealth Report* 2011 and 2015, https://www.worldwealthreport.com/.

63. As Karl Marx said, "In the way that even an accumulation of debt can appear as an accumulation of capital, we see the distortion involved in the credit system reach its culmination." *Capital*, vol. 3 (London: 1894; repr. Penguin, 1991), 607–8.

64. Greta R. Krippner, 2005, "The Financialization of the American Economy," *Socio-Economic Review* 3: 173–208.

65. Ibid., 182.

66. Ibid., 175–76.

67. Till van Treeck, 2008, *The Political Economy Debate on Financialisation: A Macroeconomic Perspective*, IMK Working Paper, http://ideas.repec.org/p/imk/wpaper/01-2008.htm, 4–5.

68. Socialist Workers Party, [1988] 1994, "What the 1987 Stock Market Crash Foretold," 1988 resolution adopted by the U.S. Socialist Workers Party, *New International* 10: 101–204, quote at 146.

69. Andrew Haldane, *How Low Can You Go?*, speech delivered to Portadown (Ireland) Chamber of Commerce, September 18, 2015, http://www.bankofengland.co.uk/publications/Documents/speeches/2015/speech840.pdf, 13.

70. Editors, "Pulled back In," *The Economist*, November 14, 2015.

71. Ousmène Mandeng, "Why Wimp Label Sticks to Emerging Nations," *Financial Times*, March 16, 2015.

72. Ibid.

73. James Kynge and Jonathan Wheatley, "Emerging Markets: The Great Unravelling," *Financial Times*, April 1, 2015.

74. IMF, *Global Financial Stability Report: Risks Rotating to Emerging Markets*, October 2015 update, https://www.Imf.Org/External/Pubs/FT/GFSR/2015/02/Pdf/Text_V3.pdf, 84.

75. James Kynge and Jonathan Wheatley, "Emerging Asia: The Ill Wind of Deflation," *Financial Times*, October 4, 2015.

76. Editors, "China Bets on Expanding Its Way Out of Debt," *Financial Times*, May 22, 2015. To give a sense of the scale of this, the *FT* editors add that annual debt servicing by Chinese firms is larger than Mexico's GDP.

77. Kynge and Wheatley, "Emerging Asia: The Ill Wind of Deflation."

78. Ibid., 86.

79. John Plender, "Relentless Capital Outflows and Sinking Currencies," *Financial Times*, September 27, 2015.

80. Jonathan Wheatley and James Kynge, "Emerging Markets: Trading Blow," *Financial Times*, June 10, 2015.

81. Kynge and Wheatley, "Emerging Asia: The Ill Wind of Deflation."

82. Jonathan Wheatley, "Corporate Bonds: Emerging Bubble," *Financial Times*, February 15, 2015.

83.   Ibid.
84.   IMF, *Global Financial Stability Report: Risks Rotating to Emerging Markets.*
85.   Editors, "The Never-Ending Story," *The Economist,* November 14, 2015.
86.   Steve Johnson, "'Enormous' Rise in EM Debt Rings Alarm Bells," *Financial Times,* August 11, 2015.
87.   Kynge and Wheatley, "Emerging Asia: The Ill Wind of Deflation."
88.   Alberto Gallo, "Prepare for a Rough Ride in EM Bonds," *Financial Times,* April 22, 2015.
89.   Editors, "Invisible Bonds," *The Economist,* November 8, 2014, http://www.economist.com/news/finance-and-economics/21631143-foreign-borrowing-emerging-market-firms-higher-it-seems-invisible-bonds.
90.   Wheatley, "Corporate Bonds: Emerging Bubble."
91.   Jonathan Wheatley, "Spectre of Bond Downgrade Hovers over Latin American Markets," *Financial Times,* November 12, 2015.
92.   Ibid.
93.   Johnson, "'Enormous' Rise in EM Debt Rings Alarm Bells."
94.   Sam Fleming, "IMF Chief Warns of 'Disappointing' Growth," *Financial Times,* September 30, 2015.
95.   Kynge and Wheatley, "Emerging Markets: The Great Unravelling."
96.   Henny Sender, "India's Happy Story Stands Out in Asia," *Financial Times,* February 10, 2015.
97.   Michael Peel, "Rising Household Debt Casts Doubt over Thailand's Economic Revival," *Financial Times,* April 16, 2015.
98.   Johnson, "'Enormous' Rise in EM Debt Rings Alarm Bells."
99.   James Kynge, "Emerging Market Capital Outflows Eclipse Financial Crisis Levels," *Financial Times,* May 7, 2015.
100. UNCTAD, FDI/TNC database, http://www.unctad.org/fdistatistics.
101. Henny Sender, "Capital Flight Now the Big Concern for Slowing China," *Financial Times,* September 6, 2015.
102. Editors, "Time Is Money for Emerging Markets," *Financial Times,* October 4, 2015.
103. Quoted in Sender, "Capital Flight Now the Big Concern for Slowing China."
104. Kynge and Wheatley, "Emerging Asia: The Ill Wind of Deflation."
105. "The expansionary fiscal response to the credit crunch is now well and truly over. The global economy is about to pass through an important inflection point, in which the fiscal stance of the major developed nations is changing from broadly expansionary to broadly contractionary." Gavyn Davies, *Financial Times* blog, October 8, 2010, http://blogs.ft.com/gavyndavies/2010/10/08/the-era-of-fiscal-consolidation-starts-here.
106. Isabel Ortiz, Jingqing Chai, and Matthew Cummins, *Austerity Measures Threaten Children and Poor Households: Recent Evidence in Public Expenditures from 128 Developing Countries,* United Nations Children's Fund (New York: UNICEF, 2011), 3–4.
107. Michael Pettis, "Competitive Devaluations Threaten a Trade War," *Financial Times,* December 1, 2009.
108. Mervyn King, *Speech to Institute of Directors,* Liverpool, October 18, 2011, http://www.bankofengland.co.uk/publications/speeches/2011/speech523.pdf.
109. Quoted in Chris Giles, "Dark Humour and Hard Talk at IMF Meetings," *Financial Times,* September 25, 2011.
110. Martin Wolf, "Time to Think the Unthinkable and Start Printing Again," *Financial Times,* September 29, 2011.

111. Martin Wolf, "Fear and Loathing in the Eurozone," *Financial Times*, September 27, 2011.

112. Martin Wolf, "We Are Trapped in a Cycle of Credit Booms," *Financial Times*, October 7, 2014.

113. Nouriel Roubini, "Mother of All Carry Trades Faces an Inevitable Bust," *Financial Times*, November 1, 2009. "Highly leveraged" refers to investors who use borrowed money to finance most of their investment, thereby gearing the profits—if a trade yields a 10 percent profit and 90 percent of the debt is borrowed money, the investor's profit is 100 percent less the funding costs. A "carry trade" is when money is borrowed in one currency and invested in another offering a higher rate of interest. This can be extremely lucrative, especially when the funding currency is depreciating (an intended consequence of ultra-low interest rates since it increases export competitiveness) and the destination currency is appreciating. For years before 2007 the Japanese government was forced to keep interest rates extremely low and the "yen carry-trade" earned untold fortunes for its investors. Now investors have a choice of funding currencies and plenty of risky bets to choose from.

114. Tony Jackson, "It's Bubbly All Round, but Really, Does Anyone Care?," *Financial Times*, December 4, 2009. He adds, "It is as if the survivors of the First World War, having paused only for a cup of tea and a sit-down, were hurling themselves into the Second."

115. Quoted in Henny Sender, "On Wall St: A Tonic that Works Too Well," *Financial Times*, December 23, 2009.

116. Karl Marx, 1859, *A Contribution to the Critique of Political Economy*, http://www.marxists.org/archive/marx/works/1859/critique-pol-economy/preface.htm.

117. Raúl Valdés Vivó, "Crisis sin salida del capitalismo," *Rebelión*, January 30, 2009, http://www.rebelion.org/noticia_pdf.php?id=79985. My translation.

Index